T0329813

LENDING TO THE BORROWER FROM HELL

THE PRINCETON ECONOMIC HISTORY
OF THE WESTERN WORLD

JOEL MOKYR, SERIES EDITOR

A list of titles in this series appears at the end of the book

LENDING TO THE BORROWER FROM HELL

DEBT, TAXES, AND DEFAULT IN THE AGE OF PHILIP II

MAURICIO DRELICHMAN AND
HANS-JOACHIM VOTH

PRINCETON UNIVERSITY PRESS
PRINCETON AND OXFORD

Drelichman, Mauricio.
Lending to the borrower from hell : debt, taxes, and default in the age of Philip II /
Mauricio Drelichman and Hans-Joachim Voth.
pages cm. — (The Princeton economic history of the western world)
Summary: "Why do lenders time and again loan money to sovereign borrowers who
promptly go bankrupt? When can this type of lending work? As the United States and many
European nations struggle with mountains of debt, historical precedents can offer valuable
insights. *Lending to the Borrower from Hell* looks at one famous case—the debts and defaults of
Philip II of Spain. Ruling over one of the largest and most powerful empires in history, King
Philip defaulted four times. Yet he never lost access to capital markets and could borrow
again within a year or two of each default. Exploring the shrewd reasoning of the lenders
who continued to offer money, Mauricio Drelichman and Hans-Joachim Voth analyze the
lessons from this important historical example. Using detailed new evidence collected from
sixteenth-century archives, Drelichman and Voth examine the incentives and returns of
lenders. They provide powerful evidence that in the right situations, lenders not only
survive despite defaults—they thrive. Drelichman and Voth also demonstrate that debt
markets cope well, despite massive fluctuations in expenditure and revenue, when lending
functions like insurance. The authors unearth unique sixteenth-century loan contracts that
offered highly effective risk sharing between the king and his lenders, with payment
obligations reduced in bad times. A fascinating story of finance and empire, *Lending to the
Borrower from Hell* offers an intelligent model for keeping economies safe in times of sovereign
debt crises and defaults"—Provided by publisher.
Includes bibliographical references and index.
ISBN 978-0-691-15149-6 (hardback)
1. Finance, Public—Spain—History—16th century. 2. Debts, Public—Spain—History—16th
century. 3. Taxation—Spain—History—16th century. 4. Philip II, King of Spain, 1527–
1598. I. Voth, Hans-Joachim. II. Title.
HJ1242.D74 2014
336.4609'031—dc23   2013027790
British Library Cataloging-in-Publication Data is available
This book has been composed in Verdigris MVB Pro Text and Gentium Plus
Printed on acid-free paper. ∞
Printed in the United States of America
1 3 5 7 9 10 8 6 4 2

TO PAULA
TO BEA

CONTENTS

ACKNOWLEDGMENTS

Blame the Midwest. Tender academic minds often need peace and quiet to get down to business. We first met in the delightful town of La Crosse, Wisconsin (also known as "Mud City, USA"), where distractions were few and far between. This is the place that the organizers of the annual Cliometrics conference had chosen as a venue in 2003. The authors got talking and quickly agreed that they should look into a joint project on the early history of sovereign borrowing. Philip II's defaults are justly famous, but had not been given their due from an economic perspective, or so we felt. Explaining why everyone before us had been wrong also seemed the best way to use two characteristic virtues of our respective nationalities—modesty, for the Argentine, and subtlety, for the German.

Money may be the sinews of power, but it is also the lifeblood of scholarship—and especially so if the project involves extensive data collection in the archives, plus the coding of hundreds of contracts written by hand in sixteenth-century script. This book would not exist without the financial support of several institutions. We have been fortunate in receiving funding by the Spanish Ministry of Science and Innovation (MICINN). Sadly, the annual treasure convoys from Madrid, laden with ducats earmarked for research and sailing, did not always arrive in full strength. Our applications almost floundered when we failed to specify whether the project required use of the Spanish research station in Antarctica, or if we would need an oceanographic research ship. The importance of linguistic accuracy was brought home to us when we discovered, minutes before submitting the research budget, that we were about to request cases of red wine (*cajas de tinto*) instead of ink-jet cartridges (*cartuchos de tinta*). Despite correcting this potentially embarrassing line item, our funding requests were often cut by 60 to 80 percent without explanation, even during Spain's boom years, while receiving the highest marks for academic merit. We are grateful for the limited funds that did arrive; the firsthand insight into the intricacies of Castilian administration also helped us to understand the bureaucratic machine that takes center stage in this book.

With Spanish treasure in variable and occasionally short supply, we moved a good part of the project to the University of British Columbia (UBC) in Vancouver, where we hired a large share of the Spanish-speaking graduate student population to transcribe and code up our data. As a result, we are now more convinced than ever that the mita, the forced labor service invented by the Spanish colonizers to exploit the rich silver mines of Potosí, had much to recommend it. In its absence, we are grateful that we could draw on generous funding by the Social Sciences and Humanities Research Council of Canada, the Canadian Institute for Advanced Research, and the UBC Hampton Fund, which did not find it odd to provide an Argentine scholar with an American PhD working in Vancouver with funds to pay for Spanish-speaking research assistants so that we could code up data from Castile.

Young scholars often imagine research as a glamorous, thrilling activity, combining exciting, Dan-Brown-like moments of discovery in dusty archives with joyful international jet-setting. Of course, this image is all wrong. Neither the siren calls of the Whistler ski resort, hiking in the Rockies and the Serra de Tramuntana in Mallorca, boating in Vancouver's English Bay, nor long lunches by Barceloneta Beach distracted us from our labors (at least most of the time).

We should also mention our gratitude for the many discomforts endured on interminable flights between Barcelona and Vancouver (as well as various conference locations), courtesy of Lufthansa, Air Canada, and a variety of American carriers. Without being confined to a narrow steel tube, rebreathing the same stale air for twelve to fourteen hours at a time, accosted by strange smells, offered inedible food, and without the front passenger's seat firmly wedged against our kneecaps, we would have found it much harder to concentrate on data analysis and the writing contained in this book—a good part of which was completed high above the Atlantic and the Great Plains of North America.

Seminar audiences at UBC Vancouver, Universitat Pompeu Fabra (UPF) in Barcelona, Northwestern, Harvard, Stanford, Caltech, Brown, the Federal Reserve Bank of New York, the University of California at Los Angeles (Anderson School and Economics), Carlos III, Rutgers, the University of California at

Davis, the University of California at Irvine, the London School of Economics, Yale School of Management, New York University Stern School of Business, the Graduate Institute at the University of Geneva, the Free University of Amsterdam, the University of Minnesota, All Souls College (Oxford), the Asian Development Bank, the Banco de España, Sciences Po, IMT Lucca, ESSEC Business School/THEMA, Utrecht, Vanderbilt, the University of Colorado at Boulder, Universidad de San Andrés, Hebrew University, Copenhagen Business School, Universidad Autónoma de Barcelona, Bocconi, American University (Washington), and the University of California at Berkeley listened to our ideas. Scholars at the Allied Social Science Association meetings in San Francisco, Center for Economic and Policy Research's (CEPR) Summer Symposium in Macroeconomics in Izmir, London Frontier Research in Economic and Social History meetings, Economic History Association meetings in Austin, joint Bundesbank–European Central Bank seminar, European Historical Economics Society conference in Lund, Vienna European Economic Association meetings, European Cliometrics meetings in Paris, two Paris School of Economics conferences on public finance, Centre de Recerca en Economia Internacional (CREI) and CEPR conference on sovereign debt in Barcelona, Warwick Political Economy Workshop, Royal Economic Society Conference in London, Bureau d'Economie Théorique et Appliquée Workshop in Historical Economics in Strasburg, National Bureau of Economic Research Summer Institute, Montevideo Congress of the Latin American Association for Economic History, Conference in Honor of Joel Mokyr in Evanston, the Canadian Network for Economic History meetings in Ottawa, Political Institutions and Economic Policy workshop at Harvard, and West Coast Workshop on International Economics at Santa Clara as well as at a string of Canadian Institute for Advanced Research meetings kindly gave us feedback. Without their continued patience and interest, sometimes bordering on excitement, we would not have had the heart to write this book.

A few heroic souls read drafts of the whole manuscript before the miniconference in Vancouver in September 2012, braving our penchant for repeating the same quotes half a dozen times. This book would be much the poorer without the generosity and advice of Mark Dincecco, Juan Gelabert, Oscar Gelderblom, Phil Hoffman, Larry Neal, Jean-Laurent Rosenthal, and Eugene White. At various stages of the project, we also benefited from the feedback of Daron Acemoglu, Carlos Alvarez Nogal, Paul Beaudry, Maristella Botticini, Fernando Broner, Bill Caferro, Ann Carlos, Albert Carreras, Christophe Chamley, Greg Clark, Brad deLong, Sebastian Edwards, John H. Elliott, Carola Frydman, Marc Flandreau, Caroline Fohlin, Xavier Gabaix, Oded Galor, Josh Gottlieb, Regina Grafe, Avner Greif, Michael Hiscox, Viktoria Hnatkovska, Hugo Hopenhayn, Kenneth Kletzer, Michael Kremer, Naomi Lamoreaux, Ed Leamer, Tim Leunig, Gary Libecap, John Londregan, Alberto Martín, Andreu Mas-Colell, Paolo Mauro, David Mitch, Kris Mitchener, Lyndon Moore, Roger Myerson, Avner Offer, Kevin O'Rourke, Sevket Pamuk, Richard Portes, Leandro Prados de la Escosura, Angela Redish, Marit Rehavi, Claudia Rei, Maria Stella Rollandi, Moritz Schularick, Chris Sims, David Stasavage, Richard Sylla, Bill Sundstrom, Nathan Sussman, Alan M. Taylor, Peter Temin, Francois Velde, Jaume Ventura, Paul Wachtel, David Weil, Mark Wright, Andrea Zannini, and Jeromin Zettelmeyer. The series editor, Joel Mokyr, helped us with his insights, enthusiasm, and good old common sense. At Princeton University Press, Seth Ditchik put the book on a fast track to publication, smoothing the administrative process as much as possible. Three anonymous referees for the press provided us with detailed feedback. At short notice and with great taste, Valeria Drelichman gave us sharp insights on cover design. At CREI, Mariona Novoa smoothed many administrative wrinkles, facilitated our various visits, and provided support at critical junctures. To those who we will have inevitably forgotten on this list, we are doubly grateful—for their contributions and forbearance.

Documents are the heart of any economic history project, but they do not surrender their secrets easily. Our efforts would have been fruitless without the guidance and advice of the archivists and scholars who helped us interpret sixteenth-century manuscripts. Among them, Isabel Aguirre Landa and Eduardo Pedruelo Martín, at the General Archive of Simancas, patiently guided us through the more than five thousand pages, sometimes written in impenetrable script; Andrea Zannini, from the University of Genoa, showed us the intricacies of early modern bookkeeping. Countless others—whose names we failed to note—facilitated our research on numerous occasions, clearing the path where we might have otherwise stumbled. To them all we extend our thanks.

Some of the work contained in this book first appeared in journals and edited volumes. For the right to reproduce our findings here, we thank the *Economic Journal*, *Journal of Economic History*, *Explorations in Economic History*, and *Journal of the European Economic Association*.

Our research assistants put in long days—and were sometimes called to duty with Skype calls in the middle of the night—to transcribe, code, and analyze reams of data that never seemed to end. At Pompeu Fabra, Hans-Christian Boy, Marc Goñi Trafach, and Diego Pereira-Garmendía mastered a wide range of crucial tasks, from archival research to complex financial modeling. At UBC, Marcos Agurto, Valeria Castellanos, Germán Pupato, Javier Torres, and Cristian Troncoso-Valverde all learned to read sixteenth-century Spanish and value early modern financial instruments, their pleas for mercy notwithstanding. When a heated discussion erupted in the graduate student lounge over the proper discount rate for *juros de resguardo*, we knew we had their fanatic devotion. Anthony Wray, the lone Anglo-Saxon on the team, became an expert in Spanish military history, tracing every last ducat used to pay the *tercios* in Flanders (or not to pay them, as the case might be). Without the professionalism, dedication to detail, and sheer hard work of all these promising young scholars, our project would not have been possible.

We dedicate this book to our partners, Paula and Beatriz, who bore our extended absences, frequent absentmindedness, and the often-frantic work on weekends, during long-planned vacations, and late into the night with good humor and patience despite the rapidly growing size of our families.

VANCOUVER AND BARCELONA, JUNE 2013

LENDING TO THE BORROWER FROM HELL

PROLOGUE

Can government borrowing be made safe? As we are finishing this book, the world is grappling with the aftermath of the financial crisis of 2008. What began as a problem in the securitized market for US mortgages became a major crisis first of banks and then governments. All over the developed world, debt levels have spiraled upward in recent years. In Europe, the cost of sovereign borrowing has become sky-high for countries whose creditworthiness is in the slightest doubt; several governments have already lost market access for their bonds. Financing troubles have spelled austerity, making the downturn worse and leading to unemployment rates in the double digits around the European periphery.

One of the motivations for writing this book was to go back in time and examine a period that has long been regarded as synonymous with continuous fiscal turmoil. We sought to learn more about the origins of state debts and sovereign default. To paraphrase the now-famous book by Carmen Reinhart and Kenneth Rogoff (2009), how different was last time? We discovered that the famous payment stops of Philip II—all four of them, making Habsburg Spain the first serial defaulter in history—were much less catastrophic than earlier authors had argued. By modern standards, defaults in the sixteenth century were on the whole remarkably mild. Only a relatively limited share of total debt was rescheduled; settlements were negotiated in less than two years (compared to an average of eight years today); terms were relatively generous; and lending resumed quickly. We also found few reasons to believe that Spain's fiscal performance was responsible for its eventual decline as a great power.

Instead of boom-and-bust cycles driven by the eternal overoptimism of financiers, we encountered a remarkably stable and effective system for financing government borrowing. There are two features at the heart of this system that may offer lessons for the present. The first concerns risk sharing between bankers and borrowers; the second involves how risks are taken and shed by financial institutions. Sovereign debt crises today produce enormous costs. In a typical debt crisis, GDP growth declines by approximately 2 to 3 percent (Panizza and Borensztein 2008).[1] Unemployment surges. Exports slump. The financial system collapses or needs massive bailouts. Just when spending cuts become particularly painful, finance ministers typically have to unveil austerity packages; the lines of the unemployed lengthen.

The debts and defaults of Philip II suggest that there is another way: prearranged reductions in what a government owes and has to pay to creditors in bad times. In fact, Philip's bankers specifically agreed on a number of repayment scenarios that depended on the health of the Crown's fiscal position. Economists have long contended that government spending that fluctuates with the economic cycle is one key reason why sovereign debt problems are so painful. In good years growth is healthy and tax receipts are plentiful. Creditworthiness looks high and markets are willing to lend at low interest rates. In bad years, however, this process goes into reverse; revenues plummet and interest rates rise. The amount of debt that can be sustained is suddenly much lower, creating a need for savage spending cuts. These austerity measures in turn undermine growth, fanning the flames of discontent. So-called state-contingent debt allows for interest and capital repayments to be reduced in times of crisis, helping to break this negative feedback loop. The cuts that make a crisis worse can therefore be avoided. Economic downturns as a result will be less severe and the risk of default declines. And yet in spite of all the intellectual appeal and conceptual elegance of the idea, there are few examples of state-contingent debt being traded in twenty-first-century debt markets. Most of them are relics of earlier defaults, intended as "sweeteners," such as the GDP bonds issued by Argentina after its dramatic payment stop in 2001. As many authors have asserted, there is a multitude of incentive problems—from the temptation to cheat to the problem of enforcement—that make it all but impossible for countries to issues bonds where repayments depend on economic conditions.

Still, all the practical problems of state-contingent debt were largely solved in the half century before 1600—more than four hundred years ago. In

---

1 The causal effect is likely less; Ugo Panizza and Eduardo Borensztein (ibid.) estimate it at around 1 percent, similar to the decline in growth rates in countries with debt crises found by Reinhart and Rogoff (2009).

this book, we show how financiers extended credit at a time of high uncertainty over a monarch's finances, sharing in both windfalls and shortfalls. Lenders agreed to forego interest or extend the maturity of loans if the king experienced a bad shock (such as the late arrival of the silver fleet). The system exhibited remarkable stability, bringing essentially the same banking dynasties together with the monarch for over half a century, providing financing and insurance. This is, in itself, a remarkable accomplishment. We ask what made it possible and consider potential lessons for the present.

The second remarkable feature of the debt issuance system evolved by Philip II and his financiers is the stability of the banking institutions. Today, banks are typically not allowed to fail because of their role in keeping the economy going. Bailouts after 2008 were motivated by a perceived need to avoid possibly dramatic repercussions in the real economy. By the same token, sovereign defaults today are considered especially risky because they damage the financial system's health. The sixteenth-century Habsburg monarchy also evolved a system where state borrowing and bankers' lending were intimately related—but one that coped with repeated payment stops.

The main innovation was an effective "risk transfer" mechanism. Savers invested in a share of a loan made by bankers, not in deposits held by the banker—an early form of syndicated lending. Investors shared in both the upside and downside of loans to the king. Bankers thus could repay the investors in *la misma moneda*—literally, "the same currency," meaning that their creditors shared losses in proportion to their investment. Had their repayment obligations remained unchanged, every payment stop could have spelled bankruptcy for the great financiers. This is, of course, the kind of risk transfer that securitized mortgage bonds such as collateralized debt obligations were meant to accomplish prior to the 2007 meltdown—an attempt that failed catastrophically. While lenders lost some money in each payment crisis, the Spanish system avoided the risks of leverage. Bankers did not end up holding the most "toxic" portion of assets, as modern-day banks did in the 2000s. Instead, losses from adverse shocks were widely shared—and so were gains in good times, ensuring a steady supply of willing savers lending to the banking dynasties that financed the Spanish monarchy.

State finances under Philip II have long been a byword for chaos and calamity. From the work of Richard Ehrenberg (1896) on the Augsburg banking house of the Fugger to the observations by Fernand Braudel (1966) in his famous book *The Mediterranean and the Mediterranean World in the Age of Philip II,* every default has been portrayed as a disaster that laid low an entire generation of lenders. Only the eternal folly of humans and hopeless overoptimism of bankers allowed the system to start again, before ending in tears one more time. Most of the earlier scholarship was not based on a detailed examination of state finances, the hard metric of sustainability and solvency, or the profitability of lending contracts. Rather, the hue and cry of bankers and officials during the restructurings themselves were often taken at face value. Reality was quite different.

Long before we began our study, many steps had already been taken to clear away the misunderstandings surrounding Spain's mythical defaults. From the 1960s onward, a generation of scholars started to amass information on the revenues and expenditures of the Habsburg monarchy, loan contracts and silver imports, and fleet arrivals and financial settlement details. Without the works by I.A.A. Thompson, John H. Elliott, Geoffrey Parker, and Modesto Ulloa, among many others, this book would not have been possible. Our first task was to systematize and survey the earlier scholarship. We quickly discovered that it was possible to reconstruct—not with certainty, but with a reasonable degree of confidence—full annual fiscal accounts during Philip II's reign. To do so, we had to obtain information on the exact amount of borrowing in each year. We therefore began by collecting much more detailed information on the short-term borrowings of Philip II than was previously available. Our new series on his short-term loans represents a major investment in archival research. These data serve as a linchpin; they allow us to reconstruct annual series on total debt, spending, and revenues.

With the statistical skeleton in place, we can examine fundamental questions on a firm empirical basis. Did Philip II's debts rise faster than his revenues? How much money was left after paying for his armies along with the pomp and circumstance of court? Did Philip II have to borrow to pay interest? The evidence strongly suggests that Habsburg finances after 1566 were in remarkably good shape: revenue rose in line with expenditure, the debt burden did not explode, and there was on average ample money left to service the debt. By most measures, Philip's empire was more fiscally sound than Britain's in the eighteenth century—a remarkable fact given the many accolades lavished on the latter. Indeed, even under conservative assumptions, the finances of Habsburg Spain were sustainable. Far from conclusive proof of a fiscal system collapsing under its own weight, the payment stops were not the result of an unbridgeable gap between expenditures and revenues. The payment stops—or *decretos*, as contemporaries called them—instead reflected temporary liquidity shocks. Years of high military expenditure combined with low revenues from the Indies could cause the king to reschedule his debts. We argue that these events—though infrequent—were largely foreseen by lenders. We also show that they did not destroy the profitability of lending to the king of Spain. Banking dynasties typically stayed the course, with the same family providing funds decade after decade. Virtually all bankers made money—and most of them earned a healthy rate of return.

Lenders may have been caught unaware when a particular decreto was issued, but the fact that payment stops could occur did not surprise them. It was not the belief that "this time is different," coupled with an endless supply of gullible bankers willing to lend to the "borrower from hell," that led to periods of irrational exuberance. Rather, bankers knew that "next time will be the same": another adverse shock could spell another suspension of payments. In exchange for accepting this risk, they were richly rewarded; average rates of return in good times were high. In this way, the lenders to Philip II were providing insurance as well as financing; in the face of adversity, the king did not have to honor all of his obligations. Importantly, defaults were excusable in the sense that they happened in genuinely bad times.[2] Combined with the contingent features embedded in a great number of contracts, the Spanish lending system survived and thrived after 1566 because it had a great deal of flexibility built into it—and not because the shocks themselves were small.

Our results suggest that the contrast between defaults and a full honoring of commitments is too stark. Instead, bankers and monarch agreed on payments conditional on a large number of different events that could take place. Some of these agreements were implicit. Theoretically possible outcomes ranged from fulfilling the obligations in the loan agreement to the letter all the way to outright repudiation. The latter never occurred; bankers were mostly paid what they had been promised, and most of the modifications that did happen were actually agreed on beforehand. Some unforeseen events could cause individual loans to deviate from the agreed-on contract; the next contract would then offer some resolution for unpaid obligations in exchange for fresh funds. When shocks were large and impossible to contract

---

2 In this regard, they are different from the general pattern in the two hundred years spanning the period 1800–2000, when the link between negative shocks and defaults was at best weak (Tomz and Wright 2007).

over in advance—such as a major military setback—the king would have to renegotiate the terms of earlier loans. As we document based on the archival record, lending proceeded apace, and without any significant changes in terms and conditions.

That the system survived the bankruptcies and continued essentially unchanged needs further explanation. The arrangement was clearly beneficial to all parties, but economic life is full of seemingly efficient, welfare-enhancing transaction structures that nonetheless fall apart because of shortsightedness and competitive avarice. That this did not happen during the crises of 1575 and 1596—the biggest defaults in Philip II's reign—is startling. The lending system functioned not least because the bankers acted as one in times of crisis, cutting the king off from fresh loans when he was not servicing old ones. Every time, the king's advisers sought to conclude a special deal with some lenders, be it the wealthy Spinola of Genoa or the Fugger of Augsburg. Every time, their special offers, normally seasoned with threats, were rejected, and no side deals were cut. Lenders acted in unison, which is why the resolution of the payment stops came to be known as *medio general*—the general settlement.[3]

Why did no lender defy the wrath of their colleagues and take a potentially highly lucrative deal? We argue that two factors were key. First, Philip's main financiers—the Genoese—maintained a tightly knit network. By lending in overlapping syndicates, few bankers did not have simultaneous obligations toward other bankers. This made it harder to break rank. Family ties and social pressure also played their role. What mattered even more, however, was the knowledge that whoever cut a special deal with the king of Spain would probably be defaulted on in turn. Incentives were such that anyone breaking a lending moratorium would induce other lenders—left out of the new deal—to offer even better terms to the king.[4] As a result, the moratoriums never broke down, despite generous offers from the royal side. By examining the rich correspondence of the Fugger brothers, we document that agents were well aware of this incentive structure.

The sovereign debt system evolved by Philip II and his bankers struck a balance between adversarial and cooperative features. Bad times saw bankers shoulder substantial burdens, and settle for "haircuts" (reductions in

---

3 The exception is the early 1557–60 bankruptcy, which we discuss in more detail in chapter 4.
4 Here we take our cue from theoretical work by Kenneth Kletzer and Brian Wright (2000).

principal and interest accrued), lower interest payments, and extended maturities. At the same time, the system only worked because bankers did not give in to the king's borrowing demands in bad times on an opportunistic basis—no fresh lending occurred while he was in default, even if he offered to exempt the financier in question from the decreto.

Spain's power and influence peaked under Charles V and Philip II, and declined thereafter. A generation of earlier authors saw the defaults as harbingers of financial failure: fiscal missteps that at least hastened (and may even have caused) Spain's eventual fall from great power status. An overtaxed economy, according to this view, sooner or later had to decline. In the final analysis, the gap between military ambitions and fiscal resources caused a deterioration of the political and strategic position. Our conclusion is the opposite: Spain declined not because of the way its fiscal policy was conducted but rather in spite of a first-rate system of public finances. As recent research has powerfully argued, Spain's economic performance until 1600 was on par with other European countries (Alvarez Nogal and Prados de la Escosura 2007). International comparisons suggest that Spanish revenues, expenditure, and debt issuance were managed at least as responsibly as in Britain, France, and the United Provinces at the height of their powers, if not more so: expenditure relative to revenues did not rise faster, nor did the debt burden peak at higher ratios.

"Imperial overstretch" was not to blame for Spain's demise from the first rank of European nations. What was? We argue that a combination of insufficient state building and bad luck on the battlefield sowed the seeds of eventual backwardness. The pressures of state financing in times of war did not create an impetus for a more unified, centralized state in Spain: "state building" and state capacity remained far below the levels seen in England or France (Epstein 2000; Grafe 2012).[5] This is partly because the country was much more fragmented to start with; it is also because, at critical junctures, silver revenues flooded in on a scale that made compromises with Castile's representative assembly—the Cortes—seemingly expendable.

Jakob Burckhardt, the influential historian of the Renaissance, once wrote that the point of history was not to be clever for the next time but instead to be "wise forever." We do not argue that financial systems today would be greatly improved if only regulators and policymakers slavishly copied

---

5 On the importance of state capacity for economic growth, see Besley and Persson 2009, 2010.

Habsburg Spain's public finance system. Many of its features, such as lending being concentrated in the hands of a small, tightly knit group of financiers and the dire need for financing as a result of numerous wars, cannot—and should not—be replicated now. What is important is the stunning success that the lenders and the king's advisers had in structuring government borrowing to minimize the risk of long-lasting, severe disruptions of credit relationships. The system seems worthy of emulation not because of each institutional feature but instead because of its effectiveness and flexibility. If incentive problems could be overcome and effective risk-sharing arrangements found in the days of the galleon and messengers on horseback, perhaps the age of the satellite, jet travel, and the Internet can discover a solution to the challenges of state-contingent debt.

CHAPTER 1

LENDING TO THE SOUND OF CANNON

A LOAN GONE AWRY

Gio Girolamo Di Negro was not a happy man as he pored over his account books in Genoa during winter 1596.[1] His company, dedicated to commercial ventures and credit operations, was making a profit—but only a small one. All told, Gio Girolamo controlled a little less than a hundred thousand Genoese lire. He was immensely rich compared to the dockworkers and his own servants. At the same time, his fortune was small compared with the financiers forming the upper classes of Genoese society. With his current profits of about 3 percent annually, Gio Girolamo would never become as rich and powerful as the many potentates in his city.[2] What could be done?

Gio Girolamo's thoughts turned to the loans that many of the leading Genoese banking dynasties had extended to the Castilian Crown. Despite some unpleasantness during the payment stop of 1575—some twenty years earlier—Genoese lenders had made a lot of money financing the Habsburg war machine. As it happened, a relative of his, Niccolò De Negro, had just offered him a chance to get into the business of lending to the king of Spain. Niccolò—or Nicolao, as he had lately taken to calling himself—was one of the four members of the Di Negro family who had established themselves in Madrid. Like most of the Genoese bankers who underwrote the short-term loans

---

1 The documentary basis of our story consists of the *asientos* signed in Madrid, the account book of the Di Negro–Pichenotti partnership, and Gio Girolamo's master account book. These allow us to establish the dates and amounts we report, and calculate the various yields and rates of return. The remaining details, whenever not specifically referenced, are fictional. No letter exchanges between the Italian and Spanish bankers have survived.

2 The master account book—*libro mastro*—of Gio Girolamo is preserved in the Archivio Doria di Genova (ADG), Inventario Doria, 192. The capital and profit figures cited here correspond to the 1596–98 period.

of the Spanish Crown—the famous *asientos*—he had Hispanicized his name.[3] There was a legal requirement that any person entering into a financial transaction with the Crown be a Castilian national; while this was never much of an impediment for the many foreigners who participated in the lending business, it helped to use a Spanish name in official dealings.[4] Being in Madrid was, of course, hugely advantageous when it came to conducting complex negotiations with the Crown.

Nicolao was new to the world of royal finance, but his family had plenty of experience. The earliest loan by a De Negro had been made almost three decades earlier—by Juan Antonio De Negro in 1567. Through the years, various members of the De Negro family lent to the Castilian Crown. Returns had been good; the family would eventually earn an average of 14 percent on its Spanish loans. Nicolao went about his business with unusual energy, extending more credit than his forebears and relatives combined. He first underwrote a loan to the king on May 5, 1595, for just under half a million ducats.[5] This was a large sum, at the upper end of what any individual banker lent.[6] Soon after, he established a partnership with Agustín Spinola, a seasoned financier and prominent member of the powerful Genoese banking family.[7] De Negro and Spinola would lend a further 1.4 million ducats in 1595 and 1596. The majority of these funds were to be delivered in Antwerp, in regular monthly installments, to the paymaster of the Army of Flanders. Once there,

---

3 Throughout the book, we will refer to the bankers by the names that appear in the archival documents. Most of these are Hispanicized names, like Nicolao De Negro. On occasion, the original Italian, German, and Portuguese names are preserved. The family name is always written in the Spanish form De Negro rather than the Italian Di Negro.

4 Several loans were concluded with bankers residing in Genoa and Lisbon. The Fugger, some of the best-known financiers of the time, did not have a family presence in Madrid for long periods. Even during the 1575 bankruptcy, they chose to conduct all negotiations through their agent, Thomas Miller.

5 Archivo General de Simancas (AGS), Contadurías Generales, Legajo 92. "El dicho Nicolas de Negro, asiento tomado con el sobre 379,039 escudos 11 sueldos 11 dineros que provee en Italia y 90,960 ducados 8 sueldos y 10 dineros en esta corte para servicios de su majestad."

6 The ducat, named after a Venetian gold coin, was the Castilian unit of account. In sixteenth-century Castile, coins with a value of 1 ducat were seldom minted and did not circulate widely. The most common form of currency were silver coins, minted either in Spain or its New World colonies. Ducats remained the standard unit of account used in official business. The average loan was just under 200,000 ducats, while the Crown's budget toward the end of the sixteenth century averaged 10 million ducats. Unskilled wages at the end of the sixteenth century in Madrid were roughly one-quarter of a ducat per day (Hamilton 1934). For more details, see chapter 4.

7 Agustín was a common name within the Spinola family. The one who partnered with De Negro was already lending in 1578.

they would be used to pay the soldiers, buy victuals, and keep the wheels of the Habsburg political and military machine turning. Spain had been fighting a bloody insurgency in the Low Countries since the 1560s—a conflict that eventually came to be known as the Eighty Years' War. Like all early modern European wars, it required "money, more money, money all the time."[8] The funds offered (and transferred) by international bankers constituted a key link in the Spanish monarchy's bid for European hegemony.

The loans extended by Spinola and De Negro in 1595 and 1596 covered nearly 15 percent of the royal budget in any one year. No prudent banker would hold that much risk in his own portfolio. De Negro therefore contacted business and family acquaintances who were looking for a good investment, including his Genoese relative, Gio Girolamo. Would he be interested in purchasing a part of his loans? The Madrid bankers charged a 1 percent intermediation fee. Gio Girolamo would then receive interest and capital repayment on the same terms as they received, which were stipulated in the original asientos.

Gio Girolamo took the offer to his occasional partners, the brothers Lazzaro and Benedetto Pichenotti. They decided to establish a separate partnership with the sole purpose of investing in Spanish asientos; Gio Girolamo put up 50 percent of the capital, with the Pichenotti brothers supplying the other half.[9] At the beginning they moved cautiously. The partnership first invested in a 208,000-ducat asiento, subscribed by Spinola and De Negro on February 24, 1596.[10] Their contribution, 5,265 ducats and 4,500 ecus, represented less than a 5 percent stake in the loan.[11] If all went smoothly, by the time the loan was fully repaid, in March 1600, they would have earned a return of 10 percent per year.[12] The Madrid bankers would send the interest and principal

---

8 This was Marshal Tribulzio's advice to Louis XII as he prepared to invade Italy (Ferguson 2001).

9 Establishing separate partnerships for different ventures facilitated accounting, while offering some protection in a world without limited liability. The master account book of the Di Negro–Pichenotti partnership is found in ADG, Inventario Doria, 193. This book was first identified by Giuseppe Felloni (1978). Our description closely follows his account.

10 AGS, Contadurías Generales, Legajo 92. "Los dichos Agustin Spinola y Nicolas de Negro, asiento tomado con ellos sobre 90,000 escuds que se han de proveer en Milan y 112,500 ducados en estos reinos."

11 Since the loan was delivered in Milan, these were Italian ecus, each equivalent to 1.065 ducats in 1596.

12 We calculate the rates of return on the basis of the cash flows implied in the contractual clauses. For a detailed description of our methodology, see chapter 6.

repayments of the loans in the same fashion as they received them from the Crown.[13] No interest or principal were due until 1598; the Genoese partners had to wait for two years to collect the first proceeds of their investment.

Back in Madrid, Spinola and De Negro were coming under increasing pressure to supply more funds. The new president of the Council of Finance, the Marquis of Poza, was taking a hard line with the bankers, demanding large sums on short notice. Word had it that he had threatened Ambrosio Spinola, the leading financier of the time, with prison if he did not make a number of previously agreed-on disbursements.[14] The reason for the marquis's short temper was obvious to anyone with an interest in political matters: in addition to the prolonged fighting in Flanders, the Anglo-Spanish War was putting extraordinary pressure on the treasury. A combined English and Dutch expeditionary force had sacked Cádiz in July 1596; the navy needed to be reinforced; and Spain's involvement in the French Wars of Religion required a constant stream of funds. Poza was impatient, but he was also offering good terms. On July 26, Spinola and De Negro agreed to lend over 1 million ducats, disbursed over fourteen months in Flanders, to be fully repaid by March 1599. The loan would yield 17.6 percent annually—a good return by any standard. Perhaps because of the more enticing terms, Gio Girolamo and the Pichenotti brothers also signed up for a share of this asiento, contributing 30,000 Flemish ecus (some 29,300 ducats).

Each asiento bore the same two words on top of its first page: "El Rey" (the king). From 1556 to 1598, this meant Philip II of Spain, his Catholic majesty, the first monarch in history on whose domains the sun truly never set. Stretching from Flanders to northern Africa and from the American continent to the Philippines, the Spanish Empire had no peers in Philip's time. The vast territories were run by a detail-loving bureaucracy, generating reams on reams of documents on the most arcane aspects of government.

---

13 There is some evidence that exchange operation gains were excluded from the profits passed on to retail investors. In the Pichenotti–Di Negro account book, the ecus are valued at the exchange rate agreed to between the king and Madrid bankers rather than at their metallic content. This suggests that the Madrid bankers kept the profits obtained in the exchange operation.

14 Ambrosio Spinola was the largest lender at the time. With the ramp up in military pressure, he began to suspect that the Crown might default, and delayed or failed to make promised disbursements on existing loan contracts. Carmen Sanz Ayán (2004) used the correspondence of the Marquis of Poza with Cristóbal de Moura, Philip II's closest minister, to document the maneuvers and threats used by Poza to make Spinola hand over the promised funds.

Philip's father, Emperor Charles V, had spent much of his life traveling from one of his European possessions to the next and leading his troops in battle. Philip II preferred to put in long hours at his desk instead, studying an impressive volume of state papers personally and deciding on all the important matters himself.[15] Often working from his austere chamber in the palace-monastery of San Lorenzo de El Escorial, he would make major strategic decisions based on detailed exposes and minutes from his advisers, delving into the tiniest minutiae, and frequently driving ministers and military commanders to desperation. In one famous example, the king first decided on the invasion attempt of England known as the Invincible Armada. The outfitting of the fleet in Lisbon took a long time, not least because the king repeatedly diverted battle-ready ships to other operations. Philip II attempted to direct every aspect of the monumental enterprise from Madrid. The fleet only reached its intended strength after four years, when Philip finally delegated full operational command to the Duke of Medina-Sidonia.[16] Reports that reached Philip's hands were always read, and were often returned full of his personal annotations in the margin. Every document that received his approval—including all the asientos—bore his unmistakable signature: "Yo, el Rey."

By 1596, Philip had slowed down. He was an old man, nearly seventy years of age, and for the past decade had been afflicted by crippling attacks of gout. He had stopped writing in his own hand; his signature, when the arthritis allowed him to put it on paper, had become an unreadable scribble. He barely left his chambers at El Escorial, which he had built to fulfill a vow made before the Battle of St. Quentin, his first victory as king. From the late 1580s, Don Cristóbal de Moura, councillor of war and state, had become his principal minister and confidante. In 1592, Philip made him his *sumiller de corps*—gentleman of the bedchamber. The *sumiller* was the first person the king saw every morning and in whose company he spent the better part of the day.[17]

---

15 For an excellent biography of Philip II, see Parker 2002.

16 On Philip II's management of the Invincible Armada, see Mattingly 1959.

17 The structure and protocol of the Habsburg court was modeled on the Burgundian one, which had been imported by Charles V. The sumiller de corps attended to the personal care of the king, which included handing him a towel and water basin every morning, serving him dinner, and pouring him his cup of wine. Sumiller is, indeed, an adaptation of the French sommelier. Sumillers were far more than personal servants; all of them held high government offices. Their power and influence was greatly increased by the unfettered access to the king afforded by their court position (Martínez Hernández 2010).

This gave Moura, born into a modest family of the Portuguese petty nobility, unrestricted access to the king and a strong say over the affairs of state. In any system of centralized government, access to the power holder is a key determinant of power (Schmitt 1954).[18] It also makes the ruler dependent on the information provided by subordinates. In theory, Philip still insisted on reserving all major decisions to himself; even at the end of his life, he only authorized his son to sign noncritical documents on his behalf. Yet Moura's influence over the king was steadily increasing. By the late 1590s, "the voice of Philip II was increasingly heard in the form of the handwriting of Don Cristóbal."[19]

It was Moura who nudged Philip II to appoint the Marquis of Poza to the presidency of the Council of Finance in June 1596. Moura and Poza were old friends, and had stayed on good terms while they both vied for favor as well as advancement at the royal court. On taking office, Poza had to deal with a dire situation. The humiliating disaster at Cádiz, beyond its psychological impact, had also resulted in the loss of a fleet ready to set sail for the Indies.[20] The war at sea required new galleons, and the soldiers in Brittany and Flanders might mutiny if they went unpaid for much longer. What really alarmed the president, though, was the short-term debt. There were 14 million ducats outstanding—or so he believed—well in excess of a full year's revenue (Castillo 1972). While this turned out to be a gross exaggeration, almost 800,000 ducats had to be repaid in July, and another 1.8 million were due between October and December.[21]

Poza was no friend of the bankers who underwrote the asientos. In his letters to Moura, he spewed invectives against their money-grabbing ways. At one point he wrote that had it been up to him, he could not have enough of their blood.[22] As soon as he took office, Poza began to hatch plans to "unen-

---

18 Interestingly, Carl Schmitt illustrates his point by using a scene from Friedrich Schiller's *Don Carlos*, in which the fictitious Marquis of Posa is allowed immediate access to Philip II. Thereafter, events take a tragic turn.

19 For a description of the role of Don Cristóbal de Moura in the last decade of Philip II's reign, see Martínez Hernández 2010.

20 For contemporary accounts of the sack of Cádiz, see De Abreu 1866.

21 All summary figures for short-term debt are calculated on the basis of our asiento series, described in chapter 3. For alternative figures, together with a chronological description of events, see De Carlos Morales 2008.

22 "Cada día boy descubriendo contra estos jinobeses casos, que si a S. Mg. y a sus ministros no nos combiniese cumplir nuestras palabras, no me bería harto de su sangre" (cited in Sanz Ayán 2004).

cumber" the king's revenues—a euphemism for stopping all payments on asientos, thereby forcing negotiations to convert them into perpetual bonds at lower interest rates.[23] He started assembling evidence of wrongdoing and overcharging by the Genoese. At the same time, Poza negotiated new, large asientos like the ones subscribed by Spinola and De Negro. Offering attractive terms was easy; at this stage, he probably had no intention of making good on them.[24] There was a relatively recent precedent: the suspension of payments in 1575. The situation then had been similar: the Dutch Revolt was raging, the Mediterranean fleet required enormous expenses to hold the strategic advantage gained at the Battle of Lepanto, revenues were flagging, and short-term debt seemed unmanageable. Despite much turmoil, the Crown had emerged in a solid financial position and had not needed to take out short-term loans for another seven years. With a steady hand, the procedure could be made to work again.

In 1574, when his ministers were urging him to issue a bankruptcy decree, Philip II had delayed it for one more year, hoping for an extraordinary shipment of silver, a lull in the wars, or some other intervention that would allow him to avoid reneging on his promises.[25] The king placed a high value on his word and did not take the decision to suspend payments lightly. This time around he embraced the idea much more quickly, perhaps thanks to Moura's influence. The monarch even suggested that his ministers and the president look at the 1575 precedent for guidance.

The decree suspending payments was issued on November 29, 1596. To the few bankers old enough to have been around in 1575, the text sounded eerily familiar. The king declared that he was saddened that few lenders were willing to continue supplying funds and shocked at the high interest they had been charging him over the last few years.[26] The document proceeded to call into question the legality and morality of the interest charges as well as that of the lending business as a whole. To rectify the situation, no asiento debt

---

23 The Spanish term, *desempeñar*, means to free up the revenue streams that had been committed to service asientos. Technically, since the loans were converted to long-term bonds, their service was merely switched to different revenue streams at lower interest rates. For a detailed discussion, see chapter 4.

24 In our account of the discussions between Moura, Poza, and Philip II, we follow the work of Sanz Ayán (2004).

25 For a detailed account of the 1575 bankruptcy and its ensuing settlement, see Lovett 1980, 1982. We further explore it in chapter 5.

26 For a summary of the events following the suspension, see Ulloa 1977, 820.

would be paid until all contracts, disbursements, and repayments had been duly scrutinized, and the interest brought into line with what was "customary." A special committee—the Junta del Decreto—was established to that end.

The timing of the suspension was strategic: over 1.2 million ducats were due just two days later. A few financiers tried to secure a special status for themselves. Some, like Ambrosio Spinola, sought to leverage their financial power, exploring whether the king might continue to service their asientos in exchange for further loans. Others, like the Sauri brothers, appealed to emotion, noting that if they were not paid, many friars, widows, and orphans (to whom they had sold loan participations) would suffer.[27] These efforts were for naught. It quickly became clear that strength was in numbers, and the bankers joined in a negotiating group that would become known as the Compañía del Medio General—the Company of the General Settlement.

Meanwhile, back in Genoa, Gio Girolamo, the Pichenotti brothers, and countless small investors like them cursed their luck. For two decades, lending to the Spanish Crown had worked well—sometimes even spectacularly well—with high returns and prompt payment, at least most of the time. Some investors, like Ambrogio Doria, took to writing increasingly angry letters to their correspondents in Spain, most of which went unanswered.[28] Others waited with trepidation. The experience of 1575 told them what to expect: there would be capital reductions and lengthened repayment terms. In all probability, they would be subject to the same losses that the bankers in Madrid were exposed to. This principle, called la misma moneda, would likely leave them with low-interest perpetuities, rather than the attractive cash returns and timely repayment of principal that their contracts had promised.[29]

---

27 This was a common theme. Writing in 1638, Venetian merchant Giovanni Domenico Peri (1672) described the effects of the 1627 bankruptcy as follows: "Oltre la rovina degli Assentisti, hanosi questi ritirato a dietro molti, che gli soccorevano di rivelantissime partite, e fra gli uni, e gli altri, sono restate esterminate molte ricche famiglie, e molte Vedove, e pupilli insiememente ridotti a miserabile povertà" (In addition to the ruin of the bankers, several other financiers who provided them with funds exited the business. Between one and the others, many rich families were exterminated, and many widows and orphans were at the same time reduced to miserable poverty).

28 ADG, Inventario Doria, 490. "Registro copialettere di Ambrogio D'Oria 1590/1597 più alcuni scritti vari posterirori del 1657/1670."

29 For an overview of the impact of the provision of la misma moneda on Genoese firms and individuals, see Neri 1989. For investors to receive their initial capital outlay, juros would need to be sold. This was possible with royal permission, which could be obtained for a fee.

The negotiations in Madrid opened with some theological pageantry. The Junta del Decreto consulted with the confessors of the king and prince, who were of the opinion that the bankers had engaged in usury and, according to an old law, should forfeit their capital. The Company of the Settlement replied with its own set of theological opinions, pointing out that the king himself had declared the interest to be legal and had suspended the application of any other laws to that effect. As intellectually stimulating as the legal and canonical jousting might have been, it did not last for long. The Crown had been prescient in amassing a small war chest to continue funding the military campaigns while the suspension was in place.[30] Nonetheless, both the Crown and bankers knew that the king would eventually need to settle in order to regain access to credit. The bankers, on their part, were also under pressure, as the moratorium brought business to a screeching halt, cutting deep into their profits.[31]

The investigations of the Junta del Decreto into the outstanding asientos yielded a pleasant surprise. When all short-term debts were added up, the total came to just over seven million ducats, about half the treasury's initial estimate. Accounting discrepancies were not unusual, as no early modern state had a treasury capable of keeping track of fiscal accounts and outstanding debt in a timely fashion. This error, however, was as large as any that there had ever been. Royal finances were much healthier than Poza had believed; perhaps the decision to declare a bankruptcy had been a mistake.[32]

There was certainly an upside to the detailed accounting exercise: the Crown realized that it had much more leeway to reach a quick settlement, and one was struck in short order. Bankers and Crown came to an agreement in November 1597. All outstanding asientos would be converted into a combination of perpetuities to be issued over the next few years. The swap implied a 20 percent loss to the bankers in present value terms. New short-term loans were arranged almost immediately. One of them included a large number of bankers from the Compañía del Medio General. Its rate of return was

---

30 The decision to suspend payments was made as early as November 9, 1596, when secret instructions were issued to embargo the treasure at the Casa de la Contratación and suspend other payments. On that date, the Casa de la Contratación sent a million ducats in bullion to Milan, and from there the Fugger bank transferred it to Flanders in April 1597 (Ulloa 1977, 820).

31 Crown bankruptcies resulted in a liquidity crunch, typically bringing payment fairs throughout Europe to a halt. See Pezzolo and Tattara 2008; Marsilio 2008.

32 The thesis that the 1596 bankruptcy was largely the result of an accounting error was first introduced by Alvaro Castillo (1972) and then taken up by Juan Gelabert (1997).

so high—89 percent—that it almost certainly was a poorly disguised form of granting additional compensation for the default.[33]

At the same time, in Genoa, Gio Girolamo and the Pichenotti brothers waited. They eventually started to receive the same mix of long-term bonds that the Madrid bankers had negotiated with the Crown. Because part of the asientos they invested in had been repaid before the default, they did not lose the full 20 percent agreed to in the settlement. Once the accounts were closed, in late 1600, they had lost 1.32 percent per year for their share in the first contract they invested in, and 5.19 percent annually for their participation in the July 26 one. Their overall annualized loss was thus 4.27 percent.[34] Di Negro must have felt gloomier than we found him at the beginning of our story. As a result of investing in the Spanish loans, his company's overall profit rate slipped to 2.4 percent. Enormous riches were now an ever more distant dream, but he probably took some comfort in his earlier prudence. Less than 10 percent of his capital had been invested in financial assets. Even as he found himself a spurned creditor of the most powerful monarch on earth, the impact on his overall financial health was small. His company would live to trade and invest another day.

ASIENTOS AND THE SYSTEM OF CASTILIAN SOVEREIGN FINANCE

The 1596 bankruptcy that affected Di Negro and the Pichenotti brothers did not represent an innovation in Philip II's financial management. The king had already defaulted three times during his reign—in 1557, 1560, and 1575. The suspensions were widely discussed by contemporaries and ultimately reached mythical status as successive generations of financial historians cited them as egregious examples of repeated sovereign default. Spain went on to become the current "world record holder" for the number of sovereign defaults in history.[35] Modern journalists like to refer to the plight of Philip II

---

33 AGS, Contadurías Generales, Legajo 93. "Francisco y Pedro de Maluenda, Nicolao Doria, Marco Antonio Judice, Nicolao de Fornari, Juan y Francisco Galeto y otros sus consortes." It is interesting to note that because this was a new loan, the extraordinary compensation accrued only to the Madrid financiers and not to their downstream investors who had been affected by the default.

34 For our exploration of the overall Pichenotti–Di Negro venture as well as its upstream and downstream impact, see Drelichman and Voth forthcoming.

35 Spain and Castile, its predecessor state, defaulted thirteen times between 1500 and the present (Reinhart and Rogoff 2009).

and his bankers as an early instance of irrational confidence and fiscal mis-management.[36] This book revolves around one central question: How could Philip II borrow so much and default so often?

The story that opens this chapter traces the funds from small investors in Genoa to the treasury of Philip II and back. We also know what the borrowed funds were used for: war. War in Flanders, war in the Mediterranean, war in the English Channel, war in the Atlantic—always war. Philip II cultivated an image of restraint and thoughtfulness that earned him the moniker "the Prudent King." And yet he was at war in every single year of his long reign.[37] Military ventures could bring much glory—such as his victories at Saint-Quentin and Lepanto—or the disgrace that followed the rout of the Armada. Battlefield successes could confer strategic advantages: the War of the Holy League confined the Ottomans to the eastern Mediterranean and secured the shipping routes of European states. They could link territories together; the famous Spanish Road that connected northern Italy with the Low Countries was a result of the 1559 treaty of Cateau-Cambrésis, which concluded the so-called Italian Wars between Spain and France. Victories could even add whole empires to a king's possessions, as in the case of the acquisition of Portugal in 1580. What wars almost never did was to bring in ready money. The financial tools pioneered by German bankers and refined by the Genoese could mobilize resources, and then transfer them where needed—but those resources had to come from somewhere else. Philip II relied on two main sources of funding: American silver and the thriving economy of Castile.

Although known the world over as the king of Spain, Philip II never held such a title. He was instead the ruler of several separate kingdoms, each with their own fiscal, judicial, and military institutions. There was no uniformity of taxes, rules, laws, or forms of representation. Among all of Philip's territories, Castile was by far the most important. It comprised some two-thirds of the land area of modern-day Spain, including virtually all of the northern Atlantic coastline, the central plateau, and Andalusia in the south. Castile also accounted for over three-quarters of population and economic activity. The Kingdom of Aragon, whose relative standing had declined steadily since its heyday in the late Middle Ages, was a distant second.

---

36 See, for example, "The Dark Side of Debt," *Economist*, September 23–29, 2006.
37 Parker (1998) tabulates the different campaigns of Philip II.

Castile experienced strong economic growth during the sixteenth century. Its population expanded from 4.8 million in the 1530s to 6.8 million in the 1590s.[38] Fiscal pressure increased at the same time, multiplying the Crown's resources. By a strange twist of fate, Castile was the sole kingdom to exert jurisdiction over Spain's possessions in the New World along with their rich silver mines.[39] This was not trivial; in the last decade of the century, taxes on treasure remittances amounted to one-quarter of the total revenue.[40] Philip II was not poor. Still, transforming Peruvian silver ores or the tithes of a town in Extremadura into powerful armies on the battlefields of Flanders required complex financial engineering.

Asientos were a formidable tool in the arsenal of early modern finance. First used by Charles V to finance the bribes that secured his election as Holy Roman emperor, they were underwritten by German, Genoese, Spanish, and Portuguese banking families. They were short-term, largely unsecured loans, with maturities stretching from a few months to a few years. Although more expensive than perpetual bonds, asientos could be combined with transfer and exchange operations that allowed the Spanish kings to access large financial resources on short notice at virtually every corner of their European dominions. Bankers offered them eagerly. Behind the attractive promised rates of return stood the flood of silver that poured into Europe from the Americas through Seville, arriving on the fabled treasure fleets, and the tax revenues of the thriving economy of Castile.[41] In a satirical poem, Francisco de Quevedo y Villegas wrote that money was born in the Indies, died in Spain, and was buried in Genoa. He forgot to add that asientos were its birth, death, and burial certificates.[42] To explain how Philip II was able to maintain uninterrupted access to credit despite his four defaults, we will need to examine in detail the nature and function of asientos.

---

38 Estimates of Castilian population in the sixteenth century vary. We use the "consensus estimates" in Alvarez Nogal and Prados de la Escosura 2007; a discussion of alternative figures can be found in this source as well. Population growth in a Malthusian world is a direct measure of economic growth (Ashraf and Galor 2011).

39 For a historical analysis of Castile's ascendancy in the sixteenth century, see chapter 2.

40 Chapter 3 provides an overview of fiscal institutions, and chapter 4 reconstructs the yearly fiscal accounts of Castile.

41 We describe Castilian debt instruments in detail in chapter 4.

42 One of the stanzas of the famous letrilla "Don Dinero" by Francisco de Quevedo reads: "Nace en las Indias honrado / donde el mundo le acompaña / viene a morir en España / y es en Génova enterrado."

DOCUMENTS AND DATA

Paper, and yet more paper. The growing bureaucracy of Philip II's empire produced it in droves, and still the Marquis of Poza happened to overestimate outstanding debt in the 1590s by a factor of two. To examine the basis of borrowing and repayment, to understand the rhythms of taxing and spending, requires information that contemporaries themselves did not have. Today, for countries with functioning statistical agencies, databases containing such information are available at the press of a button. They are vital to apply the standard tools of national accounting and international macroeconomics. Crucially, the underlying fiscal and financial data need to be reasonably complete, and be observed at regular intervals. This was beyond the administrative capabilities of decentralized fledgling national states during the early modern period. As the confusion of the Marquis of Poza illustrates, rulers and ministers often had very little idea of how much revenue they took in, how much they spent, or how much they owed. Our effort to provide a comprehensive assessment of the Castilian system of government finance therefore requires more macroeconomic data than would have been available to the president of the Council of Finance at any given time. One of this book's central tasks was to assemble estimates of the national accounts of Castile and the details of debts outstanding. The resulting database forms the core of our study.

Without the efforts of an earlier generation of scholars, our book could not have been written. Our series of revenue, for example, was constructed on the basis of Ulloa's (1977) monumental effort; his almost 900-page account of royal finances under Philip II was essential for our work.[43] Similarly, we compiled the first comprehensive view of Castilian military expenditures by aggregating data unearthed by several military historians, especially Geoffrey Parker.[44] Measures of long-term debt and population as well as estimates of national income were also gleaned from the secondary literature.[45] Finally, we incorporated into our analysis the results of the investigations that royal officials duly conducted after each suspension of payments—the last of which revealed the nature of Poza's mistake.[46]

---

43 We present our revenue series in chapter 4.
44 We present our series of military expenditures along with a full list of sources in chapter 4.
45 For two notable sources for these data, among many others, see Alvarez Nogal and Prados de la Escosura 2007; Thompson 1976, 1994a.
46 These data are found in several sources; we use Artola 1982.

Philip II never defaulted on long-term debt, and hence the analysis of his defaults must necessarily focus on short-term loans.[47] While sixteenth-century asientos have been the subject of many studies, there is no authoritative source on their overall volume.[48] Earlier authors, most notably Felipe Ruiz Martín and Ramón Carande, studied the workings of individual contracts. Despite their detailed explorations, we do not have a comprehensive analysis of asiento terms and conditions, or their evolution through time (Ruiz Martín 1965, 1968).[49] These can only be understood by examining the primary sources in detail.

The early modern Castilian state is known for generating massive amounts of documentation. Until 1561 the court had no fixed seat, and kings often took their documents with them wherever they went. Charles V was the first to find a permanent location for his personal papers, housing them in one of the towers of the castle of Simancas, near Valladolid. Philip II, who keenly understood the value of preserving state documents, decided to establish a proper archive in the castle. On his orders, the architect Juan de Herrera—also responsible for the design and execution of El Escorial—redesigned the building to serve as a repository for royal documents. The castle of Simancas thus became the first purpose-built government archive in the world; its operating instructions, issued in 1588, are similarly considered the first extant set of archival rules. Over time, until its closure in the nineteenth century, the Archive of Simancas became the resting place of all the documentation generated by the Crown.[50]

The transfer of documentation to the archive was haphazard at first, and the records of the early days of Philip II's reign are spotty.[51] Starting in 1566,

---

47 Some of the long-term bonds could be in poor standing, such as those issued against revenues from the Casa de la Contratación. These typically traded at a 40 to 50 percent discount, suggesting that interest payments were not always made as promised (Ehrenberg 1896; Ruiz Martín 1965).

48 Ulloa (1977) provides summary annual figures of short-term debt, which unfortunately suffer from double counting issues. These originated from conflating summary information for loans taken out by field commanders in Flanders with documents issued at the Court. For details, see chapter 4.

49 Ramón Carande (1987) conducted a similar effort for the reign of Charles V. More studies are available for the seventeenth century. Alvarez Nogal (1997) studied lending to the Crown in the times of Philip IV; Sanz Ayán (1998) did likewise for the reign of Charles II; and Gelabert (1999a) covered the period between 1598 and 1650.

50 AGS, Ministry of Education, Culture and Sport of Spain, 2012. http://www.mcu.es/archivos /MC/AGS/Presentacion/Historia.html (accessed August 8, 2012).

51 While the archive was for the most part well cared for throughout its history, it did see

the archive began to work in a highly systematic fashion. Nine boxes, collected by the Contaduría Mayor de Cuentas, contain a copy of every asiento issued between 1566 and 1600, among several other papers. While earlier scholars have analyzed these documents, they mostly relied on the summary description found on the first page of every contract. As we began our research, no scholar had yet attempted a comprehensive coding of the loan documents, which in many cases run to twenty or more pages. In an effort that spanned six years, we codified almost five thousand manuscript pages, clause by clause. The results, presented throughout this book, offer unprecedented insight into the world of early modern sovereign finance.[52]

THE ORIGINS OF SOVEREIGN DEBT MARKETS

Before we turn to the debts and defaults of Philip II in detail, it is useful to ask why debt existed at all. Why did states need to borrow? And how did they acquire the ability to do so? Private individuals had used credit for millennia; rules against usury are among the oldest economic regulations known to humans (Glaeser and Sheinkman 1998). And yet government debt is a relatively recent invention. Neither Rome's nor China's rulers contracted government debt on a significant scale; the Ottoman Empire for most of its history did not issue debt either.[53] Medieval kings did borrow and occasionally default on their obligations; Edward III allegedly ruined scores of Florentine bankers when he declared a payment stop in 1339. Those debts, however, were private in nature. It was only with the advent of the Italian republics that states themselves contracted debts. Late medieval Europe "invented" government debt as we know it.

From the sixteenth century onward, states accumulated debt on a modern scale, reaching 20 to 60 percent of GDP. By 1800, the most indebted (and militarily most successful) country, Britain, had debts exceeding total national production by a factor of two. Our focus is on an early stage of the process that eventually allowed states to accumulate mountains of debt and build the fiscal machinery that supported them.

---

rough times as well. It is said that during the Napoleonic invasions, French soldiers used the papers as bedding for their horses. Some of the missing documentation might have suffered this particular fate.

52 The main asiento data are fully described in chapter 4.

53 While Roman politicians were frequently deeply indebted, the Roman treasury sold no bonds or bills (Frederiksen 1966).

THE EMERGENCE OF TRANSPERSONAL STATES

Before there could be sovereign debt, there had to be sovereign states—states with clearly defined borders and a center of power, capable of asserting a monopoly of violence, administering justice, and raising taxes on a significant scale. They had to show persistence over time, control a clearly defined geographic unit, demonstrate stable, impersonal institutions, and successfully assert the need for loyalty from their subjects (Strayer 1970). By this standard, European states in 1500 were primitive. In the words of Charles Tilly (1990, 42), the continent was divided into more than five hundred "states, would-be states, statelets, and state-like organizations." Princes frequently owed allegiance to other rulers—sometimes more than one.[54] Rulers typically "lived on their own," meaning that their demesne income was the principal source of revenue. Justice was administered by local courts and vassals; armed force often had to be hired from condottieri, military entrepreneurs who would provide armies of mercenaries to the highest bidder.

David Stasavage (2011) analyzes the earliest issuance of long-dated debt in Europe. Autonomous cities succeeded in placing long-term debt well before territorial states did. The Republic of Venice, for example, began to borrow in 1262, and continued to do so with no interruptions until 1785. Genoa and Hamburg, Siena and Florence, and Basel and Cologne were not far behind. In contrast, Castile was the earliest territorial state to issue annuities and perpetuities, called *juros*, starting in the fifteenth century.[55]

Despite a lack of long-term instruments, medieval rulers could borrow, if only on a limited scale and for short periods, at high interest rates (Stasavage 2011, figure 2.2). For instance, Edward III accumulated debts from the Bardi and Peruzzi banking families in the fourteenth century (before defaulting). Medieval rulers faced two difficulties in borrowing: commitment and the personal nature of their debts. Divine rulers were not always inclined to repay. The solution to this problem was for a representative assembly to in-

---

54 As in the case of the dukes of Prussia (a fief of the Polish Crown), who also were subjects of the Holy Roman emperor.

55 Juros—annuities or perpetuities backed by specific revenue streams—had existed since at least the fourteenth century. In their early incarnations, they were royal grants given in exchange for political loyalty or military service. In the late fifteenth century, they assumed all the characteristics of sovereign debt: they were sold for cash, a seniority system was established, and they were allowed to trade in a secondary market (albeit in exchange for a fee). See Toboso Sánchez 1987. See also our discussion in chapter 3.

fluence policy "just enough" to constrain abuses of power, while allowing the emergence of a strong executive and powerful fiscal machinery—for states to become "strong" and good at taxation, but constrained.[56] Daron Acemoglu (2005) provides a theoretical discussion of this fundamental problem; empirical work by Mark Dincecco (2011) shows that constrained and centralized powers managed to raise the highest revenues in the early modern period. In effect, territorial powers ideally had to become more like the medieval city-states that pioneered borrowing: permanent, transpersonal entities with substantial resources and credible commitment.

In addition to the commitment problem, another aspect merits consideration. Initially, royal debts were personal—debts of the king, not of the kingdom. Before territorial states could borrow on a massive scale and for the long term, they had to become transpersonal. Such debts could only be contracted by entities that transcended the individual. Cities had long solved this problem; the corporatist structure of the Republic of Venice, for example, ensured that debts would be serviced long after the reigning doge had changed.

The problem for monarchs was more complicated. In a famous book titled *The King's Two Bodies*, Ernst Kantorowicz (1957) studied the medieval origins of the idea of sovereignty. He argued that in medieval political theology, the king had two bodies: the "Body natural" and the "Body politic." The former is mortal; the latter is everlasting. The death of one king implies that another one is immediately placed on the throne. This is reflected in the famous words "The king is dead! Long live the king!" originally used in the accession of Charles VII to the French throne in 1422. The same phrase was standard in England, Spain, and Denmark, among other places. *Auctoritas*—the power of the king—was instantly transferred from deceased to new ruler.

Interestingly, institutional constraints on the monarch actually played *against* the emergence of a transpersonal state. Where monarchs had to be crowned, for instance, the transfer of auctoritas was not instantaneous but instead subject to a delay. The elections of rulers—as in the Holy Roman Empire—could cause a lengthy interregnum. The fundamental problem for early modern states was to find a sweet spot, balancing the need for resources with constraints on monarchical power so that repayment was a likely prospect,

---

56 According to Stasavage (2011), the size of a state was crucial; only relatively compact territories allowed representatives to travel frequently to assemblies, voicing their concerns and overseeing spending.

while evolving a permanent institutional structure. Absolutism—not the theater of it, but rather the legal doctrine of royal power as evolved by theorists such as Jean Bodin and Samuel von Pufendorf—produced a legal conceptualization of the state that allowed it to make near-permanent commitments.[57]

THE NEED TO BORROW: WARTIME SPENDING AND THE RISE OF THE FISCAL-MILITARY STATE

The need to borrow was intimately related to the cost of war. No other activity was nearly as costly. As the early sixteenth-century writer Robert de Balsac observed, "Most important of all, success in war depends on having enough money to provide whatever the enterprise needs" (cited in Ferguson 2001). The need for ample funding—and the ability to ramp spending up quickly—was caused by technological and political changes.

After 1500, a "military revolution" transformed warfare in Europe (Parker 1976). The invention of gunpowder meant that old medieval city walls no longer offered protection; fortifications that had withstood long sieges could now be demolished in a matter of hours. The increasing use of cannon therefore required an entirely new set of protective walls, the so-called *trace italienne*. These walls typically consisted of massive bulwarks made of earth and covered with brick. The perimeter was highly jagged, as angled construction increased the resistance to an artillery attack. There was often an inner and outer set of walls, separated by a moat. The new fortifications also meant that wars became longer, with many sieges lasting more than a year.

The rise of firearms translated into a need to train soldiers. Only permanent, "standing" armies could be drilled to the level of perfection that the use of harquebuses and muskets required. Often composed of groups of mercenaries in the beginning of the early modern period, armies became increasingly professional, officered by the nobility of the home country. They also expanded in size. Relative to the population, armies after 1500 could be quite large. For example, while imperial Rome and Byzantium had no more than 0.5 to 1 percent of the population under arms, Sweden under Gustav Adolph reached a ratio of 7.5 percent—ahead of Germany in 1914 (6 percent)

57 The view that political absolutism in the early modern period was synonymous with rule by an omnipotent despot has been increasingly questioned in the literature. Instead, a closer look at the practice of government reveals that absolutism is best described as a social arrangement to the mutual benefit of both the elite and Crown (Mousnier 1979).

Table 1. Frequency of war

Century	Number of wars	Average duration (years)	Percentage of years under warfare
Sixteenth	34	1.6	95
Seventeenth	29	1.7	94
Eighteenth	17	1.0	78
Nineteenth	20	0.4	40
Twentieth	15	0.4	53

Source: Tilly 1990.
Note: A year is considered "under warfare" if there is at least one war involving the great powers taking place during any part of that year.

and not far behind the United States in 1944 (9 percent) (Gennaioli and Voth 2012). Similarly, navies that were originally composed of refitted merchant vessels became increasingly large, centralized organizations with ships designed for one aim only: to prevail in naval battle. These were immensely costly; a British ship of the line in the eighteenth century cost more than the capital of the world's biggest iron works (Brewer 1988).

Warfare was not only frequent after 1500; it became a near-permanent feature of the political landscape. Tilly (1990) calculates that for every hundred years in the sixteenth and seventeenth centuries, there was a great power war under way in ninety-five of them; the rate for the eighteenth century is only marginally lower. At the height of intensive warfare, during the Thirty Years' War, close to half of the European population was affected by military conflict in a given year, as table 1 portrays. All these changes—the arms used, the rise of permanent, large armies and navies, new fortifications, and high frequency and great length of conflict—made wars vastly more expensive. Success in war depended in the early modern period on financial resources; infinite quantities of money constituted the "sinews of power," in Marcus Tullius Cicero's famous words.[58] Successful European powers typically spent around three-quarters of tax revenue on war and related activities.[59]

---

58 "Nervos belli, pecuniam infinitam" (Brewer 1988).
59 For example, France under Louis XIV spent 20 to 30 million livre tournois per year on non-military budget items; military spending in peacetime was approximately 50 to 60 million, and reached peaks of 140 and 190 million during the Nine Years' War and the War of Spanish Succession (Velde 2003). These figures exclude debt service (which mostly went on paying debts run up during earlier wars).

Warfare during the early Middle Ages had been a relatively cheap affair; armies were small, and a large part of the labor used consisted of vassals who were obliged to follow their prince into battle. Kings had generally been able to live "on their own," using their demesne income (Landers 2003). Soon, however, rulers in the high and late medieval period began to use mercenaries on a significant scale.[60] After the Hundred Years' War, fiscal exigencies— partly driven by the increasing use of mercenaries—pushed kings to look for revenue on a much greater scale (Ormrod 1995; Verbruggen 1997). For example, Henry VIII's dissolution of the monasteries helped to cover the expense of his French campaigns. Representative assemblies all over Europe were increasingly asked to approve additional funding in the form of excises and tariffs. While many taxes were farmed out initially, later in the early modern period, the more successful states started to centralize the administration of indirect taxes.[61] No state (with the exception of England during the Napoleonic Wars), though, succeeded in introducing an effective income tax.

Over time, most states raised more revenues. Figure 1 shows the distributions of total tax revenue for different European states at various points in time.[62] Each box indicates the range from the twenty-fifth to seventy-fifth percentile at each point in time; the "whiskers" depict the entire range of the distribution, while the middle line inside the inner box shows the median. Tax revenue overall surged dramatically, from 214 tons of silver per year in 1509 to 6,800 tons in 1789. Cross-sectional dispersion increased dramatically: some states were vastly more successful in raising tax revenue than others (Besley and Persson 2010). France increased its revenues tenfold during the early modern period; the Ottoman Empire did so by only 50 percent.

While both inflation and population growth contributed a little to the higher figures, the single most important driver was taxation per capita. In 1509 the average European power extracted taxes per capita equivalent to 3.5 times the average urban worker's daily wage; by 1789, this figure had risen to twelve days' pay. Some states raised taxes even higher. In England, say, the eightyfold increase in total revenue occurred at the same time as a thirtyfold rise in taxes per capita. Most of this was not due to higher incomes.

---

60 Similarly, cities increasingly paid their citizens for military services that were initially simply an obligation associated with citizenship (Stasavage 2011).

61 One of the most effective revenue services, the British Excise and Customs Office, employed more than eight thousand officials directly by the end of the eighteenth century.

62 The states included are England, France, Venice, Prussia, Poland, the Dutch Republic, Spain, Austria, and the Ottoman Empire (taken from Karaman and Pamuk 2010).

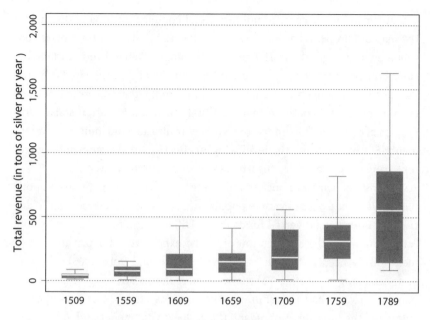

FIGURE I. Distribution of total revenue for select European states.
Source: Karaman and Pamuk 2010.

Establishing an efficient tax administration was key for surviving as a state in the early modern period. Without the ability to tax, there could be no borrowing, and without the ability to borrow, there could be no success on the battlefield.

Once rulers possessed a strong army, they could also eliminate domestic opposition. Charles V, to take one example, successfully suppressed the Comuneros Revolt in Castile in 1520–21. The royal forces vanquished the rebel militia at the Battle of Villalar, in April 1521; rebel leaders were beheaded. Castile went on to become by far the most taxed of the Habsburg territories.[63]

For all the theater associated with it, absolutism did reflect a partial shift in power. After 1500, the tendency was firmly toward centralization, the monopoly of violence, and states that could enact binding laws for all their citizens. Ancient "liberties" and tax exemptions (for the clergy or nobility) came under attack. Internal customs barriers were replaced by external tariffs and consumption taxes. Progress could stall or go into reverse—as it did under Spain's Bourbon kings—but "the tide was evidently coming in" after 1500.[64]

---

63 We review the genesis and aftermath of the Comuneros Revolt in detail in chapter 2.
64 After Alfred Lord Tennyson's line: "a single breaker may recede; but the tide is evidently

States run by a successful military-fiscal complex eventually dominated the map of Europe. What had been a patchwork of different territories consolidated into larger territorial units. For example, England and Scotland became unified after the Act of Union in 1707, and Poland disappeared from the European map altogether. Consolidation in the nineteenth century became even more rapid, as both Germany and Italy turned into nation-states. This process of consolidation interacted with centralization and military developments. States that lagged in developing an effective fiscal system and competent army were eventually absorbed by more successful powers.

The costs of war were not limited to the pressures they put on the public purse. War could cause massive population losses and severe economic disruption. Borrowing diverted funds from civilian to military uses. In Britain, "crowding out"—the substitution of public expenditure for private investment—likely occurred (Williamson 1987; Temin and Voth 2005). The medium- and long-term effects of war were more limited. In an agrarian society, population losses had a silver lining, raising per capita incomes: fewer people cultivated the same amount of land (Clark 2007; Voigtländer and Voth 2013). Wooden houses could be rebuilt quickly. Overall, there is agreement in the literature that the effects of war were not overwhelmingly negative for output. In the words of Jan De Vries (1976), "It is hard to prove that military action checked the growth of the European economy's aggregate output."[65]

Some scholars have even argued that the ruthless pursuit of military power—extended to trade relationships in the eighteenth century by mercantilists—also laid the basis for greater economic riches. Military technology advanced faster and further in Europe after 1500 than in the rest of the world—probably as a result of a highly belligerent environment (Hoffman 2011). There may have been technological spillovers to private industry.[66]

---

coming in." This is not to say that most countries overcame hurdles like internal customs barriers with ease. In Germany and Italy, territorial fragmentation lasted into the nineteenth century; in France, customs barriers persisted through the fall of the old regime. For a quantitative analysis, see Dincecco 2011.

65 Myron Gutmann (1980) argues that in areas that saw extended warfare, such as the Basse-Meuse region of France, the economic structure could successfully adapt to the presence of armies and occasional fighting.

66 Patrick O'Brien (2003) contends that Britain's rise as an industrial power owed much to its bellicose and mercantilist policies. The evidence to support this claim is at best mixed.

In the case of early modern city-states, Ehrenberg (1896, 6) argued that "credit was [the] strongest weapon in the fight for freedom." Princes similarly depended on credit to outspend and outfight their rivals. Without the ability to increase spending rapidly in wartime, military defeat loomed large—followed by losses of reputation, treasure, and territory. For each political entity, access to borrowing was a godsend. As states and cities borrowed more, however, they drove up the length, intensity, and cost of war. Fiscal exhaustion as much as defeat on the battlefield sealed the fate of the weaker contenders; as a Spanish military commander eloquently put it, "Victory will go to whoever possesses the last *escudo*" (Parker 1998).[67] It was against this backdrop that Philip II ran up enormous debts and defaulted on them four times, while continuing to expand what was already the largest empire on earth.

THE SPANISH CASE: THE DEBTS AND DEFAULTS OF PHILIP II COMPARED

Our book is a case study of a single sovereign borrower—Philip II of Spain. How does his borrowing history compare with the general pattern of cross-border debt and default between 1800 and the present? Table 2 presents summary statistics for the key indicators of sovereign debt in the past two centuries, side by side with the same figures for Philip II's reign.

The reign of Philip II registered frequent defaults; more than one year out of five saw some kind of payment suspension. And yet the tumultuous history of sovereign debt since 1800 registers similar ratios. In the data set used by Reinhart and Rogoff, roughly 20 percent of countries were in default on average in any given year. In general, countries with a history of defaults suspended payments again (Lindert and Morton 1989; Reinhart, Rogoff, and Savastano 2003); in the case of Philip II, there was a sequence of four defaults. These are explored in more detail in chapter 4, and constitute the start of what went on to become a record-setting sequence of thirteen suspensions: no country in recorded history has defaulted more times.

---

67 These are the words of Don Bernardino de Mendoza, a sixteenth-century soldier and diplomat. The escudo, or ecu, was a coin and unit of account used throughout Europe.

Table 2. Philip II and the general pattern of debt and default since 1800

Issue	General pattern	Philip II
Frequency of default	20%[a]	21.4%[i]
Serial default probability	35–80%[b]	100%
Haircuts	6.9%–72.9%[c]	20–38%[j]
Average length of restructuring period	8 years[d]	2.25 years
Interest rate penalty after default	None	None
Average debt-to-GDP ratio	52.8%[e]	~60%[k]
Fiscal revenue-to-GDP ratio	16.3%[f]	~10%[k]
Rate of return (nominal and promised ex ante)	4.9–6.9%[g]	10.3–24.1%[l]
Excess return (real and ex post)	−1.92–2.53[h]	3.16%

[a] Reinhart and Rogoff 2009. Michael Tomz and Mark Wright (2007) calculate that there were 250 defaults in a set of 175 countries since 1820. This implies a much lower default rate; if the average duration of a default was eight years, then there would have been a default in only 6.3 percent of the country years. The reasons for the discrepancy are most likely that many of the 175 countries in their database are relatively young and that the true number of potential default years is much lower than implied in our calculation.

[b] Tomz and Wright 2007. Calculated as the frequency of default, given an earlier default episode.

[c] Sturzenegger and Zettelmayer 2008.

[d] Benjamin and Wright 2009.

[e] World Development Indicators. Includes countries with information on central government balance as well as general government debt.

[f] World Development Indicators. Average for all countries with observations in 1960–2000.

[g] Lindert and Morton 1989.

[h] Lindert and Morton 1989.

[i] Philip II reigned for forty-two years and was in default during nine of them (across four bankruptcies).

[j] Third and fourth defaults only.

[k] GDP figures are highly uncertain; we use estimates in Alvarez Nogal and Prados de la Escosura 2007.

[l] Twenty-fifth to seventy-fifth percentile of the modified internal rate of return (MIRR).

Throughout history, the size of haircuts has varied by at least a factor of ten—from less than 7 percent to more than 70 percent. Philip II's defaults were relatively mild by modern standards; the biggest and most severe rescheduling, the medio general of 1575, led to average losses of 38 percent. The 1596 default was even milder and resulted in losses of 20 percent in net present value (NPV) terms.

Restructurings under Philip II were also surprisingly swift. The average renegotiation in the recent past took eight years (Tomz and Wright 2007).[68] Philip II and his bankers typically settled within twenty-six months—a length of time that declined with each default. The 1596 episode was resolved within a year. Interestingly, countries that defaulted in the past typically did not experience an increase in the interest rates at which they could borrow after a resumption of lending (Lindert and Morton 1989). This was also true in the case of Philip II, where lending conditions remained broadly unchanged before and after the well-documented defaults of 1575 and 1596.[69]

Debt-to-GDP ratios have fluctuated greatly in the past. On average, countries have been able to borrow just over 50 percent of their output. Philip II accumulated substantial debts by the standards of the age. With the total value of outstanding debt close to 60 percent of GDP, Habsburg Spain could have qualified for initial euro membership, but only just. For an early modern state, accumulating such debts should perhaps be thought of as a sign of success—of an administrative machine producing fiscal revenues on a scale large enough to make repayments a distinct possibility in the eyes of lenders (Besley and Persson 2010). Certainly the ability of the Spanish monarchy to raise and allocate around 10 percent of GDP in taxes and contributions was unusual at the time, and must be recognized as a major accomplishment.

On average since the nineteenth century, lending to sovereigns has been profitable, but this generally positive experience has been punctuated by periods of sharp losses. The same was true of lending to Philip II. We calculate that bankers on average made greater profits than what was available elsewhere (chapter 6). These were also slightly higher than those found in the more recent past.[70] While Peter Lindert and Peter Morton (1989) document excess returns of up to 2.5 percent a year, we find an annual value of 3.16 percent over a thirty-year period.[71]

To sum up, the borrowings of Philip II of Spain seem remarkably familiar to the modern eye. The debt levels, size of haircuts, rates of return, interest

---

68 Reinhart and Rogoff (2009) show that the range since 1845 is one to seventy-eight years, with a median of six years before 1946 and three years thereafter.

69 For a detailed discussion of this point, see chapters 6 and 7.

70 There are some cases of sovereign lending in the late twentieth century that were even more profitable for investors (over relatively short periods) than lending to Philip II; we discuss them in more detail in chapter 8.

71 While Philip II ruled for over forty years, we only have data for thirty-one years of his reign.

rate penalties after payment suspensions, and default frequencies were not fundamentally different from what scholars have documented for the two centuries after 1800. That so many outcomes are similar suggests that the forces at work today are the same ones that allowed the market for sovereign debt to thrive in sixteenth-century Habsburg Spain.

THE FOUR QUESTIONS

This book's central concern—why Philip II could borrow so much while defaulting so often—is broad and complex. We break it down into smaller, more digestible issues and structure the book around four key questions. Did Philip II have enough resources to pay back his debts? If yes, what prevented him from behaving opportunistically? (That is, why did he not just default to make himself better off?) What were the benefits for the bankers? How can we interpret the recurring defaults? In the language of economics, these questions address the sustainability of debt, the compatibility of incentives, the profitability of lending, and the nature of contracting.

COULD PHILIP II PAY BACK HIS DEBTS?

Our first order of business is to establish whether the Crown of Castile had the capacity to actually service and repay its debts. If bankers lent to a monarch who could not have possibly repaid his debts, then bankruptcies are a foregone conclusion. Financiers would have to be irrational (in an economic sense) to extend credit to such a sovereign, but this would hardly be the first—or last—time that lenders did not act in their own best interests. Indeed, repeated defaults have been invoked as a sign of irrationality by many historians and economists.[72]

In macroeconomics, the term "sustainability" describes a situation when debts can be serviced indefinitely into the future. We therefore ask whether Castile's debt load was sustainable, using the standard tools and tests of modern international finance. To that end, we construct a set of national accounts for Castile at an annual frequency between 1566 and 1596. This thirty-

---

72 For two prominent examples, see Braudel 1966; Reinhart and Rogoff 2009.

one-year data series is the earliest of its kind for any sovereign state in history completed so far.

Armed with our fiscal data, we show that Castile passes several tests of debt sustainability, and that these results resist various robustness checks. In many ways, the results of our accounting exercises are too pessimistic to judge the actions of sixteenth-century actors. Our sustainability standard is the same one applied by the International Monetary Fund (IMF) when evaluating the fiscal solvency of modern states. It is both stringent as well as ahistorical; Philip II's finances pass this test with flying colors.

Castile in the second half of the sixteenth century raised much more money in taxes than it spent on the armies, royal court, and law enforcement. In other words, it ran massive primary surpluses, which could be—and were—used for debt service. On average, Castile's growing debts between 1550 and 1600 were well supported by rising tax revenues; as the debt burden grew, the country generated higher and higher primary surpluses. Both tax increases and silver revenues from the Americas helped to keep the weight of rising debt in check. The Castilian debt burden in the sixteenth century was no higher overall than that of highly successful nineteenth- and twentieth-century economies.

Castile also spent much more than could be expected on its wars, while receiving almost no monetary returns from them. Had some campaigns been more successful or just shorter, the decline in expenditure would have vastly improved the Crown's already-adequate ability to service its loans. Lenders were not wrong in expecting that Philip II would have enough resources to pay them back in the long run. Although there were periods when liquidity was tight, on average the money to service the asientos was there. The Crown's success in supporting functioning markets for the various types of debt it issued is testimony to its sound fiscal footing.

WHY DID PHILIP II WANT TO PAY BACK HIS DEBTS?

The Crown may have been able to service all its debts in the long run, but this doesn't mean that it was in its best interest to do so. A sovereign is a special kind of borrower—one that cannot be taken to court or otherwise forced to honor their contracts. This can lead to opportunistic behavior. Plenty of European monarchs refused to pay back their debts, sometimes taking the lives of creditors—as well as their money—in the process. If Philip II faced the

same incentives, lending to him could have been not just economically irrational but also downright foolish. When a monarch averages one default a
decade, there is enough evidence to suspect opportunistic behavior.

Opportunistic defaults only work if a borrower has an outside option. The
king, after confiscating the loans from a set of lenders, must either be able to
turn to someone else capable of satisfying their financing needs or attempt
to provide for them in-house. Neither option was available to Philip II. Lending in the sixteenth century occurred in an "anarchic" environment (Kletzer
and Wright 2000); neither king nor bankers could credibly commit. In actual
fact, both bankers and king defaulted on the letter of agreements; one banker
went bankrupt, never returning the funds deposited by Philip. This means
that the king could not simply default, save the interest, and draw down the
balance whenever the need arose. If there is also no alternative lender to
turn to, then maintaining a good reputation—by faithfully servicing one's
debts—is the only way to maintain access to smoothing services (Cole and
Kehoe 1995).

The Genoese bankers clearly understood this and acted accordingly. The
archival documents we explore show a tightly interwoven network of bankers. The incentives among lenders were carefully structured to ensure mutual support. Crucially, no member cut side deals during payment suspensions; moratoriums on lending to the king had "bite" because no other lender
entered the market. This is true of Genoese network members; it is also true
of outsiders, such as the Augsburg banking house of Fugger. Their correspondence suggests that a "cheat-the-cheater" mechanism (Kletzer and Wright
2000) was responsible for this—the very real fear that if they extended fresh
credit while the king had suspended payments on the Genoese, they would
be next in being defaulted on.[73] This ensured that the incentives of the king
and bankers were aligned, and that debts were repaid as soon as the resources
to do so were available.[74]

Why was being cut off from loans so painful to Philip II? The answer, in one
word, is war. All borrowing is about breaking the link between revenue and
spending; to shift expenditure from one period to the next is particularly useful in times of war, when financial demands can be urgent indeed. Philip II

---

73 We present the evidence for this argument in detail in chapter 5.
74 For the standard application of cheat-the-cheater strategies to sovereign lending, see
Kletzer and Wright 2000. The Genoese network itself was a coalition in the style described by
Avner Greif (1993).

lived in one of the most belligerent periods in all of recorded history. The ability to ramp up spending in times of military necessity was valuable; without a viable alternative, a working relationship with the Genoese bankers was essential.

James Conklin (1998) has argued that the reason why Philip II repaid his debts was that the Genoese could impose costly sanctions on him. In his interpretation, the suspension of transfers following the default of 1575 caused a sharp reversal of Spain's military fortunes in the Netherlands; unpaid troops mutinied and sacked the loyal city of Antwerp, causing a massive backlash against Spanish rule. Afterward, the king quickly settled. We do not find support for Conklin's interpretation. A close reading of the documentary record shows that the "transfer stop" by the Genoese had no bite, transfers continued unabated, and the king's treasurer in the Netherlands had ample funds to pay the mutinous troops. A power vacuum caused by the death of the governor-general in Flanders instead allowed matters to get out of hand. This explains the mutinies and why the events in Antwerp had little impact on the eventual default settlement.

WHY DID BANKERS LEND?

The king could pay, and had the incentives to do so, but any lending relationship needs two willing participants. The suspension of 1575 imposed an average loss of 38 percent on all outstanding debt—a large hit that could have discouraged lenders from trying their luck again. Yet our data show that bankers from the same families lent to Philip for the duration of his reign, regardless of how many of their members were caught in a default or how much of their capital was compromised. Why was lending to the first serial defaulter in history so attractive?

To answer this question, we analyze the asientos clause by clause, reconstructing their agreed-on cash flows. This allows us to calculate the promised rates of return, which we then modify depending on whether a contract was affected by a default. When we aggregate the loans by banking family, the puzzle is resolved. Returns during normal times were high—very high. By any standard, they more than made up for the losses incurred during the bankruptcies. A suspension could inflict severe short-term losses, but these would be amply compensated as long as the family continued to lend to the king for a sufficiently long time. By the standards of the time, it was notable that no banker lost his life lending to Philip II (the murderous thoughts of the Marquis of Poza notwithstanding).[75] We find something even more astounding: despite the less than stellar repayment record of the Crown, almost no banking family lost money.

WHAT WAS THE NATURE OF THE DEFAULTS?

Castilian debts were sustainable, the king had appropriate incentives to honor them, and bankers made healthy profits on their loans. Why, then, did Philip II default four times during his reign, and how should we think about these episodes? Understanding the nature of these defaults as well as their implications for theories of sovereign finance is the ultimate goal of our book.

Today, a country is technically in default as soon as it misses a single payment on any of the obligations that compose its debt stock.[76] Sixteenth-century standards were much more flexible. Both the king and his lenders routinely deviated from the letter of the contracts. Payments and disbursements could be delayed or made only in part, with successive agreements compensating for the missed portions of earlier ones. The situation looked much like what Jeremy Bulow and Kenneth Rogoff (1989) call "constant recontracting"—contracts served more as guidelines than ironclad commitments to be honored regardless of the situation.[77] Under these circumstances, the concept of default becomes somewhat blurred. Few contracts were fulfilled to the letter. Similarly, no contract was completely repudiated. Many fell in an intermediate category: some parts were observed as agreed, and others were renegotiated as needed. The structure of the contracts opens a window into how this uncertainty was managed. Given how casually clauses

---

75 The king was also not above killing his opponents, as is illustrated by the case of the Counts of Egmont and Horn. They were decapitated in Brussels after a rigged trial.

76 The Greek debt crisis of 2011 has shown that creditors are willing to relax this standard somewhat, agreeing to some amount of debt relief—and hence a noncompliance with assumed obligations—to avoid an outright default.

77 In the theory of constant recontracting, the only firm commitments that the parties can make are the payments being exchanged at the signing. Everything else is an expression of intent, which might or might not be honored. In the parlance of economics, these expressions of intent are called "cheap talk." We avoid the term because it conveys that the letter of the contracts is worthless. In reality, it represented the best guess that bankers and the Crown could make about a highly uncertain future. In chapter 5, we review the theory of sovereign debt, including the role of constant recontracting in it.

were treated once a contract had been signed, it is remarkable that both sides went to great lengths to stipulate what would happen in certain eventualities. A large number of loans contain clauses trying to account for contingencies that might arise—a delayed treasure fleet, nonperforming tax stream, or sudden need of liquidity on the part of the king. If the events triggering these clauses occurred, payments were rescheduled, and interest rates were reduced or increased depending on the situation.

Philip II and his bankers were contracting in a highly uncertain environment. They were fully aware that the future could bring a wide variety of situations, and had developed formal tools to deal with them. Some contingencies, like a delay in the arrival of a treasure fleet, could be reasonably expected, written down, and planned for. Others, like the riot of the Morisco population that destroyed the silk industry in Granada in 1568, were virtually impossible to anticipate. Yet others were distinct possibilities, but probably too damaging to set on paper. It is hard to imagine, for example, any royal official drafting a contract that began with, "Should our Great Armada be completely destroyed by our enemies. . . ."

When a contracted-on contingency was triggered, payments were rescheduled and interest rates were modified. The essence of bankruptcies was no different. When Castile's finances were affected by a major, unforeseen event, both the Crown and bankers understood that a restructuring was necessary. Just as with the contingency clauses, maturities were lengthened through a bond swap, while returns were reduced accordingly. The sovereign debt literature calls this type of default excusable since the ruler is not behaving opportunistically (Grossman and Van Huyck 1988). Such defaults usually result in moderate principal reductions and a quick resumption of lending; creditors do not hold the borrower responsible for the default, and hence do not exclude them from capital markets for lengthy periods. Excusable defaults must be triggered by observable events outside the control of the borrower. In Castile's case, these were large shortfall in silver remittances or the combination of several military setbacks.

Bankers knew that they were financing risky military ventures and that large, negative shocks to the king's fiscal position were possible. Anticipating them, they charged a premium for their loans. This generated relatively high profits in tranquil times. Once a bankruptcy was triggered, bankers could afford to postpone collecting on their loans and reduce the interest rates. In effect, the bankers offered insurance to the king, collecting premiums in good times and paying out in bad times. We show that Philip II's defaults were excusable and, in all likelihood, largely anticipated by his lenders. This explains the moderate and quick settlements reached as well as the continued participation in the market by the same banking families over a period of decades.

THE MODERN ANGLE

Throughout our work, we have collected more data than could have ever been accessed by the king and his ministers at any given time. We set fiscal figures in relation to macroeconomic aggregates that were unknown at the time. We compute measures of debt sustainability and loan yields using methods that were not developed until centuries later. It is only fair to ask whether our findings suffer from a problem of perspective. Might our results be far from the mark because we use anachronistic tools to evaluate economic behavior?

Our first point is that the financial sophistication of the Crown and its bankers should not be underestimated. The clauses in the asientos, for example, make it clear that the concept of present value was well established. Compound interest, although seldom used because of usury restrictions, was similarly well understood. Annuities and perpetuities were correctly priced, and even took into account the partial period between issuance and the first interest payment. This should allay concerns over our use of present value formulas to calculate the profitability of individual contracts. Even if contemporaries could not work out the full valuation of the most complicated contracts due to a lack of computing power, all they would have missed out on is a fine ranking between alternative types of instruments. Whether a contract was profitable or not was apparent all along.[78]

Sustainability is a different matter. There was no obvious understanding of the relationship between aggregate debt and fiscal capacity, let alone of what constituted a sustainable debt path. It is, however, not necessary for decision makers to have been aware of these concepts. If Castilian debts were sustainable, the Crown should have found itself with enough cash to service them. If

---

78 There is convincing evidence that economic agents can valuate complex financial derivatives quite accurately, even in the absence of the necessary mathematical knowledge. For an example involving the pricing of warrants before the development of the Black-Scholes formula, see Moore and Juh 2006.

they were unsustainable, it would have run out of money. The appropriate fiscal adjustments could be directed by simple observations of the year-over-year financial requirements. Despite our modern tools, our conclusions are mere statements of fact, and hence do not rely on the state of knowledge at the time.

BEYOND FINANCE: POLITICAL AND ECONOMIC CONSEQUENCES

Our discussion so far has focused on understanding Castile's system of sovereign finance and explaining the defaults of Philip II. In the last chapter of the book, we turn to the implications for the long-run development of Spain. Castile stands out among its peers because of its ability to issue a large amount of debt while preserving access to capital markets after each of its defaults. These feats, though, have often been singled out as one of the reasons that held back Spain's economic development. After all, Castile entered the early modern age as a thriving economy and fearsome military power. Two hundred years later, it was a shadow of its former self, an economic also-ran, and its Crown was being fought over by rival European powers in the War of the Spanish Succession. Spain's economic performance would not catch up with comparable European countries until the last third of the twentieth century. What went wrong, and did government finance play a role in it?

Despite stereotypes to the contrary, the government institutions of Castile in the early sixteenth century were better than those of most of its competitors.[79] Kings were fairly constrained throughout the sixteenth and seventeenth centuries. There was no real feudal system, and the merchant elites of the Castilian cities wielded a large amount of power through the institution of the Cortes, their representative assembly. Among other prerogatives, the Cortes had the ability to veto tax increases and limit the issues of long-term debt.[80] Without reaching the level of independence of English common law courts, the judiciary was also fairly independent, while dispensing justice ef-

---

79 Douglass North and Robert Paul Thomas (1973) used Spain as an example of a rent-seeking society. Daron Acemoglu, Simon Johnson, and James Robinson (2005) code Castile as being an absolutist state. For additional instances of this view, see Landes 1998; De Long and Shleifer 1993; Ekelund and Tollison 1997. North (1991) subsequently qualified his position to reflect that the king was in fact constrained by the Cortes.
80 Chapter 3 explores the balance of power between the Crown and Cortes.

fectively.[81] Early on, the Castilian state exhibited all the markers that the new institutional economics associates with successful economic outcomes. Yet after a relatively brief period of splendor in the mid-sixteenth century, Castile entered a phase of long-term underperformance.

One line of argument blames the "decline" of Castile on the fiscal mismanagement of the Habsburgs and excessive imperial ambitions. This implicitly accepts the conventional wisdom about Castilian institutions. Unconstrained monarchs—the reasoning goes—were allowed to run up huge debts while spending the proceeds on unproductive wars. The resulting fiscal pressure distorted the economy, leading to an inferior long-run outcome. The problem with this story line is that its first premise cannot stand up to a closer look: Castilian kings were just as constrained as any other early modern monarch.

There was nonetheless a loophole. Medieval law granted the king exclusive control over the taxing and spending of mineral resources. While this was usually a prerogative of little consequence, the discovery of the silver mines in America made it critically important for Spain. Its kings suddenly gained access to a large source of revenue—one that was not subject to the control of cities, nobles, or merchant elites. Silver taxes could be pledged as a source of repayment for asientos, allowing monarchs to leverage themselves and undertake large military adventures without much supervision or challenge from the Cortes. Part of the institutionalist assertion, then, survives in modified form: Castilian institutions were not "bad" at the beginning of the sixteenth century, but their quality deteriorated because of the silver discoveries.

We next challenge the second premise of the contention: that the debt load of the state crushed the Castilian economy. Europe after 1500 saw only a few bids for supremacy; Habsburg Spain's was one of the more determined ones. Paul Kennedy (1987) famously argued that imperial overstretch—an excessively ambitious program of territorial expansion and military buildup—doomed powers such as Spain (and many others). According to this view, the cost of empire eventually undermined the dynamism of the domestic economy. The growing gap between imperial ambition and fiscal resources led first to the accumulation of debt, and then to default. To test this claim, our starting point is a set of international comparisons. We take three other early modern powers—England, the Netherlands, and France—and analyze their

---

81 For an overview, see Kagan 1981. For an example of how judicial decision making influenced economic efficiency, see Drelichman 2009.

fiscal situations at the height of their powers.[82] In each comparison, Castile's finances are either unremarkable or even appear in a favorable light. Notably, English debt burdens were always higher than Castilian ones, while sustainability indicators were lower. There is no evidence that Britain or any other early modern nation for that matter exhibited greater fiscal responsibility than Castile under Philip II. Even if institutions were far from optimal by the end of the sixteenth century, it is not clear that they produced fiscal outcomes that differed much from those of other powers.

If the fiscal situation of Castile was not fundamentally different from that of other early modern powers, why did the Spanish juggernaut lose momentum from the seventeenth century onward? Silver did much to stop the drive toward state building that lay at the core of British success (Brewer 1988). Equally important was the fragmented system of local and regional political power, which resisted each and every attempt at meaningful centralization (Grafe 2012).

A third, though equally crucial factor stands out: Britain won its wars, while Spain lost many. Battlefield success was not predetermined; luck—emphasized by Napoléon as the single most important attribute of a good general—plays a critical role. Both France and Spain defaulted frequently, while Britain did not—and it triumphed in the end. We argue that causality goes in the opposite direction of the one implied by imperial overstretch. Spain and France lost out as a result of military misfortunes, such as the Armada and the disastrous invasion of Russia. Britain, on the other hand, got lucky. Had Waterloo turned out differently, Britain—having accumulated debts equivalent to more than 200 percent of GDP—would have defaulted (and lost a good deal of its empire), too. Throughout the book, we explore some of the determinants of military outcomes and ponder whether better fortunes on the battlefield might have resulted in a different ending for the first empire on which the sun never set.

THE BOOK'S PLAN

In chapter 2, we provide a brief history of Castilian ascendancy from the late Middle Ages through the end of Philip II's reign. Chapter 3 describes the fiscal institutions and borrowing instruments available to the Crown, and pre-

---

82 This choice was largely dictated by data availability, but it also makes sense. Looking at each state during its period of peak power offers a more comparable scenario than using the same period as a baseline. For a detailed analysis, see chapter 8.

sents our asiento data in detail. Next, we start answering our four core questions. Chapter 4 addresses the sustainability of debt, while chapter 5 deals with repayment incentives. Chapter 6 looks at the profitability of banking families, and chapter 7 analyzes the role of contingent scenarios and nature of the defaults. Chapter 8 supplies international comparisons and examines the impact of debt leveraging on the long-run development of Castile.

CHAPTER 2

PHILIP'S EMPIRE

THE FOUNDATIONS OF EMPIRE

It was a cold autumn night in October 1469. Two Castilian gentlemen sat down at an inn near the Aragonese border and ordered a hot meal after a long day of travel. Their servant, a shabbily dressed young man in his late teens, took their traveling clothes and then went to tend to the mules outside. A few tables over, two scruffy characters were drinking cheap wine and gambling at cards. What could have been an everyday scene in any inn on the Iberian Peninsula contained the seeds of high political drama. The seedy-looking men were actually working for Bishop Pedro González de Mendoza, a powerful Castilian nobleman close to King Henry IV. They as well as many other spies were keeping a close eye on any unusual travelers about to cross the border. Little did they know that the man they were looking for was right there under their very eyes, sleeping in the stall with the mules. The gentlemen whose servant he pretended to be were Gutierre de Cárdenas and Alonso de Palencia, trusted advisers of Isabella, crown princess of Castile. Their young charge, unrecognizable in his dirty muleteer rags, was none other than Prince Ferdinand of Aragon. Isabella, ignoring the wishes of most of the Iberian Peninsula's political establishment, had chosen him as her husband.[1]

Isabella had no shortage of suitors. King Henry IV, Isabella's half brother, favored a union with the crown of Portugal through a marriage with King Alphonse V, which also had the support of a large part of the Castilian nobility. Other candidates included the king of Navarre and the Duke of Berry, brother to Louis XI of France. Isabella's advisers had been secretly negotiat-

---

1 Ferdinand's voyage and his wedding to Isabella are reconstructed in Rubin 2004. Although our scene at the inn is fictional, all the other details are historically accurate.

ing the conditions of her marriage to Ferdinand with King Juan of Aragon since January 1469. In May, the princess, who had been closely watched by King Henry's men in the town of Ocaña, managed to escape to Valladolid under false pretenses. There she lived at the fortified palace of the Vivero family while waiting for Ferdinand. The groom finally arrived in early October. After the introductions and all-important signing of the marriage capitulations, they were married on October 19. While traditional accounts speak of a "secret" wedding, the description scarcely fits the celebration: some two thousand guests attended the exchanging of vows. The marriage of Ferdinand and Isabella was soon to have crucial repercussions the world over.

By displaying a mind of their own, Isabella and Ferdinand made a bold move. They alienated Henry IV, from whom Isabella had agreed to obtain consent before marrying. They also risked an ecclesiastical annulment, as they were second cousins and the pope had been reluctant to grant a dispensation for fear of angering Henry.[2] More important, by going against the desires of the Castilian nobles, they all but guaranteed a war of succession after Henry's death. Their victory and consolidation as the joint monarchs of Castile and Aragon would not come until 1479, when a peace treaty with Portugal settled the dynastic claims to the Castilian Crown.

Bold and unusual as the marriage of Isabella and Ferdinand was, its most significant consequences could not have been foreseen at the time. The great overseas discoveries and power struggles associated with them were still more than two decades in the future. Had Isabella married Alphonse V of Portugal, there might have been a single Iberian merchant empire in the centuries to come. Yet Castile and Portugal continued their rivalry, with the treaty of Tordesillas demarcating their areas of influence in the New World in 1494. Moreover, after the marriage of Ferdinand and Isabella, a series of agreements—both tacit and explicit—recognized Castile's exclusive sovereignty over all territories conquered in the future.[3] Conquest in medieval and early modern Europe typically involved small territories, and the negotiators clearly had in mind the completion of the Reconquista, or minor acquisitions in North

---

2 Isabella had actually refused to marry Ferdinand until a papal dispensation bull was obtained. The papal envoy, Antonio Veneris, provided an extrasacramental dispensation, which was falsely presented as a legitimate bull during the ceremony. A proper dispensation bull was finally issued in 1471 by Pope Sixtus IV.

3 For a discussion of the origin and interpretation of Castile's sovereignty over newly conquered territories, see García Gallo 1950.

Africa. They could hardly have imagined that within three short decades, vast parts of the globe on three continents would come under Castilian influence.

In general, the relationship between Castile and Aragon was structured as an association of equals, with each retaining their separate crowns, councils, and representative assemblies. Their combined might and the elimination of their rivalry, however, allowed Ferdinand and Isabella to concentrate substantial powers in their hands. This strengthened the institution of the monarchy. Ferdinand and Isabella shed many of the medieval structures of administration, modernizing the apparatus of the state and preparing it for the coming expansion.

The first step was to bring the nobility under control. Shortly after acceding to the throne, Isabella and Ferdinand launched a sweeping reform of the annuities from which many noble families derived a substantial part of their income. The *reforma de mercedes* of 1480 had the double impact of rescinding many of these annuities—hence limiting the economic power of the upper nobility—while also wrestling their administration from tax farmers and placing it into the hands of royal accountants.[4] The monarchs also revoked most of the petty nobility privileges that Henry IV had granted in an attempt to shore up support for his reign.[5] Finally, the creation of a national militia— the Santa Hermandad—and professional army units—the famed tercios— stripped nobles of their central feudal role as military entrepreneurs.[6] The Santa Hermandad resulted from an agglomeration of the local militias, or *hermandades*, that were organized in the Middle Ages as a form of local law enforcement. They were often seen as symbols of the resistance of townships against seigniorial power. The Catholic Kings united them in a kingdom-wide organization with a more solid financial structure.[7] Tercios, first used in the Italian wars of the 1490s, were professionally staffed regiments designed to stand up to cavalry charges by adopting an improved version of the Swiss pikemen fighting technique. They became fearsome units during the Dutch War of Independence. While the nobility did retain considerable influence, that influence was increasingly ordained, vetted, and regulated by the mon-

---

4 For a discussion of the reforma de mercedes, see Haliczer 1975.

5 The privileges of *hidalguía*, or petty nobility, would return with vigor in the second half of the sixteenth century, when they were used (and abused) in several struggles for local political control (Drelichman 2007).

6 See, for example, Parker 1972.

7 On the Santa Hermandad, see Lunenfeld 1970.

archy, rather than stemming from military and financial functions within the structure of the state.

A second major step in state building was to bring the church more firmly under royal control. Since the fourteenth century, radical elements in the ecclesiastical hierarchy had expressed their discontent with the Crown by staging pogroms against Jews and Muslims. By providing a formal channel to repress religious minorities, the establishment of the Inquisition in 1484 put an end to the popular uprisings. Firmly entrenched in the Crown's orbit, the Inquisition thus transformed a challenge to monarchical control into a tool to project royal power.[8] Isabella and Ferdinand were staunch defenders of the Inquisition in its early years—a stance that contributed to Pope Alexander VI granting them the title of Catholic Kings. Next, Ferdinand obtained the right of royal patronage in 1508. This gave the king vast powers over the operations of the church, including the appointment of its authorities, the funding of its works and activities, and control over some of its revenue streams. More than half a century later, Philip II would build on this authority to effectively convert the church into a fiscal arm of the Crown.

Dynastic policy was the third and final pillar of state building by the Catholic Kings. Like all princes, Ferdinand strived to marry his children and grandchildren into the reigning houses of Europe. Unlike most, he succeeded brilliantly. Of significance were the marriages of Catherine of Aragon to the future Henry VIII, and that of Joanna of Castile, the crown princess, to Philip "the Handsome" of Habsburg. On Isabella's death, Joanna became queen of Castile, while Ferdinand retained only the crown of Aragon. The death of Philip the Handsome—already Philip I of Castile—in 1506 left Joanna to reign on her own. Grief stricken at the death of her husband, the story goes, Joanna went "mad." Whether the queen was mentally ill, depressed, or just overwhelmed has been the subject of endless debates. What is certain is that her condition gave Ferdinand the excuse to lock his daughter up in a castle, declare himself regent, and effectively rule Castile for another ten years. Joanna's six children with Philip I were the real payoff for the Catholic Kings' dynastic strategy. Both sons became Holy Roman emperors—Charles V and Ferdinand I—while all four daughters married kings (one of them twice). The

---

8 See, for example, Rawlings 2006; Pérez 2003; Kamen 1999. In a literature as vast as that on the Inquisition, the view that its role was primarily that of a channel to project royal power is not uncontested. The main opposition to it sees the Inquisition as a fundamentally cultural phenomenon (see, for example, Netanyahu 2001).

Habsburg inheritance of Philip I would be the main basis of Charles V's election to the imperial throne in 1519. Castile would benefit again from Ferdinand's dynastic shrewdness in 1580, when the repeated intermarriages between several generations of Castilian and Portuguese royals served as the legal basis for Philip II's successful claim to the crown of Portugal.

The marriage of Ferdinand and Isabella proved decisive for the fortunes of Spain. After Ferdinand's death in 1516, separate monarchs never again ruled Castile and Aragon. The two kingdoms nevertheless remained independent, each with their own representative assemblies, administrative structures, and judicial and fiscal institutions. Between 1516 and 1700, they were held in "personal union" by all the Habsburg monarchs. Aragon's separate institutions would be abolished only in 1707, with the *Decretos de Nueva Planta* issued by Philip V during the War of the Spanish Succession.

While domestic disturbances and regional uprisings recurred periodically, the constant low-level warfare on the Iberian Peninsula that had characterized the late Middle Ages was now a thing of the past. The new political framework stopped short of full integration; the persistence of separate institutions would eventually become a critical factor in the long-run economic underperformance of Spain.[9] But at the dawn of the early modern age, Ferdinand and Isabella had succeeded in giving their kingdoms a relatively strong monarchy and streamlined state institutions. Castile, where the reforms were particularly deep and the peace dividend sizable, flourished economically. It began to project its power throughout the known world and forcefully push into the unknown.

ECONOMIC PERFORMANCE

Starting in the 1490s, most areas of Spain entered a period of remarkable growth that would last until the end of the sixteenth century. Within this general upward trend, regional patterns of economic development varied widely. Philip II decided to make Madrid his capital; New Castile, the area surrounding it, experienced the fastest growth, with rates that may have surpassed 1 percent per year.[10] In contrast, the kingdom of Aragon began a long

---

9 This point has been most recently articulated in Grafe 2012.
10 In this discussion we follow Alvarez Nogal and Prados de la Escosura (2007), who provide a thorough reconstruction of the population, urbanization rates, sectoral output, and aggregate growth for all Spanish regions.

relative decline, with Valencia and Catalonia barely registering any increases in output. Population in the aggregate grew at a brisk pace. Spain as a whole counted about 4.8 million people in 1530—a figure that rose to about 6.8 million by 1590.[11] This represents a sustained growth rate of 0.58 percent for the period—a high figure for a premodern economy. Urbanization rates—a common measure of economic development in premodern times—also increased across the board, from roughly 12 percent in 1530 to about 20 percent in 1590 for the whole of Spain. In parts of Andalusia, which received a strong impulse from Seville's monopoly over trade with the Americas, urbanization may have been as high as 50 percent.[12]

Agriculture was the mainstay of economic activity. In addition, Spain was well positioned to benefit from the rise in trade across the Atlantic.[13] During the first half of the sixteenth century, the Spanish kingdoms saw the growth of vibrant merchant economies. Castile's principal export was high-grade merino wool, which supplied the cloth industry in the Low Countries.[14] Although the industry was not as strong as it had been in its medieval heyday, wool exports through the northern ports still amounted to 30,000 sacks per year (over 2.4 million kilograms) in the 1550s, with the southern ports possibly exporting a similar amount (Casado Alonso 1994).[15] Iron and leather manufactures were also important as well as hides and oil. Andalusia, which constituted a separate customs area, was a large producer of wine and olive oil. The Basque Country supplied European markets with cod, alum, and iron, while the kingdom of Aragon's main exports were silk, rice, and salt (Rich and Wilson 1967; Braudel 1966; Lynch 1991; Grafe 2001). While the silver trade would steal the show in the second half of the sixteenth century, the economies of several Spanish regions displayed a strong, healthy growth well before the commercial development of mineral resources in the colonies.

11 Population estimates vary widely in the literature. We use the consensus figures in Alvarez Nogal and Prados de la Escosura 2007. See also Nicolau 2005; Carreras 2003; Nadal i Oller 1984. Paul Bairoch, Jean Batou, and Pierre Chèvre (1988) provide much higher figures—about 7.5 million in 1530—but their numbers are no longer considered reliable.

12 For alternative urbanization figures between the eighth and the fifteenth centuries based on the Bairoch, Batou, and Chèvre data, see Buringh and Van Zanden 2009.

13 Daron Acemoglu, Simon Johnson, and James Robinson (2005) show how the combination of access to the Atlantic and participatory institutions was a key factor in Europe's rise to dominance.

14 For the standard reference on the Spanish wool industry, see Phillips and Phillips 1997. See also Ruiz Martín and García Sanz 1998; Grafe 2001; Munro 2005; Drelichman 2009.

15 Data from the southern ports are not available, and hence the magnitude of exports through them is merely an educated guess.

The opening of transatlantic and Indian Ocean routes brought profound changes for Spanish industry and trade. Silver imports from the Indies—at first a trickle and then a veritable flood—caused a large shift in comparative advantage, putting traditional exports at a disadvantage. At the same time, they created a large demand for luxury imports from the Far East.[16] Sugar and cochineal, both colonial reexports, also gained prominence in international markets (Rich and Wilson 1967).

The combination of a healthy agricultural economy, a growing population, and rapidly rising trade in silver and colonial products provided the resources that were to fuel Spain's imperial expansion. We will explore the fiscal aspect of that expansion in detail in chapter 3.

CHARLES V AND THE BEGINNINGS OF THE EMPIRE

Before the empire, there was the Emperor. Charles of Habsburg inherited the crowns of Castile and Aragon on the death of his grandfather, Ferdinand the Catholic, in 1516. His accession was not without controversy; his mother, Joanna the Mad, remained the legitimate queen, even while confined to her castle in Tordesillas. The Castilian nobility was reluctant to accept a foreign prince who did not speak Spanish, and viewed Charles's cadre of Flemish advisers and ministers with suspicion. When the crown of the Holy Roman Empire fell vacant in 1519, Charles was the leading candidate to succeed his paternal grandfather, Emperor Maximilian. He effectively bought the election with the help of the Fugger banking family. The Fugger advanced the money to bribe the grand electors, while refusing to cash the bills of exchange from Charles's main competitor, Francis I of France (Parker 1999).[17] Charles thus became Charles V, the name by which history remembers him. In Spain, where he reigned as Carlos I, he would soon be referred to simply as *el emperador*.

Charles's election created apprehension in Castilian society. The electors had stipulated that no imperial revenues could be spent outside the empire's confines. In addition, the Golden Bull—the Holy Roman Empire's constitu-

---

16 Drelichman (2005) documents the loss of comparative advantage in traditional Spanish exports. Flynn and Giráldez (2004) explore the nature of the global trading networks in Spanish silver.

17 Henry Cohn (2001) argues that the bribes paid to the electors did not influence the outcome, with military and political considerations carrying more weight.

tional document since 1356—specified that tolls, mineral wealth, coinage, and taxes on the Jews remained under the exclusive domain of the German princes (Henderson 2010). This meant that Charles's wars would have to be financed from other sources; the obvious alternative was Castile and its thriving economy.[18] The situation came to a head when Charles convened a special session of the Cortes in Santiago de Compostela to request funds for his coronation voyage. The representatives eventually voted in favor of Charles's trip.

While the outcome was not unexpected, it created major discontent. The urban lower nobility and well-to-do bourgeoisie of Castilian cities saw their economic as well as social standing threatened by the concentration of power in the hands of the monarchy and its supporters.[19] Unrest erupted in the revolt of the comunidades. It began in May 1520 and lasted until April 1521, when royalist forces decisively defeated the rebel militia at the Battle of Villalar. At the rebellion's peak, thirteen cities openly defied royal authority. As the year wore on, however, the antiaristocratic nature of the movement convinced the previously indifferent upper nobility to support the king. This sealed the fate of the Comuneros Revolt. Charles's victory consolidated his military sway over Castile, established royal supremacy over the cities, and curtailed the ability of the Cortes to control royal expenditures. It also made Castile the main funding source for the costs of the empire.

Throughout his reign, Charles aspired to create a unified Christian empire in western Europe.[20] Military and political realities would make this goal impossible. Instead of pursuing heretics and infidels, he found himself spending enormous resources to fight Catholic France in the Italian wars. Despite defeating the Protestant princes of Germany in the Battle of Mühlberg, he was

---

18 In general, it was expected that the all territories under the same ruler would come to his aid in times of crisis (Rodríguez-Salgado 1988). The German princes effectively solved the collective action problem, which allowed them to present a united front and extricate themselves from this position, thereby increasing the burden on Charles's other domains.

19 See Pérez 1970; Haliczer 1981. This interpretation stands in contrast with the one handed down by Marxist historiography, which viewed the comunidades as an uprising of oppressed masses against royal power and a foreshadower of the Communist revolutions of the twentieth century (Maravall 1963).

20 The reign of Charles V has been studied exhaustively from a variety of angles. For just a few recent English-language general treatments, see Tracy 2002; Blockmans 2001; Blockmans and Mout 2005. For a comprehensive bibliography, see Biblioteca Cervantes Virtual, http://bib .cervantesvirtual.com/historia/CarlosV/fuentes_y_biblio.shtml. Manuel Fernández Alvarez (1979) has transcribed and edited an impressive amount of documentation related to Charles's reign in his *Corpus Documental de Carlos V*.

eventually forced to come to terms with them at the Peace of Augsburg in 1555. The treaty enshrined the principle of *cuius regio eius religio*, effectively recognizing the legal status of Protestant princes and subjects in the nominally "Holy" and "Roman" Empire.[21]

In early modern Europe, war was the single most expensive activity that a ruler could engage in. Rulers typically spent three-quarters of their revenue on armed forces in the centuries between 1500 and 1800. While a military conflict was under way, expenditures almost always exceeded revenues by a large margin. Charles's wars strained the finances of his various domains. He relied heavily on his Burgundian inheritance—the Low Countries—where he increased taxes. This sowed the seeds of discontent, which would eventually lead to the Dutch Revolt during the reign of his son, Philip II. He also tapped the kingdom of Naples, part of the Aragonese territories he received from his grandfather Ferdinand the Catholic. Nonetheless, Charles leaned heavily on Castile.[22] When current taxes became insufficient to finance war expenditures, Charles resorted to many fiscal measures that upset formal and informal property rights. These included the sale of Crown lands that had long been used for communal production, the granting of privileges of lordship over formerly free towns, and the confiscation of remittances of precious metals. Most important, Charles contracted major debts with international bankers, including the German banking houses of the Fugger and Welser families.[23] These loans were granted in the expectation that Castilian resources would be used to honor them. Even when Philip II eventually defaulted in 1557 and 1560, claims were settled with the transfer of Castilian assets to the bankers, including the profitable masterships of the military orders and strategic mercury mines at Almadén.

The exploration of the New World, started by Christopher Columbus's voyages in the 1490s, had proceeded apace during the reign of the Catholic Kings. The first voyages yielded only a small amount of loot, mainly in the form of ornamental gold plundered from the natives. The lure of gold and silver, however, was always strong for those setting sail for the vast, uncharted

---

21 M. J. Rodríguez-Salgado (1988) writes that Ferdinand the Catholic had warned Charles, in his youth, to resist the urge to engage in a protracted war with France. Charles did not heed this advice; his pyrrhic victories came at the price of forfeiting his dream of vanquishing the enemies of Catholicism.

22 James Tracy (2002) provides an analysis of the relative contribution of Charles's several territories to his war efforts.

23 For the standard source on Charles's loans with international bankers, see Carande 1987.

American continent. The indigenous populations soon recognized the Spaniards' obsession with gold. They often made up stories of untold treasures in remote places as a way to get rid of the unwanted visitors. This was, for example, the origin of the legend of El Dorado—the golden man—in whose quest many generations of explorers spent their best years, fortunes, and sometimes lives.

The first two decades of exploration were mostly focused on the Caribbean islands. Columbus had established his first base in Hispaniola. By the early 1510s Spaniards were settling Cuba; though poor in mineral resources, the island was where the newcomers first learned about tobacco and its uses. Havana was founded in 1514, and would soon become the main base for further exploration. When Charles V ascended to the throne in 1516, the conquistadores were preparing to move on to the American mainland and capture the real prizes: the Aztec and Inca empires.

The clashes between the Spaniards and two major Mesoamerican civilizations came to symbolize the enormous superiority of Europeans in the age of exploration. In both cases, large, relatively advanced political and military systems collapsed in a matter of months when confronted by an invader who arrived with only a handful of men under arms. Jared Diamond (1997) famously argued that "guns, germs, and steel" gave Spaniards the upper hand. Superior military techniques and advanced weaponry allowed the conquistadores a tactical advantage. European germs decimated the ranks of the natives, given that they had no immunity to them, and created enormous turmoil. This was true even at the top of the political structure. When Francisco Pizarro arrived in Peru, he took advantage of a civil war to subdue the Inca Empire. The war was being fought over the succession of Emperor Huayna Capac, who had died of smallpox—a disease that had reached the Americas in Spanish ships.

Hernán Cortés, who arrived on the Mexican mainland on Good Friday 1519, led the Spanish conquest of the Aztec Empire. He soon forged an alliance with local tribes, boosting his military strength. In November he entered Tenochtitlan, the Aztec capital, invited by Emperor Moctezuma, who may have believed that Cortés was a god. The Spaniards soon seized Moctezuma, holding him captive in order to guarantee their own safety. The population grew restless, and the emperor was eventually killed during a clash between Spaniards and locals. The Spaniards were forced to leave the city, losing many of their men to the Aztecs on the *noche triste* of June 30, 1520.

Tenochtitlan finally fell to the Spaniards in August 1521. Cortés defeated the last emperor, Cuathemoc, after an eight-month siege, using a purpose-built flotilla on Lake Tlateloco and an army composed mostly of his Tlaxcala allies.[24] Cortés's victory yielded much glory, but little treasure. The Aztecs had a limited amount of ornamental gold, which the Spaniards duly looted, but no major hoards or mines.

The other large conquest was that of the Inca Empire, which extended from modern-day central Chile to southern Colombia. Francisco Pizarro and Diego de Almagro first arrived in Inca territory in 1528. A civil war was raging between two sons of Emperor Huayna Capac, Atahualpa and Huascar. Pizarro returned to Spain, where he obtained a royal charter to conquer the central territory of the Inca Empire and become its governor.[25] He returned to Inca territory in 1531 and slowly made his way to the heartland of the empire, reaching Atahualpa at his summer retreat in Cajamarca in November 1532. The traditional account of the clash is well known. The emperor agreed to meet the Spaniards in the city square on the morning of November 16, and waited there with thousands of soldiers. A deputy of Pizarro and a friar approached him, demanding that he recognize Catholicism as the true religion and handing him a Bible. The emperor, confused about what was being asked of him, threw the book away, sparking the attack. The Spanish horses sowed panic among the defenders, who had never seen such large animals. Firearms and a few pieces of artillery were used to great effect. The Spaniards slaughtered Atahualpa's guards and, copying Cortés's strategy, captured the emperor to guarantee their own safety. Atahualpa offered his captors a ransom, consisting of the volume of his cell filled with gold up to the height of his extended arm, if they would spare his life and free him. The Spaniards accepted, collecting the ransom without ever intending to keep their promise. In the meantime, Huascar, the other contender to the throne, was assassinated. Atahualpa was executed in 1533. Although Atahualpa's ransom was much richer than the gold plundered from the Aztecs, the Inca Empire could not supply a steady stream of gold either. The families of Pizarro and Almagro soon engaged in internecine fighting; both conquistadores were killed in the conflict, leading Charles V to eliminate the governorships they had held and create the Viceroyalty of Peru in 1542.

---

24 The most famous account of Cortés's conquest of Mexico is the "Verdadera historia de la conquista de la Nueva España"—a chronicle by his subordinate Bernal Díaz del Castillo.
25 This document is known as the Capitulaciones de Toledo.

As soon as American treasure reached Spain, it was used to pay for military expenditures. The first shipment of Aztec gold had arrived in Barcelona in 1520. Charles V utilized it to pay for his imperial coronation voyage, after the Comuneros Revolt had left the royal treasury seriously depleted. In 1534, the proceeds from the ransom of Atahualpa were used to pay for the campaign of Tunis, Charles's most successful military venture (Parker 1999). No major hoards arrived after the demise of the Inca Empire, but the opening of the gold mines of New Granada continued to provide a modest flow of specie that kept exploration viable.[26]

Despite the occasional windfall, mineral wealth was never a major source of income for Castile before 1550.[27] The large silver deposits at Potosí and Zacatecas were only discovered in 1545 and 1546, respectively. The technical challenges associated with exploiting them on a commercial scale took more than a decade to resolve. American precious metals began reaching Spain in large quantities only in the mid-1550s, toward the end of Charles's reign.

Ultimately, the Spanish Empire would end up looking very different from Charles's vision. There would no longer be an emperor ruling the Spanish lands, as the Holy Roman Crown passed into the hands of Charles's brother, Ferdinand I of Habsburg. Philip II nonetheless was the first Spanish ruler who could truthfully claim that the sun never set on his domains; his empire contained possessions on every known continent. Castile under Philip continued to try to impose its political will in Europe. In addition to Spain's considerable economic resources, it could now count on a seemingly endless stream of revenue from its overseas possessions. The bullion remittances became a key element of the short-term debt system. The funds thus mobilized paid for Philip's armies and fleets, financing military campaigns that defined his reign, and eventually sealed the fate of his empire.

EUROPEAN CONFLICTS DURING PHILIP'S REIGN

During his long reign, Philip's domains were never completely at peace.[28] War mattered because it could bring glory or shame as well as riches or fiscal ruin. The continuous need to raise funds for the next war—or pay the debts

---

26 New Granada corresponds to modern-day Colombia and parts of Venezuela.
27 For the standard sources on the volume of precious metal imports into Castile, see Hamilton 1934; Morineau 1985.
28 Geoffrey Parker (1998) charted Philip's campaigns, showing that throughout his forty-two-year reign, only a period of six months in the year 1577 was without a major military conflict.

of the last one—weighed heavily on the minds of rulers everywhere after 1500. Covering all of Philip's campaigns—the focus of many scholarly studies—lies beyond our scope. Here we review the enterprises that had the most significant fiscal implications for Castile: the War of the Holy League, the Dutch Revolt, and the Invincible Armada and its aftermath.[29] At the end of this chapter, we discuss how they fit in the logic of empire and, in turn, molded its shape.

FROM SAINT-QUENTIN TO LEPANTO

In late 1555, an increasingly frail and downcast Charles V finalized plans to divest his possessions. The Austrian domains passed on to his brother Ferdinand, who was also in line to succeed Charles as Holy Roman emperor. To Philip, Charles left the Iberian kingdoms and their colonies, the Low Countries, Sicily, Naples, and Milan—territories that, together, became known as the Spanish Empire.

Charles V viewed himself as a medieval warrior leading his troops into battle. Titian's famous portrait of him following his victory in the Battle of Mühlberg shows the emperor in shining armor, lance in hand, riding an enormous black horse. Philip II, in contrast, was a consummate administrator. He preferred the study to the battlefield, working his way through thousands of documents, many of which he annotated in his own hand. He micromanaged the affairs of government, and dealt with his officials, stakeholders, and sources of political and economic support on a day-to-day basis.[30] Philip was fond of absorbing all aspects of an issue, soliciting and carefully weighing many different opinions before finally reaching a decision. This detail-oriented approach to decision making earned him the moniker "the prudent king." His portrait—also by Titian—depicts him inside a palace, standing in front of a desk, and not in the fray of battle.

Philip had been thoroughly groomed for his position, immersing himself in international affairs and administrative practices during his long educa-

---

29 While technically the Armada was launched in the context of the Dutch Revolt, its sheer size, scope, and financial demands gave it a life of its own, and the historical literature has often treated it as a separate unit of analysis.

30 For an excellent account of the last decade of Charles's reign, the transformation of the empire, the political and personal differences between Charles and Philip, and the personal imprint that Philip II would put on the empire in the early years of his monarchy, see Rodríguez-Salgado 1988.

FIGURE 2. Charles V

tion abroad. He was intimately acquainted with matters of government, having served as coregent of the Spanish kingdoms since 1551. While less keen on the personal warrior role than his father, he engaged in almost-constant warfare. Immediately after ascending to the throne, he was forced to confront Henry II of France, who attempted to seize the Habsburgs' Italian possessions. Philip's forces won decisive victories at Saint-Quentin in 1557 and Gravelines in 1558. While Philip could have marched on Paris, he did not do so because funding for the war's continuation was uncertain. The treaty of

FIGURE 3. Philip II

Cateau-Cambrésis in 1559 put an end to the Italian wars, restoring the territorial balance that had existed before the hostilities. This reflected the financial exhaustion of both adversaries. The peace was sealed with Philip's marriage to Henry's daughter, Isabel of Valois. Known in Spain as Isabel of the Peace, she was Philip's third wife, after Maria Manuela of Portugal and Mary I of England.

After securing peace with France, Philip took up residence in Castile, making Madrid his permanent capital in 1561. By spending most of his time in Spain and attending personally to government affairs, Philip built connections with the Castilian elites in a way that Charles had never managed. His constant interaction with grandees and government officials, either directly or through his secretaries, resulted in a closer alignment of the monarch's interests with those of his supporters. This cultural transformation facilitated the political and financial transactions that kept the wheels of empire turning more or less smoothly throughout Philip's reign.

Philip's military track record was a mix of costly victories and disastrous defeats, similar to that of his father's reign. His star was shining brightly in 1571, after the naval victory of Lepanto. The combined navies of the Spanish kingdoms, Venice, Genoa, the Papal States, and other smaller powers had defeated the Ottoman fleet in what was to be the last great battle between galleys. Castile and Philip's other kingdoms had shouldered the largest share of the total cost, spending five million ducats to finance the combined fleets.[31] With the victory won, though, disputes broke out between the members of the Holy League over how to preserve the gains in the eastern Mediterranean. The Ottomans took advantage of the disagreements to recover most of the outposts and fortresses they had lost. Within a few years, they were once again raiding the coast of Sicily. Lepanto eventually came to mark a turning point in the balance of power in the Mediterranean in favor of Christian Europe. Yet in its immediate aftermath, there seemingly was little to show for the costs and pains of the war (Kamen 2003).

---

31 Parker (1979) reconstructs the costs of the Battle of Lepanto as well as the ongoing outlays needed to maintain the gains achieved. He concludes that fighting the battle itself was the only reasonable course of action in the face of the Ottoman threat, and that its total cost ended up being moderate. The continuing charges for the maintenance of the Mediterranean fleet, however, were a major drain on the treasury.

THE DUTCH REVOLT AND THE INVINCIBLE ARMADA

The Dutch Revolt began in the late 1560s. It only ended with the formal recognition of Dutch independence at the Peace of Westphalia in 1648. Known as the Eighty Years' War, the revolt consumed enormous resources. Spain's best fighting units, military commanders, diplomats, and much of Castile's free cash and credit were at one time or another employed in Flanders. Ultimately, the best effort of the sixteenth century's only superpower failed. Spain's decline and eventual fall as a major player in the European concert of powers—gradual at first, and rapid after the 1650s—can be traced back to its defeat in Flanders.

Since the late Middle Ages, the Low Countries had been a part of the Duchy of Burgundy. The Duchy ceased to exist as an independent polity in the late 1400s, with its southern lands absorbed into France. The Low Countries went to Mary of Burgundy, and from her into the Habsburg inheritance through her marriage with Maximilian II, Charles V's grandfather. Charles himself was born and raised in the Flemish city of Ghent, and considered his Burgundian upbringing a core part of his identity (Fernández Alvarez 2004).[32] The combination of active commerce and industry, a favorable geography, good governance, and an emerging system of public and private credit made the Dutch and Flemish cities some of the richest in the Habsburg domains.[33] It therefore is not surprising that Charles and Philip frequently turned to them in their search for funding.

The Low Countries had a long tradition of strong city governments. They did not hesitate to show their discontent when they perceived that their sovereign was overstepping his powers (Boone 2007). Even Charles V saw his birthplace of Ghent revolt against him in 1537, after he demanded additional taxes and military service to fight France. Charles personally traveled to the city to stamp out the revolt in 1540, executing the rebel leaders, humiliating the remaining public officials, and revoking a number of town privileges. Despite this, Charles continued to be perceived as a ruler with the interests of the Low Countries close to his heart; Philip, in contrast, was widely seen as

---

32 The Burgundian protocol was used in the Spanish court throughout the reigns of both Charles V and Philip II.

33 For some excellent general treatments of the dynamism of the Low Countries in the early modern age, see Tracy 1985, 1990; Gelderblom 2013.

more distant, indifferent to local concerns, and potentially hostile because of growing Protestantism in the Dutch provinces (Parker 1977).

Unrest started in the early 1560s, during the regency of Philip's half sister, Margaret of Parma. The States General demanded the withdrawal of the Spanish troops that garrisoned the Netherlands after the end of the war with France. Complaints over taxation, religious intolerance, military presence, and unpopular government officials escalated steadily over the next few years. Philip paid little attention to the Dutch remonstrances. For the most part, he ordered Margaret to ignore or repress the demands of the nobles.[34] In late 1566, the *beeldenstorm*—a series of iconoclastic attacks on Catholic churches—convinced Philip to intervene. He appointed the Duke of Alba, a hard-liner, as governor-general of the Netherlands. Alba arrived with an army of twelve thousand troops and sought to restore order. William of Orange, the main leader of the revolt, fled to Germany. Soon he would start to organize a military force. Alba established a special court in Brussels to prosecute the rebels. In addition to a large number of Calvinists, the court also tried and executed two popular Catholic noblemen, the Counts of Egmont and Horn. Together with William of Orange, they had led the opposition to Philip's policies, while (as the Dutch national anthem still proclaims today) remaining loyal to the king. Their execution hardened opposition to Spanish rule in the Low Countries, eliminated the best hope for a brokered peace, and opened the path to the Eighty Years' War.

Alba pursued the war with the same harshness with which he had persecuted the rebels in Brussels. Surrendering rebel cities were sacked; sometimes, cities that resisted saw their entire populations put to the sword. Some towns abandoned the rebel cause in a bid to save themselves; in others, resistance grew more determined. While Alba made progress on the battlefield, the costs were enormous. Eventually Philip II replaced him with Luis de Requesens in 1573. Requesens tried a more moderate line, but Philip's unwillingness to contemplate religious tolerance for the provinces closed the doors to any peace treaty. Requesens died in 1576, while he was trying to resolve one of the many mutinies among his troops as a result of unpaid wages. Without a governor-general to negotiate with, and with payment many months in

---

34 Parker (1979) attributes this apparently erratic behavior to Philip's perception of the Dutch issues as secondary, while his energies were fully committed to the naval warfare in the Mediterranean that would eventually lead to the War of the Holy League.

the future, mutinying soldiers sacked Antwerp on November 4, 1576.[35] The horror of Spanish soldiers plundering a loyal city and killing many citizens prompted all the provinces—loyal and rebel—to sign the Pacification of Ghent, an agreement with the purpose of driving the Spanish troops from the Low Countries and stopping the religious persecutions. Philip, temporarily unable to fund the war and faced with a united front, withdrew his troops for a brief period. In 1578 he also lost his second governor-general in two years, his half brother Don John of Austria.

By 1579 the tide started to turn. The settlement of the 1575 bankruptcy, increased silver remittances from the New World, and the waning of the war in the Mediterranean allowed Philip to fund another bid for reconquest in the Netherlands. Peace negotiations sponsored by Emperor Rudolph II had broken down, and the Dutch provinces split into the Union of Arras (loyal) and Union of Utrecht (rebel). New army units were dispatched to the Low Countries. Philip's new governor, the Duke of Parma, slowly recaptured the southern provinces. It took him six years to finally secure Antwerp and start making inroads into the rebel heartland.

In the meantime, the northern provinces formally rejected Philip as sovereign in the Act of Abjuration of 1581. They offered the crown to a variety of other rulers, but could find no prince willing to take it; acceptance would spell instant conflict with Christendom's most powerful monarch. Without any takers, the northern provinces eventually decided to govern themselves as a republic. The "Spanish surge," combined with the assassination of William of Orange in 1584, threw the politics of the northern provinces into turmoil. In an attempt to strengthen their military position, they agreed to the Treaty of Nonsuch with England, accepting the Earl of Leicester as governor-general in exchange for military assistance. This turned out to be an unhappy arrangement. The States General and the stadtholder, Maurice of Nassau, began clawing back administrative and military competencies almost immediately; after some mixed successes in military and diplomatic campaigns, Leicester returned to England in 1587. Combined with the damaging raids by English privateers on Spanish trade, an increase in English aid to the Dutch rebels, and Sir Francis Drake's raid on Cádiz in 1587, the Treaty of Nonsuch helped to strengthen Philip's determination to invade England. The idea was

---

35 See chapter 5, where we explore the reasons behind the Sack of Antwerp in detail. See also the online appendix in Drelichman and Voth 2011a.

to cut the lifeline for the rebels and perhaps force a religious change in a Protestant monarchy (De Lamar 1988).

The *Grande y Felicísima Armada*, which the English scornfully christened "Invincible" after its rout, was the brainchild of Alvaro de Bazán, Marquis of Santa Cruz. Bazán was a consummate naval strategist who had distinguished himself in numerous naval campaigns, including Lepanto. As the mastermind behind the system of armed convoys carrying silver across the Atlantic, he was no stranger to complex operations that combined large numbers of military and transport ships. The plan for the Armada, hatched as early as 1583, went through numerous iterations. There were setbacks, redesigns, and diversions, as Santa Cruz, Parma, and the king sought to coordinate a gigantic enterprise. On occasion, the partially assembled fleet was dispatched to pursue alternative endeavors, setting the invasion plan back by many months.[36] In its final form, the plan called for 127 ships to carry all the supplies necessary for an invasion of England. The fleet would sail from Spain to the Netherlands. From there it would escort an army of 16,000 troops under the Duke of Parma, crossing in flat-bottomed barges. The Spaniards would land in the vicinity of Kent, from where they would then march on London.

Victory on land was a virtual certainty; the untrained English militia would be no match for Parma's battle-hardened veterans. The English acknowledged as much. In 1614, Sir Walter Raleigh—who, together with Sir Richard Grenville, had been charged with the defense of Devon and Cornwall—wrote that his troops were "of no such force as to encounter an Armie like unto that, wherewith it was intended that the prince of Parma should have landed in England." As Parker put it, if the Armada had landed, Spain stood to reap substantial benefits and the operation would have been regarded as Philip's finest hour.[37]

The difficulty, of course, was in making the landing happen. The outfitting of the fleet was delayed by the slow disbursements of funds, the constant wavering by Philip and his commanders as to the size as well as objectives, the 1587 English raid on Cádiz, and Santa Cruz's inability to secure enough ships while maintaining them seaworthy in the face of the multiyear delays. On the Dutch front, Parma was also having trouble keeping his invasion army combat ready, fed, and paid while waiting for ships that, season after season, did not come.

---

36 For an account of the multiple overlapping plans for the Armada, and a discussion of the delays and setbacks it experienced, see De Lamar 1988.

37 Raleigh's quote and Parker's appraisal appear in Parker 1979.

In winter 1588, Bazán died unexpectedly. Having already decided that the operation would go ahead that year regardless of the cost or peril, the king put the Duke of Medina-Sidonia in charge. Though reviled by his contemporaries and later generations of historians as an incompetent nobleman who lost the Armada, Medina-Sidonia had actually made his name as an excellent military organizer and administrator. He managed to complete the outfitting of the fleet in a matter of months and headed for Flanders in the spring.

Medina-Sidonia was a prudent commander, and not the bumbling, seasick buffoon described by generations of earlier writers. His actions were fully in line with the objectives for the Armada. The enterprise was risky, as everyone—including Philip—knew. The risk was worth taking in the eyes of the Spanish because the potential gains were enormous. That the fleet met an ignominious end was not the result of incompetence. It reflected the logistical difficulties in carrying out the plan, coupled with a series of unexpected, negative shocks during its execution.[38]

In July 1588, the Armada sailed through the channel and reached Flanders. It came within forty-eight hours of joining forces with Parma's invasion army, but never actually managed to do so. Scattered by ill winds and English fireships after the Battle of Gravelines, the fleet was forced to circumnavigate the British Isles, suffering many shipwrecks off the coasts of Scotland and Ireland. The most recent calculations peg the numbers of lost or damaged ships at forty-three, or roughly one-third of the fleet (Casado Soto 1988). Loss of life is harder to quantify, as it is not possible to establish how many sailors and soldiers sailed in the first place. Rough estimates place casualties at eighty-seven hundred, or about 50 percent of the initial strength.[39] In a remarkable twist of fate, most of the nimble, efficient English ships that routed the Spanish fleet dated from the 1550s. They had been built following a recommendation to the Privy Council by the then king consort of England—none other than Philip II himself (Parker 1996, 91).[40]

The defeat of the Armada was far less damaging to Spain's military position than the fleet's standing in the popular imagination as a major disaster

38 This view can already be found in Mattingly 1959; Thompson 1969. Rodríguez-Salgado (1990) surveys more recent work supporting the idea that the disaster of the Armada had more to do with negative risk realizations than with hubris and incompetence.
39 Rodríguez-Salgado (1990) provides a survey of existing estimates.
40 Philip was married to Mary I of England between 1554 (when he was still prince) and 1558, when Mary died. She was Philip's second wife.

suggests. Within a year, the Armada's strength had been replenished and the threat of an English counterattack effectively checked. The operation was still extremely expensive. The whole campaign and its aftermath cost upward of ten million ducats, or fully two years' worth of royal revenue. And yet the plan's failure did not lead to a bankruptcy.[41] That Philip II's empire could absorb such a financial loss and live to fight another day speaks volumes about the immense resources that it could muster. The risk of defeat was fully taken into account in financial and military decision making. The failure of the Drake-Norris expedition—also known as the Counter Armada—in 1589 gave the Spaniards breathing room, and the two nations continued to trade naval attacks and raids on coastal towns. Hostilities reached a peak in the period 1596–97, when an English expedition occupied Cádiz for two weeks. Philip sent two retaliatory Armadas, which suffered fates similar to that of their Invincible predecessor. The war of attrition, combined with the ongoing hostilities with Henry IV of France, eventually took its toll on Castile's finances. Acknowledging Castile's inability to continue the fight on two fronts, Philip's envoys concluded the Peace of Vervins. This ended the war with France in 1598. Philip III would ultimately wind down the war with England in 1604.[42]

TERRITORIAL EXPANSION UNDER PHILIP II

Philip spent most of his resources waging wars that produced few territorial gains. On the other hand, the greatest expansions of Spain's empire were relatively cheap. Two merit special attention: the colonies in America and Asia, and the acquisition of Portugal and its empire.

THE OVERSEAS POSSESSIONS

Soon after Columbus's voyages, the Spanish conquest of the New World began. In this endeavor Spain faced no European rivals; the English only disturbed Spain with privateering raids in the second half of the sixteenth century and would not stake territorial claims until the seventeenth. The French

---

41 The defeat nevertheless served to focus the mind of the Cortes into voting for new excises—the *millones*—to provide for the defense of the kingdom. For an in-depth analysis, see chapter 3.
42 On the role of the 1596 bankruptcy and royal finances in the Peace of Vervins, see Gelabert 2013.

focused mostly on New France and, except for the short-lived settlement of Fort Caroline in Florida, did not clash with Spain. The only other contender for a portion of the newly discovered continent was Portugal. The relationship between the two Iberian neighbors was regulated by the 1494 treaty of Tordesillas, which kept them on different sides of a mutually agreed-on line. The low threat of conflict with other European powers in the New World allowed Castile to conduct the exploration, conquest, and colonization of the continent at a relatively low cost, using a system of private enterprise. Explorers—*adelantados*—obtained charters from the Crown. These gave them the rights to govern territories or capture loot. The expeditions were for the most part privately financed. The Crown enforced a colonial trading monopoly through the city of Seville, supervised by the Casa de Contratación. It charged a flat 20 percent tax—the royal fifth—on precious metal flows between America and Spain, and a 2.5 percent levy—the *avería*—on all other commercial goods. An additional tax, the *Almojarifazgo Mayor de Sevilla*, was collected on trade between Seville and the rest of Castile.

As Spain's footprint in the New World grew, so did the value of transatlantic trade. Establishing a bureaucratic and military presence became a matter of urgency. One of the most important concerns was to protect the ships; laden with precious metals and valuable commodities, they were tempting targets for privateers. Armed galleons began to escort the ships while crossing the Atlantic. Protection was financed out of the avería. The escorts increased in frequency and size, eventually evolving into a system of treasure fleets. From 1565 on, these sailed twice a year between Seville and the colonies (Hamilton 1929). The armed convoys also ensured that ships on the return voyage docked in Seville, where their cargo could be assayed and taxed. Smuggling was nonetheless substantial. Captains were willing to accept bribes in order to carry undeclared treasure, which was off-loaded during the nighttime at the mouth of the Guadalquivir River, just before the last leg of the journey to the Casa de la Contratación.[43]

---

43 Michel Morineau (1985) reports that bribes were around 7 percent of the value of undeclared treasure. The net saving was therefore 13 percent (the "saved" royal fifth minus 7 percent). There also might have been a slight timing advantage, as the House of Trade often retained treasure for up to a month. Being caught with undeclared treasure carried a penalty of four times its value (Hamilton 1929). The risk of detection seems to have been fairly low. There are few notices about confiscated contraband, and Dutch commercial publications and Italian diplomatic correspondence discuss contraband amounts at length.

Government also advanced inexorably in the New World, but it did so in what Regina Grafe and María Alejandra Irigoín (2006) call the importation of "an eclectic mixture of institutional precedents from various parts of the Spanish monarchy." Explorers and conquerors soon gave way to career bureaucrats. The governorships created during the conquest were grouped into the viceroyalties of New Spain and Peru.[44] Courts were established to settle disputes, and colonial *cajas* collected taxes. In 1524 the Council of the Indies—a royal institution residing in the court in Spain—was created to oversee the government of the New World. In practice, colonial units retained a large degree of autonomy. The "tyranny of distance" made direct rule impossible. Letters from Peru to Spain took several months to arrive, if sent at the optimal time given sailing schedules. An answer would take at least a year, and often much longer.

Growing economic clout added to the power of colonial officials. As the colonial period progressed, the local administrations developed a network of taxes and fiscal transfers that operated with only nominal reference to the central government in Spain. Nevertheless, the New World generated substantial surpluses for Castile. Salaries—the largest expenditure in the colonial administration—accounted for only 3 percent of New Spain's revenues, and 12 percent of New Granada's and Peru's during the sixteenth century.[45] Castile also collected taxes on trade and treasure on landing in Seville. Hence, the relative burden of administrative cost was even lower and the net gains from the American colonies were even greater. The overall costs of running the colonies were low compared with the benefits that Castile reaped from them.[46]

The Philippines were Castile's second important colonial outpost. First surveyed by Ferdinand Magellan in 1521, they became a permanent base for the Spaniards in 1565. Manila was founded in 1571. It mainly served as a trading port to satisfy the enormous Chinese appetite for silver from Seville (and later on, directly from Acapulco). Gold and various luxury items made the return trip to Spain, and from there some went on to the colonies. Governing the archipelago, however, was to prove very different from managing the

---

44 New Spain refers to modern-day Mexico.

45 For an excellent discussion of the institutional characteristics, intergovernmental transfers, and administrative costs in Spanish America, see Grafe and Irigoín 2006.

46 Not all the treasure was taxed in Seville, however. Part of it was assayed, taxed, and sometimes coined in the colonies. This proportion increased as the colonies' demand for taxes and coinage grew.

American viceroyalties. The local populations were militarily more advanced and the geography was more complex, leading to constant skirmishes, raids, and massacres. As a result of the high security costs and lack of a resource-based economy, the colony struggled to break even. Its economic benefit to the empire came in the form of closing the "circle of silver," facilitating an arbitrage that yielded enormous profits for Spanish merchants and the Castilian Crown.[47]

PORTUGAL

In 1578 the young King Sebastian of Portugal, unmarried and childless, died in the Battle of Alcacer Quibir. His death sparked a succession crisis. The prize was nothing less than the largest merchant empire in the world. Sebastian was succeeded by his great uncle, Henry "the Chaste," who, as a cardinal of the church, had no legitimate heirs of his own. His death two years later ushered in several competing claims to the throne.

The Portuguese succession illustrates the complicated dynastic scheming and inbreeding prevalent in European royal households. The regnant families of Castile and Portugal had intermarried several times during the last three generations. Maria of Aragon, daughter of the Catholic Kings, married Manuel I of Portugal. Their son, King John III of Portugal, married Catherine of Austria, a daughter of Joanna the Mad and Philip the Handsome, and hence John III's first cousin. Their son, John Manuel, married Joan of Austria, the daughter of Charles V and Isabel of Portugal (who was in turn the daughter of Manuel I and Maria of Aragon). John Manuel died before becoming king, with the throne ultimately passing to Sebastian. Philip II, who claimed the crown, was himself Sebastian's uncle. At Sebastian's death, the dynastically stronger claims to succeed him were those of the House of Braganza, because its members, Catherine of Braganza and Ranuccio Farnese, descended from King Manuel I via a male line.[48] Philip II was a descendant of Manuel I through his mother, Isabel, thereby making his claim weaker. Another claimant, the

---

47 For a discussion of the role of the Philippines in the universe of Spanish trade, see Flynn and Giráldez 2004.
48 Ranuccio was the son of Alexander Farnese, Duke of Parma and governor of the Netherlands. Given his father's status as a direct subordinate of Philip II, Ranuccio's rights were not pursued. His aunt, Catherine of Braganza, tried in vain to convince Philip to support her cause. At the dissolution of the Iberian Union in 1640, Catherine's descendants would be acclaimed as the legitimate rulers of Portugal.

Prior of Crato, was a direct grandson of King Manuel I, but he had been born out of wedlock.[49]

The crisis resulted from a split in the nobility, which reflected a deep discontent with more than a decade of weak and corrupt administration, rising taxes, and a flagging economy. A nationalist faction that wished to keep the crown on a Portuguese head sided with the Prior of Crato, but he lacked popular support. The merchant aristocracy fled to Spain and threw its support behind Philip, seeking to import what it saw as the superior model of Castilian administration. Ignoring the weakness of his dynastic claims, Philip recalled the Duke of Alba from retirement and placed him at the head of an invasion army. Alba easily defeated the poorly trained forces of the Prior of Crato at the Battle of Alcantara, and the Cortes de Tomar swore Philip in as the king of Portugal in late 1580. In exchange for the nobility's support, Philip promised to respect the independence of Portugal in terms of language, coinage, noble privileges, and financial management. The merchant empire would continue to be run by Portuguese nationals; as Portuguese king, Philip could not confer privileges on Spaniards, nor could he appoint any Spaniard (save for members of the royal household) to positions of power. The crowns remained strictly segregated for the remainder of Philip's reign, with no direct transfers between the treasuries or other major interference in Portuguese financial management.

Portugal did bear a major cost from the Iberian Union: the loss of an independent foreign policy. It now had to provide military support to Philip—an obligation that became burdensome at the time of the Armada. Bazán assembled the fleet in Portuguese ports using local resources and naval expertise. Portugal supplied a fifth of the ships sailing in the Armada, staffed by forty-five hundred sailors and soldiers (Boyajian 1993). Portuguese merchants also became the target of English privateers. Raids on smaller ports and the occasional threat to Lisbon continued until the end of the Anglo-Spanish War.

A second effect of the Iberian Union on the Portuguese economy was the decline of the Asian trade. Eventually, Portugal was replaced by the Netherlands as the dominant merchant empire in the East. Castile organized its colonial expansion on the basis of free enterprise; individual explorers, char-

---

49 Our account in this section follows Marques (1979) and Serrão (1982), two classic sources on Portuguese history.

tered by the Crown, assumed all the risk and received the largest share of the profits. The Portuguese Empire, on the other hand, was built and adminis-tered directly by the Crown (Rei 2011). When the Spaniards took over the Portuguese Empire, they were ill equipped to deal with its business model; Asian trade languished as a result.

Portugal's elites would ultimately become unhappy with their country's marriage to Castile in the seventeenth century. Yet Philip II—known in Por-tugal as Philip I—respected his end of the bargain, keeping the two crowns strictly separate (Serrão 1982). Portugal contributed enough on the military front, and the combined Iberian trading empires, while starting to face chal-lenges in Asia, still had no rival in either the East or West. The Iberian Union was a highly cost-effective expansion of Philip's empire. It came at the ex-pense of a single, limited military operation even as it added a world of trade, power, and naval might to the king's personal holdings, and a welcome help-ing hand to Castile's military campaigns.

THE LOGIC OF EMPIRE

MILITARY CHOICES

Philip II's financial troubles have been frequently blamed on his imperial ambitions. Spain's path from hegemonic superpower in the sixteenth cen-tury to a mere prize to be fought over by France, England, and the Nether-lands at the dawn of the eighteenth century has also been attributed to im-perial overstretch. The argument is simple: at the height of its power, Spain failed to reform as well as centralize its fiscal and administrative structures along the lines pioneered by other European powers. Depending on the ac-count, this failure was caused either by a combination of complacency, in-competence, and superstition, or a sense that after expending so many lives and resources, changing course was not an option. In John H. Elliott's (1963a) words, at the critical junctures where the imperial enterprise could have been scaled back, Castile appeared to find itself "in a position where it seemed that readjustment to the new economic realities could be achieved only at the price of sacrificing its most cherished ideals."[50] Caught in the logic of past choices, Spain suffered and finally crumbled under the weight

---

50 For another exponent of the imperial overstretch, see Kennedy 1987.

of an unattainable ambition from which it didn't have the strength or will to back away.

A more recent literature instead sees the empire as a multinational enterprise, headquartered in Castile, and composed of fairly autonomous "business units."[51] Decisions on where to push the boundaries were dictated by a combination of opportunity and expected gains. This was a necessary feature, since most of the imperial ventures were supported, financed, and carried out by third parties, which had to tie their fortunes to those of Spain. Henry Kamen (2003) points out that the Spanish Empire was built by German, Genoese, and Neapolitan financiers, Flemish, Dutch, and Portuguese shipbuilders, traders from all corners of Europe and Asia, and soldiers of every nationality, including indigenous peoples in the Americas and mercenaries from Spain's own enemies. Each of them, in their own way, risked life and fortune on ventures that seemed promising at the time. When a Genoese banker delivered a large loan to the paymaster of the Army of Flanders, he knew full well what the funds would be used for and had a reasonably good idea of which portions of the empire the repayment would come from. Military commanders planned and fought for victory. Even in the most iconic defeat, that of the Armada, the consensus of military historians is that its objectives—establishing a beachhead in Kent and forcing England into a negotiated peace—were feasible and could have been attained with high probability.

Military historians have also examined the pattern of confrontations that Philip II entered into. Parker proposes a "domino theory."[52] The European portions of the empire, though geographically disperse, had no slack built into them. Given that the Low Countries and northern Italy were rich possessions that had to be defended, the "Spanish Road" linking them was essential. This created a sense of encirclement for French rulers, contributing to an almost-permanent state of conflict between the two powers. If the Netherlands were to be pacified, then there was little choice about confronting England as well. Similarly, when the Ottomans pushed westward into the Mediterranean, the dominant option from both a military and economic point of view was to fight back. It is true that Philip refused to give up any

---

51 Parker (1998) first espoused this theory in the context of elucidating the guiding principle of Philip II's imperial strategy. Kamen (2003) expanded it to the entire the Spanish Empire.

52 Here we largely follow Parker 1972, 1998. Pierson (1989) makes a similar point about the strategic choices that led to the Armada.

territory because he considered it part of his inheritance, ultimately bestowed on him by God. It is also true, however, that he couldn't have surrendered any part of his empire without jeopardizing the rest.

While the Spanish Empire today evokes visions of overstretch and decline, it is worth remembering that few harbingers of its protracted dismemberment were evident during Philip II's long reign. Castile continued its expansion in the seventeenth century, even pushing deep into the Netherlands during the reign of Philip IV. Nor did Castile have to win every single confrontation into which it entered. Some negative outcomes would not doom the enterprise, and loss-making ventures were acceptable if they contributed to the integrity of the whole.

BACK TO CASTILE

The Spanish Empire's day-to-day operations were often remarkably decentralized. As a general rule, territories were expected to raise their own revenues, pay for most of their own expenses—including defense—and support the monarch when asked to do so (Rodríguez-Salgado 1988).[53] The execution of imperial military and geopolitical strategy, though, frequently required large transfers of resources between territories. Those transfers were decided at the highest level of government and handled directly by the central treasury in Castile. The Castilian Crown also underwrote the loans and exchange operations necessary to make those transfers happen. Payment for those loans came almost exclusively from Castilian taxes, levied on Castile's colonial remittances, domestic production and consumption, and growing international trade as well as directly on its subjects. Castile therefore was both the central clearinghouse and paymaster of last resort.[54] To keep the wheels of empire turning required a well-oiled fiscal and financial machinery in Castile. It is to that machinery that we turn our attention in the remainder of the book.

---

53 An exception to this rule were the New World colonies, as illustrated in Grafe and Irigoín 2006. The enormous geographic barriers between Spain and the Americas likely played a large part in the emergence of the system of intercolonial transfers that arose there.

54 P.G.M. Dickson (1987) makes a similar point regarding the Habsburg German possessions: the central territories bore the brunt of taxation, while dominions had a light fiscal load. After losing Silesia to Frederick the Great in the War of Austrian Succession, Maria Theresia's advisers were stunned at how Frederick managed to radically increase taxation in the territory.

CHAPTER 3

TAXES, DEBTS, AND INSTITUTIONS

Early modern kings evoke images of absolute rule, crystallized in the famous statement attributed to Louis XIV: *"L'État, c'est moi."* Modern economic research often refers to this image when characterizing European states between 1500 and 1800.[1] As a generation of revisionist historians has convincingly argued, royal power in the early modern period was in practice never unconstrained.[2] Instead, "absolutism" is probably best viewed as a social arrangement to the mutual benefit of both the elite and the Crown, with the former providing crucial support to the latter.[3] For the celebrated case of France, Roland Mousnier (1974) famously showed that Louis XIV and his successors governed largely by consensus; absolutism was more theater than reality. In each country different regional histories continued to shape the boundaries between the king and the rights and freedoms of his subjects to a varying extent.

In sixteenth-century Castile, the limits of royal authority were heavily influenced by the Reconquista's long shadow. During the Middle Ages, after every push into Arab territory, Christian kings had faced the problem of how to hold on to their gains. To encourage the repopulation of conquered land, they endowed towns and cities with sizable commons and extensive political liberties. Religious orders, in similar fashion, were granted large territories in exchange for establishing monasteries, which served as both spiritual centers and economic engines. At the dawn of the early modern age, these entitlements had seriously limited the Crown's resources. The royal demesne was

---

1 Acemoglu, Johnson, and Robinson (2005), for example, code Spain as being an "absolutist" state.

2 See, for example, the definition of absolutism by Richard Bonney (1987).

3 We cannot review the entire literature on the reality of absolutism here. For good overviews, see Oestreich 1969; Parker 1983.

the largest source of income in most of Europe. In Castile, lands given to towns and religious orders had reduced its size, curtailing royal revenues. Municipal freedoms resulted in a weak feudal order, depriving kings of direct military support and forcing them to negotiate directly with the cities about taxes.

After the end of the Reconquista, the Catholic Kings moved to reassert royal authority—a process that continued under Charles V and Philip II. This push, however, was conditioned internally by the strength of the cities (and to some extent, the nobility and the church) and externally by the military needs of the Crown. To obtain additional resources, kings had to bargain with the cities in a process that could be lengthy and often required costly concessions. The result was far from the centrally controlled system epitomized in the figure of an absolute monarch. And yet by the end of the sixteenth century, Castile had managed to increase its tax revenues and fiscal pressure to levels far above those of competing powers.[4]

In this chapter, we describe the evolution of Castile's political and fiscal institutions under the Habsburg monarchs, focusing on the mechanisms and events that made its remarkable expansion possible. We then present the main fiscal and financial data of this book. Two series are key. First, relying on published sources, we carefully reconstruct fiscal revenues between 1555 and 1596. Next, using new, hand-collected data from the archives, we compile a new series of short-term loans—asientos. Both series underpin the analysis in the remainder of our book.

POLITICAL ORGANIZATION

CROWN AND KINGDOM

The Crown—or government—was personified in the figure of the king, and consisted of a system of councils with executive responsibility over the different areas of public administration.[5] This system evolved during the late

---

4 We provide a full set of international comparisons in chapter 8.

5 Technically all executive decisions emanated from the king, while councils were limited to the consultative function implied in their name (*consilium*). The actions of the councils were called *consultas*, which implied a request for or offer of advice. In practice, the sheer volume of state business meant that all but the most crucial decisions were taken by the councils and rubberstamped by the king.

Middle Ages and consolidated under the Habsburgs in the sixteenth century.[6] The most important matters requiring executive action were heard and decided in the Council of Castile, which also served as the highest court of appeal. Most territories in the monarchy had their own councils (Aragon, Navarre, Italy, Flanders, Portugal, and the Indies). The Council of Finance (Consejo de Hacienda) was responsible for most fiscal and financial matters.[7] The councils of war, inquisition, and military orders, and the Council of the Chamber rounded up the higher-order executive bodies.

In contrast to the Crown, the "Kingdom" was the set of different social strata, corporations, municipalities, and organizations of the realm. The institution that gave life to the Kingdom was the Cortes, a representative assembly that dated back at least to the twelfth century.[8] From the fourteenth century on, voting in the Cortes was reserved for the representatives of Castilian cities, with the clergy and nobility excluded. The number of voting cities was fixed at seventeen in the first half of the fifteenth century, with Granada becoming the eighteenth vote after its capture in 1492. From the late Middle Ages onward, the Cortes became the standard-bearer of the urban elites. Although in the fifteenth century the Cortes was convened at irregular intervals, from the sixteenth century on it sat on average every three years.[9]

Following the tradition of medieval curiae, the function of the Cortes was to provide *auxilium et consilium*—resources and advice—to the king. This took the form of granting revenue along with submitting a list of complaints and requests for the monarch's consideration. A number of taxes required Cortes approval. The most important among them was the sales taxes known as *alcabalas*, closely followed by the personal taxes called *servicios* (both discussed below). The Cortes could be reasonably expected to renew the previous level

6 In our description of the system of councils, we follow Artola 1988.
7 Certain revenue streams were administered by bodies other than the Council of Finance. This was the case of revenues collected through the church, which were overseen by the Council of Crusade; later on, the excises known as the *millones* would be overseen by the Diputación, an organ of the Cortes.
8 The Cortes has been the subject of a large body of scholarly research, with novel contributions appearing to this day. For some general treatments centered on the early modern period, see Carretero Zamora 1988; Thompson 1976, 1993, 1994a; Fortea Pérez 2009; proceedings of the Congreso Científico sobre la Historia de las Cortes de Castilla y León (1989). The first documented meeting of the Cortes took place in León in 1188.
9 The Cortes had to be called by the king and could not convene of its own accord. A number of taxes would technically lapse, though, if not renewed by the Cortes, and hence monarchs had powerful incentives to call regular meetings of the assembly.

of taxes; refusing to do so would have been considered an act of rebellion. The most the Cortes dared to do to confront the king when it came to renewing existing tax levels was to attempt to have its complaints addressed before voting on funding. Even in this limited objective, it was almost never successful. The closest the Cortes came to obtaining redress to its complaints before voting on supply was in 1576, when it requested a lowering of the rate on the alcabala. After much haggling, the king agreed to consider the request, implying that he would approve it provided that the Cortes renewed the previous level of funding first. The Cortes dutifully played its part; the previous taxes were first renewed and then graciously lowered by the king.[10]

When the king requested an increase in taxes, however, the Cortes could and did refuse to provide it, delay it, or request concessions in return. A case in point is that of the Cortes of 1575, when the assembly refused the king's request for tripling the sales tax. The proceedings dragged on for several months, with the deteriorating financial position of the Crown and demands of the war in the Low Countries looming large over the impasse. An agreement to double the tax was finally reached, but the proceeds came too late to help avert the bankruptcy of that year. For a monarch who has been characterized as "absolute," Philip II was constrained indeed.

The Cortes was most powerful in times of crisis, usually prompted by difficult military situations. Its ability to resist royal pressure in other circumstances, though, was much diminished after the standoff between Charles V and the Cortes of 1519, which had been convened to authorize a levy to pay for Charles's trip to accept the Holy Roman Crown. Knowing that Charles's imperial ambitions were likely to be financed out of Castilian tax revenues, the cities resisted the move. Several of them explicitly refused to grant full powers to their representatives, requiring them to instead consult with city governments before approving any levies. The Cortes was originally convened in Santiago de Compostela, and Charles subsequently moved the sessions to even more remote La Coruña, where he strong-armed the representatives into compliance.[11] Tellingly, the ensuing revolt of the comunidades began when a mob in Segovia lynched a delegate returning from the Cortes.

---

10 See Jago 1985; Fortea Pérez 2009.
11 These events support David Stasavage's (2011) conjecture that geographic distance could be a major obstacle for a representative assembly trying to monitor and constrain a monarch in the early modern period.

Although the revolt raged on for a year, Charles eventually quashed the uprising without much difficulty.

One key feature of the Cortes's role in granting financial support was the designation of an income stream as "ordinary" or "extraordinary." In medieval times, ordinary streams were permanent ones, while extraordinary revenues had to be reauthorized at every sitting. By the early modern period, both types of revenues were renewed as a matter of course, but the distinction still mattered, as long-term debt could only be issued against ordinary revenues. The Cortes, therefore, held one important tool of fiscal control. By refusing to approve new ordinary revenues or convert extraordinary revenues into ordinary ones, it could effectively set a ceiling for the long-term debt issued by the Crown.

NOBILITY

The structure of the Castilian nobility was, as in virtually every emerging European state, a product of its military history during the Middle Ages.[12] Newly incorporated villages and cities were granted extensive liberties in areas conquered from the Arabs. This process resulted in a weak feudal structure, with the powers of the lord (señor) of a town severely restricted by the privileges previously granted to the municipal corporation. Some groups of towns, called behetrías, were even granted the ability to select their own feudal lord. Many territories did not become subject to a lord altogether, remaining in the king's demesne—but free from feudal dues—as late as the second half of the sixteenth century. Afterward, the Crown began to sell them to noble families to raise funds.[13] A related fund-raising strategy was the sale of tierras baldías—literally, "empty lands." Although these lands were technically part of the royal demesne, towns and peasants had used them as commons for centuries. Their privatization caused serious disruptions to the local economies, creating problems not unlike those that would emerge with the enclosure movement in Britain.[14]

---

12 For an overview of early modern Castilian nobility, see Domínguez Ortiz 1985.

13 The sale of privileges of lordships over formerly free towns caused serious distress for local economies, as towns lost income streams to their new overlords or saw their fiscal pressure increase. Several towns enacted extraordinary levies in an effort to buy their own privileges and remain free from external overlordship. For a discussion on the sale of towns under the Habsburgs, see Nader 1990.

14 For more on the privatization of tierras baldías, see Vassberg 1975, 1984; García Sanz 1980.

From the late Middle Ages onward, the rights of feudal lords—who constituted the upper nobility—were usually limited to collecting rent over their lands as well as certain other feudal dues. The administration of justice transitioned into royal hands early on, as did military service, which by the fifteenth century was entirely professional or mercenary. The nobility was thus drawn closer to the king, who kept it in check by carefully distributing key government posts among different noble lineages, assigning nobles to military command posts, and periodically extracting monetary contributions.

During the reigns of Charles V and Philip II, there was also a large increase in the number of petty nobles—the hidalgos of Don Quixote fame. Traditional historiography assumed that the newly minted hidalgos were after the tax exemptions that came with ennoblement. Since nobles were not supposed to engage in manual labor, it was also assumed that the newly ennobled left the labor force in droves. Braudel (1966, 517) famously called this phenomenon "the treason of the bourgeoisie." In reality, the value of the tax exemptions was small compared to the cost of obtaining noble status, and most hidalgos could not afford to leave the labor force. Their main reason for seeking ennoblement was to take advantage of a provision that reserved one-half of all municipal positions for nobles—the *mitad de los oficios*. While a few succeeded in securing a profitable appointment, the large number of new hidalgos meant that most were thwarted in their quest. Life for them continued as usual, except for a court document certifying their status. Although significant from a cultural point of view, this expansion of the nobility had virtually no fiscal or political consequences.[15]

THE CHURCH

The Catholic Church played a key role in the political and financial fortunes of Spain. When the Arabs overran most of the Iberian Peninsula in the eighth century, Christianity was one of the few common traits the defeated Visigothic kingdoms could find to form a unified front against the invader. During the seven centuries of the Reconquista, religion and the Crown developed an almost-symbiotic relationship. The church was part of the military machine in the form of the four religious-military orders of Santiago, Alcántara,

---

15 For an analysis of the expansion of the number of hidalgos in the sixteenth century, see Drelichman 2007.

Calatrava, and Montesa, which were rewarded with large shares of the land they helped recover from the Muslims. The establishment of monasteries was also an effective way of cementing a presence in a newly conquered country devoid of enough settlers, and the Crown willingly ceded the surrounding lands to the new convents. As the country was slowly resettled by Christians, parishes were pressed into fiscal service, collecting a number of taxes and levies on behalf of the Crown. Priests were likely to know in detail the resources of their parishioners and, holding moral sway over them, also had a better chance than royal collectors in ensuring that they paid their due.

An idea of the influence and reach of the church can be gleaned by surveying its property holdings. Church property, once acquired, could not be sold, mortgaged, or alienated in any way. One way to acquire and entail new properties were the bequests of wealthy landowners—a common occurrence in a society that saw good deeds on earth as a way to achieve eternal salvation. Much more important, however, was the role played by ecclesiastical organizations in providing long-term financial arrangements for owners of small- and medium-size fields. During economic downturns, it was common for landowners to sell their land to a cathedral or monastery; in exchange they received a sum of money and entered into a perpetual lease (*censo*). By the end of the seventeenth century the church was the largest landowner in Spain, and a large portion of its income was derived from land rents and mortgage payments. Cadastral data from the mid-eighteenth century reveal that the church held 12.3 percent of the land in the crown of Castile and accounted for 19.5 percent of agricultural production. When the personal holdings of ecclesiastics are added, the amount of land controlled by "dead hands" reached 24 percent. Yet the cadastral surveys only identified the person directly exploiting the land rather than the holder of eminent domain. Many plots that belonged to the church but were held in tenancy or perpetual leases by peasants therefore would have been wrongly classified as belonging to those peasants. As large as the 24 percent figure may seem, it was just a lower end on the share of real estate accumulated by convents, hospitals, cathedrals, monasteries, and ecclesiastics themselves over the centuries (Marcos Martín 2000).

Although no cadastral data are available for the sixteenth century, the *Censo de los Millones*, taken for the purpose of allocating the new excises voted in 1591, offers an idea of the relative economic weight of the church. According to its findings, the church concentrated roughly one-sixth of the landed wealth of Castile, although clergy constituted a much smaller share of the population.[16] As an example, in 1500 a full 20 percent of the buildings in the city of Seville belonged to churches and clergy; by 1561, the cathedral and second-largest church alone owned 23.9 percent of all buildings in the city. In Toledo, the Cathedral chapter owned about 30 percent of the buildings in the city by the end of the sixteenth century.[17]

Starting with Ferdinand the Catholic, the kings of Spain became close allies and staunch supporters of the Papacy. In chapter 2, we discussed how this earned Ferdinand and his successors the privilege of royal patronage, which entailed the authority to appoint bishops and prelates. Church positions were profitable; their endowments and revenue streams made them highly coveted by members of noble families. Royal patronage therefore gave the Crown yet another tool with which to keep a short leash on both the nobility and clergy. As an extension of the right of patronage, Ferdinand also claimed the masterships of the military orders along with the sizable rents they generated. The Papacy formally recognized the takeover with a bull in 1523.

Finally, the Inquisition was a formidable tool of social and political control in both Spain and the colonies.[18] It depended directly on the Crown, which had a dedicated council to oversee it. The inquisitors, designated by the monarch and vested with full judicial powers, busied themselves with eradicating heresy, unholiness, and moral deviations. Between the establishment of the Inquisition in 1484 and its dissolution in 1837, perhaps some 125,000 individuals suffered its scrutiny. Death sentences were rare, imposed perhaps in less than 1 percent of the cases, and even then not always carried out.[19] Physical torture and punishment, however, were liberally used to elicit confessions as well as ensure that morals were respected and the tenets of the faith

---

16   The share of clerics was estimated at 1.5 percent of the population. The number rings small, possibly because ecclesiastics succeeded in underreporting their numbers and hence lowering their contribution to the new tax. The figure is still an order of magnitude lower than the percentage of land controlled by the church.

17   For the figures for Seville, see Benassar 2001. For Toledo, see Drelichman and González Agudo 2013.

18   Jordi Vidal-Robert (2011) provides an economic analysis of the Spanish Inquisition as a tool of social control.

19   For a modern estimate of the victims of the Inquisition and composition of the sentences handed out, see Pérez 2003.

were not challenged. The Inquisition was completely autonomous from a financial point of view. It relied exclusively on the fines it imposed and goods it expropriated to finance itself, without either receiving or making transfers to the Crown.

REVENUES

At the beginning of the sixteenth century, the Crown had a wide variety of revenue streams at its disposal. As Castile entered its imperial period, new taxes and income sources were added, while the existing ones were expanded or otherwise modified as the need and opportunity presented themselves. The balance between different sources of income was the result of complicated historical processes; custom, vested interests, and the relative strength between the Crown and kingdom all contributed to the particular fiscal structure of Castile. We now provide an overview of the most significant revenue streams and trace their evolution throughout the reign of Philip II.[20]

DIRECT TAXES

The medieval fiscal structure relied heavily on direct taxes. The most important among these were the servicios—contributions voted by the Cortes and apportioned among the different municipalities of the kingdom. Each municipality was free to collect its quota as it best saw fit; poll taxes and impositions proportional to wealth were both common. These received the collective name of *pechos*, and the contributors thus were called *pecheros*—a word that became synonymous with commoners. Nobles, clergy, and the indigent were exempt. Servicios were the original taxes supplied to the king by the Cortes, and they had both an ordinary and extraordinary component (in the sense discussed above). Their approval, which was valid for a multiyear period, normally signaled the culmination of an assembly. Although symbolically important, the nominal amount of servicios did not change much during the second half of the sixteenth century. In 1555, they accounted for about 14 percent of the total revenue; by 1596, this had shrunk to 3.5 percent as a result of inflation and fiscal expansion.

---

20 The discussion of revenue sources is based on Thompson 1976; Ulloa 1977; Artola 1982, 1988. Quantitative data are drawn from our previous work in Drelichman and Voth 2010.

Revenues Collected through the Church

From the early thirteenth century, the Crown had frequently collected one-third of the ecclesiastical tithes (*tercias*) as a levy to finance crusade operations. King Alfonso X the Learned made the tercias permanent in 1255, fixing them at two-ninths of the tithes collected by every parish. Subsequent papal bulls added the *cruzada* (1485), a contribution that rewarded the kingdoms that fought against the infidel; the *excusado* (1565), the full amount of the tithes of the second-richest parishioner in each parish; and the *subsidio* (1568), one-tenth of the income of ecclesiastics.[21] Because of the difficulty of assessing the value of the latter two taxes, the Crown regularly negotiated a yearly lump-sum payment with the bishops in their stead. The cruzada, subsidio, and excusado were collectively known as *tres gracias*—the three graces. Overall, revenues collected through the church fluctuated between 13 and 18 percent of royal income in the second half of the sixteenth century.

Indirect Taxes

The main indirect tax—and indeed, the most important source of revenue—was the alcabala, or sales tax. Legally, the alcabala was payable by everybody regardless of social status and was applicable to every transaction at the same rate of 10 percent. In practice this was never applied, as for an early modern economy, it would have been both extremely onerous and impractical to collect. Instead of direct collection, the Crown opted for one of two systems, which were employed in different periods or sometimes concurrently in different parts of the kingdom. The first option was farming out the collection of the tax in a figure called *arrendamiento*. The cities often objected to it, since the arrangement made the tax farmers the residual claimants of the collected amounts, which prompted them to behave in an overzealous or downright abusive manner in the hopes of squeezing additional taxes out of the populace. The alternative, which became increasingly common in the

---

21 Originally the excusado was to be equal to the tithe of the richest parishioner. In a reflection of the extreme skewness of the income distribution, the bishops fought hard to have it changed to the tithe of the second-richest parishioner. Since the Crown and bishops negotiated a lump-sum payment in lieu of the tax, the point was moot in regard to Crown revenue. It nonetheless remained important for local excusados, such as those used to finance the *fabricae* of large cathedrals.

sixteenth century, consisted of a negotiated yearly payment between the king and Cortes, which then apportioned the total amount among the different jurisdictions. This system was called *encabezamiento*. Participant cities were free to collect their quota in any way they saw fit; they usually did so by taxing only certain easy-to-monitor goods, such as those sold through licensed establishments. Sales taxes under the encabezamiento averaged a rate between 2 and 3 percent.

In the second half of the sixteenth century, the alcabala eclipsed all other sources of revenue, representing roughly a third of royal income. Because of this, the value of the encabezamiento was the main bargaining tool that the Cortes had when trying to extract concessions from the king. This could result in tense standoffs, such as the one that emerged in the Cortes of 1573, when the king requested a tripling in the encabezamiento's value. When the Cortes balked, the king threatened it with pulling out of the agreement altogether and collecting the tax at the 10 percent statutory rate. Knowing that he did not have the fiscal structure to follow through with it and that any attempt at forcibly raising taxes would be unpopular, the Cortes called the king's bluff. The negotiations dragged into 1575, and the impasse became a determining factor in that year's bankruptcy. With a default in royal debt looming, both the king and Cortes compromised, agreeing to a doubling of the encabezamiento, which nonetheless came too late to avoid a suspension of payments. Only two years later, the Cortes complained that the tax was too high a burden on economic activity; having settled his debts and finding himself in a better financial position, the king agreed to a minor reduction.

Another major increase in indirect taxes came after the defeat of the Armada in 1588. The outfitting of the fleet had cost a full two years' worth of revenue. The destruction of a good portion of it coupled with the impending threat of British and French invasion required that its power be restored as quickly as possible. The Cortes was asked to vote a new set of excises, known as the *servicio de los ocho millones* (or simply, *millones*), after the eight million ducats it was supposed to raise over six years. The tax was approved in 1591, but not before the Cortes extracted a degree of control over its use. This was the first time that the powers of a representative assembly in a large European state included control over expenditure, but it was not to last (Stasavage 2011). Within a decade, the king managed to pack the commission overseeing the millones, which retained control only in name. The Cortes was asked to reauthorize the tax repeatedly. The millones soon became permanent for all practical purposes.

There were also several taxes on specific large-scale economic activities. The most important were those on the production of silk in Granada (*renta de la seda*) and the taxes on migratory sheep flocks (*servicio y montazgo*). These taxes, however, reached their peak in the late fifteenth and early sixteenth centuries, and were in frank decline by the time Philip II took power.[22]

After the excises, the most important indirect taxes were the internal and external customs. The former, called *puertos secos* (literally, "dry ports"— internal customs collection points), experienced relative stagnation and decline throughout the modern period. At the same time, the large expansion in Atlantic trade switched the center of gravity to the import and reexport duties collected at the port of Seville as well as, to a lesser extent, at the northern ports. There were several duties imposed at different times and ports; the most crucial ones were the almojarifazgo and avería. Also significant was the *derecho de las lanas*, which taxed exports of merino wool. By 1596, custom duties amounted to approximately 10 percent of the total revenue. The granting of monopolies was also a modest revenue source during Philip's reign, accounting for between 7 and 13 percent of revenue throughout the period.

There were also a large number of minor income streams—many of them carryovers from medieval times. Since taxes were stipulated in nominal terms, most of these were progressively eroded in value as a result of the silver inflation of the sixteenth century.

AMERICAN SILVER

Early Spanish conquistadores in the New World were single-minded in their quest for precious metals. Their initial military ventures yielded considerable quantities of gold and silver, accumulated by Inca and Aztec rulers. And yet the hoards seized by Cortes, Pizarro, and their men were nothing com-

---

22 Migratory sheepherding entered a declining phase in the second half of the sixteenth century and dropped precipitously after 1580. The activity had long ceased to be a source of significant Crown revenue by then (Drelichman 2009). The 1568 rebellion of the Morisco population in the Alpujarras region resulted in both the diaspora of the Moriscos and destruction of mulberry trees, fatally damaging both the silk industry and the taxes it generated.

pared to the torrent of treasure that eventually poured out of the rich silver mines in Potosí and Zacatecas. The city of Potosí's sixteenth-century coat of arms did not exaggerate when it boasted:

> I am rich Potosí
> Treasure of the world
> The king of all mountains
> And the envy of all kings.

The Potosí and Zacatecas deposits were discovered in the mid-1540s. Before silver could be extracted in a viable way, some technical issues had to be resolved. Since classical Greek times it had been known that mercury formed an amalgam with certain types of silver and iron sulphides, which could then be separated from the raw ores and purified by evaporating the mercury. American ores, however, would not amalgamate with mercury, making their refining difficult and inefficient. Ten years passed until Bartolomé de Medina, a Spanish merchant, discovered that he could solve the problem by adding copper to the ore. American ores were in fact poor in copper, which is a required catalyst for mercury and silver to amalgam. This refining method became known as the patio process, because it required the amalgamated ore to rest for weeks on a hot and sunny stone-paved area, which was usually fenced or walled to ward off intruders. In colder Peru the refining took place in small rooms with a central fire, but the process nonetheless retained its name.[23]

Once silver was smelted in Potosí, it made its way on mule back to Lima to be assayed. From there, a fleet carried the bullion to Panama. It was then transported over the isthmus and onward to Havana. Mexican silver, produced in Zacatecas, was transported overland to Veracruz and then by sea to Havana as well. There, the precious cargo would accumulate until the next treasure fleet sailed for Seville. The fleets would initially ride the Gulf Stream, sailing in parallel with Florida's coast. Then, having reached as far north as modern-day Virginia Beach (near Cape Hatteras), they started to sail east. They would pass Bermuda and then make their way to Spain, escorted by

---

23 The mercury amalgam smelting process permitted the cost-efficient refining of low-grade ores. It was described in Agricola's *De Re Metallica*, published in 1556, and it seems certain that Medina had access to this knowledge before setting out for Mexico in 1554. The chemistry of the patio process has only recently been replicated in a laboratory setting and thoroughly dissected. For a technical treatment, see Johnson and Whittle 1999.

large armed convoys that protected them from enemy fleets, pirates, and privateers.

The vast majority of silver production was in private hands. The Crown enforced a trading monopoly; all silver as well as any other goods of colonial provenance had to make their way through the city of Seville, where they were deposited in the House of Trade to be assessed and taxed.[24] Only after the king had collected his share were they released to their owners. The convoys that protected the treasure ships also ensured that they all sailed into port to be taxed. While small amounts of contraband were always present, they did not reach a significant scale until the seventeenth century, when the king's penchant for confiscating the private holdings of silver deposited in the House of Trade made smuggling treasure more attractive.[25]

Silver reaching Seville was taxed at a flat rate of 20 percent—the royal fifth. In the second half of the sixteenth century, silver revenue grew to reach 25 percent of all royal income, second only to the alcabala. Bullion flows were highly volatile. Production at the American mines suffered from large swings, caused mostly by mortality among the workforce. The sailing of the silver fleets was strongly dependent on Caribbean weather patterns. In many years fleets were delayed or forced to cancel their sailing altogether; on a few occasions both yearly fleets were prevented from leaving Havana, resulting in a cash crunch on the peninsula. This caused wide swings in the amounts of silver reaching the House of Trade year after year, and hence in the royal revenues they generated.

Sometimes the Crown would seize silver shipments, to be used for urgent spending needs. Such seizures had a long lineage, going back to the days of Charles V. The first confiscation occurred as early as 1523, when two hundred thousand ducats were taken to pay for the army that would fight the rebel king of Navarre. The practice, though sporadic at first, slowly became a standard feature of royal policy. The total share of private treasure confiscated fluctuated with the Crown's spending needs, but on several occasions affected the entire treasure landed in Seville. Instead of their bullion, the disgruntled owners of the confiscated silver normally received nonredeemable

---

24   Earl Hamilton's classic account of silver imports into Castile relied on official records from the House of Trade. While these records do not reflect contraband, they capture royal silver income accurately. See Hamilton 1934; Ulloa 1977.

25   See the discussion in chapter 2. Morineau (1985) does not find significant discrepancies between declared amounts and total shipments reconstructed from Dutch gazettes until the 1580s, leading to the conclusion that smuggling was limited up to that time.

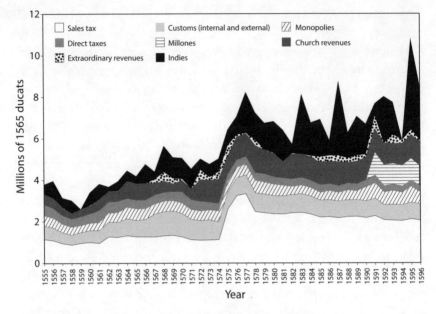

FIGURE 4. Crown revenues, 1555–96

juros yielding between 5.5 and 7.14 percent (Ruiz Martín 1965). Under Philip II, such forced conversions of treasure into juros were rare.

A RECONSTRUCTION OF YEARLY REVENUES, 1555–96

In figure 4, we present the evolution of Crown revenue between 1555 and 1596 in real terms.[26] The coverage period, dictated by data availability, consists of Philip II's entire reign except for the last two years.

The graph tells the story of Castilian revenues in clear terms. Most income streams were stable as a result of tax farming or lump-sum payment negotiations with the cities or the church. Direct taxes, monopolies, and customs revenue barely show any variations throughout the period. Revenues collected through the church rise substantially when the subsidio and the excusado are introduced in 1571. The sales taxes—alcabalas—jump in 1575–77 after the Cortes approved a doubling of rates plus a one-time surcharge. This

---

26 For the full reconstruction, including yearly data, see Drelichman and Voth 2010. For individual revenue stream data, see Thompson 1976; Ulloa 1977. The deflator is the price index for Old Castile reported in Drelichman 2005.

was followed by a reduction as a result of bargaining between the king and Cortes in 1576.[27] The year 1591 saw the introduction of the millones—new excises worth a total of eight million ducats, spread over six years.

The least stable of all revenue streams was silver taxation. This value was modest until the early 1570s. It reflected difficulties in attracting workers for exploiting the mines. The Spaniards eventually introduced the *mita*, or forced labor service, which was used extensively to provide workers for the mines, and production increased quickly. The jagged profile of the annual revenue series also reflects the irregularities in the sailings of the Atlantic fleets. Years of low silver revenue were normally the result of one of the two fleets failing to make the crossing, either because of insufficient production or adverse weather. While a missed sailing created short-term liquidity problems, it did not cause a serious financial setback. Silver that did not cross the Atlantic one year would likely arrive the next, and a wide array of lenders and financial intermediaries was ready to make up the shortfall in the meantime.

DEBT

The large fluctuations in income and expenditures required the extensive use of debt instruments. Since the late Middle Ages, the Crown borrowed in long-term debt markets. In the early sixteenth century, Charles V started borrowing from international bankers short term as well. Throughout the sixteenth century, the credit system of the Spanish Crown acquired many of the characteristics associated with modern sovereign debt. While there were no freely transferable bearer bonds, liquidly traded in secondary markets (developed a century later in the Netherlands), the Genoese introduced contingent clauses and complex collateralization in their loans to Philip II. These elements have only reemerged as financial instruments for sovereigns in the early twenty-first century.

JUROS

The Crown's main way of borrowing was to issue juros—annuities or perpetual bonds. These instruments were akin to French *rentes*, Dutch *renten*, and

---

27 The Cortes of 1574 was studied by A. W. Lovett (1980). Charles Jago (1985) and José Ignacio Fortea Pérez (2009) provide accounts of the Cortes of 1576.

Genoese *compere*. They originated in the medieval period, when they were used by monarchs to reward distinguished service by their subjects. At that time, juros mostly took the form of lifetime pensions, payable from specific revenue streams. By the fourteenth century, juros were regularly used as a way of raising funds in exchange for surrendering the right to future revenue. Juros gradually saw their term being lengthened to two lives and eventually in perpetuity.[28]

The value of juros was determined by a number of characteristics. Chief among them were their term (lifetime or perpetual), their yearly payment, and the revenue stream backing them. Juros were referred to by the inverse ratio of their yearly payment to their nominal amount. For example, a bond that paid 5 percent interest on its face value would be designated as being of "veinte mil al millar," or a thousand units of interest for each twenty thousand of principal. The actual yield of juros, of course, depended on the price at which they were sold. Throughout the sixteenth century, most bonds traded at par, and their median yield was 7.14 percent, or one unit of interest for every fourteen of capital. Juros issued as part of bankruptcy settlements usually paid 5 percent interest.

To offer the Crown a chance to benefit from a fall in interest rates, most juros were redeemable at the sovereign's discretion; a few were not callable. All juros were issued to a specific person, who was the only one authorized to collect the annual payments. The Crown, however, regularly granted requests for the transfer of title of perpetual juros in exchange for a fee.[29] Thus, while juros were never true bearer bonds, there is ample evidence of a healthy secondary market for them.

One important feature of juros was that they only bound the monarch to service them as long as the tax stream backing them produced sufficient funds. In that sense they represented a contingent claim on fiscal resources, with the lender bearing the downside risk. Juros carried different levels of seniority, indicating the order in which they would be paid. Seniority had an impact on the price at which juros could be sold. Junior bonds fetched lower prices, and the gradient became steeper the more doubts there were about

---

28 For an overview of juros and their history, see Toboso Sánchez 1987. The practice of granting rights to future fiscal revenue in exchange for an upfront payment seems to have first originated in twelfth-century Genoa, although the final characteristics of juros are observed evolving simultaneously in several European locations.

29 Lifetime juros could only be transferred in special circumstances, as their value depended on the age of the holder.

the health of a given tax stream. Because the possibility of nonpayment was already part of the original loan contract, when specific tax revenues dried up, it did not constitute bankruptcy to fail to service juros.

The sixteenth century was a golden era for Castilian long-term debt. During the reigns of Charles V and of Philip II, juros were considered among the safest investments in Europe. They could be found in the portfolios of banks and sophisticated investors throughout the continent. A number of factors contributed to the prominent standing of juros among international financial assets. First, as discussed above, they could only be issued against tax streams designated by the Cortes as ordinary. These revenues were typically stable. Second, although juros could be found in investment portfolios throughout Europe, the vast bulk of them were held by Castilian elites. Defaulting on juros would have had a large political cost for the king. Finally, while the king was technically not responsible for the consequences of underperforming revenue streams, the Crown's actions show that there was an implicit guarantee against catastrophic losses. When the taxes on silk production in Granada collapsed due to the Morisco rebellion of 1568, for example, the king compensated the holders of the tax farm by releasing them from their obligations and granted them juros for the value they had already paid.[30] Throughout the sixteenth century, juros accounted for the vast majority of Castilian borrowing, averaging well over 80 percent of outstanding debt.

Data on juros are scant, and the nature of the archival record makes it difficult to reconstruct their stock on a yearly basis. Only a small proportion of the relevant holdings are cataloged; compiling estimates of outstanding debt on an annual basis has so far proven impossible.[31] Instead, we have snapshot data for select years.

Table 3 shows the available estimates for the stock of juros and their service. These were obtained through official inquiries commissioned by the king. The fact that he ordered these surveys demonstrates how difficult it

---

30   The agreement is detailed in a contract between the king and Jerónimo de Salamanca, Lucas Justiniano, and Bautista Spinola dated May 19, 1569. AGS Contadurías Generales, Legajo 85.

31   There is no central registry of juros. The cataloging does not allow us to identify bonds belonging to a particular period; this can only be done poring by hand through each document. Furthermore, the available juros are not a random sample; only bonds that were resold at some point in time are included. A bond that was resold many times would register several duplicate instances in the archival record, with little information to link them together. On the other hand, ecclesiastical institutions and noble families were large investors, and many were unlikely to ever trade the bonds they held, and hence their juros would be missing from any attempt at a reconstruction.

Table 3. Juros and their service (in millions of current ducats)

Year	Outstanding juros	Juros servicing outlays	Average cost of juro service	Revenue
1560	19	1.468	7.7%	3.155
1565	25			4.192
1566		1.861	7.4%†	4.770
1573		2.752		5.433
1575	42.5	2.730	6.4%	7.606
1584		3.273		7.806
1598	68	4.634	6.8%	11.328††

Source: Debt estimates for 1560, 1565, and 1598 are from Artola 1982. The figure for 1575 is from De Carlos Morales 2008. Service estimates are from Ruiz Martín 1965; Ulloa 1977.
† Calculated using 1565 stock of juros
†† Figure from 1596

was for the royal treasury to keep track of the stock of outstanding debt. Surveys were particularly important around the defaults, which explains their timing. In chapter 4, we use these estimates, our new series of short-term borrowing, our reconstruction of military expenditures, and the logic of the fiscal budget constraint to construct estimates of the annual stock of juros for the duration of Philip II's reign.

Juros were sold in a variety of ways. Initially they were acquired directly by wealthy nobles and institutions. As the market thickened, the king's secretaries would conduct an informal auction, in which they sounded out potential investors in order to place a new bond on the most favorable terms possible. Starting in the 1560s, though, most juros were sold through the same Genoese bankers who underwrote the king's short-term loans. Bankers often chose to accept juros as repayment for a loan and then sold the bonds to their clients abroad. Finally, large amounts of juros were issued as part of the debt conversions agreed to in the settlements of the Crown's bankruptcies.

Table 3 depicts a progressive decline in the average yield of juros during the second half of the sixteenth century. This reflects a combination of factors. First, interest rates were experiencing a long secular decline in Europe. Castile benefited from the overall trend (Stasavage 2011). Second, strong Castilian economic growth made juros a safe investment. Finally, the settlements of the 1575 and 1596 defaults added a sizable amount of juros carrying 5 percent interest to the existing stock, thus lowering the average interest cost of long-term debt. Still, it should be noted that interest costs were already coming down well before these settlements.

ASIENTOS

While juros accounted for the bulk of the Crown's borrowing, short-term lending instruments, called asientos, attracted most of the attention of contemporaries and modern-day scholars alike. Juros could only be issued against a little more than half of all revenues—again, those designated by the Cortes as ordinary. This left a sizable free cash flow, which could be leveraged using short-term debt. While doing so, the Crown and its bankers created a sophisticated, flexible financing instrument that would be inextricably linked to Castile's financial fortunes for a century.

The term "asiento" literally means "contract," and it was used to refer to a wide variety of agreements. The most famous was the one chartering the slave trade. Whenever we speak of asientos in this book, we mean financial contracts between the king and private bankers. Charles V first used asientos to seal short-term lending agreements with the German Fugger and Welser families.[32] The first Fugger loan famously allowed Charles to outspend Francis I in buying electoral votes and thus secure the imperial Crown in 1519. Later asientos helped to finance military campaigns all over the continent. At a time when American silver production was still in its early stages, it was the growing economy of Castile that supplied the resources to service asientos.

The asientos between Charles V and the German bankers were largely personal loans. The king took them out in his own name, and the links between the German banking families and House of Habsburg certainly played a big role in the negotiations. The contractual forms were typically straightforward—a delivery of funds, followed by one or several repayments with interest. Many times, there also would be a currency conversion advantageous to the banker.

Toward the end of Charles's reign, Genoese bankers had already begun to provide funding on a scale comparable to that of the Fugger family. As the crisis resulting from the insurgency of Moritz of Saxony deepened, the emperor had to ask for extensions of his repayment dates. Anton Fugger, writing in 1553, was not impressed with the way in which the Spanish court dealt

---

32 For the standard source on the asientos of Charles V, see Carande 1987.

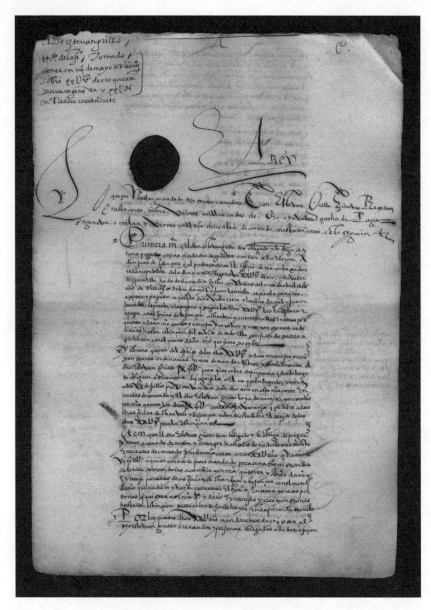

FIGURE 5. The first page of an asiento. *Source*: General Archive of Simancas, Ministry of Culture, Spain, CCG, 86.

with old debts, complaining about "the recklessness with which debts are not paid" (Ehrenberg 1896). He suggested bribing the king's personal secretary, Francisco Eraso, to speed up repayment. As a matter of fact, only the timely arrival of American silver rescued Charles V's financial position. Despite these difficulties, Charles V had staked his reputation on the servicing of his loans. In the secret instructions left to Philip II on his abdication, the emperor sought to impress on his son the need to honor his financial commitments, even at the expense of obligations to his own subjects (Fernández Alvarez 2004, 1979).[33]

On taking the throne, Philip found an accumulation of old debts and limited resources to service them. He did not follow his father's advice for long; the crisis he inherited resulted in a first payment stop on asientos in 1557, soon followed by the second one in 1560. The Genoese appear to have settled their claims quickly and on advantageous terms. The greater—and more complicated—debts of the German bankers, especially the Fugger, took much longer to negotiate. Hans Fugger had to travel from Augsburg to Madrid in person to settle the matter, which he accomplished by August 1562. The agreement saw the interest rate on debts reduced to 5–9 percent per year, plus an extension of the debt maturity. One-fifth of the debts was settled with juros from the Casa de la Contratación, which soon lost about half of their face value; another fifth came from silver revenue; an additional fifth was from rent payments of the military orders in Spain (*maestrazgos*); only 10 percent arrived in the form of cash (Kellenbenz 1967). The king also agreed to repay in part by handing over the right to exploit the rich mercury mines at Almadén. Even when payments were made, taking them out of Spain was difficult, as silver exports required an additional permit. While there is no exact way to calculate the net losses to lenders in the 1557–60 settlement, there is no question that the Fugger in particular were left with a worse deal than the Genoese, receiving less money and over a longer period than their competitors.[34]

---

33 This is not to say that Charles V serviced every single loan at all times; for example, the Fugger were still waiting for repayment of debts from the Schmalkaldian War in 1551 some seven years later (Ehrenberg 1896).

34 The Fugger balance sheet for 1563 shows lending of 4.44 million florins to the king of Spain, with 1 million either doubtful or written off, for a (maximum) loss rate of 22.56 percent. We do not consider this figure comparable to our later "haircut" calculations for Philip II's other defaults, first because it only concerns one family, and second because we do not know which share of doubtful debts was eventually recovered (Ehrenberg 1896).

Short-term lending had resumed in full by 1566, with several Genoese families now accounting for the bulk of the debt market. The Genoese introduced a number of innovations that made asientos less risky, allowed for a wide variety of contingencies, and aligned the king's repayment incentives with those of the bankers.[35] The first and perhaps most important change introduced by the Genoese involved spreading the risk of short-term loans. Rather than commit the bulk of their financial fortunes to the volatile repayment record of the Crown, the Genoese sold off most of each loan to smaller investors. After agreeing to underwrite an asiento for the king, bankers would offer shares in it at the European payment fairs as well as to smaller investors in Genoa. This practice allowed them to transfer as much risk as they wished while collecting a financial intermediation fee that averaged 1 percent. In this way, the Genoese bankers leveraged their network of business associates and ability to tap into international capital markets. As a result of early-modern "financial engineering," the large families that underwrote the asientos usually had only a limited and controlled exposure to the Crown. When Philip II defaulted on 14.6 million ducats of short-term debt in 1575, for instance, only four families had an exposure in excess of 100,000 ducats of their own capital.[36] This spreading of risk was multitiered. The smaller banks buying shares in the asientos would in turn offer fractions in their own participation to retail customers in Genoa, in other Italian cities, and at the local exchange fairs. The short-term financing of the Spanish Crown thus became a multinational affair, trickling down to all levels of society with the ability to aggregate individually modest amounts into large loans. The similarities with modern-day financing structures are striking. Genoese bankers "securitized" loans to the king by selling them to other investors, much as the Wall Street firms do to this day. The aggregation of savings in multiple steps is reminiscent of modern bond funds, with the savings of many collected in larger pools so as to finance large bond issues.

Interestingly, the Genoese system of risk transfer differed radically from the one used by the German banking families. The Fugger, for example, bor-

---

35 Marie-Thérèse Boyer-Xambeu, Ghislain Deleplace, and Lucien Gillard (1994) argue that asientos were developed in response to the closing of the Laredo-Antwerp sea route in 1568–69. Our data speak against this interpretation. The Genoese system was already fully in place by 1566, and contracts signed between 1566 and 1568 already show the full range of innovations associated with Genoese finance.
36 The bankers were Constantín Gentil, Lucián Centurión, Nicolao de Grimaldo, and the Spinola family (De Carlos Morales 2008).

rowed themselves against their name and net worth, and then lent to their creditors in the classic way of bankers. For instance, in 1563, the bank's capital amounted to 5.4 million florins, of which 2 million was equity and 3.4 million were debts of various kinds. For a long time, Fugger debt (*Fugger-Briefe*, literally "Fugger letters"—debt obligations issued by the Augsburg banking house) was considered almost risk free.[37] As late as the mid-1550s, the Fugger could borrow at rates of 8–10 percent in Antwerp—less than almost any other borrower, including the city of Antwerp itself (Ehrenberg 1896). When problems mounted as a result of Philip II's first bankruptcy, rolling over these debts became increasingly difficult; members of the Fugger family ultimately had to add funds from their personal fortunes and borrow at much higher interest rates.[38]

The Genoese also used other clauses to increase the effective return of their asientos. Usury laws were in force and periodically invoked. As a consequence, no one was willing to explicitly charge interest in excess of the legal maximum. This limit varied between 8 percent at the beginning of Philip's reign and 16 percent by the time of his death. Many asientos commanded far higher rates. Some of this excess return was obtained in the old-fashioned way by contracting in different currencies and inflating the exchange rate. Contracts also specified disbursement and repayment in different precious metals; the differences in their relative valuation across European cities afforded arbitrage opportunities for informed lenders. The Genoese, however, created an even more important channel for generating additional profits through their preeminent position in the juros market.[39]

When they entered the world of Castilian sovereign finance, the Genoese brought with them over 150 years of experience in managing the state debts of Genoa through the Casa di San Giorgio. This institution acted as a central clearinghouse for long-term loans, called compere, which shared essentially all the characteristics of Castilian juros in the sixteenth century.[40] The Geno-

---

37 These should not be confused with the letters from various parts of Europe compiled by the Fugger.

38 Ironically, they also had to borrow from Juan Curiel de la Torre, one of the principal lenders to Philip II—at high interest rates (Ehrenberg 1896). The cost of credit for this transaction was 22 percent per year—much higher than the rates at which the Fugger had lent to various princes.

39 Chapter 5 discusses the significance of the Genoese position in the juros market for debt sustainability.

40 Among the vast literature on the Casa di San Giorgio and its central place in the history of public finance, see Greif 1994; Epstein 2001; Felloni 2006a, 2006b. For a brief overview and literature survey, see Marsilio 2013.

ese, therefore, had on their side a vast expertise in dealing with the nuances of tax-backed securities; they could readily assess the health of tax streams securing the loans, calculate yields based on the characteristics of each issue, and split large issues for resell to retail investors. This knowledge was put to good profit in dealing with the Crown. In many asientos, the bankers requested that the king post collateral in the form of juros as a repayment guarantee for the principal and interest. If the king failed to repay the short-term loan as agreed, the bankers could then sell the collateral juros (called *de resguardo*) on the open market and recoup their investment. If the king repaid, the bankers had to return juros of the same value. The bankers used their clout with the king to demand the best available juros as collateral. Often they would then be allowed to substitute the original bonds for others of the same face value and seniority, but backed by inferior revenue streams. These bonds could be purchased below par on the open market, thus presenting an arbitrage opportunity to the banker.

The practice of swapping discounted bonds for others trading at par was common during the failed experiment to issue juros against the revenue of the Casa de la Contratación in 1565. The revenues of the Casa de la Contratación—one-fifth of all silver remittances arriving in Seville—were a royal prerogative, and hence not subject to the Cortes's approval. This in theory rendered taxes on silver ineligible to back juros, but the king nonetheless pushed ahead. It soon became clear, however, that the bullion was being transferred to the central treasury or otherwise spent before it could be made available to service the bonds. As a result, the juros quickly lost up to 50 percent of their value. Genoese bankers specialized in buying them on the open market at a discount and had them credited at par when returning them as part of the collateral on asientos. The episode highlighted the wisdom of only issuing long-term debt on revenues controlled by the Cortes. Juros were never again issued on extraordinary income or over royal prerogatives.[41]

Another innovation introduced by the Genoese in their asientos was the use of contingency clauses. Most contracts specified the source of funds intended for repayment, but also stipulated alternative scenarios. For example, a banker might be promised a hundred thousand ducats from the silver brought by the first fleet arriving from the Indies. The contract might fur-

41 For more on the juros of the Casa de la Contratación, see Ruiz Martín 1965.

ther stipulate that if the fleet did not arrive by a specific date, the banker might be entitled to a penalty rate, collect payment from other sources, or liquidate the collateral. The combination of contingency and collateral clauses allowed the king and bankers to contract over a wide variety of states of the world at a time when long-distance trade and large-scale military enterprises created large volatility in the Crown's cash flow. Adverse events— such as the late arrival of a fleet or failure of a particular tax stream—allowed the king to lengthen the repayment period of a contract, switch collection locations, and even lower overall payments. In other cases, the bankers were given the option to obtain early repayment by selling the collateral even if the loan was in good standing or cancel additional disbursements of funds.

By their very nature, asientos were riskier than juros. Although the contracts might specify the intended sources of repayment, no funds were specifically earmarked on signing. If the cash flow situation was critical, the treasurer might delay issuing the repayment orders. Even after excluding contracts affected by the defaults, over 20 percent of asientos issued during Philip II's reign were not repaid by the deadline originally specified. Payments could be delayed from a few weeks to several years. In many cases, the king and bankers would negotiate a consolidation of outstanding payments into a new asiento, with additional interest added to compensate for earlier, unmet obligations.

A NEW SERIES OF ASIENTOS

In terms of data, an important contribution of this book is a new series of asientos, consisting of every contract between Philip II and his bankers between 1566 and 1598. Two additional years from the reign of Philip III, 1599 and 1600, were added to allow for a better exploration of the effects of the 1596 bankruptcy.

Studying asientos is vital to understand the financing of the early modern Castilian state as well as the workings of the early Spanish Empire. While asientos represent a minority share in total debt, ranging between 10 and 25 percent of all obligations, they are the segment that exhibits by far the greater volatility. Asientos are where the action is. They also experience a wide array of rescheduling and recontracting. While juros were pretty much honored on time and in full throughout the sixteenth century, the letter of asientos was not observed to some degree almost 30 percent of the time.

Their continued popularity in the face of this volatility as well as their apparent insecurity seems at odds with the conventional wisdom of modern international finance, calling for a deeper investigation. Finally, knowing the aggregate value of asientos issued each year is an essential step in determining the fiscal position of early modern Castile. In a context of scant aggregate macroeconomic indicators, our series serves as the linchpin that allows us to perform the earliest reconstruction of full yearly national accounts for any sovereign state in history.

Asientos were issued in duplicate. The original document, signed by the king, was given to the bankers who provided the funds, while a copy was kept in the Contaduría Mayor de Cuentas—the body in charge of auditing all the financial transactions of the Crown. These copies have been preserved in the Archive of Simancas, where a relatively recent cataloging effort has produced a complete series of asientos beginning in 1566.[42] We collected every asiento in this series up to the year 1600—amounting to 438 documents and over 5,000 manuscript pages—and transcribed their every single clause. We recorded up to 90 variables for each contract, including the date, the bankers' names, the amounts involved, the delivery and repayment locations, the tax streams that were supposed to provide the repayment, the type and amount of collateral (if any), whether the contract involved an exchange operation, the presence and nature of contingency clauses, and a variety of other descriptors. We then used the text in the clauses to reconstruct the agreed-on cash flow for each contract, which will help us establish their actual rates of return.[43]

Ours is not the first effort to describe short-term borrowing during Philip II's reign. Ulloa (1977) compiled a series of asientos between 1566 and 1596, relying on the same documents we used, but his work suffers from serious shortcomings. First, Ulloa overestimates the total amount of short-term borrowing as a result of including asientos entered into by field commanders in Flanders with the agents of Genoese or Spanish banking houses. These loans were typically consolidated into larger contracts in Madrid, and hence are counted twice in Ulloa's series.[44] Next, Ulloa relied only on the summary information given in the first page of the contracts. Asientos were used for a

---

42 AGS, Contadurías Generales, Legajos 86–93.
43 We first introduced these data in Drelichman and Voth 2010, where we reported lending amounts. We added banker identities in Drelichman and Voth 2011a, full cash flows in Drelichman and Voth 2011b, and information on contingent clauses in Drelichman and Voth 2012.
44 For an example of the consolidation of asientos, see Lapeyre 1953.

variety of purposes, including lending, transferring money, farming out tax revenues, and chartering monopolies. A single contract would often involve two or more of these transaction types; the lending and transferring combination was particularly widespread. The summary information on the first page lists the total monetary amounts involved without distinguishing among transactions. By relying on these headline figures, Ulloa overestimated the total amounts lent. By actually reading the contractual clauses, we are able to separate borrowed amounts from all the other transactions involved. Finally, Ulloa did not collect any information on terms and conditions, interest rates, or other variables that might shed light on the workings of asientos.

Earlier scholars have already compiled time series of asientos outstanding for the period before Philip's reign. Carande (1987) pioneered the study of time series with his work on the loans of Charles V. Charles's documents are still today not organized into a series; collecting them was a painstaking multiyear effort, in which it was necessary to track down every individual contract. While it is unfortunate that Carande's study does not include enough information to calculate the interest rate on the contracts, his work nevertheless remains a standard source on Castilian short-term borrowing between 1519 and 1555.[45] The archival record between 1555 and 1566 is incomplete, and has not been systematically cataloged; estimating the amount of short-term debt subscribed during this period is difficult.[46] Carlos Alvarez Nogal (1997), Sanz Ayán (1998), and Juan Gelabert (1999b) have compiled series on the short-term borrowing of Philip III and Philip IV.

Figure 6 shows the annual real value of asiento issues between 1566 and 1600, separating their gross value from their loan component.[47] The first striking feature is the lack of a trend—Philip II borrowed as much per year at the end of his reign as he did at the beginning. Next, the bankruptcies of 1575 and 1596 only result in short interruptions in lending. New issues resume in 1577 and 1597, respectively. The high borrowing volumes in these last two years reflect the new loans negotiated with bankers as part of the respective settlements.

---

45 Carande only reports the total amount disbursed by the bankers and total amount repaid. There is no information on the timing of the payments, thereby making it impossible to establish a rate of return.

46 For an account of the 1555–59 period, see Rodríguez Salgado 1988.

47 The deflator used throughout the book is the Old Castile price series from Drelichman 2005. Using alternative deflators results in immaterial changes.

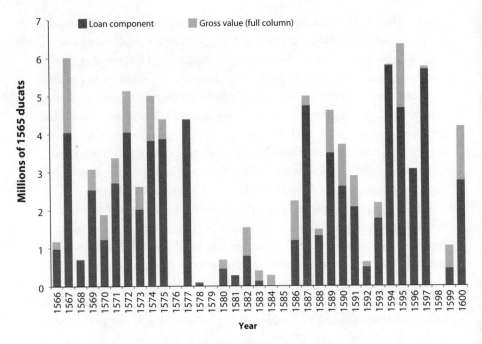

FIGURE 6. Yearly asiento issues, 1566–1600

Annual short-term borrowing decreased substantially between 1577 and 1584, and again in 1597–99, relative to the previous trends. Did access to credit suffer after the defaults? This is unlikely, for two reasons. For one, with each settlement Philip received a fresh loan, worth 5 million current ducats in 1577 and 7.2 million in 1597. These amounts, captured in the respective columns of figure 6, are comparable to the peak volume of predefault lending. Furthermore, both ordinary tax revenues and silver remittances were unusually strong in the years 1576–81 (figure 4). Revenue from sales taxes grew from 1.1 million ducats in 1575 to 3.2 million in 1576 and 1577 before settling down to an annual rate of 2.4 million—more than twice its predefault level. Silver revenue also surged, amounting to almost 2 million ducats in 1577 (compared with an average of 0.7 million between 1570 and 1575). Overall, lending during the eight years after 1576 declined by 2.1 million ducats annually compared to the prior period. Annual revenue was up by 1.8 million ducats. In addition, warfare in the Low Countries declined following the Pacification of Ghent. Lower borrowing does not imply that the Crown was shut out of credit markets. Rather, the elimination of the deficit through a combination of revenue windfalls and lower expenditure made further borrowing unnecessary.

Asiento issues reflected military events. In 1567, the start of the Dutch Revolt drove up short-term borrowing to its highest value in the entire period. Issuance remained high throughout the early 1570s, with Castile fighting in both the Low Countries and Mediterranean. The temporary withdrawal from Flanders after the Pacification of Ghent resulted in a large "peace dividend": borrowing was much lower in 1576–84. The resumption of hostilities in Flanders along with the outfitting and rebuilding of the Armada increased borrowing once again to high levels in 1585–91. Renewed fighting against England and France spelled sustained high asiento issuance until Philip II's death and beyond.

CONCLUSION

When Philip II acceded to the throne in 1566, Castile was already a major player on the European political and military scene. The reforms of the Catholic Kings in the later part of the fifteenth century were instrumental in increasing state capacity early on. The military campaigns of Charles V, though expensive and of mixed military value, put European powers on notice of Castile's power and imperial ambitions. These were backed by a fast-growing economy that, along with a variety of fiscal instruments, allowed a comparatively nimble bureaucratic machinery to increase revenues and use them to project military might. The state itself was built on a broad support base, with the Crown keeping a large but not unchecked role. Through their participation in the Cortes, mercantile interests could and did limit the king's ability to tax. Fiscal negotiations were meaningful. Whenever the reason for additional revenues was not convincing, the Cortes used its effective veto power. At critical junctures, when the survival of the state was at stake, additional revenues were granted in exchange for administrative and supervisory powers as well as other concessions. The Cortes also placed a limit on the revenues that could be used to guarantee the payment of juros, effectively setting a ceiling for long-term debt. These features provide little support for the literature's characterization of Castile as an unqualified absolutist state.[48]

---

48 The king did retain control over expenditure and foreign policy; while this would have important consequences for warfare and government finance, it is hard to argue that those features alone make a state absolutist.

The Castilian portfolio of fiscal and financial instruments was remarkably complete for its time. The revenue technology was a mix of useful adaptations of medieval legacy taxes combined with newer excises and trade duties. As the economy grew, the focus of taxation shifted increasingly to internal and overseas trade, with American silver eventually providing up to 25 percent of all fiscal revenues. On the financing side, the Crown had both long- and short-term debt instruments at its disposal. Although the long-term juros were technically nominative, they were widely traded in the secondary market, supplying a key element for the correct pricing of debt. Since they were held by Castilian elites and backed by earmarked revenues, they were perceived to be safe. This perception proved correct, as juros were strictly honored throughout the sixteenth century. On the short-term front, asientos allowed the Crown to smooth the volatile silver revenues, leverage income outside the purview of the Cortes, and quickly shift resources throughout the empire. The contractual complexity of these loans, allowing for a variety of contingent delivery and repayment scenarios while spreading the risk among multiple layers of lenders, rivals that of sophisticated modern instruments.

Castilian asientos did not become famous because of their innovative contractual structures. They instead earned their celebrity status through their central role in the seven bankruptcies declared by the Crown between 1557 and 1647. In the chapters that follow, we reconstruct their anatomy, analyze their causes and consequences, and shed light on the role they played in the international financial architecture built around the most powerful empire of its time.

CHAPTER 4

THE SUSTAINABLE DEBTS OF PHILIP II

For a long time, Philip II's defaults have been blamed on a disastrous combination of the Crown's unsustainable fiscal situation, on the one hand, and myopic lenders, on the other. Braudel famously argued that each bankruptcy ruined different bankers, who were quickly replaced by another, equally irrational wave of entrants. He concluded that "every time the state declared itself bankrupt, bringing contracts to a violent end, there were always some actors who lost, fell through a trap-door, or tiptoed away towards the wings" (Braudel 1966, 362).

Assessing lender rationality is a complex problem, which we address in the following chapters. We focus here on fiscal sustainability, the first test that any borrower must pass for a lending transaction to be sound. Did the Castilian Crown have enough resources to honor its debts in the long run? Or to put it simply: Could Philip pay?

Evaluating the health of a state's finances requires a reliable set of long-term fiscal accounts. These include measures of revenue, expenditure, debt service, and variations in the stock of debt. Assembling them for sixteenth-century Castile is a daunting task. Like virtually every fledgling national state, the Castilian administration did not keep centralized financial records. Revenues were often spent at their collection point or transferred to other parts of the empire without passing through the central treasury. No unified tally of expenses was kept, nor were debt payments generally added up and accounted for. The treasury functioned more as a residual claimant than an efficient administrator of tax revenues. The information needed to present a comprehensive view of state finances must therefore be pieced together from a multitude of different sources, all of which vary in quality.

This chapter is based on Drelichman and Voth 2010.

In chapter 3, we introduced our new series of short-term debt as well as some estimates of long-term debt for benchmark years. We also pieced together a new series of revenues, constructed on the basis of individual income streams. Here we add calculations of military expenditure and short-term debt service. In combination with carefully chosen assumptions, we can then estimate the missing data and correct for the effect of the bankruptcies. The result is a full set of annual fiscal accounts for Castile between 1566 and 1596, the earliest such reconstruction for any sovereign state. While the exercise is conjectural rather than precise, it nonetheless will allow us to explore the financial health of the Crown in more depth than has previously been possible.

Sustainability means that a country is able to service its debts indefinitely, given current fiscal parameters. Solvency is a less stringent criterion; it simply implies that there are plausible future paths of revenue and expenditure that will lead to sustainable outcomes. To assess if debts are sustainable or a country is solvent thus requires a number of assumptions about the evolution of fiscal variables. These in turn depend on economic growth, policy measures, and unforeseen events. Not surprisingly, there is little consensus about how to exactly determine whether a sovereign is likely to honor their debts. We adopt the most common approach—that used by the IMF. At every step, we use the most conservative assumptions possible, and further complement the analysis with a number of robustness checks and counterfactual thought experiments.

MORE DATA

MILITARY EXPENDITURE

Civil expenditures in early modern states were small. The payroll of the central administration was tiny. The administration of justice was largely funded at the local level, frequently through user fees.[1] Poor relief was the domain of religious and charitable organizations. To be sure, the pomp and circumstance of monarchy—the palaces and lavish feasts, royal visits, and upkeep of the royal household in general—cost money. Yet they absorbed only a small share of government revenues. Rising national states spent the overwhelming majority of their resources on a single endeavor: war.

Philip II was at war in every single year of his reign, as described in chapter 2. Because of their geopolitical significance, each of Castile's campaigns has

---

1 For an overview of Castile's justice system, see Kagan 1981.

been thoroughly studied by military historians.[2] We use their work to reconstruct the impact of warfare on the finances of Castile.

Military operations were funded at the local level as far as possible. Flemish and Italian revenue covered part of the large military costs in those territories. Shortfalls were met with transfers from Castile, usually through a financial intermediary. These transfers could grow quickly whenever things went awry, as they did repeatedly during the Dutch Revolt. The total cost of war is equivalent to the amounts spent from both sources. Since Castilian debt was paid only from Castilian revenues, however, only the transfers from Castile matter when evaluating fiscal sustainability. Given this, our first step is to classify military expenditures according to the source of the funds. This is fortunate, as the Castilian accounts are remarkably complete, while data on costs defrayed from local sources are considerably spottier.

To construct an annual series of military expenditures paid by the Castilian treasury, only one strong assumption is needed. The contributions to the Army of Flanders between 1580 and 1596, reported by Parker (1998), are only available as quinquennial totals. In this case, though, we have good yearly data for the contributions paid by the Flemish treasury. To apportion the quinquennial contributions from the Castilian treasury to individual years, we assume that they followed the same annual pattern as Flemish contributions; the latter are therefore expected to capture short-term fluctuations in total expenditure on the Dutch War. To check for robustness, we dropped the Flemish expenditures as a source of variation and used the alternative assumption that the yearly contributions of the Castilian treasury were one-fifth of the quinquennial totals. This did not alter the sustainability results in any significant way.

Figure 7 presents our estimates of military expenditure between 1565 and 1596. Where the cost of an individual campaign differs across sources, we chose the estimate supported by better documentation. Of the 146 million ducats spent on war during Philip's reign, fully 77 million (some 53 percent of the total) were spent on the Army of Flanders.[3] Because the Dutch Revolt was such a large item in Castile's military budget, we differentiate it from the other campaigns.

In the early 1570s, the War of the Holy League and growing intensity of the Dutch Revolt led to a spike in military outlays, which peaked in 1574.

2 In particular, we rely on Dandelet 1995, 2001; De Lamar 1964, 1988; Koenigsberger 1951; Lynch 1961; Parker 1970, 1977, 1979, 1998, 2004; Tenace 1997, 2003; Thompson 1976, 1992.
3 Magnitudes are given in 1566 constant prices.

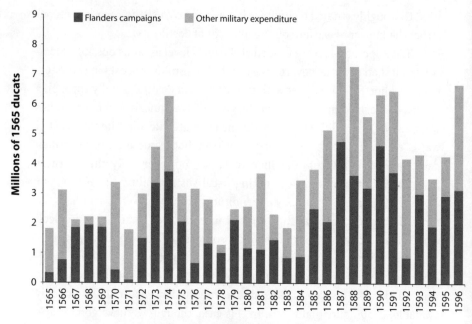

FIGURE 7. Military expenditure paid from Castilian sources

The 1575 bankruptcy followed immediately after. The following decade saw relatively limited military expenditure. This changed with the resumption of hostilities in the Netherlands in 1583. Expenditure continued to rise in the run-up to and aftermath of the Armada. Outfitting it cost approximately 10 million ducats, roughly two years of total revenue. Following the disaster, a similar sum was spent on rebuilding the fleet to defend Spain against French and British attack. The 1596 peak—the last year for which our sources allow a comprehensive assessment—reflects the continuing expenses in Flanders and the response to the English naval threat.

SHORT-TERM DEBT SERVICE

Another important component of national accounts is the cost of servicing debts. We presented what little information is available on juros in chapter 3; we will derive estimates of the yearly interest paid on them in the next section. Our data on asientos, on the other hand, is detailed enough to allow us to calculate servicing costs with reasonable precision.

Asientos were convenient as a short-term borrowing device; they allowed the Crown to obtain money quickly and transfer it to virtually any point in its European dominions. They were also expensive. Their median gross rate of return was 13.8 percent, and many contracts cost more than 20 percent. This included compensation for currency conversions, overseas deliveries, transportation costs, and the risk of late payment and subsequent renegotiation. Many asientos used convoluted contractual forms. A good part of the return resulted from exchange transactions at favorable rates, advance payments by the Crown without interest, and swaps of financial instruments. Further complicating matters, scheduled payments seldom specified whether they were for interest or repayment of capital. Debt service, then, is not observable directly. We use an indirect estimation methodology instead.

First, we transcribe every clause in each asiento contracted between 1566 and 1596, and use them to reconstruct the agreed-on monthly cash flows. From the overall set of cash flows, it is possible to calculate the rate of return of each contract (chapter 6 discusses the methodology in detail). We then estimate the total interest for each asiento by multiplying its loan component by the rate of return. Because we do not know which payments are for interest and which ones are for capital repayment, we assume that each payment from the king to the bankers is composed of interest and capital amortization in constant proportions throughout the life of the loan. This is in line with what the few asientos separating interest and principal repayment specify.[4] Annual short-term debt service of the Crown is then the sum of the interest payments for all asiento contracts in force in any single year. The default of September 1575 stopped payments on all asientos. The settlement was only reached in late 1577, and there were no new loan repayments until 1578. Therefore, we assign a value of zero to 1576 and 1577 asiento service. The default of 1596, in contrast, lasted less than a year, and so there are positive amounts of debt service in both 1596 and 1597.

THE BANKRUPTCIES

Each of Philip II's defaults resulted in a negotiated reduction of outstanding debt. As such, they affected the fiscal position directly, and thus need to be taken into account when calculating the balance of revenues and expendi-

---

4 Because the cash flows are clearly specified, modifying this assumption by either fully front loading or fully back loading the interest does not significantly alter the results.

tures. We have little data on the 1557 and 1560 episodes—dates for which we also do not know revenues or expenditures. Yet we can assess the scale of the 1575 and 1596 suspensions as well as the conditions of their settlements in detail.

A bankruptcy always started with a decree of suspension, the decreto. After some legal skirmishes and the gathering of relevant information, both the Crown and bankers created negotiating groups. In the case of the bankers, the goal was to have the delegates speak for as large a share of outstanding debt as possible, and hence confront the king with substantial market power. When an agreement was reached, a settlement—called medio general—was subscribed. This document specified the amounts to be repaid, payment instruments to be used, timing of repayments, and conditions of any fresh loans supplied by the bankers.

The first default covered by our data started with a decree of suspension issued on September 1, 1575. A settlement was reached with the medio general in late 1577.[5] The king recognized outstanding obligations for 15.1 million ducats, divided into 14.6 million ducats of outstanding principal as of September 1, 1575, and 584,000 ducats in interest accrued between September 1 and December 1, 1575. It is not clear why this interest was added; in any event, the first provision of the settlement was to write it off. We work from the outstanding capital at the time of the suspension: 14.6 million ducats.

Of the total outstanding asientos, 5.6 million ducats were collateralized by perpetual juros with a yield of 7.14 percent, guaranteed by ordinary revenues. The holders of these juros were allowed to keep them, but their annuity rate was reduced to 5 percent. Compared to the 7.14 percent that had been contracted, the reduction in the annuity rate amounts to a write-off of 1.6 million ducats. A further 4.4 million ducats worth of asientos were collateralized by perpetual juros with a yield of 5 percent guaranteed by the revenues of the Casa de la Contratación. Because too many juros had been issued against these revenues, they were often not serviced; in the secondary market they traded at around 50 percent of their face value.[6] The Crown recognized 55 percent of *juros de contratación* at face value by converting them to 5 percent perpetuities. The remaining 45 percent, 1.96 million ducats' worth, were treated as uncollateralized debt.

---

5 *Asiento y Medio General de la Hacienda.* AGS, Consejo y Juntas de Hacienda, Libro 42.
6 On this point, see Ruiz Martín 1965.

Uncollateralized debt, which amounted to 6.6 million ducats including the juros de contratación, suffered the harshest treatment. Two-thirds of it was converted into perpetuities of the same face value with a yield of 3.3 percent. The remaining third was converted into tax farms on small towns (*vasallos*) with a nominal yield of 2.3 percent. The write-off on this portion of the debt relative to a 7.14 percent interest rate amounts to 3.8 million ducats. In total, the 1575 medio general rescheduled a total of 14.6 million ducats of short-term debt. It imposed a 5.5-million-ducat haircut in present value terms, or 37.7 percent of the loans in default.

The 1596 bankruptcy, which we described in chapter 1 following Ulloa (1977, 823), Enrica Neri (1989, 109), and Sanz Ayán (2004), was mild in comparison. The 1597 settlement rescheduled a total 7.05 million ducats. Two-thirds, or 4.7 million ducats' worth, were converted into 5 percent perpetual juros. Using the same interest rate assumption as for the 1575 settlement, this would imply a haircut of 1.41 million ducats. The remaining third was guaranteed by 12.5 percent lifetime juros in possession of the bankers; these lifetime bonds had been issued in 1580, and hence were halfway through their accounting life expectancy of thirty-three years. The settlement stipulated that they were to be swapped for 7.14 percent perpetual juros; the bankers would be given enough perpetual juros so as not to alter the present value of the principal. In short, this portion of the outstanding debt suffered no write off; the king lengthened the repayment schedule in exchange for a higher face value of the bonds. The total write-off of the 1597 settlement amounted to 1.41 million ducats, or exactly 20 percent of the amount defaulted on.

Christophe Chamley and Carlos Alvarez Nogal (2012) offer a different interpretation of Philip II's bankruptcies. They point out that juros were redeemable at the request of the king. So if prevailing interest rates fell, it was in the king's interest to buy back all juros and issue new ones at lower rates. In their view, the defaults were just a way to accomplish this; the 1575 and 1596 settlements accomplished nothing more than to swap asientos collateralized by high-interest juros for new, lower-interest perpetuities. There was no actual haircut, as the king was merely exercising an option to which he had a right all along. The historical record strongly contradicts this explanation; the bankruptcies were not consensual events and involved acrimonious negotiations. Equally important is the fact that most redeemable juros—those that were not attached to asientos—were not converted to lower-interest ones.[7] We nonetheless note that should Chamley and Alvarez Nogal's interpretation be correct, this would actually reduce Castile's debt burden, and the results we detail below would be strengthened.

DOWNWARD BIAS

Before we proceed, it is worth noting that all the assumptions we made in constructing the fiscal database are as cautious as possible. Whenever it was necessary to make a choice regarding the collection methodology or fill in missing data, we chose the path that resulted in lower revenues or higher costs. This introduces a bias against our argument, reducing the chance that we will find sustainability. In particular, we worked with confirmed revenues (as opposed to agreed-on ones). When facing a missing observation, we imputed the lowest of the closest values available. Conversely, we use the agreed-on asiento servicing costs, even though we know that many contracts were subject to individual renegotiations that lowered their yield. In the next section we will use a similar approach to estimate the debt service on juros, applying the average yield to every bond even though some of them may not have been paid in full because they were attached to an underperforming revenue stream. We cannot be sure that our military expenditure series captures every last ducat spent on military operations, but the logic of fiscal accounting implies that whatever we missed in this category will be added to civil expenditure. Overall, our data reflect a conservative take on Castile's financial position. The calculations will therefore yield a lower bound on the sustainability of sovereign debt.

ANNUAL FISCAL ACCOUNTS

SOLVING THE PUZZLE

Before explaining how we reconstruct the fiscal position of Castile on an annual basis, it is useful to review some basic concepts of national accounting. The government's fiscal balance is defined as the sum of all its revenues minus its expenditures. If the number is positive, the budget is in surplus; if

---

7 This stands in stark contrast to England's debt conversions, also studied by Chamley (2011), which proceeded in an orderly fashion.

it is negative, it is in deficit. Any deficit must be covered by the issuance of additional debt, while any surplus adds to the government's assets and hence reduces the net stock of debt. We can therefore write

$$R_t - G_t = -\Delta D_t, \tag{1}$$

where R stands for revenues, G represents all government expenditures, and D is the stock of debt.

Government expenditures are divided into ordinary expenditure and debt service, while the stock of debt is composed by the sum of long- and short-term debt:

$$R_t - E_t - DS_t = -\Delta D_t. \tag{2}$$

E now represents ordinary expenditures, while DS stands for debt service. The first two terms of the equation, revenue minus ordinary expenditure, represent the primary surplus, a key element in debt sustainability calculations. When the primary surplus is negative—a primary deficit—the government is borrowing just to be able to pay interest on old debts. The mechanics of compound interest mean that primary deficits can quickly cause the stock of debt to spiral out of control. Positive and large primary surpluses are needed for debt to be sustainable.

For our purposes, it is also useful to disaggregate debt service into long and short term, and ordinary expenditure into military and nonmilitary:

$$R_t - ME_t - NME_t - DS_t^l - DS_t^s = PS_t - DS_t = -\Delta(D_t^l + D_t^s). \tag{3}$$

Here DS^l and DS^s denote long- and short-term debt service, ME is military expenditure, NME is nonmilitary expenditure, and PS is the primary surplus. In chapter 3, we presented series of revenue and short-term debt issues. We added series of military expenditure and short-term debt service in this chapter. We are left with three unknowns: nonmilitary expenditure, long-term debt service, and variations in the stock of long-term debt. To solve for them, we will rely on the following two assumptions:

- Assumption 1: long-term debt service grew smoothly between observations
- Assumption 2: real nonmilitary expenditure was constant throughout the period

Table 4. Juros and their service (in millions of current ducats)

Year	Outstanding juros	Juros servicing outlays	Average cost of juro service	Revenue
1560	19	1.468	7.7%	3.155
1565	25			4.192
1566		1.861	7.4%†	4.770
1573		2.752		5.433
1575	42.5	2.730	6.4%	7.606
1584		3.273		7.806
1598	68	4.634	6.8%	11.328††

Source: Debt estimates for 1560, 1565, and 1598 are from Artola 1982. The figure for 1575 is from De Carlos Morales 2008. Service estimates are from Ruiz Martín 1965; Ulloa 1977.
† Calculated using 1565 stock of juros
†† Figure from 1596

We begin with long-term debt service. For convenience, we reproduce the table from chapter 3 reporting the scant available data on juros and their service. The table reports juros service for six different years. Following our first assumption, we fill the missing years by interpolating linearly. The assumption is plausible: because of the large stock of juros, the average interest paid on them could not vary abruptly from year to year. The issuance of juros was also capped by ordinary revenue, which grew slowly and gradually. The major exception to this trend was the year 1575, when the Cortes authorized a large increase in ordinary revenue. We have an actual observation for that year, so our procedure still captures the break in the trend. While some measurement error will remain, it will be small relative to the overall size of the budget. This approach, then, gives us a usable series for DS^l.

We have data for the stock of outstanding juros for 1565, 1575, and 1598. The latter two dates correspond to the third and fourth bankruptcies of Philip II. Because of the nature of the reschedulings, there was no asiento debt in these years, and so the amount of outstanding juros was equivalent to the total debt. For 1565 we have no hard data on short-term debt. Since the Fugger settlement had not yet been fully negotiated, though, and since the Genoese bankers did not enter the market in earnest until 1566, the amount of any outstanding asientos would have been small. It seems reasonable to assume that asiento debt was negligible relative to juros in 1565 and juros represented almost all the debt outstanding. Because we can guess the total debt outstanding in 1565 and 1598 with reasonable accuracy, we also know how much debt grew between those years: by 43 million ducats.

It is now useful to sum up equation (3) over time:

$$\Sigma_t R_t - \Sigma_t ME_t - \Sigma_t NME_t - \Sigma_t DS_t^l - \Sigma_t DS_t^s = \Sigma_t \Delta D_t. \qquad (4)$$

We just calculated the last term of this expression—the change in total debt over the entire period. Our first assumption gave us the series for long-term debt service, and we have data for revenue, military expenditure, and short-term debt service. All of these can be easily summed up as well. With this in hand, it is straightforward to solve for the sum of nonmilitary expenditure over the whole period. This turns out to be 18.7 million ducats, compared to a total of 146.2 million ducats of military expenditure—equivalent to 11.3 percent of the combined total.

Next we use our second assumption to assign yearly values to nonmilitary expenditure, spreading it out over the whole period while letting its nominal value grow at the rate of inflation. This is again plausible, as most of the expenses on the civil administration and internal law enforcement were fixed. Since nonmilitary expenditure is small compared to the size of the budget, modifying this assumption does not affect our results in any significant way.

Because we estimated military expenditure by adding up the costs of different campaigns relying on a patchwork of sources, one might worry about important outlays being overlooked. In order to allay this concern, it is worth noting that because civil expenditure is calculated as a residual, underestimating military expenditure would simply result in higher values for nonmilitary outlays. Overall expenditure would not change; "missing" military expenditures have no effect on sustainability. That said, our estimate of civil expenditure is low, and hence it is unlikely that we have underestimated military expenditure by a large margin. The government's budget identity suggests that our series must be capturing virtually all of the outlays associated with Castile's military campaigns.

We now have annual series for revenue, military expenditure, nonmilitary expenditure, long- and short-term debt service as well as the total stock of debt in the initial and final years. Using equation (3), it is easy to compute a yearly series of changes in the debt stock. Adding them to the initial debt

Table 5. Fiscal accounts, 1566–96 (period averages)

	1566–74	1575–84	1585–96
Panel A (nominal, million of ducats)			
Revenues	5.17	7.88	9.60
Military expenditure	3.40	3.04	6.95
Nonmilitary expenditure	0.54	0.59	0.66
Primary surplus	1.24	4.25	1.99
Long-term debt service	2.35	3.00	3.91
Short-term debt service	0.77	0.47	0.79
Fiscal balance	−1.89	0.78	−2.71
Outstanding debt	30.35	37.37	54.07
Panel B (real, million of 1565 ducats)			
Revenue	4.93	6.96	7.52
Military expenditure	3.18	2.67	5.48
Nonmilitary expenditure	0.52	0.52	0.52
Primary surplus	1.23	3.77	1.53
Long-term debt service	2.23	2.65	3.06
Short-term debt service	0.72	0.41	0.62
Fiscal balance	−1.72	0.71	−2.15
Outstanding debt	28.75	32.96	42.24
Panel C (% of revenue)			
Military expenditure	65.8%	38.6%	72.4%
Nonmilitary expenditure	10.4%	7.5%	6.9%
Primary surplus	24.0%	53.9%	20.7%
Long-term debt service	45.5%	38.1%	40.7%
Short-term debt service	14.9%	6.0%	8.2%
Fiscal balance	−36.6%	9.9%	−28.2%
Outstanding debt	587.0%	474.2%	563.2%

gives a time series of total debt outstanding. This completes our full set of annual fiscal accounts for Castile, which we summarize in table 5.

BASIC TRENDS

Before assessing whether Castile's debt was sustainable, it is useful to discuss the basic trends. Large issuance of short-term debt did not always coincide with major increases in the total debt stock. Nominal debt increased by 40.9

million ducats between 1565 and 1596. Over the same period, the Crown entered into asiento loans for 92.1 million ducats. Thus, on average, around half of asiento borrowing was either rolled over into new short-term loans or consolidated into long-term debt; the rest was used to repay lenders. A large portion of short-term borrowing covered transitory fluctuations in income and expenditure rather than adding to overall indebtedness. As a robustness check, our total debt series closely matches the intermediate estimates for individual years in table 4.

The next key result is that revenues throughout Philip's reign were markedly higher than military and nonmilitary expenditure combined—that is, the Crown on average ran a primary surplus. Spending excluding debt-servicing costs amounted to 76 percent of revenue in the 1560s and early 1570s, fell to 46 percent in the late 1570s and early 1590s, and then increased to 79 percent. Once we take debt-servicing costs into account, the budget was on average in deficit during Philip's second and fourth decade on the throne, and in surplus during the third one.

In panel B of table 5, we report period average fiscal accounts in real terms. Castilian economic performance was strong in the third quarter of the sixteenth century. This allowed the Crown to push through a remarkable fiscal expansion. Revenues grew by 41 percent in real terms between 1566–74 and 1575–84. Even more surprisingly, revenues increased by an additional 8 percent during the last decade of Philip's reign, despite the marked deceleration in Castilian economic performance. Over the entire period, Crown income grew by 53 percent, while nondebt expenditure increased by 62 percent.

In 1575–84, real military spending had fallen 14 percent relative to 1566–74. Philip earned a "peace dividend" after the successful Battle of Lepanto and the lull in the Dutch Revolt. Castile's budget swung into surplus as a result, having been in deficit during 1566–74. This surplus gave way to annual deficits of more than 2 million ducats (in 1565 prices) in the period 1585–96. Military spending then more than doubled, driven by the Armada and renewed fighting in the Low Countries. In real terms, Philip's overall debts rose by 47 percent between the second and fourth decade of his reign—less than the increase in revenues.

Panel C of table 5 shows our fiscal accounts as a percentage of annual revenue. Our choice of scaling variable requires some explanation. Arguably, the right way to measure the burden of military commitments and debt is to scale them by the economy's total output. Yet estimating sixteenth-century

GDP is difficult; the latest published estimates differ by more than 200 percent between their upper and lower bounds (Alvarez Nogal and Prados de la Escosura 2007). In addition to the substantial uncertainty surrounding Castilian GDP, there are reasons to use revenue as a scaling variable. While modern states exert control over large portions of GDP, early modern ones did not. To assess sustainability is to examine potentially available resources for servicing debts; therefore, actual fiscal revenues are a better indicator in the early modern period than GDP. Creditors, for good reason, would have cared more about the Crown's revenue than about the economy's total output when assessing a country's creditworthiness.

Military spending fluctuated strongly from year to year, but its long-term share was broadly stable. The debt burden displayed an overall negative trend. The total debt-servicing cost amounted to 60 percent of revenue in the first decade. This fell to 44 percent in the second one, and rose slightly to 49 percent in the last one—still finishing with a lower value than it started. For the period as a whole, Philip II ran average fiscal deficits of approximately 20 percent of revenue. While the average deficit in the first period amounted to 37 percent, the second one witnessed surpluses of 10 percent of revenue. The decade of the Armada saw a return to deficits of, on average, 28 percent.

Figure 8 shows the primary surplus and fiscal balance side by side. The run-up to the bankruptcy in 1575 and the Armada are associated with primary deficits. After the rescheduling in 1577 and the big tax hike agreed to by the Cortes, surpluses became substantial, varying between 50 and 70 percent of revenue. Lower military expenditure helped with the return to large (primary and overall) surpluses. Similarly, the introduction of the millones in the 1590s improved Castile's fiscal position. During Philip's reign as a whole, Castile ran primary surpluses equivalent to 32 percent of revenues. Despite almost continuous warfare, Philip II almost never borrowed to pay interest. A substantial proportion of his revenue was instead available for servicing his debts, year after year. The only exceptions to this were periods of exceptional military effort—the great Dutch offensive of the early 1570s and the Armada.[8]

War did not only dominate overall spending; it also cast a long shadow over Castile's fiscal balance. Revenues could fluctuate from year to year, and

---

8 Figure 8 also speaks against the main conclusions of the "serial default" literature. Following the 1575 payment stop, we do not see the downward spiral of weakening fiscal institutions predicted by Carmen Reinhart, Kenneth Rogoff, and Miguel Savastano (2003). Rather, due to fiscal restraint and tax hikes, the primary surplus went up.

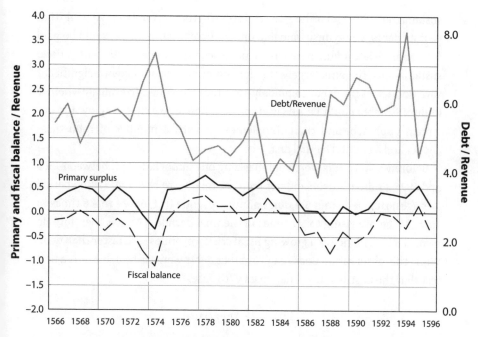

FIGURE 8. Fiscal balance and debt relative to revenue

did so largely as a result of silver windfalls or shortfalls. Debt-servicing costs also fluctuated, depending on the mix of short- and long-term debt along with the financing conditions in each market. Yet the prime determinant of the Crown's fiscal position was the scale of its military effort.[9] Our international comparisons, which we present in chapter 8, further suggest that long-term sustainability and growth were tied more to success on the battlefield than to "responsible" fiscal behavior.

SUSTAINABILITY

For public debt to be sustainable, revenues and expenditures have to allow all debts to be serviced in perpetuity. Similarly, the ratio of debt to income should not rise above sensible levels, defined by the development of the tax system and public debt administration. Beyond this broad definition, however, there is little theoretical consensus on how to calculate the maximum

---

9 If we regress ps_t on ME_t, we obtain a coefficient of -1.07 (t-statistic 9.4). This implies that the primary surplus moved almost exactly 1:1 with military spending.

sustainable debt level or how to establish whether a country is solvent (that is, if its debts, while unsustainable under current parameters, could be paid with appropriate adjustments in the fiscal accounts). The assessment of fiscal sustainability remains largely the domain of practitioners, with significant variation across the major commonly accepted techniques. To evaluate whether Philip II's debts could be serviced in the long run we first employ a mainstream approach, and then complement it with a number of robustness checks and a counterfactual analysis.

Before we start, it is worth emphasizing one important fact. Between 1566 and 1596, Philip II's debts did not increase relative to revenue. Taking period averages, they fell from 5.9 times annual revenue in 1566–74 to 4.8 times in 1575–84, before rising to 5.7 times in the final decade. There is therefore no prima facie evidence of a growing fiscal crisis; revenues rose faster than debt. While this observation does not prove that debts were sustainable, it is a first test that the Castilian fiscal data pass with ease.

THE IMF APPROACH

A more systematic approach, favored by the IMF (2003), calculates the primary surpluses necessary to stabilize the debt-to-GDP ratio. The basic idea is that debts will continue to be serviceable as long as the growth rate of debt does not exceed the growth rate of output. This requires a primary surplus—keeping expenditure (net of the cost of debt service) below revenue. Thus, revenue growth combined with cheap borrowing can lead to a favorable outcome even if debts continue to increase.

We explore this approach more rigorously using the debt accumulation equation from Joshua Aizenman and Brian Pinto (2005),

$$\Delta d_t = pd_t + \frac{(r_t - g_t)}{(1 + g_t)} d_{t-1},$$ (5)

where Δd is the change in the debt as a percentage of GDP, r is the (nominal) rate of interest, g is the growth rate of GDP, and pd is the primary deficit as a percentage of GDP. Equation (5) says that the increase in the debt-to-income ratio equals the current period primary deficit plus the interest on previous period debt, adjusted by the growth rate of the economy. Because sustainability requires that debt does not increase as a percentage of GDP, we set Δd to zero and obtain

$$-pd^*_t = ps^*_t = \frac{(r_t - g_t)}{(1 + g_t)} d_{t-1},$$ (6)

where ps^* is the primary surplus that will hold the debt-to-GDP ratio constant and hence meet the sustainability requirement. Lagging the equation one period, setting d_{t-1} equal to d_t, and assuming that r and g do not change over time yields

$$d^* = ps/(r - g),$$ (7)

where d^* is the sustainable debt level relative to GDP. The right-hand side is simply the discounted value of future primary surpluses, where the discount rate is calculated as the difference between the interest and growth rates of the economy. The higher the primary surplus, and the higher the growth rate of income, the larger the debt that can reliably be serviced.

This approach to sustainability assumes that the state can lay claim to a constant share of GDP in the form of taxation. This was definitely not the case in sixteenth-century Castile. As the Crown consolidated its power in the early sixteenth century, its tax revenues grew faster than the economy. Negotiations between the king and Cortes of 1575 and 1591 led to large tax hikes. One may wonder how sustainable a fiscal position can be that depends on government revenues growing faster than the economy at large. Taxing income above subsistence income is markedly easier than taxing incomes below a minimum consumption threshold. As total incomes increased, surplus incomes grew much faster—merely because average income at the beginning of the period was close to subsistence. Fast revenue growth after 1500 simply meant that early modern states laid claim to a high share of rapidly growing "surplus" income (Voigtländer and Voth 2013).

In the case of Castile, revenues from the Indies were also rising rapidly. Overall, in the thirty-one years covered by our data, revenues increased by 53 percent—a growth rate that output cannot possibly have matched. This reinforces our choice of revenue as a scaling variable instead of GDP; lenders surely cared more about the actual income of the Crown rather than a notional upper limit of national production. Given this, we perform all our sustainability calculations scaling our variables by revenue. We will nonetheless repeat the analysis using various estimates of GDP when discussing robustness.

Table 6 shows our baseline sustainability results, comparing required and actual primary surpluses as well as possible and actual debt levels. The analy-

Table 6. Sustainability calculations: Baseline results

	g	r	ps*	ps	ps-ps*	d*	d	d-d*
1565–74	3.38%	10.20%	0.394	0.249	−0.145	3.645	5.863	2.218
1574–84	3.28%	9.30%	0.433	0.454	0.020	7.534	4.787	−2.748
1584–96	3.44%	8.80%	0.227	0.201	−0.026	3.744	5.728	1.983
1565–96	3.37%	9.40%	0.348	0.315	−0.033	5.229	5.476	0.246

Note: G is the growth rate of revenue, r is the average interest rate on government debt, ps is the actual primary surplus relative to revenue, ps* is the surplus required for stabilizing the debt-to-revenue ratio, d is actual debt to revenue, and d* is the debt-to-revenue ratio that can be sustained given actual primary surpluses. Growth rates are calculated as annualized compounded rates of growth between benchmark dates. Hence, the overall rate is not equivalent to the weighted average of the growth rates in subperiods.

sis is performed by decade and for the entire period covered by our data. Primary surpluses for the period as a whole were sufficient to keep upward pressure on the debt-to-revenue ratio in check. The primary surplus ps* required to stabilize the debt-to-revenue ratio was 35 percent of revenue, which is only slightly higher than the 31.5 percent actually attained. At the time of Philip's death, the Crown's debt in relation to revenue (d) stood where it had been thirty-three years earlier—at a multiple of less than 6. The average sustainable debt (d*) was 5.2 times revenue, and actual levels stood at 5.5 times, which is a minor difference.

During the first decade, primary surpluses were about two-thirds of the level necessary for stability. Interest rates were relatively high, and revenue grew moderately. Debt levels were higher than could be sustained indefinitely. The second decade, from 1575 to 1584, showed a decline in interest rates and higher growth rate of revenue. Reduced military spending allowed primary surpluses to increase markedly. These surpluses were now higher than necessary to stabilize debt levels. Actual indebtedness was below the maximum sustainable level. In the final decade, military events caused expenditure to increase again. The primary surplus required for stability fell to 0.23, which is three percentage points (of revenue) higher than the actual number. For the period as a whole, sustainability was not compromised despite near-continuous warfare and major military efforts in the last two decades of the sixteenth century.

ROBUSTNESS

Our conclusion that Philip II's finances were largely sustainable rests on newly collected data, a reworking of existing estimates, and the derivation of information from combining these different series. At each step, we made assumptions that may impact our assessment. We now examine how our conclusions are affected if we use alternative indicators or assumptions.

ALTERNATIVE REVENUE GROWTH RATES

The revenue growth rates we used so far were calculated as the compound growth rate between end points. Results are therefore sensitive to the choice of the first and last year of the period considered. An alternative is to regress the natural logarithm of revenue on a time trend. The coefficient on the time variable will then be a measure of the average annual growth rate taking into account intraperiod fluctuations. In table 7, we show the results for the period as a whole if we use the alternative measure of revenue increases. Overall growth is somewhat lower, increasing the gap between the actual and required primary surplus. The difference nonetheless remains relatively small. The gap between sustainable and actual debt levels also increases, but it remains less than the revenues of an average year.

ALTERNATIVE GDP SERIES

GDP is the standard scaling variable for fiscal variables. While we argue that revenue is a better yardstick in the case of an early modern economy, here we demonstrate that our main conclusion is robust to the use of GDP. The most recent GDP estimates for Castile, by Carlos Alvarez Nogal and Leandro Prados de la Escosura (2007), are presented as an upper and lower bound on GDP. The difference between the two can be large; they vary on average by a factor of 3. In table 7, we repeat our sustainability calculations using both the upper and lower bound as well as the midpoint. As a further check, we use a different set of GDP figures from Albert Carreras (2003).

Our conclusions are unaffected if we use GDP as a scaling variable, independent of the particular series employed. In each case, we find that the required and actual primary surpluses are nearly identical. With Carreras's

Table 7. Robustness

	g	r	ps*	ps	ps-ps*	d*	d	d-d*
Revenue-based								
Benchmark	3.37%	9.40%	0.348	0.315	−0.033	5.229	5.476	0.246
Regression-based	2.83%	9.40%	0.345	0.315	−0.030	4.800	5.476	0.676
GDP-based								
Carreras	1.90%	9.40%	0.032	0.032	0.000	0.423	0.514	0.091
Alvarez-Prados - midpoint	3.40%	9.40%	0.014	0.014	0.000	0.232	0.223	−0.009
Alvarez-Prados - lower bound	3.40%	9.40%	0.028	0.029	0.001	0.480	0.461	−0.018
Alvarez-Prados - upper bound	3.40%	9.40%	0.009	0.009	0.000	0.153	0.147	−0.006

Note: G is the growth rate of revenue, r is the interest rate, ps is the actual primary surplus relative to revenue, ps* is the surplus required for stabilizing the debt-to-revenue ratio, d is actual debt to revenue, and d* is the debt-to-revenue ratio that can be sustained given actual primary surpluses. Growth rates are calculated as annualized compounded rates of growth between benchmark dates. Hence, the overall rate is not equivalent to the weighted average of the growth rates in subperiods.

GDP estimates, which are relatively pessimistic, there is a 9 percent gap between actual and sustainable debt. In any of the variations of the Alvarez Nogal and Prados de la Escosura figures, we find full sustainability. We do not take a stand on whether 1.9 or 3.4 percent growth of output is the correct number for sixteenth-century Castile, but note that even with the most pessimistic figures, the gap d-d* is small.

NO PRINCIPAL REDUCTIONS DURING DEFAULTS

It can be asserted that one particular aspect of our analysis stacks the odds in favor of finding sustainability. During the 1575 and 1596 defaults, lenders saw the present value of their principal reduced. The debt outstanding would have been higher without these adjustments. How much of the "health" of Philip II's finances derived from the write-downs after the defaults?

We calculate a counterfactual debt series by adding debt service on the defaulted asientos plus principal to the debt stock. After applying this correction, the counterfactual debt in 1577, the year of the medio general, is 5.5 million ducats higher than the actual level. We then scale up debt service charges in line with the new debt stock in the preceding year. This reduces primary surpluses and increases the primary deficits. Likewise, in 1596, we add the write-down from the medio general to the debt stock outstanding, raising it by 1.4 million ducats. Even without the default of 1577, the new taxes would have been adequate to bring debt back under control in the 1580s. The debt to revenue would have remained around a factor of 6 until the 1590s, before rising to a factor of 8. After the Armada, debt would have increased much more rapidly without the 1575 default. The final debt stock could have been higher by the equivalent of two years' revenue.

Arguably, even this extremely pessimistic scenario would still not imply a lack of sustainability; Britain's debts in 1815, for example, stood at 185 percent of GDP (Barro 1987).[10] Yet it is likely that the rapid rise in debt ratios after 1588 in our counterfactual could have raised questions about Castile's ability to service debts in the long run, a sequence of primary surpluses in the 1590s notwithstanding. In other words, up to the Armada, Spanish government finances would have been sustainable even without the default of 1575 and haircut imposed on lenders. After 1588, in contrast, Philip's actual fiscal position was more manageable partly because of the 1575 default.

ALTERNATIVE ASIENTO-SERVICING COST

For our baseline scenario, we calculated the cost of servicing asientos from the agreed-on cash flows in each year, based on the evidence in the complete set of contracts. While this allows for precise comparisons between individual loans, the overall cost estimate relies on our chosen measure of profitability: the modified internal rate of return (MIRR). One alternative is to use average financing costs and duration when converting asiento borrowing into debt-servicing costs. We assume that all (transfers, exchange, and financing) costs accrue in the first year of a loan's life. Since the average asiento had a duration of eighteen months, this involves a certain amount of front loading, which increases the debt burden. To further stack the odds against our main conclusion—that the king's debts were sustainable—we also use the gross value of the asiento (including transfers), not just the borrowing component. Finally, we use a high value for the interest rate: 16 percent.

---

10 Since some debt was issued below par, it is not quite clear which value one should use: the nominal value of debt or the amounts actually raised. If we used the nominal value of the debt, the burden would have exceeded 200 percent of GDP.

This is our calculated median rate of return on asiento lending plus a premium of 2 percent. The new estimate for annual asiento-servicing costs is

$$ds_t^s = d_t^s \times 1.5 \times 0.16,$$

where d^s is the total value of asientos contracted. Under this assumption, the debt-to-revenue ratio would have increased to 6.4 instead of 5.9. The difference remains small, even if this approach clearly raises the debt burden. We can be fairly certain that this approach is too pessimistic. It implies a debt level of 73 million ducats by 1598, for instance, when the actual observed amount is 66 million. Our original methodology yields much more accurate results.

THE VALUE OF VICTORY IN THE LOW COUNTRIES

One important consideration in assessing sustainability is whether the downturns in Castile's fiscal position reflected fiscally irresponsible policies or bad luck—unanticipated shocks. As we will see in the next few chapters, financial markets treat these two situations quite differently, reacting in a more lenient way to shocks that are perceived to be outside the sovereign's control. On the other hand, if a country runs up large debts to engage in current consumption and has no sensible plan to raise future revenues, it is hard to contend that the fiscal situation is sustainable. We now examine the two major shocks to Philip II's fiscal position: the loss of the Invincible Armada and protracted campaign in the Netherlands. Both of them had large potential upsides and hence should not be considered as examples of reckless fiscal policy.

With hindsight, we know that the Armada marked a turning point in Philip II's fortunes. And yet we know that "under the sun . . . the race is not to the swift, nor the battle to the strong . . . but time and chance happeneth to them all" (Ecclesiastes 9.11, King James version). Ex ante, it was by no means clear that Spain—which had recently routed the Ottoman fleet in a major naval battle at Lepanto—would fail in its attempt to invade England. As we discussed in chapter 2, contemporaries took the Armada seriously. Sir Walter Raleigh, among other prominent figures, openly worried that England would have been left defenseless had the fleet managed a successful landing. As Parker (1979) observes, even if the Armada had only achieved its minimum goal of establishing a beachhead in Kent, Spain would have reaped large benefits. Success, while not guaranteed by any means, was far from unthinkable. By the same token, the scale of the disaster—one-third of the fleet and half the lives lost at sea, and no landing in England at all—must have been toward the most pessimistic end of the range of possible outcomes.

We argue that the large financial losses incurred by Castile as a result of the Armada were an unexpected shock. While defeat is always a possibility in war, complete military and financial disaster was probably more like the proverbial "black swan" events in financial markets—an unlikely and damaging negative outcome.

Attempting to subdue the Dutch rebellion was arguably different. The Armada was a single throw of dice; the Dutch War represented a continuous, expensive, and seemingly interminable commitment of fighting power and financial resources. While the Armada was inspired by the need to make progress in Flanders, protracted attempts to conquer Holland and Zeeland cannot be construed as an unexpected expenditure shock. The continued demands of this war placed enormous strain on Castile's finances for the last three decades of Philip's reign and were a key factor in the accumulation of debt. We will argue that the expected benefits from eventual victory and subsequent peace in the Netherlands were such that they justify Spain's prolonged and expensive efforts, even in a narrow economic sense. Victory in any form, even at a late stage, would have rapidly improved Philip II's finances.

Spain ultimately lost its bid for control of the Netherlands. If there was *any* chance of success at any point, then the fiscal outcome that we documented above constitutes a *lower bound* on the sustainability of Castilian finances— one that reflects what must have been the worst-case scenario in military terms based on the available information. Ex ante, Philip and his advisers had good reason to hope that they might succeed in suppressing the Dutch Revolt. Few large, populous areas had ever broken away from their rulers in Europe; Switzerland was the only notable exception. Philip's empire was the superpower of the age. Many contemporaries were convinced that Philip II's fearsome tercios, which had repeatedly vanquished their opponents, would eventually prevail. The Dutch rebels themselves were fully aware that the effort to discard their ruler and become independent was extraordinary. After the Spanish victory at the Battle of Mook in 1574, William of Orange declared that "we have done what no other nation has done before us, to wit that we have defended and maintained ourselves in such a small country against the great and horrible assaults of mighty enemies, without any help." Indeed, leaders of the revolt like Orange were convinced that they would eventually lose without outside intervention (Swart 1978, 24). The bankers that bankrolled Spain's military operations must have had similar thoughts.

We now gauge how much of a difference victory in Flanders would have made to Philip's finances. A successful conclusion to Philip II's campaign in the Low Countries would have reduced military expenditure. In addition, it may have yielded extra revenue through taxing the rebellious provinces. We hazard conservative guesses for both figures. These strongly suggest that even relatively small changes to actual expenditure and revenue would have had a considerable impact on the Crown's overall fiscal position.

After the Sack of Antwerp in 1576, there was a lull in the fighting. This situation illustrates how quickly Castilian finances recovered once military spending fell. During the period 1566–96, Philip II spent 163 million ducats on nondebt expenditures, of which 144.3 were military expenses. Of these, fully 53 percent—77.3 million ducats—was spent on the Army of Flanders. During the Armada and its aftermath, from 1587 to 1596, expenditure in the Low Countries amounted to 40.6 million ducats. During the ten preceding years, when no major military operations took place, the total expenditure on the Army of Flanders was only 16.8 million ducats, amounting to 59 percent less.

In our counterfactual, we assume that a breakthrough in the Netherlands might have been achieved by the late 1580s, following the Duke of Parma's big push into Dutch territory (an earlier victory—by the Duke of Alba, for example—would have yielded even more favorable outcomes). We use 1588, the year of the Armada, as a reference point. This choice is dictated by the availability of data—1588 is as late a date as we can choose and still have enough data afterward for a counterfactual to be meaningful. We assume that military expenditure following a Spanish victory would have been similar to the figures for 1577–86. Thus, some 17.6 million ducats could probably have been saved from 1589 on. Note that our calculations provide a lower bound on the reduction in expenses that would have followed this success, as our figures continue to count the full cost of rebuilding the decimated Armada. Excluding it could have saved another 5.56 million ducats after 1588 (Parker 1998).[11]

---

11 The only sense in which victory in Flanders could have worsened Philip's fiscal position would have been a continuation of high-intensity warfare with England. While not impossible, we consider this unlikely.

Additional tax revenues are a more speculative source of improvement in Philip II's finances. Victory over the rebellious provinces would have allowed Philip to tax them.[12] We take the estimates of tax revenue in Holland compiled by Wantjie Fritschy (2003). To err on the side of caution, we assume that Castile would not have been as efficient in taxing its reluctant subjects compared to how efficient they were themselves. We therefore reduced the tax estimates by 50 percent. Accordingly, most of the change in Philip's fiscal position would have reflected lower expenditure (saving 2.5 million ducats in 1596) rather than higher revenue (adding 0.53 million).[13]

To examine the impact of lower expenditure and higher revenue, we recalculate overall expenditure, the fiscal balance, primary surpluses, and total debt for each year. As a result of victory in the Low Countries, Philip could have ended his reign with debts of 39 million ducats instead of 66 million. The debt-to-revenue ratio would have resumed the downward trend it was on before the plan for the Armada was hatched. Figure 9 shows the two counterfactuals. The first uses only lower military expenditure, while the second adds possible revenue from Holland. There is little difference between the two; the key reason why Philip's finances would have looked healthy by the end of his reign would have been less war, not more taxes. Thus, the Armada and the renewed Dutch campaign could have made good sense in fiscal terms at the time the decisions were taken. This is not to say that fiscal considerations were paramount among Philip's advisers. It simply implies that religious or strategic considerations need not be the only reasons why attacking England and the Netherlands seemed like promising projects at the time.

CONCLUSION

Could Philip II repay his debts? Our reconstructed fiscal accounts suggest that he could have done so. While liquidity was scarce during periods of in-

---

12 Since there are no good estimates for the total value of debt issued by the rebellious provinces before their uprising, we abstract from the fact that the tax revenue of conquered territories would not have been entirely unencumbered after a Spanish triumph. For example, so-called *Rentmeisterbriefe* (long-term debts similar to juros) had been issued in Holland and Zeeland. The Fugger held a good number of these—and never received payment for them (Ehrenberg 1896). These debts would have been recognized and serviced after a Spanish victory, reducing the net gain in tax capacity.

13 This is a highly conservative calculation. Dutch revenues increased rapidly in the seventeenth century, averaging 2.6 million ducats per year between 1600 and 1650. This is four times the amount we use in our counterfactual.

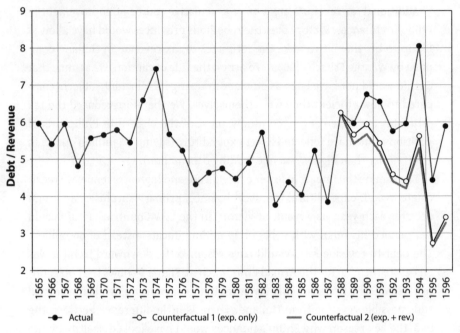

FIGURE 9. Victory in Flanders: Counterfactual debt-to-revenue paths

tense warfare, years of relative peace brought large surpluses. A systematic analysis based on the IMF's methodology to evaluate fiscal sustainability shows that Castile was able to service its debts in the long run. Because our data were constructed with a bias against finding sustainability, this result represents a lower bound for the actual health of Crown finances. Our conclusions are not affected by employing a variety of scaling variables, alternative growth rates for revenue, a more aggressive way of calculating debt service, or ignoring the debt reductions negotiated during the defaults. Bankers and investors were not lured into lending their money to an insolvent state; Castile was able to honor the king's debts.

To perform our analysis, we reconstructed Castile's annual fiscal accounts. This is a complex task for the early modern period; it requires high-frequency information on virtually all the financial activities of the state. Such information was not collected at the time. Our data collection effort produced new yearly series of revenue, military expenditure, short-term debt issues, and short-term debt service. Using conservative assumptions and the logic of the government's budget constraint, we derived figures for long-term debt service, civil expenditures, and overall debt stocks. The resulting database spans a full thirty-one-year period—enough to employ modern quantitative techniques.

We also asked whether the events that led to major downturns in Castile's financial fortunes could have been anticipated. Based on contemporary assessments, we conclude that the Armada had a reasonable chance of success. While defeat was a possibility, the actual scale of the disaster that unfolded must have seemed highly unlikely ex ante. The expenses associated with rebuilding the fleet were an unexpected shock. Furthermore, fighting the Dutch rebels was economically rational. Castile was heavily favored to win the war, and even limited success would have resulted in a large peace dividend.

Overall, our analysis provides strong evidence that Castile's fiscal position in the second half of the sixteenth century was on a solid footing. The resources to service debt were available. Why, then, did bankruptcies continue to take place? Was Philip II an opportunistic borrower, defaulting on his commitments when he could have made good on them? Were there inherent failures in the sovereign debt market? Or were other mechanisms at work, with payment stops playing an integral role in a complex system of international finance? The next chapter addresses these questions.

CHAPTER 5

LENDING TO THE BORROWER
FROM HELL

CREDIT AND THE KING'S SWORD

On Thursday, October 12, 1307, the Grand Master of the Order of Templars, Jacques de Molay, was carrying a heavy burden: he was a pallbearer at the funeral of Catherine of Courtenay, sister-in-law to Philip IV of France. The young noble woman had died at the age of thirty-two. Only nobles in favor at court were accorded the special honor of acting as pallbearers. Also present at the funeral were the king and every member of the royal family as well as most of the leading officials.

The next morning, bailiffs woke de Molay before dawn, bearing a warrant for his arrest. The Templars, or so the king alleged, were heretics who in their initiation rites denied Christ and spat on the cross, and then engaged in homoerotic rituals—"an abominable work, a detestable disgrace, a thing almost inhuman, indeed set apart from all humanity" (Barber 2001). At the same time, hundreds of Knights Templar were arrested all over France. Under torture, the grand master confessed to the Templars' sins (before recanting). Seven years later, after a drawn-out legal process, he met his end on the Isle des Juifs in Paris, near the garden of the royal palace. He was burned at the stake on March 19, 1314, together with Geoffroi de Charney, the former master of Normandy for the Templars.

There can be no question that the charges against de Molay and the Templars were trumped up. Similar persecutions had already been brought against French Jews (expelled in 1306) and the Lombards. The reason for these judicial murders was the same: the Templars, Jews, and Lombards had lent money to the king. Philip IV was in desperate need of funds, having

---

Portions of this chapter are based on Drelichman and Voth 2011a.

fought a major war with England only shortly before. Few regular tax revenues underwrote the king's finances; he was largely expected to live off his
demesne income. Loans regularly filled the gap between expenditure and
revenue, especially at times of major financial demands such as during the
campaigns in southwestern France against the English. After his attack on
the Templars, Philip IV unsurprisingly found few willing lenders. Two hundred and fifty years later, the advisers of another king called Philip—who also
happened to be strapped for cash while fighting expensive wars and borrowing heavily—voiced similarly murderous sentiments. In 1596, the Marquis of
Poza, president of the Council of Finance of Castile, noted in writing that he
would like to put the Genoese bankers lending to Philip II of Spain to the
sword: "Every day, we discover new evidence against the Genoese.... I
couldn't possibly have enough of their blood" (Sanz Ayán 2004).[1]

Lending to kings could indeed be a perilous business.[2] And yet in contrast
to the events in Paris in 1307–14, the dark mutterings of the Marquis of Poza
did not result in bloodshed. No banker to the Crown of Castile lost their life
because of royally sanctioned violence. What had changed? Not only did the
Genoese escape with their throats intact; they also made good money. A more
enlightened approach to the lives of subjects or sudden aversion to killing
was certainly not the cause; Philip II was perfectly capable of executing alleged troublemakers if it suited him. Even loyal subjects like the Counts
Egmont and Horn, who opposed Spanish policy in the Netherlands, were
summarily executed.

How can we explain the vast difference in outcomes—the violent persecu-
tion of the Templars, Jews, and Lombards, on the one hand, and prosperous
security of the Genoese, on the other? Continued lending under Philip II of
Spain stands in stark contrast to the collapse of royal credit under Philip IV
of France. De Molay's fate illustrates the heart of the problem of sovereign
lending. Because the borrower is also the supreme judge and lawmaker, there
can be no appeal to higher authorities if contracts are broken. Medieval kings
repeatedly engaged in repudiations and confiscations on a grand scale. While
some new lenders can sometimes be convinced that their fate is going to be

---

1 "Cada día boy descubriendo contra estos jinobeses casos, que si a S. Mg. y a sus ministros no
nos combiniese cumplir nuestras palabras, no me bería harto de su sangre."

2 For example, Braudel (1966) cites the case of Michael Cantacuzenus, who was hanged on the
orders of the sultan in 1578 in order to seize his wealth. Cases such as these—similar to the pro-
scriptions that dealt such a blow to Roman aristocracy in the late republic (Mommsen 1881)—
became exceedingly rare in western Europe after 1500.

different than that of the last group, few were willing to lend to Philip IV after the Templars' end. In fact, in both medieval England and France, where monarchs had defaulted and turned on their creditors, royals found it hard to borrow afterward. Philip II had to reschedule his debts several times, but his creditors were never persecuted. As we will see, the spirit of loan agreements was upheld consistently (even if the king did not always fulfill them to the letter).

Sustaining sovereign borrowing on a vast scale—indeed, a modern scale—cannot be taken for granted. In this chapter we put forward our explanation: Philip II's borrowing needs were so large that he could not do without future loans by Genoese lenders. Since these lenders were strongly connected among themselves, they "acted as one" in times of crisis; none cut a side deal, despite numerous offers from the royal camp. Attempts to lure in bankers from outside the circle of Genoese came to nothing. Faced with a dominant "coalition" that could effectively deny him the means to borrow and fight in the future, Philip II always came back to the negotiating table, offering solutions to his bankers that were fair and broadly in line with the original agreements. Sovereign lending—and the lives and limbs of his creditors—were effectively protected by their market power.

Our argument is based on a close analysis of our full database of asientos combined with bankers' correspondence and the eventual settlement of the 1575 bankruptcy. This shows that bankers imposed effective lending moratoriums when the king failed to service old debts. Additional sanctions—though perhaps attempted—were ineffective. Genoese bankers provided two-thirds of short-term loans in overlapping partnerships, effectively forming a network or coalition. This lending structure created a web of multilateral obligations. As a result, lending moratoriums stopped the king's access to credit: no network members broke rank; no preexisting lender from outside the network lent to him; and no new bankers supplied funds. The reason, we contend, is that bankers who "cheated" by lending during the moratorium would have faced severe penalties. Network members could hurt each other financially by seizing cross-posted collateral or failing to make payments due. Outsiders also did not enter since they feared being defaulted on by the king.

Philip II's borrowing can be explained without punishments or banker irrationality. Instead, we document the importance of lenders' incentive structures and banker collusion, using archival evidence. Our results are among the first to provide empirical support for models of sovereign lending that rely only on the borrower's need for intertemporal smoothing and lateral enforcement among creditors. This finding is significant because it offers direct empirical proof for reputation-based models of sovereign lending where cheat-the-cheater incentives play a major role.

We begin our analysis summarizing how debt has worked over the last two centuries and how economic theory has approached the issue of sovereign debt in general. In the second part of this chapter, we demonstrate how lender collusion among the Genoese, cooperating in a network structure, kept the system of government borrowing going.

THE FUNDAMENTAL PROBLEM OF SOVEREIGN DEBT: THE ABILITY TO BORROW

> An economist is someone who sees something that works
> in practice and wonders if it would work in theory.
> —Ronald Reagan

For modern-day economics, the existence of sovereign (cross-border) debt contracts is a puzzle. Government spending can be financed by a mix of borrowing, taxes, and seigniorage. Borrowing today implies that revenue from the latter two sources of funding needs to increase in the future if the debt is to be repaid. Default on domestically issued debt can also be avoided, for example, by changing the tax treatment of bondholders. Within a country, government debt mainly has a redistributive effect, shifting the burden of funding the government between taxpayers, lenders, and holders of currency. The origins of government borrowing actually lie in a semicoercive structure: Italian city-states such as Venice initially forced their elites to lend. These loans could then be traded in secondary markets, and interest was paid on them (Kirshner 1996; Stasavage 2011).[3]

The defining problem of sovereign debt is that foreign governments are normally not subject to contract enforcement by courts in other countries (Panizza, Sturzenegger, and Zettelmeyer 2009). Cross-border borrowing is different from domestic transactions because the bondholders are not under the rule of the borrower.[4] International loans are extended not because the

---

3 In addition, cities in northern France and the Low Countries sold annuities from the thirteenth century onward (Tracy 1985).

4 One (important) caveat is that states have successfully restructured bonds issued under their own national law, but held by foreigners. Greece in 2012 is a case in point.

alternative is taxation or expropriation; rulers have no direct power to co-erce lenders into offering any funds. Foreign lenders need to be convinced that they will obtain a return on their investment.

HOW DEBT HAS WORKED

Over the last two centuries, sovereign debt has on the whole been profitable for lenders. Based on a comprehensive data collection exercise, Lindert and Morton (1989) analyze the returns for bondholders during the period 1850–1970. They find that on average, creditors made money, despite the fact that 106 countries defaulted a total of 250 times in the last two centuries (Tomz and Wright 2007). The excess return compared to loans to a benchmark "home" sovereign (the United Kingdom or United States) amounted to 0.42 percent. This is much less than the 1.81 percent return differential promised by the original loan contracts, but it implies risk-neutral investors clearly benefited from exposure to cross-border lending.[5]

This is not to say that there weren't severe losses; many bondholders lost their shirts over the centuries. For instance, investors in Argentine debt lost on average 17 percent annually during the period 1992–2001 (Sturzenegger and Zettelmeyer 2008). Elsewhere, investors earned extremely rich returns. Holders of Egyptian debt in the last two centuries, for example, were prom-ised 6.7 percent annually and received 6.2 percent—a full 253 basis points above the return on alternative benchmark bonds issued by the investors' domestic government (Lindert and Morton 1989). Similarly, investors in Bra-zilian bonds between 1992 and 2001 earned an annual return of over 16 per-cent. Barry Eichengreen and Richard Portes (1989a) analyzed returns on ster-ling and dollar bonds during the 1920s and 1930s. They also find modest, though positive, compensation for risk overall.[6]

If sovereign debt on average "works," how do we make sense of its success? The theoretical literature grapples with the question of why sovereign lend-ing can exist at all. It can be divided into two broad approaches: sanctions and reputation. Papers in the reputation tradition argue that the need to

---

5 The argument is strengthened if we take into account the diversification benefits of foreign lending (Chabot and Kurz 2010).
6 They also conclude that British investors fared markedly better than US ones, who mainly lent to the countries that experienced trouble in the 1930s. In part, the UK policy of steering investment toward the British Empire helped to avoid the worst losses.

smooth consumption is key: if a borrower fails to honor their contract, credit will dry up. The borrower will be markedly worse off, being unable to borrow in hard times. In contrast, the sanctions literature argues that without penalties above and beyond the mere exclusion from future borrowing, sovereign lending cannot exist. Sanctions range from trade embargoes to military intervention. Here we review the theory and evidence supporting each approach, and also discuss what happens when restructuring becomes necessary. Finally, we put the case of Habsburg Spain in the context of predictions from the modern literature.

SANCTIONS

Without sanctions, no sovereign debt can be issued. This is the argument made by Jeremy Bulow and Kenneth Rogoff (1989), who analyze a model in which the principal benefit of servicing debt is consumption smoothing. When a sovereign can sign insurance contracts, purchase assets, or make deposits in a bank, he can always make himself better off by first defaulting and then using "self-insurance" (ibid.). The implication of this reasoning is that no sovereign debt can exist in equilibrium, no matter how great the need to smooth is, if there are alternative ways to transfer resources across time. In Bulow and Rogoff's setup, sanctions are the only factor that can make borrowing possible. If lenders receive help from their own governments—dispatching gunboats, say—then penalties can be so painful that loans will be repaid. Importantly, penalties have to go beyond the withholding of credit: punishment *in addition to a moratorium by the existing lender* is necessary to make sovereign borrowing feasible.

Over the last two hundred years, there are examples of both trade sanctions and armed intervention—but they are exceedingly rare. Carlos Díaz-Alejandro (1983) argued that Argentina did not default in the 1930s to avoid trade restrictions from lenders, but the claim is controversial (Tomz 2007). In other episodes, the mere *threat* of trade sanctions and expropriation of trade revenues may have improved outcomes for creditors. In the 1930s, for instance, the United Kingdom threatened to interfere with German trade if bondholders were not paid; Germany backed away from defaulting on its payments to British creditors (Eichengreen and Portes 1989a).

Direct military intervention constituted an effective punishment strategy. For example, Egypt first lost control of its customs revenues after suspending payments in the 1870s. Britain took over the running of the khedive's finances, before making Egypt a part of the empire (Mitchener and Weidenmier 2010). So-called supersanctions—interventions with military force or the threat thereof—effectively reduced bond spreads. In 1904, the United States extended the Monroe Doctrine—the "Roosevelt Corollary." It called for intervention in case of debt delinquency; Latin American bonds rallied sharply in response (Mitchener and Weidenmier 2005). Supersanctions were effective but uncommon. The British government generally held to the "doctrine that if investors choose to buy the bonds of a foreign country carrying a high rate of interest in preference to British Government Bonds . . . they cannot claim that the British government is bound to intervene in the event of default."[7]

Andrew Rose (2005) argues that defaults coincide with a collapse in trade (contributing to lower output), and that this effectively constitutes a "punishment." This is in line with Phillip Lane's (2004) finding that countries more open to trade can support greater external debts. Rose shows that the volume of exports and imports between creditor and debtor countries shrinks substantially during a payment stop.[8] Eduardo Borensztein and Ugo Panizza (2009) analyze a more comprehensive data set on trade at the industry level; they discover that exporters suffer—but only for relatively short periods. This effect is compensated for by a decline in competing imports for domestic industries (Lanau 2008).

The sanctions view receives support from calibrated models of sovereign borrowing. Even permanent exclusion from debt markets can only support relatively low levels of debt (Arellano and Heathcote 2010). Mark Aguiar and Gita Gopinath (2006) demonstrate that in their model, the value of smoothing consumption around a stable long-term trend is small and cannot sustain much lending.[9] If there is an additional output penalty of 2 percentage points of GDP during a default, however, then feasible debt payments increase sharply. These payments can then reach 20 percent of GDP—implying a debt-to-GDP ratio above 100 percent.

---

7 Sir John Simon, British field officer, 1934, cited in Eichengreen and Portes 1989a.
8 His data also suggest that much of the trade lost between creditor and debtor countries is compensated for by higher exports to other countries. Trade diversion may have welfare costs, but these are typically too small to explain the scale of output declines found in the literature.
9 Laura Alfaro and Fabio Kanczuk (2005) present a similar finding in their calibration of a contingent debt service model.

Output losses in times of default can rationalize why positive and significant borrowing occurs. Calibrated models have more problems matching the frequency of default. The Aguiar and Gopinath model predicts that up to 50 percent of countries will restructure or be in default during peak years. In actual fact, the number is closer to 10–20 percent of countries (Reinhart and Rogoff 2009).[10]

The empirical literature typically finds significant declines in GDP during payment stops (Barro 2001; Cohen 1992). What is less clear is why they happen. Defaults may simply reflect "hard times." In a paper studying the incidence of payments stops for the last two hundred years, Michael Tomz and Mark Wright (2007) show that countries typically default during downturns; more than 60 percent of the default episodes in their sample occurred while output was below trend. Yet the relationship is surprisingly weak: while some 32 percent of all defaults occurred in the 5 percent of observations in their sample with the biggest output declines, fully one-fifth happened in countries with mild downturns.[11]

To sum up, it is apparent that painful sanctions have been used to ensure the repayment of sovereign debt. This is consistent with the predictions from models in the style of Bulow and Rogoff (1989). What is less obvious is if the magnitudes and frequency of sanctions are sufficient to explain the existence of sovereign debt in the first place—and if reputation is not a better explanation for cross-border lending on average.

REPUTATION

The reputation camp argues that the threat to cut off future lending is sufficient to make sovereign borrowing feasible (Eaton and Gersovitz 1981; Eaton and Fernandez 1995). If a borrower defaults, there may be no way to punish them, but withholding future funds can be sufficient to force compliance. The need to smooth consumption is a sufficiently strong motivating force. If a borrower defaults now, their access to funds in the future will suffer. This is going to be painful because access to credit matters the most in hard times.

---

10 Scaled by output, the average is lower—around 5 percent—although the peak during the 1930s still approaches 40 percent.

11 Using higher-frequency data, Eduardo Levy-Yeyati and Ugo Panizza (2011) demonstrate that defaults typically occur at the lowest point of output during a recession and that many recoveries start in the next quarter.

Jonathan Eaton and Mark Gersovitz (1981) offer one of the earliest and most influential contributions to this literature. They assume that a defaulter can never borrow again.[12] The threat of exclusion from credit markets consequently can sustain lending. As the authors acknowledge, permanent exclusion is an unrealistic assumption. In the language of game theory, such a strategy is not "renegotiation proof"; both borrower and lender will probably be better off if the defaulter is permitted access to loans eventually. Defaults, in reality, have always been followed by renegotiations. While these can take a long time, there are no examples of permanent exclusion from lending markets (Benjamin and Wright 2009; Reinhart and Rogoff 2009).

With renegotiation, inefficient penalties can be avoided, but the amount of debt that can be sustained will be lower (Bulow and Rogoff 1989). The need to impose unrealistic, permanent exclusion from credit markets is also avoided if defaults are "excusable." Herschel Grossman and John Van Huyck (1988) present a model where lenders try to determine the nature of borrowers. These borrowers come in two types: good and bad. Both can default. The former simply want to smooth consumption; if shocks are extreme, they may be better off defaulting. The latter will be inclined to default in all states of the world. Permanent exclusion makes no business sense for the "good" borrowers; they were simply unlucky. The "bad" types, on the other hand, will rationally be excluded permanently. They may have received funds in the first place, owing to uncertainty and asymmetric information, but they cannot tap the market again.

Excusable defaults are, in effect, a form of insurance against adverse shocks; lenders know in advance that there is a chance that times will turn out to be sufficiently bad for the borrower to default. In that case, they will price the loan accordingly, in the same way as an insurance company will charge a premium in exchange for having to pay out substantial amounts of money when, say, a fire devastates a building. The excusable default argument has the advantage that it can reconcile the existence of sovereign lending with the history of frequent (and repeated) defaults since 1500 (Reinhart, Rogoff, and Savastano 2003). Excusable defaults are a de facto way of making sovereign debt state dependent, thereby allowing governments to reduce the burden of debt in bad states of the world.

---

12 Kenneth Kletzer (1984) supplies another early example of a reputation-based model. Jonathan Eaton and Raquel Fernandez (1995) provide a survey of this literature.

The existence of multiple lenders can modify incentives. A lending relationship may unravel if new lenders enter the market; without sanctions, the new lender may be able to "steal" the customer, offering mutually beneficial arrangements after a default. The old lender is not paid, and the new one splits the gains from intertemporal trade with the borrower. In a classic paper, Kenneth Kletzer and Brian Wright (2000) analyze the incentive structure in an anarchic environment when neither borrower no lender can credibly commit. There, the existence of an additional lender can be shown to produce no breakdown of the lending relationship. The reason is that there is a strong incentive for existing lenders to "cheat the cheater"—that is, offer even better terms to the borrower if a new lender enters and breaks a moratorium.

Sovereign debt theory has typically treated domestic and foreign borrowers as clearly distinct. This is not necessarily accurate; bonds are tradable, and can be passed from, for instance, a bondholder abroad to one in the same jurisdiction as the borrower. Since there are some reasons for governments to treat investors in the same country more generously, the imperfect nature of market segmentation may actually help to rationalize the existence of cross-border debt markets. If in a crisis foreigners can always sell to domestic investors, then the absence of third-party enforcement is much less important (Broner, Martin, and Ventura 2010).

In the sovereign debt literature, the commitment problem is typically on the borrower's side. One alternative to servicing debt in the Bulow and Rogoff approach is to save and draw down balances in bad times. This requires access to a safe "storage technology" for savings. If bankers can also default, however, this will affect the sustainability of debt; smoothing can now only be achieved by maintaining access to credit. In this case, the reputation of the borrower matters more and may be sufficient to allow cross-border lending (Cole and Kehoe 1995). Intuitively, in a world with "Swiss bankers," Bulow and Rogoff's no-lending result goes through; in a world without them, only those borrowers who establish profitable relationships with their (untrustworthy) bankers can borrow.

In Kletzer and Wright's (2000) approach, banks cannot commit to offering deposit contracts in the style of Bulow and Rogoff; hence, reputational concerns and cheat-the-cheater mechanisms can ensure that lending exists in equilibrium. Going even further, Wright (2002) shows that if banks have some degree of market power, lending can be sustained even if banks can offer any type of insurance contract. In a modification of Eaton and Gersovitz's model, Wright demonstrates that as long as there are important benefits from syndicated lending (that is, a single bank cannot satisfy all the needs of a borrower), cooperation between banks is necessary. The more they "act as one," the easier it is to extend credit, even if alternative ways of insuring income risks exist. Reputation, in this context, matters, yet it is the reputation of intermediaries for cooperating in punishing recalcitrant borrowers and not the reputation of borrowers that is critical.

Harold Cole and Patrick Kehoe (1998) analyze an alternative way in which reputation alone can sustain large amounts of debts. They examine a model in which reputation in one area—such as debt repayment—spills over into reputation in other interactions. The more an opportunistic default damages the ability to conduct essential business in other areas, the more lending will be feasible in equilibrium.

Both the sanctions and reputations approaches—in their simplest form—imply that defaults should never be observed in equilibrium. There are two ways to rationalize their existence. One approach uses informational frictions and contends that payment suspensions are basically "misunderstandings"—mainly because the borrower did not understand the consequences of not paying (Atkeson 1991). The second alternative is to consider defaults as a way to make lending markets "complete." Most loan covenants do not contemplate alternative states of the world, forcing the borrower to repay regardless of their financial health. Negative shocks to a borrower's servicing capacity can therefore make the cost of repaying debt extremely high. Under such conditions, it is often better for the borrower not to pay. Lenders realize this at the time they make the loan (Grossman and Van Huyck 1988). As long as ex ante expectations are not violated, there is no reason for the credit intermediation process to unravel. Signs of an excusable default are that they occur in verifiably bad states of the world.

So far we have only discussed those cases where borrowers unilaterally decide to default or not. Cole and Kehoe (1996) focus on a case where lenders must decide to roll over the maturing debt of a sovereign. If they decide to lend, the borrower will honor their debts, and if they do not extend fresh credit to replace the ones falling due, it can be in the sovereign's interest to default. In particular, if the maturity of debt is low, countries will find it optimal to stop payments if there is a "run" on their debt. This gives rise to multiple equilibriums. If all lenders are happy to extend credit, a country will not default; if some are worried that they will not be repaid and refuse to roll over debt, a generalized run can break the incentive-compatibility of the initial contract.

IMPLICATIONS FOR EMPIRICAL RESEARCH

Both the reputation and sanctions views can marshal a measure of empirical support, but many doubts remain. If the search for a single theoretical model of sovereign debt and default that fits all facts in all time periods is in vain, we should study what made sovereign lending feasible during key episodes. Confronting the predictions of theoretical models of sovereign debt with data is, by its very nature, difficult; many of the predictions concern incentives for players, not their observable actions.

Sanctions models at least offer easily testable predictions once defaults occur. Reputation models, in contrast, are even harder to examine in light of empirical evidence. Recent models of contracting under anarchy, where enforcement and punishment reflect the incentive structure among lenders, are equally difficult to test. The case of Habsburg Spain is especially important because the quality of information allows us to examine the implications of reputation models in detail. Uniquely, we are able to observe incentives directly for a borrower whose case has historical significance.

Imperial Spain has already served as a testing ground for different sovereign debt models. The school of thought that sees banker folly behind defaults claims Philip II's case as key evidence. Much work on Philip II's borrowing has emphasized the Crown's hopeless financial position.[13] Braudel famously argued that the king's payment stops resulted in major losses for his lenders. To this day, journalists use Castile's bankruptcies to illustrate banker irrationality (*The Economist*, September 23–29, 2006). Also, Reinhart and Rogoff (2009) argue that lending to serial defaulters may not be fully rational, and cite the repeated defaults of Spain as a case in point.[14]

In contrast, Conklin (1998) concluded that effective sanctions sustained lending to Philip. In his view, Imperial Spain's debts in the second half of the sixteenth century provide important support for the sanctions view of international borrowing. When Philip II stopped payments in 1575, his bankers halted all transfers. This stopped wage payments to the Army of Flanders, which mutinied. A sharp setback for Spain ensued and forced the king to settle.

---

13 See, among others, Braudel 1966; Thompson 1994a, 1994b; Lovett 1982.
14 Roland Benabou (forthcoming) offers a model of (individually) rational reality denial.

Table 8. Key predictions of debt models

	Reputation	Sentiment	Sanctions	Cheat-the-cheater
Example	Eaton and Gersovitz 1981	Braudel 1966; Reinhart and Rogoff 2009	Bulow and Rogoff 1989	Kletzer and Wright 2000
Punishment	Lending withheld	None	Sanctions *outside lending relationship*	Lending withheld
Duration	Permanent		Temporary	Temporary, reversed quickly
Defaults observed in equilibrium?	No		No	Yes
Commitment		None	Borrowers cannot commit, but lenders can	None
Banker turnover	Low	High	Low	Low

The purpose of this chapter is to confront theoretical predictions with the Spanish evidence. There are a number of clear implications about what we should expect to see; table 8 gives an overview of the approaches guiding our analysis.

In our view, the data do not support earlier interpretations of Philip's bankruptcies. Sanctions were not effective, and bankers were not irrational in lending to the king. Before we explain why these approaches fall short, we review the specific aspects of the data that we use in building our argument.

DATA

To better understand why Philip II received and retained access to credit, we turn to the new series of asientos we introduced in chapter 3. The series starts in 1566, which means that we have no data on the first two defaults (1557 and 1560).[15] We use the complete set of existing contracts until 1600, two years after Philip's death. While earlier authors used information on

---

15 Rodríguez-Salgado (1988) provides an account of the 1557 default as well as the run-up to the 1560 one.

lending volume (summarized on the first page of each document), the actual loans contain a wealth of additional information that has never been exploited: the identity of lenders, services performed, and other contractual arrangements.[16] We utilize this detailed microdata later in the chapter.

Financial transactions between the bankers and king involved transfers, loans, or exchange operations—usually in combination. Transfers allowed funds to be disbursed in distant locations. Exchange operations normally specified the currencies involved, the exchange rate to be used, and permits for exporting specie. Other details include the place of delivery and repayment, the tax stream for repayment, and transfer and exchange fees. Occasionally, the king posted collateral in exchange for a loan. Other benefits could include lifetime pensions or noble titles. The time of repayment frequently depended on the king's fiscal position (for example, as a function of the silver fleet's annual arrival).[17]

Regular borrowing in Philip's reign started after the resolution of his second bankruptcy. After 1566, the king concluded an average of 12.5 asientos per year—sometimes none, and in other years as many as 38. Their duration varied between a few months and several years (with a maximum of 134 months). The largest contract was for 2.1 million ducats (equivalent to 30 percent of the annual fiscal revenue at the time).[18] The smallest contract was for a mere 1,663 ducats. Table 9 summarizes the key features of our data.

Foreign exchange transactions appear in 42 percent of all contracts. The nominal interest rate stated in the loan documents averages 9.9 percent. It could be as low as 0 percent (in special cases where the loan funded the construction of ecclesiastical buildings) or as high as 16 percent. The actual yield of contracts could sometimes be much higher, depending on the exchange rates used, the valuation of payment instruments, and ad hoc clauses. In one-third of all cases, the king posted collateral (typically juros).

Philip II borrowed from several banking families throughout his reign. No fewer than nine members of the Lomelín family lent to him. The Spinola family contributed twelve lenders, the Gentil ten, the Centurión six, and the Fug-

---

16 The standard series in use is by Ulloa (1977). It suffers from the double counting of asientos contracted by field commanders in Flanders, which left most details to be negotiated later in consolidated contracts between the king and bankers' representatives in Madrid. Our database includes only the final agreements, which superseded those made elsewhere, and fully specified all terms and conditions. For more details, see chapter 3.

17 We discuss these conditional clauses in detail in chapter 7.

18 We exclude the 5 million ducat loan that accompanied the general settlement of 1577 as well as the 7.2 million ducat one that followed the resolution of the 1597 bankruptcy.

Table 9. Descriptive statistics

	Mean	Standard deviation	Minimum	Maximum	N
Principal	190,080	275,853	1,663[a]	2,386,755[b]	438
FX	0.418	0.494	0	1	438
Duration	22.605	20.286	0	134	438
Stated r	0.099	0.039	0	0.16	318
Collateral	0.320	0.467	0	1	438

Note: Principal is given in constant 1565 ducats; FX is a dummy variable for the presence of a foreign exchange transaction; duration is given in months, r is the nominal rate stated in the contract; and collateral is a dummy variable for the presence of collateral.

[a] The minimum value for principal is calculated excluding nine contracts that merely restructured old loans; because they did not result in fresh cash for the king, they are deemed to have a principal of zero.

[b] The maximum loan corresponds to a portion of the general settlement of 1577, which was apportioned between four banking syndicates. The largest contract excluding the settlement was for 2.08 million ducats.

ger five.[19] Often, several members of the same banking family lent in a single contract. On March 13, 1572, for instance, we find Gerónimo and Esteban Grillo providing a loan of 100,000 ecus.[20] The brothers Augustín, Tadeo, and Pablo Gentil join forces in several contracts between 1567 and 1569.[21] Lending in small syndicates composed of members of different families was also common. Of 438 total transactions, 141 had multiple lenders. They account for 30 percent of all money lent.

Lending was heavily concentrated. While 130 individuals from 63 families lent to Philip II, a few account for the bulk of the funds. The top 10 banking families were responsible for more than 70 percent of all money lent. The Spinola, Grimaldo, and Fugger families extended 40 percent of all loans. In contrast, the bottom 48 lenders combined provided less credit than the Spinola family alone. Figure 10 plots the cumulative percentage of the total amount lent to the Crown against the rank of the banking family. A Gini coefficient of 0.73 indicates a highly unequal distribution.

---

19 For bankers residing in Spain, we use the Spanish spelling of the banking families' names throughout. For those residing abroad, such as the Fugger family, we keep the original-language spelling.

20 AGS, Contadurías Generales, Legajo 85. "Gerónimo Grillo y Esteban Grillo. Traslado del asiento con ellos tomado a 13 de marzo de 1572."

21 AGS, Contadurías Generales, Legajos 84 and 85.

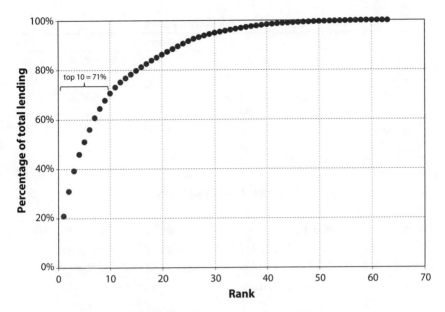

FIGURE 10. Cumulative lending to Philip II by rank of lending family, 1566–1600

Lending relationships proved to be enduring. The Fugger started lending to Charles V early in the century and continued to do so until the death of Philip II in 1596. Jakob Fugger lent in 1519. His nephew, Anton Fugger, did the same in the 1550s, and in 1590 we find Jakob's great-grandson, Marcos Fugger, also supplying credit to the king of Castile.[22] The Grimaldo family lent 27 times between 1566 and 1589. The record holders in terms of frequency were the Spinola, whose members participated in a total of 98 loan contracts over the period 1566–99.

Table 10 summarizes the place of delivery of funds by bankers before and after the 1575 default. Fully 62 percent of the amount borrowed was delivered outside Castile. Flanders was the most important foreign destination for funds. Italy was a distant second, as the Mediterranean fleets were partly funded by local revenue (Parker 1998, 135). Repayment typically took place in Castile. The Spanish Empire, for all its size and might, was mainly financed by the Castilian economy—the strongest in Europe at the time (Alvarez Nogal and Prados de la Escosura 2007).

---

22 The Fugger family never stopped lending for more than nine consecutive years.

Table 10. Place of delivery of asientos

Location	Delivery	
	In 1566 ducats	In percent
Castile	31,407,408	37.8%
Flanders	30,383,774	36.5%
Italy	16,588,412	19.9%
Elsewhere	4,808,984	5.8%
Total	83,188,578	100%

WRONG EXPLANATIONS

Before we put forward our interpretation, we will discuss alternative solutions to the problem of "Why lend to a monarch?" Two are particularly prominent in the literature: banker irrationality and the idea that penalties were crucial for sustaining lending.

IRRATIONALITY AND BANKER TURNOVER

Braudel (1966) argued that Philip II managed to borrow massively, stop payments often, and pay back little because he succeeded in fooling one group of bankers after another.[23] Sequential default and financial ruin of this kind require that each group of financiers thought they would be treated better than the last ones—a form of banker irrationality. Journalistic references to Philip's defaults frequently make this point, arguing that "Genoese lenders' indulgence of Philip II of Spain's expensive taste for warfare caused not only the first sovereign bankruptcy in 1557, but the second, third and fourth as well" (*The Economist*, September 23–29, 2006).

Did successive waves of lemming-like lenders—first from Germany, then from Italy, and finally from Portugal and Spain—enter the borrowing game? We examine the nationality of bankers and turnover ratios in our database,

---

23 Braudel (1966, 362) argued that each bankruptcy ruined another group of lenders. These were then in turn promptly replaced by a new group (and nationality), which, lemming-like, readily extended credit to the king. He also argued that "the Fugger and their acolytes . . . were to withdraw (apart from brief reappearances in 1575 and 1595) from the dangerous business of the asientos," and that "the decree of 1st September, 1575, then, was a blow struck at the entire fortunes of the Genoese. . . . To the Genoese this brought massive losses" (ibid., 351–52, 355). We argue that Braudel is mistaken in both cases.

taking the default of 1575 as a potential breakpoint. The 438 loan transactions demonstrate that the composition of financiers remained stable throughout. After 1575, the share of Spaniards declined from 28.8 to 25.6 percent. The German bankers, who were allegedly burned by the first bankruptcy, acted as a continuous source of funding. Their share more than doubled—from 4.3 to 10.9 percent—after the third bankruptcy. The Genoese provided 67 percent of the loans before the 1575 bankruptcy and 64 percent after it. Thus there is little to suggest that the king's access to credit depended on the repeated fooling of bankers from different countries.

Was the frequency of repeat business unusually low after the bankruptcy? We define repeat lenders as those who offered funds during one of the preceding 50 transactions. This gives us a time-varying measure of banker turnover. The volume of lending by bankers without a prior relationship was small throughout. During the period as a whole, an average of 85.4 percent of borrowing came from bankers who had lent recently. In the seven years before the 1575 suspension, 91 percent of lending was repeat business; for the seven years thereafter, this figure was 89 percent.[24] Repeat lending continued after 1575, and much of Philip's borrowed money came from bankers who had lent to him earlier. This is inconsistent with the idea that the king's default brought ruin to successive waves of lenders.

Despite the frequency of repeat business, a group of financiers whose expectations were disappointed by the bankruptcy and its resolution may have decided to cease lending. To examine this possibility, we look at *exits* from the pool of active bankers. Figure 11 shows the evolution of funds provided by bankers that will not lend again.

Few lenders terminated their lending relationship with Philip II. Conditional on having lent in a single transaction, the same banker had an 88 percent chance of entering into another contract. Crucially, the period before the bankruptcy of 1575 does not show a spike in bankers who subsequently exit our sample. Bankers who lent before the bankruptcy had a 3.8 percent likelihood of dropping out of the business, compared with 4.4 percent afterward. Because our data set ends in 1600, those lending for the first time later in our sample period have less of a chance to enter into repeat business. This explains the gradual increase of the proportion in the "never again" category

---

24 For a complete yearly chart of repeat lending, see the appendix in Drelichman and Voth 2011a.

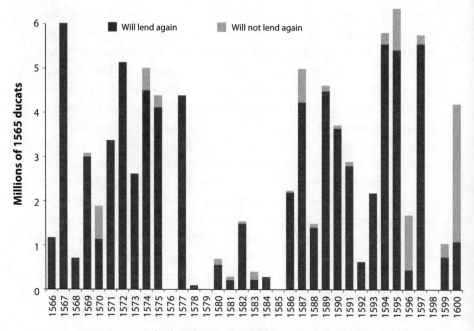

FIGURE 11. Annual volume lent in terms of future interactions with the king

over the final few years. There was no discontinuity after the payment stop, which suggests that expectations cannot have been disappointed on a major scale.

In figure 12 we refine the analysis; we examine how many of the lenders to Philip II after 1575 already had been lenders beforehand (and hence were probably affected by the payment stop). We see that the overwhelming majority of funds lent after the default actually came from bankers who had been lending to Castile before the decreto. The proportion declines over time, as new entrants also lend to the king. Still, well into the 1590s, up to half of all money advanced to the king came from lenders who were already in business before 1575. Based on this evidence, it cannot be the folly of bankers—lured into lending by the king, only to be ruined by repeated defaults—that accounts for the continued access to cross-border financing.

Our results suggest that banker irrationality is not a probable explanation for continued lending to Philip II. The same banking families, from the same countries, supplied funds to the monarch throughout his reign. They did so regardless of the defaults: the rate of banker turnover did not change after

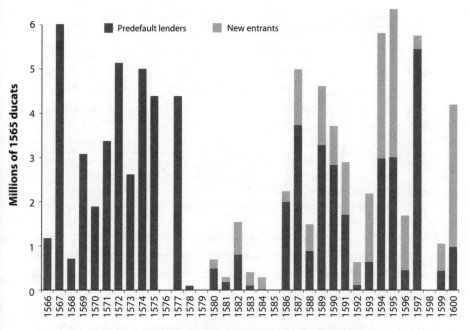

FIGURE 12. Value of lending by new entrants and by bankers with
a pre-default relationship, 1566–1600

the payment stops. This makes it unlikely that excessively optimistic lender sentiment, as proposed by Braudel, was responsible for the king's access to funds.

PENALTIES: THE "TRANSFER STOP" THAT WASN'T

Conklin (1998) held that sovereign lending to Philip II was sustainable because Genoese bankers had a powerful sanctioning mechanism: stopping transfers to Flanders. After the 1575 bankruptcy, bankers would have used this penalty, cutting off funding for the Army of Flanders. This would in turn have caused the 1576 mutiny, which culminated in the Sack of Antwerp. A. W. Lovett (1982, 2) similarly concluded that "the financial prostration of the monarchy led directly to the Sack of Antwerp by Spanish mutineers in the early days of November 1576." The mutiny and ensuing massacre were highly damaging to the Spanish position. Both the loyal and rebel provinces joined forces in the Pacification of Ghent; Spanish troops were expelled from the

Table 11. Amounts transferred to Flanders by bankers (in ducats)

Year	Transfers	Year	Transfers
1566	390,111	1572	434,248
1567	1,830,243	1573	925,937
1568	92,040	1574	1,479,735
1569	180,394	1575	1,610,422
1570	130,384	1576	889,988[a]
1571	0	1577	1,192,933

Sources: AGS, Contadurías Generales, Legajos 86–93; Vázquez de Prada 1962, 330–33.
Note: The 1577 value is the amount transferred before the medio general.
[a] In addition to this amount, Conklin reports that the Crown physically transported slightly under four hundred thousand ducats to Flanders in 1576.

Low Countries. Of all the events that facilitated the eventual independence of the Unified Provinces, the Sack of Antwerp is arguably among the most important. It took until 1584 for Spain just to regain its previous footing in terms of territory controlled. Having learned his lesson, the king would have quickly settled with his bankers. According to Conklin, the Sack of Antwerp constitutes a "sanction" in the sense of the modern sovereign debt literature: a painful penalty, beyond a simple exclusion from capital markets, that ultimately forced the king to service his debts.

To test if a dramatic shortfall of cash was responsible for the Sack of Antwerp, we reconstruct total transfers from the asientos in our database and complement them with transfers not contained in lending contracts, as reported by Valentín Vázquez de Prada (1962). Table 11 shows the volumes transferred to Flanders between 1566 and 1577, as derived from the archival record.[25]

After the decree suspending payments from September 1575, the Genoese indeed stopped all lending and transfers. Transferring funds by sea or overland was nearly impossible (Lovett 1982).[26] Other bankers did not lend, but they moved funds. In total, German and Spanish bankers transferred 2.1 million ducats during the two years of the suspension (Ulloa 1977, 795–96). Combined with the 400,000 ducats transported directly to Flanders, an average of

25 Our coding of the asientos in the archive of Simancas allows us to separate the transfers to Flanders from those to other destinations, which were not part of the penalty suggested by Conklin. For other discussions of the transfers during the bankruptcy years, see Lapeyre 1953, 22; Vázquez de Prada 1962, 330–33; Ulloa 1977, 795–96.
26 In 1569, funds earmarked for the Duke of Alba's troops were seized by Elizabeth II after the ships had to contend with adverse weather in the English Channel (Lovett 1982).

1.25 million ducats per year was available.[27] This was plenty; in the four years prior to the decree, average remittances ran at only 1.1 million per annum. Thus, after 1575, the Crown had access to more money than before in Flanders. Only the peak remittances of 1574–75 were higher than transfers in 1576 and 1577.

As with many early modern armies, troops in Flanders often went unpaid for extended periods. Mutinies were a regular occurrence; Spanish troops there rebelled thirty-two times during the reign of Philip II. During the mutiny of the garrison of Antwerp in 1598, for example, one man was owed back pay since 1584. Even if this was extreme, pay received was normally only a fraction of what was owed. For instance, mutineers at Zechem in 1594 had received 66 percent of the promised wages during 1582–90 (Parker 1972).

There are therefore two diametrically opposed interpretations of the mutinies in the Army of Flanders. One sees them as a desperate response to a dramatic shortfall in financial resources, with the mutiny leading to the Sack of Antwerp as its most egregious case (as argued by Conklin). The alternative sees mutinies as a form of wage bargaining. The scope for settlement should increase when the size of the pie grows. The savage attack of Antwerp is not the logical extension of this arrangement but rather a dramatic illustration of the system breaking down.

To distinguish between these two hypotheses, we use annual data on the frequency of mutinies and transfers to Flanders. If the first hypothesis is correct, mutinies should increase in frequency as transfers fall short. If they are in effect an attempt at bargaining over (back) pay, then an increase in royal resources in the Low Countries should create more conflict. To explore whether mutinies in general were associated with low transfer levels, we compile the number of mutinies declared in the Army of Flanders each year between 1573 and 1598. In table 12, we regress these data on several variables that may have affected the rebelliousness of Spanish soldiers. These include the amount transferred to Flanders, both in the current year and previous ones; the total cost of the Flanders campaign; and the cost of settling mutinies.[28]

---

27 Note that the only evidence for this transfer is Conklin (1998). The source that he cites does not contain information on this particular transaction.

28 Both the transfers to Flanders and cost of the Flanders campaign exclude the cost of settling mutinies. For the data on mutinies and their cost, see Parker 2004; Tenace 1997. The cost of the Flanders campaign is part of the military expenditure series presented in chapter 4. The data on transfers are from our database of asientos.

Table 12. Determinants of mutinies, 1573–98

	Dependent variable is number of mutinies				
	(1)	(2)	(3)	(4)	(5)
Transfers	0.349**	0.058	0.076	-0.027	0.109
	(2.14)	(0.24)	(0.30)	(-0.10)	(0.37)
Transfers (t-1)		0.469**	0.484*	0.418*	0.169
		(2.18)	(1.89)	(1.85)	(0.64)
Transfers (t-2)			0.013		
			(0.06)		
Flanders cost				0.162	0.153
				(0.76)	(0.68)
Mutiny costs					1.693**
					(2.22)
Constant	-0.452	-0.716**	-0.842**	-1.008*	-1.215**
	(-1.53)	(-2.10)	(-2.13)	(-1.89)	(-2.09)
N	25	25	25	25	25
Pseudo-R^2	0.06	0.14	0.16	0.15	0.22

Note: Poisson regressions. Values in parentheses are z-statistics. Significance levels are * <10% and ** <5%. All independent variables are expressed in millions of ducats.

The first three columns regress the number of mutinies on the value of transfers in the same year and with up to two lags. The few significant coefficients have a positive sign; mutinies follow years of exceptionally large transfers. This effect persists if we add the total cost of the Flanders campaign, which itself is not significant (column [4]). In column (5), we add the cost of settling mutinies. This last variable is positive and significant, as expected: when mutinies break out, the cost of settling them increases. Furthermore, including it eliminates the importance of the transfers and military expenditure variables. We conclude that mutinies were not caused by a reduction in transfers from Castile. If anything, mutinies occurred in years with larger than normal transfers. This strongly suggests that mutinies were not violent responses to a dramatic shortfall in resources; as their common occurrence suggests, they were part and parcel of the bargaining process between field commanders, the king, and ordinary soldiers.

As a matter of fact, as a result of frequent mutinies, the system had evolved a highly standardized procedure for dealing with the issue of back pay and soldier grievances. In normal times, the mutinous troops would elect a leader, expel all those who were not joining forces with them, and enter into direct negotiations with the government. Demands could include, in addition to back pay, a pardon for the mutineers, a general muster (giving soldiers a chance to join another regiment), a hospital, religious care, and cheap provisions from government granaries (Parker 1972). If resolving a mutiny took time, the government would normally move mutineers to a town of lesser military importance and provide a minimum allowance (*sustento*) until enough money had arrived to pay off the troops. Mutineers were typically even paid for the months during which they had refused orders. It is unsurprising, then, that as Parker (1973) put it, "few fighting forces could boast of as many mutinies or of mutinies better organized than the Army of Flanders."

In the run-up to the Sack of Antwerp, the 1576 mutiny was neither the biggest one (in terms of the number of soldiers involved), nor the longest, nor the most costly to resolve (based on the final settlement for the mutinous troops). It began when unpaid troops demanded their due after successfully taking the town of Zierikzee. The mutiny was more expensive than preceding ones, but not by a large margin; the final cost was 633,000 ecus—some 89,000 higher than the previous one (also in Antwerp, in 1574). Many of the subsequent mutinies were larger, involved more people, lasted longer, and resulted in higher demands for back pay. By the standards of the Eighty Years' War, the amount owed in 1576 was not unusually large. If transfers were ample and mutinies a common occurrence, what explains the unusual violence of 1576 and its grave political and military consequences for Spain?

In contrast to the civilized negotiation process that soldiers and administrators typically engaged in during a mutiny, the culmination of the 1576 episode was dramatic indeed. After storming the city walls of Antwerp on November 4, 1576, Spanish mercenaries raped, burned, and pillaged indiscriminately for three days. More than seven thousand inhabitants in a previously loyal city lost their lives. Citizens who escaped with life and part of their property often had to pay protection money. The events became known as the Spanish Fury and greased the wheels of Protestant anti-Spanish propaganda.[29]

Why did an everyday mutiny turn into a massacre and major setback for Spanish ambitions in the Low Countries? What was missing were loyal officials willing to carry out Philip II's orders, disbursing cash sent and finding a settlement with the mutineers (as the king repeatedly urged his appointees

---

29 The Sack of Antwerp further enhanced Spain's Black Legend—the view that Spain acted in both the colonies and Europe with greater moral callousness than other powers.

FIGURE 13. The Sack of Antwerp. *Scenes of the Spanish Fury at Antorff, 1576,*
Flemish school, sixteenth century.

to do). The untimely death of the governor-general, Don Luis de Requesens,
in March 1576 created a power vacuum. As recognized in some of the historical literature, Don John of Austria's delay in taking up his post as the
new governor-general allowed anti-Spanish sentiment to gain strength.[30]
Based on a close reading of the letters between the king and local officials,
we are able to take the argument further. The Council of State, dominated by
Dutch nobles, saw the mutiny as an opportunity to end the war by thwarting
Spain's military ambitions. It therefore decided not to employ the funds
sent for the purpose of pacifying the mutineers. To demonstrate the sa-
lience of this view, we first show that the Crown never lacked the funds to
pay off the mutineers, and then explore the tension between the king and
Council of State.

---

30 "It was the outbreak of a large-scale mutiny . . . in conjunction with the increasingly strong
desire for peace in the southern Netherlands and Don John's procrastination in taking up this
post as governor-general, which, in July and August 1576, led to a spectacular improvement of
the rebel position" (Swart 1978, 25).

In August 1576, Spain's total debt with the mutineers stood at 123,000 ecus.[31] Between May and August 1576, Philip II had sent 400,000 ecus to Flanders—300,000 of which were earmarked for the mutineers. On August 27, 1576, the king wrote to the Council of State:

> In an attempt to remedy matters as much as possible, we [the king] have sent a few days ago a bill of exchange for 200,000 ecus, in addition to the other 100,000 ecus already sent, so that you have the means to satisfy the demands of the soldiers. (Gachard 1861, doc. 1699)

By mid-September, the Fugger family alone had transferred 600,000 ecus to the Netherlands on Philip's behalf. The total transferred after the bankruptcy and before the Sack of Antwerp amounted to 732,000 ecus. This is approximately five times more than the debt at that time with the mutineers and, in fact, more than the eventual settlement. Philip II thus never lacked the funds to put an end to the mutiny or the means to transfer them to the Low Countries. The mutiny and Sack of Antwerp do not reflect a catastrophic shortfall of cash, caused by the bankruptcy of 1575. The money was in Flanders already. It just failed to reach the soldiers owing to political brinkmanship, as we show next.

In August, the king urged the caretaker government to deal generously with the mutineers. He insisted that "it is necessary to avoid this [further conflict with the mutineers] by all possible means, as we expect you will do, by negotiating with one and the other, as well as using the money that we have sent to you in the past days" (ibid., doc. 1699). Yet on August 17, 1576, the Council of State wrote to the king, telling him that all attempts to subdue the provinces fighting under the lead of the Prince of Orange had failed. The only way forward, it urged, was to settle with the rebels. If the king did not agree, the council asked to be dismissed (ibid., doc. 1692).

By mid-September, the king was in despair. He complained to the council of its lack of "obedience and good intelligence, which ministers should have" because the mutiny had not yet been settled with the funds sent. He then commanded the council to use the 200,000 ecus already provided with the express purpose of satisfying the mutineers (ibid., doc. 1712). In a letter to Gerónimo de Roda, one of Philip's officials in the Low Countries, he empha-

---

31 The Flemish ecu was worth approximately 0.98 ducats at the time. The eventual cost of the settlement was larger, since the mutineers were joined by others and because they received back pay for the months of the mutiny.

sized that there was no problem in transferring funds. In his letter from August 27, the king wrote that he would "try to find other sources of funds, to send via the same [said] person, in order not to leave anything undone, so that with divine kindness it will be possible to achieve the true pacification of our good country over there" (ibid.). Clearly the king's ability to obtain money was the key difficulty—not transferring it. The king underscored that he had good ways of transferring funds through a trusted intermediary with all the right qualities. Money had been available since August 21; it was Philip's express command that it be used to pay off the Spanish and Walloon mutineers.

Again, the Council of State failed to do as it was told. By October 18, Roda reported that the mutineers had received no more than 43,000 ecus, and that without a further 80,000 plus the two months' pay since August, they were unwilling to return to the colors (ibid., doc. 1744). Meanwhile, the Estates of Flanders and Brabant had authorized the raising of local troops to defend against the mutineers. Led by a local nobleman, Jacque de Glimes, these troops then arrested the Council of State and expelled the Spanish members. The Estates next published an edict declaring the Spanish mutineers outlaws who must be put to death (ibid., doc. 1729). Instead of negotiating over back pay in a structured and peaceful way, as was typical, the mutineers were suddenly declared criminals subject to summary execution. This left them with no choice but to use force.

The correspondence between Philip II and his ministers in the Low Countries shows that political events—the untimely death of the governor-general as well as the independent agendas of the local assemblies and nobles—determined why a run-of-the-mill mutiny was not quelled quickly. Philip II was fully aware that paying the troops was important to avoid a major setback. He sent more than enough cash and repeatedly urged his officials to use the standard remedies to mutiny in the Army of Flanders—kindness to the soldiers, disbursement of back pay, and avoidance of conflict. All financial means necessary for a settlement were available from August 1576 onward, three months before the Sack of Antwerp. Instead of following the king's orders, the Council of State along with the Estates of Flanders and Brabant used the mutiny (and death of the governor-general) to pursue their own agenda—making peace with the rebels in Holland and Zeeland, thereby unifying the Low Country provinces with a view to expelling the Spaniards altogether. Deprived of a chance to seek redress from the government in the normal way, the troops were left with few options. They therefore began to sack loyal cities violently—first Aalst and then Antwerp. For the Dutch nobles, this strategy paid off in political terms. After the Sack of Antwerp, the previously loyal cities turned against Spanish rule. As a result of the Pacification of Ghent, the rebellious provinces and formerly loyal ones now joined forces, promulgated religious tolerance, and united in the aim to drive out the Spanish. Don John of Austria, when he finally arrived to take up his post of governor-general, could only do so on the condition that all Spanish troops left.

Did the threat of sanctions or their actual imposition compel Philip II to service their debts? Our new evidence strongly suggests that this is not the case. The decision by the Genoese to stop transfers was not only ineffective; it also made no difference to the mutiny, considered by Conklin as the crucial punishment. Philip II's financial position in 1576 was clearly not comfortable. Yet sanctions proper require a punishment *beyond a stop to normal lending*, and such sanctions never materialized. Whatever the Genoese did in addition to suspending lending obviously did not work.

MARKET POWER AND REPUTATION

Philip II exempted one banking family from the bankruptcy decree: the Fugger. They were essential for transfers between 1575 and 1577, when the vast majority of royal funds that reached Flanders did so through their correspondents. Yet not even the Fugger family lent after 1575. We now describe how this simple fact can help us shed light on what sustained lending to a sovereign monarch such as Philip II.

Lending to the king of Spain happened in an "anarchic" environment, in the sense of Kletzer and Wright (2000). The monarch could not credibly commit to repay his lenders. In many cases, he failed to honor the letter of the contract: more than 20 percent of the loan documents contain detailed references to promised payments that had not been made as agreed in earlier contracts with the same lender. This even applied to juros, widely considered a particularly safe asset. While Philip II never rescheduled juros, payments could be less than promised if they were secured against a poor tax stream.[32]

---

32 At various junctures, the king and his advisers considered forced conversions of juros, but ultimately decided against them. Juro interest reduction would eventually take place in the seventeenth century.

The king had access to few smoothing mechanisms: short-term borrowing, depositing funds with bankers, and long-term borrowing. Given urgent, volatile spending needs, only the first of these mechanisms was practical. Foreign bankers could and did default on the king's deposits. Enforcement across borders was slow and complicated. For example, we know of a case where a Genoese banker failed to return a deposit of 300,000 ducats that he held on behalf of the king. The issue was then settled through the intervention of a second banker, who agreed to lend an equivalent sum at a preferential rate in exchange for the king dropping the proceedings against the banker who defaulted.[33] In such an environment, depositing funds with a banker was not an alternative to borrowing.[34] Issuing juros was not a viable alternative either. New issues required the authorization of the Cortes, and even when authorized, their sale was a drawn-out process. In addition, the same Genoese bankers who dominated the asiento business also enjoyed a near monopoly over the intermediation of juro issuance (Castillo 1963). With more than 150 years of experience operating the Casa di San Giorgio, the Genoese had a keen understanding of a sole financial agent's power when lending to a sovereign. While Castile had no comparable arrangement, Genoese bankers maneuvered to gain a commanding position in both short- and long-term debt markets. When the king defaulted on short-term debt, he found that lenders also held a tight grip on juros—his only alternative way to borrow. Finally, placing long-term debt is usually a more involved operation than contracting short-term loans. Even economies with much more developed financial and economic systems in the twentieth century typically financed wars initially with short-term debt, which they then later consolidated into long-term bonds (Roesler 1967). Just like other warring princes, Philip II could effectively ramp up spending ahead of revenue only through short-term borrowing.

THE GENOESE COALITION

To keep the king from defaulting, incentives other than direct penalties must have been at work. Our data suggest that the lending structure was key. The

33 See AGS, Contadurías Generales, Legajo 84. "Tomás de Marín. Asiento tomado con Pirro Boqui en su nombre."
34 In this sense, the alternative considered by Bulow and Rogoff (1989) was not available to the king.

Genoese provided funds in overlapping groups. Approximately one-third of all transactions involved more than a single banking family.[35] This created a de facto network or alliance of financiers who would act as one—a lenders' coalition. Contemporaries referred to the Genoese as a close-knit group, subject to the same treatment by the king, and acting largely in concert.[36]

Some of the co-lending relationships involved multiple loans by stable groups of bankers. For example, Lucián Centurión and Agustín Spinola together lent no fewer than seven times during 1566–67. In other cases, the co-lending occurred only once. Most of the network members were engaged in repeated interactions with each other. The Grimaldo and Spinola families often co-lent, as did the Judice, Doria, Centurión, and De Negro families. One family stands out as the "spider in the web": the Spinola. Their transactions involved sixteen other banking families as partners. The Doria family, the next most influential, joined forces with seven other dynasties. The Doria and Spinola networks were linked through mutually provided loans as well as by the fact that both families co-lent with the Grimaldo, Lercaro, Marín, and Maluenda families. Many of these families also played a leading role in Genoese politics beginning in the 1270s. Figure 14 provides an overview of the network's structure.

The numbers below family names show the total lending in thousands of 1566 ducats. The thicker lines indicate higher average lending (scaled by the log of lending volume). The Grimaldo, Lomelín, de la Torre, Centurión, Spinola, Grillo, Cattaneo, Lercaro, and Gentil families are all linked in the four contracts stipulated in the medio general, but for clarity of exposition those links are not shown here.

We define all transactions by bankers who co-lent—either through joint loans or sharing business partners—as network lending. This must constitute a lower bound on the actual business and family relationships between bankers. Even under this restrictive definition, bankers in the network accounted for a large share of transactions and lending volume. There are only twenty-seven families (out of sixty-three in total) in the largest network we identify,

---

35 Whether the Genoese with their high degree of collaboration constituted a cartel has been debated in the historical literature (Alvarez Nogal 2003). We do not take a view on their pricing behavior. We refer to them as a network simply because of their co-lending and behavior during the defaults.

36 See, for example, the Fugger correspondence summarized in Karnehm 2003. See also several pieces of official correspondence in De Carlos Morales 2008.

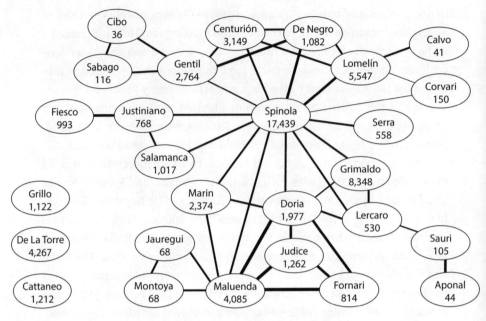

FIGURE 14. The Genoese network

but they account for 72 percent of the principal and almost the same proportion of all transactions (see table 13).

Figure 15 shows network and nonnetwork lending by year. Over time, the size of the network was broadly stable. Before the bankruptcy of 1575, network members accounted for 80 percent of lending; after it, they accounted for 67 percent. There were two years when the king borrowed or transferred funds without any support of network members. In 1576, no banker was

Table 13. Network lending (millions of 1566 ducats)

	Number of		
	Families	Transactions	Volume lent
Network	27	308	59.9
Nonnetwork	36	130	23.2
Total	63	438	83.1
Network	43%	70%	72%
Nonnetwork	57%	30%	28%

Source: AGS, Contadurías Generales, Legajos 86–93.

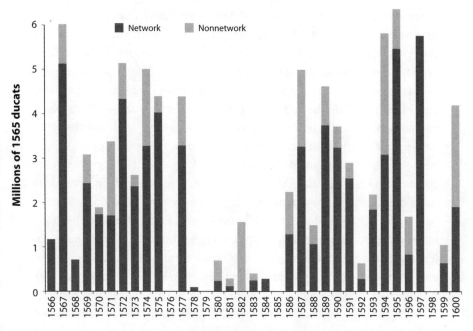

FIGURE 15. Lending by network members, 1566–1600

lending to the king, and the entire amount transacted consisted of transfers by nonnetwork members. In 1582, the king borrowed almost exclusively from the Fugger, the most prominent family outside the network.[37]

Co-lending was not the only way in which the network operated. In many cases, collateral was passed from one banker to the next.[38] This practice made it much more difficult for the king to selectively default on members of the Genoese coalition. Lenders left out of a deal could seize cross-posted collateral. Thus, network cohesion was enhanced by the use of juros. Collecting debts on behalf of other bankers was also common. Often, the king borrowed from one banker and agreed to repay another banker's loan as part of the new deal. The king also promised repayment through other bankers. All these agency relationships hindered side deals.

---

37 The largest loan by the Fugger was for 1.3 million ducats in 1594—a year in which the silver fleets did not sail.

38 See, for example, AGS, Contadurías Generales, Legajo 85, where several loans made by Lorenzo Spinola are collateralized with bonds held by Nicolao de Grimaldo.

For example, the king borrowed 80,000 ducats from Lucián Centurión and Agustín Spinola in 1569.[39] Half the repayment was promised in the form of tax revenue; the other half was from a group of seven Genoese bankers.[40] This type of arrangement made it difficult for the king to default and then enter into a special deal with the Spinola family. The Spinola were substantial backers of Philip, lending the largest quantity (17 million ducats) of all the banking families. Yet in these two contracts alone, had the Spinola cut the other bankers out of any arrangement, funds equal to half the principal could have been seized. Similarly, on March 5, 1595, the king agreed to borrow 330,000 ducats from Francisco and Pedro de Maluenda. Repayment was promised via Adán de Vivaldo, from whom the king also borrowed. Vivaldo, a Spanish banker, did not co-lend with the Genoese in any of our contracts. This illustrates that multilateral relationships among bankers transcended mere co-lending. Some of the relationships that emerge from our sources link members of the network that did not co-lend. The Lomelín and Grimaldo families never joined the same syndicates. Nonetheless, as part of a lending contract between the king and Baltasar Lomelín, in 1588 both Esteban Lomelín and Doña Sasandra de Grimaldo were allowed to change the tax stream against which their long-dated debt was secured (a transaction that increased the value of the debt they held).

Cooperation among bankers also extended beyond lending. In 1567, for instance, Tomás de Marín accepted a deposit of 300,000 ducats from the king in Milan, but then failed to repay. Nicolao de Grimaldo stepped in, agreeing to lend the king the same amount if the case against Marín was dropped. The deposit at Marín's bank was converted into a perpetual rent in favor of the king at 8 percent interest.[41] As another example, in 1587 the king entered into an asiento for a million ducats with Agustín Spinola. In it, the king agreed to drop a number of lawsuits against three other bankers, Lucián Centurión, Antonio Alvarez de Alcócer, and Manuel Caldera.[42] Bankers also used their

---

39 AGS, Contadurías Generales, Legajo 85. "Lucián Centurión y Agustín Spinola. Traslado del asiento con ellos tomado a 2 de mayo de 1569."

40 These bankers were Nicolás and Visconte Cattaneo, Alberto Pinelo, Miguel de Mena, Constantin Gentil, Benito Sabago, and Juan Antonio De Negro. Many of them also lent through syndicated loans with the Spinola and Centurión families.

41 AGS, Contadurías Generales, Legajo 84. "Tomás de Marín. Asiento tomado con Pirro Boqui en su nombre." We never observe Grimaldo and Marín lending together to the king. Still, they both belonged to the network because they extended loans jointly with other bankers.

42 AGS, Contadurías Generales, Legajo 88. "Agustín Spinola, hijo de Francisco difunto. Asiento tomado con él sobre un millón de ducados que provee en Italia."

network clout to force the king to honor his commitments. A 30,000-ecu loan by Francisco Spinola in 1588, say, included a clause that required the king to settle an old debt with Lorenzo Lomelín.[43]

We argue that network membership and syndicated lending were crucial in sustaining sovereign borrowing. For this contention to stick, there should be no other reasons for co-lending. For example, larger loans might require greater resources than those available to a single banking family. Pooling therefore could reflect capacity constraints. The data, however, do not support such an interpretation. Single-family loans are actually slightly larger (by 1 percent) than multifamily loans. Loan duration was similar too—26.4 months for single-family loans versus 25.5 months for the rest. Transfers, another possible reason for co-lending, are also more common in the single-family loans than in the multifamily ones. All other observables, including interest rates, the use of collateral, and contingency clauses, show no major differences. We conclude that loan requirements or simple capacity constraints on the part of lenders cannot be the reason for co-lending.

Just like the European nobility and ruling dynasties, banking families frequently use marriage as a tool to strengthen business links.[44] We use the partial genealogies for seven Genoese banking families documented in the Doria Archive of Genoa to explore the intermarriage among them (Saginati 2004). In figure 16, we add information on intermarriage within the Genoese network. Importantly, there was overlap between co-lending and intermarriage; the connections between the Spinola and the Grimaldo, Gentil, Centurión, and Doria were particularly strong, as were those between the Centurión and the De Negro. In each case, these links involved both financial and family "co-investments." There were also fresh links between network members who had not lent together, such as the Sabago and Doria. Even though our intermarriage data cover only seven families, we find that the six that intermarried among each other while also co-syndicating loans accounted for 47 percent of all network lending.

There were also five other families that intermarried with other network members, but did not co-lend with the families they married into. They con-

---

43 AGS, Contadurías Generales, Legajo 88. "Lo que por mi mandado se asienta y concierta con Francisco Spinola genovés sobre 30,000 escudos."
44 The text of the medio general, for example, specifies that Esteban Lomelín is Nicolao de Grimaldo's son-in-law. AGS, Consejo y Juntas de Hacienda, Libro 42. Similar family relationships are occasionally mentioned in the text of the asientos.

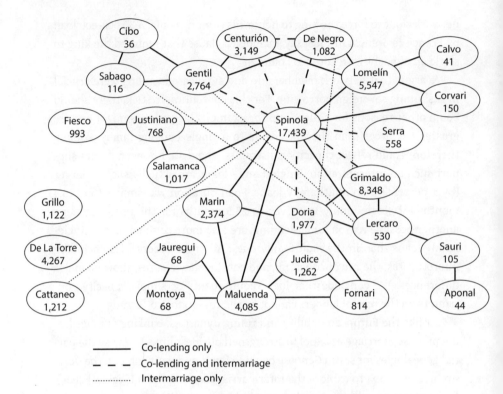

FIGURE 16. Structure of the network based on co-lending and intermarriage

tributed 9.5 percent of total network lending.[45] Co-lending was only one dimension of other key connections. Since our genealogical data is limited, these results constitute a lower bound on the ties that transcended joint lending.

CHEAT-THE-CHEATER ENFORCEMENT

Two factors interacted to make lending to Philip II sustainable: the stability of the bankers' network and its dominant role in lending. The Genoese coordinated their actions closely. Because of his financing needs, Philip II could not do without the Genoese coalition. Therefore, he eventually had to settle with the bankers when they imposed a moratorium on him. This also made it

---

45 Three families both intermarried with network members with who they co-lent and with other network members who did not feature on the same loan documents.

unappealing for outsiders to start lending. This illustrates the significance of market structure, along the lines articulated by Natalia Kovrijnykh and Balázs Szentes (2007) and Mark Wright (2002).

Genoese market power derived from control over the only means that allowed "intertemporal barter" (Kletzer and Wright 2000), especially within the (short) time horizons necessitated by wartime financing. Because of the Genoese's controlling positions in both the markets for juros and asientos, the king basically had no alternative but to obtain financing from them. Crucially, there was no entry of new lenders and no disintegration of the dominant Genoese network. Our preferred interpretation emphasizes cheat-the-cheater enforcement, with *the risk of being cheated as a result of other lenders' actions* as the main reason for no new bankers entering.

A crisis defines the value of a coalition. In our data, we observe the Genoese lenders going through two crises: the defaults of 1575 and 1596.[46] In both, the king needed cash urgently. The Sack of Antwerp had weakened Spain's position in the Low Countries, and victory began to look unlikely. Similarly, the threat of an English invasion in 1596 forced heavy spending to build fleets, outfit armies, and strengthen fortifications, while expenditures in Flanders proceeded apace. During these episodes, both the Crown and individual bankers from the network explored the possibility of a side deal. None was concluded, nor did any new lenders enter into one. A combination of social enforcement mechanisms (among the Genoese) and incentives (for the Genoese and all other potential lenders) was responsible for this outcome.

During the debt renegotiations of 1576–77 and 1596–97, the king's representatives attempted to undermine the coalition's cohesion. They focused on the Spinola family as well as selected large bankers. Despite offering preferential treatment of old debts in exchange for fresh loans, no deal was concluded. In 1576, Lorenzo Spinola and Nicolao de Grimaldo engaged in protracted private negotiations, but failed to come to an agreement with the Crown (Lovett 1982, 12–13; De Carlos Morales 2008, 170). Eventually Nicolao took part in the medio general. Although Lorenzo did not participate in the negotiations of the general settlement, his brother Agustín (a member of the family partnership) did. Overall, 93 percent of the loans in default were rescheduled. The remaining ones were contracts with small bankers who did

---

46 The earlier defaults affected loans by the Fugger and Welser to Charles V. The settlements involved large transfers of physical assets—including mines, land, and tax farms—that are difficult to value. Furthermore, our series of asientos extend back only to 1566.

not take part in the negotiations but instead were offered the same terms at a later date. In 1596, Ambrosio Spinola played a double game. He negotiated on behalf of other network members while discussing a special deal for himself. The Crown also offered favored treatment to a small syndicate. In the end, all bankers again settled on identical terms through a general agreement (Sanz Ayán 2004, 34–36). We do not know exactly what was on the minds of the Genoese banking families as they decided to maintain the moratorium, but it seems likely that the tight network of mutual commercial and other relationships kept opportunistic behavior by select banking families in check.

By analyzing the behavior and writings of bankers outside the coalition, we can gain further insight into the motivations of both the Genoese and other lenders. Throughout the second half of the sixteenth century, Philip borrowed from thirty-six families that did not belong to the Genoese network—a "competitive fringe" in the jargon of industrial organization. The most important bankers outside the network were the Fugger, who were responsible for the majority of transfers to Flanders during the 1575 suspension. The Crown clearly considered these services when it decided to continue to service its debt with the Fugger. The Royal adviser Dávalos de Sotomayor said as much: "Your majesty has the inexcusable obligation . . . of paying back the Fugger, who are not affected by the decree, somewhat less than two [million ducats]" (cited in Lovett 1982, 13).

The fact that the Fugger debt was still serviced despite the decreto, the general suspension of payments, could be seen as supporting the sanctions view—that the ability to cut off transfers to Flanders sustained lending. This is not correct. As the last lenders who had not been defaulted on the Fugger had greater market power since they were still willing to transfer funds. At the same time, and despite their advantageous position, they did not extend fresh funds at the hour of greatest need for the Spanish monarchy. What the absence of any lending operations by the Fugger family demonstrates is that lending and transfers were kept strictly separate; the threat of sanctions was not enough to support continuous access to credit.[47]

---

47 There is one possible exception: the transfer of a hundred thousand ducats to Flanders in 1576. The initial request by Francisco Garnica, one of the king's officials, was for fifty thousand ducats to be advanced by the Crown with the rest to be paid from the next year's tax increase. Although such an arrangement would constitute a loan, there is no evidence that the Fugger actually advanced any money.

The Fugger tried to benefit from the crisis in the Netherlands and the Crown's need for funds. Their agent in Spain, Tomás Miller, actually suggested a loan to pay Spanish troops in the Low Countries (Lovett 1982, 13).[48] In the end, there was no new lending by the Fugger until 1580. Their private correspondence tells us about the reasons why they did not seize the seemingly attractive opportunity to lend to the king when the latter was desperate for cash. What stopped them was the fear of being defaulted on if they lent during the moratorium.

The Fugger family in Germany took a dim view of the new loan proposed by Miller. Hans Fugger maintained a lively correspondence with his brother Marx, in which they discussed everything from high finance and politics to hunting dogs and the merits of sweet Italian wines. In a crucial exchange, Hans told Marx in emphatic terms that Miller had to be stopped. Otherwise, the Fugger would be cheated and would eventually end up being affected by the payment stop:

> Day after day, we have to render more and more services to the king (of Spain). . . . [T]his makes it imperative that Tomás Miller is stopped; if not, we will fraudulently and mockingly be thrown into the decree [affected by the payment stop].[49]

If a new loan were to be extended, Hans feared that

> the Spaniards will forever take advantage of us, they will suck us dry and exploit our position, and *if we don't do everything they say*, they will throw us into the decree, and . . . mistreat us like the Genoese, whose fate we have before our own eyes.[50]

---

48 The Fugger had a history of agents actually extending credit to the king of Spain in the 1550s. Some of the loans extended by those agents were caught in the 1556–60 default. After this episode, rules were tightened and agents could no longer lend without authorization from "headquarters" (Ehrenberg 1896).

49 "Du siehst, daß sich von Tag zu Tag die Servitios, so wir dem Künig [von Spanien] thun müeßen hauffen." . . . [W]irds ain grosse Notturfft erfordern, dem T[omás] Miller ain Bys einzulegen, wir khummen sonst burlando ins Decret." Karnehm 2003, 408–9. According to Charles Karnehm (ibid.), "burlare" here means "fraudulently"; an alternative translation is "mockingly."

50 "Die Sp[ani]er [werden sich] unser zu ewigen Zeitten . . . bedienen wellen, uns aussaugen, und nött[igen], wan wir dann nit jederzeit thun werden, was Sie wellen, so wirdt man uns das Decret fürwerffen, und sagen, man wöll uns darein schließen und tractieren wie die Genueser, wie dan schon vor Augen." Letter from Hans Fugger to Marx Fugger, September 5, 1576, cited in Karnehm 2003, 408–9; emphasis added. Nor was the idea that the king would strong-arm the Fugger into ever-more concessions idle speculation. Several transfers from Spain during the crisis were organized by the Fugger agent in Madrid, in direct contravention of the orders from Augsburg—because Miller could see no way to say "no" to the king and his advisers in the hour of need (Ehrenberg 1896).

What was on Hans's mind is clear enough: after receiving fresh funds, the king would default on them, too. Thus, the Augsburg banking family decided to do as the Genoese were doing—cut off lending—even though they had not suffered a default. They did so despite the fact that they were still offering transfer services to the king of Spain. The Fugger's concern illustrates what Kletzer and Wright (2000) call a cheat-the-cheater mechanism. Because they would not be able to satisfy all the king's demands, the Fugger considered it a virtual certainty that they would be cheated and defaulted on. The reason they could not satisfy every possible demand by Philip is also clear: his smoothing needs were simply too large. Eventually the king would have to settle with the Genoese. Then the Fugger family would lose everything. The Genoese were already furious with the Fugger for transferring funds to the Low Countries and in retaliation "tried to do them at Court all the harm they could" (Ehrenberg 1896). There is every reason to believe that the same logic that kept the Fugger from lending was constraining the behavior of other bankers. Thus, the power of the cheat-the-cheater mechanism reflected the Genoese coalition's market power, deterring insider defections as well as outsiders. Syndicated lending was a key factor sustaining the market power of the dominant banker coalition.[51]

SOVEREIGN LENDING SUSTAINED: MARKET POWER AND COHESION IN TIMES OF CRISIS

Philip II of Spain accumulated towering debts, and four times he stopped all payments to his bankers. Nonetheless, he continued to retain access to fresh loans for most of his reign—in the overwhelming majority of cases, from the same lenders he defaulted on. What explains this puzzling symbiosis between the first serial defaulter in history and his financiers?

Using our new data set collected from the General Archive of Simancas, we document a unique way in which Philip II's Genoese bankers overcame enforcement and collective action problems: lending in overlapping syndicates. Effective coordination between lenders gave this coalition substantial market power vis-à-vis the king. Because of his enormous borrowing needs, the king's demand for loans could not be satisfied by any other group of lenders; in effect, Philip II had access to only a few lenders, who acted in unison. Net-

---

51 The logic here is related to the argument in Wright 2002.

works based on social affiliations can solve the problem of incomplete contracting in a variety of contexts, creating in effect a private-order institution (Greif 2006). Examples include contract enforcement among diamond dealers and securities traders, merchants engaged in long-distance trade, as well as the running of common resources.[52] In the case of Philip II, the largest and most important bankers acted as if they were a single financial entity—a lenders' coalition. Ultimately, cheat-the-cheater incentives (Kletzer and Wright 2000) ensured that a simple lending moratorium of the Genoese was sufficient to force a powerful monarch like Philip II to pay his debts.

The crucial test for our hypothesis comes during the default of 1575. No outside power could come to aid of the Genoese, as the US Marine Corps had done in Santo Domingo in 1904 on behalf of European creditors; Philip II commanded the military of the world's only superpower at the time. Lenders had few ways to sanction Philip II by means other than a stop to lending. They attempted to impose a transfer stop that would have cut off funding for the troops in Flanders. We document that this penalty was ineffective; ample funds still flowed there. Crucially, Spain's major setback in the Netherlands in 1576 was not driven by a funding crisis but instead by the volatile politics of the time. The Fugger and other bankers continued to transfer funds for the Spanish sovereign, and enough money was made available in the Netherlands to pay off the mutineers. The case of Philip II, then, cannot be claimed as an example of sanctions in the Bulow and Rogoff style. Banker irrationality or sentiment also played no role in lending to the Spanish monarch. Contrary to the argument made by Braudel (1966), banker turnover was minimal. There was no mass exodus of lenders following the defaults. This suggests that expectations were not massively disappointed by the temporary payment stops and general settlements with bankers.

When the payment stop of 1575 came, neither new nor existing lenders undermined the Genoese lenders' moratorium. To offer the Crown fresh funds would have been a bad idea for any lender. The king's borrowing needs were so high that he would eventually have to settle with the Genoese coalition. Because the Genoese acted in unison, any lender who offered funds to Philip II during the moratorium would most likely have been cheated, in line with the predictions of Kletzer and Wright (2000). As a detailed analysis of the correspondence between the Fugger makes apparent, this consideration

---

52 Examples include Wade 1987; Baker 1984; Bernstein 1992; Greif 1993.

was certainly important for bankers at the time—and a key reason why the famous Augsburg banking dynasty chose not to offer new loans.

Lending occurred under conditions of anarchy, with neither side being able to make firm, binding commitments. Why established lenders in the Genoese coalition repeatedly agreed to debt reductions and a resumption of lending is also probably best explained by the market power derived from the group's cohesion (Kovrijnykh and Szentes 2007). This ensured that even after earlier debts had been reduced, future profits would be ample.[53] Far from indicating banker irrationality and the significance of lender sentiment, the boom-and-bust cycles of the sixteenth-century Spanish monarchy reflect the efficiency and flexibility of private-order institutional arrangements.

---

53 We examine the profitability of lenders in detail in chapter 6.

CHAPTER 6

SERIAL DEFAULTS, SERIAL PROFITS

The king continued to borrow massively throughout his reign, using the help of bankers to raise short-term financing. The Genoese banking network kept incentives aligned; the king's best strategy was to service his debts, so that he had access to capital markets in the future. Here we look at the bankers' side: How much did they profit as a result of "lender power"? We calculate returns on lending to the Castilian crown, taking into account defaults and the bankers' cost of funds. Our calculations demonstrate that loans to Philip II were highly profitable. Defaults and reschedulings reduced the rate of return, but profitability net of these losses was still high—and markedly higher than the return on alternative investments. This was true on average and also applied to the vast majority of banking dynasties individually. As a consequence, few financiers ever stopped lending to Philip II. Profitable lending also explains why the number of exits from the stage after the 1575 default was no greater than before.

MEASURING RETURNS

To estimate rates of return, we need to reconstruct the cash flows of each contract. The database of asientos described in chapter 3 contains detailed information about the agreed-on cash flows, collateral and foreign exchange clauses, payment dates, and fringe benefits. These can be used to calculate the rate of return for each lending contract.

We now illustrate this process with an example. The brothers Pedro and Francisco de Maluenda entered into a contract with the king on July 13,

---

This chapter is based on Drelichman and Voth 2011b, 2012.

1595.[1] They agreed to deliver 349,464 ducats in Lisbon in thirteen payments.[2] The first payment, for 26,856 ducats, was due eight days after the contract date. The remaining twelve payments, of 26,884 ducats each, were due at the end of each month, starting in July 1595. The king promised to repay as follows:

- A payment of 75,000 ducats from the general treasury in November 1595
- A payment of 97,000 ducats one month after the arrival of the first treasure fleet
- The amounts in the first two payments would accrue 1 percent monthly (simple, not compounding) interest starting from the month of August
- A payment of 1,950 ducats in October 1595 to cover miscellaneous transaction costs; the bankers did not have to itemize expenses
- A final payment one month after the arrival of the fleet of 1596; this payment was calculated on the basis of the outstanding 177,000 ducats, plus 1 percent monthly interest from October 1595, plus an additional 2 percent of the base amount for "other costs"

If the fleet of 1596 failed to reach Seville by December, the bankers could ask for lifetime juros of the same face value as the outstanding payment, with a maximum rate of 7.14 percent. Finally, there was a standard set of clauses allowing the bankers to export bullion (needed to disburse funds abroad).

The Maluenda contract is relatively simple. Because the deliveries were made through letters of exchange denominated in Castilian ducats and the repayments were made in Castile itself, no currency conversion was necessary. The fleet arrival was the only source of uncertainty. We assume that the bankers expected the fleets to reach Spain in September—their median arrival month. Payment therefore should have occurred in October. If the fleet arrived later, a monthly 1 percent interest charge would accrue until the payments were made or the bankers received juros. The option of receiving lifetime juros is not relevant for present value calculations under normal condi-

---

1 AGS, Contadurías Generales, Legajo 92. "Los dichos Francisco y Pedro de Maluenda. Asiento tomado con ellos en 13 de julio de 1595 sobre 439,500 ducados que han de proveer en Lisboa."
2 The summary on the front page of the contract describes the principal as consisting of 349,500 ducats. These small discrepancies, in all likelihood introduced for rounding convenience, are not uncommon. The relevant amounts, which we use throughout our empirical exercises, are those in the specific clauses.

tions, given that lifetime juros have a present value lower than their face value. When a default was imminent, the option could have been useful; in normal times, it would not be exercised. We therefore disregard the possibility of taking lifetime juros in lieu of payment when calculating ex ante returns.[3] The cash flows implied by our method are reported in table 14.

In constructing the cash flows, we needed to adopt several conventions. The asiento described above illustrates our treatment of payments tied to the arrival of the fleets. Other assumptions relate to the valuation of juros used for repayment. As a general rule, we use the cash flows of the juros themselves and calculate their NPV.[4]

We use two different profitability measures to derive rates of returns: the MIRR and profit index (PI). Virtually all our findings are robust to the choice of measure.[5]

The MIRR is defined as the ratio between the future value of positive cash flows and present value of negative cash flows. The formula is

$$MIRR = \sqrt{\frac{-FV(\text{positive cash flows}, r_r)}{PV(\text{negative cash flows}, r_f)}} - 1, \tag{1}$$

where n is the number of periods in the contract. If the lender receives positive cash flows before the end of the contract, the assumption is that these cash flows can be reinvested at rate r_r. Negative cash flows after the start of the loan are discounted at rate r_f.

Using the MIRR is attractive because of the nature of asiento contracts. The cash flow of many asientos turned from positive to negative and back several times over the lifetime of a loan. Our sample contract with the Maluenda brothers is a case in point. The obvious alternative to the MIRR is the internal rate of return (IRR), a common measure in corporate finance. The IRR is defined as the discount rate that makes the NPV of a series of cash flows equal to zero. It is unsuitable given the nature of our data. The IRR performs well only in the case of simple cash flows, with a single disbursement followed by a single repayment. Whenever there are intermediate cash flows,

---

3 Bankers could request juros yielding a maximum of 7.14 percent. Under our discount rate assumption (also 7.14 percent), the present value of lifetime juros of any allowed yield would have been lower than their face value.

4 For a full description of all the assumptions we used, see the appendix in Drelichman and Voth 2011b.

5 In chapter 4, we used the MIRR as a measure of asiento rates of return.

Table 14. Agreed-on cash flows in the Maluenda brothers' contract

Month	Disbursements	Repayments	Net cash flow	Description
July 1595	53,740		-53,740	Initial disbursement of 26,856 ducats; first monthly disbursement of 26,884 ducats
August 1595	26,884		-26,884	Monthly disbursement
September 1595	26,884		-26,884	Monthly disbursement
October 1595	26,884	100,890	74,006	Monthly disbursement; repayment of 1,950 ducats; repayment of 97,000 ducats plus 1% simple interest for two months
November 1595	26,884	77,250	50,366	Monthly disbursement; repayment of 75,000 ducats plus 1% simple interest for three months
December 1595	26,884		-26,884	Monthly disbursement
January 1596	26,884		-26,884	Monthly disbursement
February 1596	26,884		-26,884	Monthly disbursement
March 1596	26,884		-26,884	Monthly disbursement
April 1596	26,884		-26,884	Monthly disbursement
May 1596	26,884		-26,884	Monthly disbursement
June 1596	26,884		-26,884	Monthly disbursement
July 1596	0		0	
August 1596	0		0	
September 1596	0		0	
October 1596	0	201,780	201,780	Final repayment of 177,000 ducats plus 1% simple interest for twelve months plus 2% lump-sum bonus

two problems arise. First, the IRR formula assumes that any intermediate positive cash flows can be reinvested at the same rate of return as the entire project. This is unrealistic; there was not an infinitely elastic demand for loan contracts by the Crown. The banker's obvious alternative was to invest repayments in juros. Because juros yielded less than asientos, the IRR would overestimate the profitability of the contract. Second, intermediate negative cash flows can cause the IRR formula to yield multiple solutions or none at all. Since most asientos specified staggered disbursements and intermediate repayments, we do not use the IRR.

The MIRR has the advantage of yielding a unique solution. In the absence of intermediate cash flows, it is identical to the IRR. Just as the IRR, it can be interpreted as the rate of return that makes the NPV of the project equal to zero. The MIRR requires explicit assumptions about the reinvestment as well as the finance rate. For our benchmark estimates, we use the juro yield of 7.14 percent as the reinvestment rate and 5 percent as the finance rate. These are conservative choices intended to produce lower-bound estimates of profitability.[6] We also conduct sensitivity analysis with alternative parameter values.

The profit index is defined as the NPV of a contract divided by the capital at risk. Its advantage over the MIRR is that it only requires specifying one discount rate. The drawback is that the concept of capital at risk is not well defined when there are multiple staggered disbursements and repayments. Disbursements increase the capital at risk, while repayments diminish it. A long contract with a single repayment at the end exposes the lender to more risk than contracts with intermediate repayments spread across the same period. We measure the capital at risk as the total amount disbursed over the life of the contract. This overstates the true exposure, which was reduced by intermediate repayments. We also do not discount future disbursements but rather use their full value. In combination, these assumptions introduce a downward bias.

---

6 The obvious choice for a reinvestment rate is the juro yield of 7.14 percent. Juros were relatively safe investments that could be traded on a fairly liquid market. Bankers could possibly do better, in which case our estimate produces a lower bound on profitability. Specifying the finance rate is trickier. We bias the results against finding profitability by specifying the finance rate at 5 percent for our benchmark estimates. This was the lowest yield of any juro that was not part of a forced conversion and clearly below the average yield of long-term debt. We also conduct sensitivity analysis by lowering the finance rate all the way to zero. Since intermediate negative cash flows are substantially smaller than intermediate positive ones, the impact of any finance rate assumption will be limited.

The main difference between the MIRR and PI is that the former is a gross measure, while the latter is net of opportunity cost—which we take to be the juro yield. To compare them, the juro rate must be first subtracted from the MIRR. Next, the discount rates used differ conceptually. In the MIRR, the re-investment and finance rates refer to the yield of alternative assets. In the PI, the discount rate is a subjective measure that combines the opportunity cost of funds and risk aversion of the investor. Finally, as we discuss in the analysis, the MIRR is not well suited to evaluating long loans. When maturity is relevant, we use the PI instead.

SCENARIOS

We derive our data from the contracts as agreed between king and bankers. In many cases, the original agreement was not respected to the letter. The 1575 or 1596 bankruptcy impacted 119 contracts. Delays in both disbursements and repayments were common even in normal times. Almost 20 percent of loans contain clauses rescheduling previously unfulfilled obligations. Without observing the cash flows, we cannot derive precise measures of ex post profitability. Nonetheless, we can bound the likely returns. We do so by using our knowledge of the defaults and their settlements to approximate actual cash flows.

First, we calculate the profitability of each contract assuming that its clauses were respected to the letter. This is our upper bound. We then consider what would have happened if the king had repudiated all the outstanding debt in the 1575 and 1596 bankruptcies. This yields a (low) lower bound.[7] Finally, we approximate the actual cash flows by estimating the settlement payments made by the king on each contract affected by the defaults. To illustrate the three scenarios, we return to the contract with the Maluenda brothers.

The first column in table 15 reproduces the agreed-on cash flows in the original contract. Using our benchmark reinvestment and finance rate, the expected MIRR was 12.5 percent, or a healthy 5.4 percent above the juro rate. The PI was 6.8 percent. In November 1596, however, the king issued the fourth suspension decree of his reign. The treasure that had arrived with the

---

7 Note that it is not realistic to assume that any one banker could have earned a return as low as the one implied by this scenario; the banker would in all likelihood not have lent again after 1575.

Table 15. Cash flows and profitability of the Maluenda brothers' contract

	Original agreement	Settlements	Repudiation
July 1595	-53,740	-53,740	-53,740
August 1595	-26,884	-26,884	-26,884
September 1595	-26,884	-26,884	-26,884
October 1595	74,006	74,006	74,006
November 1595	50,366	50,366	50,366
December 1595	-26,884	-26,884	-26,884
January 1596	-26,884	-26,884	-26,884
February 1596	-26,884	-26,884	-26,884
March 1596	-26,884	-26,884	-26,884
April 1596	-26,884	-26,884	-26,884
May 1596	-26,884	-26,884	-26,884
June 1596	-26,884	-26,884	-26,884
July 1596			
August 1596			
September 1596			
October 1596	201,780		
⋮		⋮	
October 1597		137,059	
Yearly MIRR	12.5%	-5.3%	-61.1%
Yearly PI	6.8%	-14.8%	-55.4%

1596 fleet was embargoed at the Casa de la Contratación; the final payment of the contract did not take place.[8] Had the king repudiated the outstanding debt, the returns would have been strongly negative. Note that the majority of contracts would not have had such poor returns even under repudiation. Most were repaid partially or fully before the defaults took place. Bankers who had not disbursed the full loan amount could stop further payments. The Maluenda contract illustrates what could have happened in a worst-case scenario to an especially unlucky set of bankers. In actual fact, such a dire scenario did not materialize. The king agreed to repay 80 percent of the outstanding debts in October 1597. The settlement column reports our estimate of the actual cash flow. Since the language in most contracts does not distinguish between capital repayment and interest, we assume that all payments

8 We use the dates of arrival of the fleets in Morineau 1985.

go toward capital amortization first. This produces a lower bound for outstanding capital at the time of the default and hence the settlement payment. By this methodology, as of October 1596, the king would have owed the Maluenda brothers 171,324 ducats from this particular contract.[9] We multiply this amount by 0.8—the settlement ratio—and enter it as a positive cash flow in October 1597. This yields a MIRR of -5.3 percent (quite comparable to the PI of -14.8 percent).[10]

While the 1597 settlement imposed a uniform 20 percent reduction on outstanding claims, the terms in 1575 varied according to how a contract was collateralized.[11] Bankers who held standard juros as collateral recovered 70 percent of their claims; bankers holding juros guaranteed by the Casa de la Contratación received 55 percent; uncollateralized loans were granted 42 percent. For contracts affected by the 1575 default, we calculate the recovery rates for each contract based on the type of collateral used.

OVERALL PROFITABILITY OF LENDING

Our first question is whether bankers on the whole made money by lending to the king. To this end, we aggregate all lenders into a fictitious single financial entity for the years 1566–1600. Contractually agreed-on (ex ante) rates of return are only a first step in assessing the profitability of bank lending, as the case of the asiento of the Maluenda brothers demonstrates. We can learn about actual cash flows from three types of evidence. First, we have detailed information on the settlements after the defaults: we know who the king defaulted on and how the impasse was resolved. Second, the contracts themselves are meticulous in recording the king's payment behavior on earlier contracts. When an old loan was not paid in accordance with the letter of the original contract, the next one would often provide compensation. Third, when the same bankers offered loan after loan, it is unlikely that they received returns far below their opportunity cost of capital.

---

9 Because the clause structure in this particular contract is detailed, it is possible to calculate that the outstanding capital at the time of the default was 177,000 ducats. Its MIRR therefore would have been -4.6 percent. Few contracts contain similar detail. Thus we apply the "capital amortization first" methodology uniformly.

10 While the Maluenda brothers lost money on this particular contract, their overall relationship with the king was profitable. They lent over 4.3 million ducats to Philip II, realizing a MIRR of 20.6 percent after taking into account the effects of the defaults.

11 We describe the terms of each medio general in chapter 4.

The king could deviate from loan agreements in two different ways. For one, he might fall behind on payments on a particular loan. The payment in this case of the arrears would be rescheduled in a new contract with the banker. Although the return might not be as high as originally agreed, bankers seldom lost part of the principal and frequently received some compensatory interest. Second, the king could declare a bankruptcy and suspend payments on all outstanding loans at the same time. Philip did so four times during his reign, and our data cover the last two. Defaults like these would be renegotiated with all bankers in a general settlement, which specified principal and interest write-offs. The total ex post returns can therefore be written as

$$R = R_e - p_r L_r - p_d L_d,$$

where R is the total ex post return, R_e is the contracted rate, p_r is the proportion of debt rescheduled in individual contracts, L_r is the loss rate for rescheduled debt, p_d is the proportion of debt defaulted on in general bankruptcies, and L_d is the loss rate in the defaults.

Based on the expected returns, R_e is 20.3 percent. Obligations from earlier loan contracts were rescheduled in ninety-six cases. The king typically acknowledged the earlier debt and then offered various sweeteners in the new loan contract. This procedure affected 10 percent of the total amount lent—hence p_r is 0.1. Rescheduling earlier obligations typically increased returns for the new contract by 2 to 3 percent.[12]

How high was the recovery rate on rescheduled loans? The most optimistic interpretation implies that the additional returns to subsequent lending fully compensated lenders for what they had lost. A more cautious approach would assume that lenders received no interest on their earlier loans. This would reduce average profitability linearly, in line with the proportion of loans that were rescheduled. L_r would be 0.203, the same as the average return on loans. Hence, returns would have been 0.1*0.203 = 0.0203 lower than the ex ante contracted rate because of the subsequent recontracting.

Next, we need to derive values for the proportion of loans defaulted on and the recovery rates. Philip's four defaults were not of equal magnitude. The two earlier ones, in 1557 and 1560, mainly involved German bankers. They

---

12 Both quantile and robust regressions show an excess return of 2.5 to 3.2 percent for contracts that rescheduled earlier obligations (t-statistics 1.5 and 1.6, respectively—marginally below the level required for significance at the 10 percent level).

largely concerned debts contracted by Philip's father, Charles V, and were settled by transferring revenue-yielding assets. The famous quicksilver mines of Almadén, for instance, were given to the Fugger in exchange for debt cancellation. Since the original loans were not part of our data set, we were not able to examine the revenue impact of these two payment stops.

In 1575, the king suspended payment on 14.6 million ducats of outstanding loans. The majority of bankers negotiated a comprehensive settlement with the Crown. It resulted in write-offs of 30 to 58 percent. On average, the king agreed to honor 62 percent of the outstanding principal of short-dated loans and the associated interest payments. Long-term bonds escaped unscathed. In 1596, the king defaulted on 7 million ducats of debt, and the haircut imposed was 20 percent. We know that total asiento lending was 99.7 million nominal ducats over the period of these last two defaults, and that no more than 21.6 million worth of loans were affected by them—just over 21 percent of all contracts. The weighted recovery rate for the third and fourth defaults is 68 percent. The cost of the defaults to lenders is thus $p_d L_d = 0.21*0.32 = 0.067$. The average write-offs from the defaults on loans amounted to less than 7 percent of lending over the period. Defaults hence reduced profitability twice as strongly as our pessimistic calculations for ordinary reschedulings suggest.

Based on the figures just derived, we calculate

$$R = R_e - p_r L_r - p_d L_d = 0.203 - 0.1*0.203 - $$
$$- 0.21*0.32 = 0.203 - 0.0203 - 0.067 = 0.116$$

How profitable was lending? The fiscal turmoil that characterized Philip II's reign cost lenders less than half their potential profits, according to our calculations. Their average rate of return was 4.43 percent above the juro rate, indicating that they earned profits over and above their opportunity costs.

This result is derived from a calculation with many unknowns. We have tried to err on the side of caution, using estimates that are, if anything, too pessimistic about bankers' profits. How robust is our finding? Since the amount of rescheduled debt is relatively well established, we examine what happens when we vary the write-off rates. To reduce average profitability to zero, given the losses on ordinary reschedulings, the write-off during the defaults would have had to be 87 percent instead of the 32 percent actually suffered. Alternatively, write-offs on the reschedulings would have to be greater than 100 percent (135 percent) instead of the 20.3 percent we calculated (taking the estimated losses during defaults as given). Only extremely large deviations from the estimated loss rates and rescheduled amounts could reduce ex post rates of return to zero.

Profitability by Family

While the results presented so far show that lending to Philip II was profitable on average (even under unfavorable assumptions), this could mask considerable variation across lenders. We now examine rates of return by family. Between 1566 and 1596, 145 different bankers belonging to 78 families engaged in business with Philip II. Still, only 127 bankers, belonging to 60 families, ever risked capital. The rest provided intermediation services without putting their own resources on the line. We focus on the 60 families that extended credit.

Table 16 reports the MIRR by family for the period 1566–1600. The families are ranked by the total amount lent over the period as a whole. The provision of credit was heavily concentrated. The Spinola family, which counted 12 active members, lent over 20 percent of all funds. The top 10 families provided just short of 70 percent of all loans, and 19 families lent over 1 million ducats each.

The rates of return varied considerably. No family agreed to compensation below the 7.14 percent juro rate.[13] In the event of a complete repudiation, 18 families would have lost money. The remaining 42 families, however, would have realized positive rates of return; 37 of them would have earned more than the juro rate.[14]

According to our best estimate of actual profitability, reported in the settlements column, only 9 families failed to earn their opportunity cost; fully 51 earned more than the long-term bond yield. Of the 5 families that actually lost money, 3 invested little—2,080, 6,110, and 28,601 ducats respectively. All 5 entered into one or two contracts with the king, closely before the defaults. The Galletto and Salinas families sustained losses on somewhat-larger contracts, but their rates of return, -11.3 and -10.5 percent, respectively, are

---

13 This validates our choice of the juro rate as an upper bound for the opportunity cost of funds.

14 Note that families that were not affected by the defaults have the same rate of return under each of the three scenarios.

Table 16. MIRR by family (1566–1600, annualized rates)

Family name	Original agreement	Settlements	Repudiation	Total amount ever disbursed
Spinola	20.6%	19.3%	16.8%	16,359,959
Grimaldo	18.6%	11.7%	2.6%	7,306,110
Lomelín	23.8%	17.3%	0.8%	5,219,088
Fucar	11.4%	6.2%	-3.8%	4,951,107
Maluenda	26.1%	20.6%	10.9%	4,360,131
Torre	22.2%	16.1%	3.0%	4,142,326
Espinosa	12.0%	8.4%	6.8%	3,405,119
Centurión	19.3%	17.2%	10.9%	3,253,726
Gentil	19.9%	15.6%	8.8%	2,927,399
Marin	20.1%	20.0%	19.3%	2,646,472
Vitoria	19.4%	10.4%	-19.7%	2,063,816
Doria	23.8%	13.8%	-4.1%	2,027,106
Judice	27.0%	27.0%	27.0%	1,697,703
Latorre	11.5%	11.5%	11.5%	1,489,818
Carlessequi	16.1%	16.1%	16.1%	1,425,315
Cataneo	21.5%	7.6%	-5.1%	1,226,934
Isunza	25.0%	24.8%	23.6%	1,171,464
Ruiz	9.9%	7.5%	-7.9%	1,140,276
Salamanca	11.8%	11.8%	11.8%	1,005,657
Fiesco	24.5%	16.6%	-5.0%	995,290
Fornari	16.7%	8.1%	-8.6%	940,188
Grillo	27.8%	21.4%	12.6%	930,411
Justiniano	25.9%	15.9%	-11.4%	786,673
De Negro	18.1%	13.8%	-12.9%	769,407
Pasqual	21.8%	16.1%	16.1%	582,976
Lercaro	12.4%	3.1%	-13.2%	551,300
Suarez	22.2%	21.0%	20.5%	525,413
Isla	10.8%	10.8%	10.8%	497,175
Serra	8.0%	2.9%	-12.3%	458,178
Herrera	10.8%	10.8%	10.8%	451,234
Galletto	13.9%	-11.3%	-100.0%	407,817
Carmona	17.8%	17.8%	17.8%	395,333
Salazar	17.8%	17.8%	17.8%	395,333

Table 16. (*continued*)

Family name	Original agreement	Settlements	Repudiation	Total amount ever disbursed
Pinelo	15.8%	15.8%	15.8%	341,405
Mena	17.0%	10.6%	−6.0%	306,982
Murain	8.1%	8.1%	8.1%	299,000
Cambi	9.6%	8.3%	6.7%	275,549
Salinas	17.3%	−10.5%	−22.7%	264,440
Adorno	31.0%	31.0%	31.0%	230,938
Curiel de la Torre	151.1%	151.1%	151.1%	186,309
Sauri	21.7%	5.8%	−30.0%	126,605
Corvari	23.4%	23.4%	23.4%	119,224
Diaz Aguilar	9.9%	9.9%	9.9%	118,480
Sabago	16.5%	16.5%	16.5%	100,155
Obada	8.3%	8.3%	8.3%	100,000
Franquis	9.4%	9.4%	9.4%	83,000
Villaldo	20.5%	20.5%	20.5%	77,409
Aponal	32.1%	32.1%	32.1%	67,026
Salucio	78.2%	78.2%	78.2%	60,027
Interiano	31.1%	31.1%	31.1%	53,333
Calvo	12.4%	12.4%	12.4%	50,000
Serna	12.9%	12.9%	12.9%	30,581
Vicuña	12.9%	12.9%	12.9%	30,581
Palavecin	8.6%	−5.5%	−50.7%	28,601
Cibo	67.3%	67.3%	67.3%	19,624
Picamillo	15.6%	15.6%	15.6%	16,184
Rastrogago	19.1%	19.1%	19.1%	15,000
Lago	19.1%	19.1%	19.1%	15,000
San Vitores	8.6%	−4.9%	−45.3%	6,110
Bobadilla	10.0%	−0.6%	−14.8%	2,080

Note: The reinvestment rate is assumed to be 7.14 percent, and the finance rate 5 percent. The amounts disbursed are expressed in ducats. We use the Spanish spellings of the family names, as they appear in the archival documents.

hardly catastrophic. In fact, the Galletto family signed its only contract just four days before the 1596 bankruptcy. In all likelihood the disbursement was never made and the family did not suffer any losses. We nonetheless assume the contract was fulfilled in order to bias our results against finding profitability. The repudiation scenario therefore shows a profitability of -100 percent; the family would have lost the entire amount disbursed. The absolute losses of these 5 families amounted to just over 75,000 ducats. This is less than 0.1 percent of the total short-term lending to Philip II.

According to the settlement scenario, 4 families did not lose money in absolute value, but failed to earn the juro rate. One of these was the Fucar (Fugger) banking dynasty. As a matter of fact, the Fugger were the only family exempted from the provisions of the 1575 bankruptcy. Their actual rate of return was the originally contracted 11.4 percent. The other 3 families were the Lercaro (3.1 percent), Serra (2.9 percent), and Sauri (5.8 percent). The last 2 families had only a sporadic relationship with the king and happened to lend just prior to the defaults. The Lercaro lent somewhat-larger amounts throughout the entire period—just over 550,000 ducats. These loans were provided in the run-up to the bankruptcies, and the reduction in payment obligations caused the Lercaro to earn less than they would have by investing in juros.

Three of the MIRRs reported in table 16 are unusually high. Juan Curiel de la Torre earned over 151 percent on lending some 186,000 ducats. The Salucio and Cibo families also earned in excess of 50 percent. Curiel de la Torre achieved such a high return through a combination of factors. He had high returns on small contracts, and kept his exposure to a minimum by staggering disbursements and repayments.[15] The Salucio and Cibo lent little, and hence did not obtain large absolute gains.

CORRELATES OF RETURNS

Table 16 reveals considerable heterogeneity in the rate of returns at the family level. Across individual loans, differences in outcomes are even more marked. What explains the cross-section of returns to lending? Were some

---

15 We calculate profitability using the net disbursements as weights for each individual contract. Curiel de la Torre's disbursements were timed to coincide with repayments from the king. Even though the contracts were nominally for large amounts, Curiel de la Torre's actual net exposure was low and hence his returns on capital at risk were high. The effect is particularly noticeable because he did not lend large amounts.

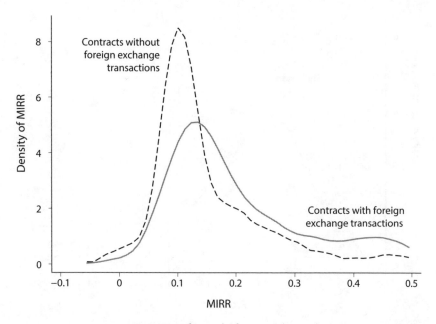

FIGURE 17. Density of MIRRs by foreign exchange clauses

bankers obtaining preferential treatment? Or does the variation mostly reflect the different characteristics of each loan?

We begin by examining some of the patterns of association between contract characteristics and the agreed-on lending rate. The first factor to note is that many loans contained a foreign exchange component. These were, on average, more expensive.

Figure 17 plots the distributions of loan profitability with and without an explicit foreign currency clause. While there is a lot of variation in the interest rates charged, the difference in the means and modes is clear. Loans with a foreign exchange component had an unweighted mean (median) interest rate of 27 percent (17 percent); those without had an unweighted mean (median) interest rate of 19 percent (11 percent). At first pass, then, contracting debts that involved disbursement in foreign specie raised the cost of a loan. Depending on the method used, we find increases of up to 9 percent.

Maturity also influenced the cost of loans. Since the MIRR is not well suited to evaluate loans of long maturity, we use the PI instead.[16] Loans with above-

---

16 The MIRR assumes that all intermediate positive cash flows are reinvested at the exogenously assumed reinvestment rate until the end of the contract. For long loans, this biases the estimated profitability toward the reinvestment rate. The PI is independent of loan maturity.

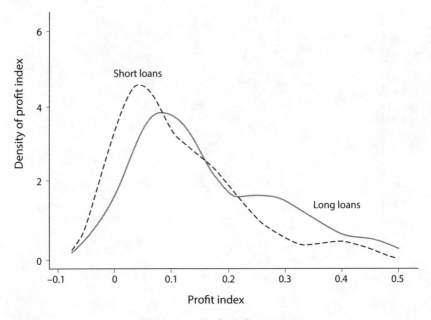

FIGURE 18. Density of PI by loan maturity

median maturity (more than twenty-two months) often attracted higher interest rates. Figure 18 plots the distributions. The unweighted mean (median) PI for long loans was 24 percent (13 percent), while it was 17 percent (11 percent) for short loans.

Table 17 summarizes the profitability of loans conditional on their characteristics. Those with a foreign exchange clause had 3 to 5 percent higher returns.[17] Contracts with collateral did not attract a significantly higher rate of return. Transfers themselves (without accounting for the use of foreign exchange clauses) also did not attract higher returns. Large loans were somewhat cheaper than small ones, but the difference is only clear for means, not medians. Finally, lenders' nationality affected profitability. German lenders received a lower rate of return, although their loans were frequently serviced during the defaults and hence were less risky. The Genoese earned (median) returns that were higher than the rest by about 2 percent, but their average returns were indistinguishable.[18]

---

17 If we control for other characteristics in a multivariate setting, this premium rises to 6.5 to 9.3 percent (Drelichman and Voth 2011b).

18 The regression exercise does not allow us to determine if the higher returns for Spaniards

Table 17. Conditional profitability

Characteristics	Mean	Median	Standard deviation	N
All contracts	23.6	13.8	32.5	401
Foreign exchange clause	29.3	17.1	33.2	166
Collateral	22.5	15.3	23.8	133
Transfers	20.3	13.5	16.7	164
Above-average principal	20.4	13.9	17.0	102
Below-average principal	24.7	13.7	36.3	299
Above-average duration	14.5	12.0	9.9	159
Below-average duration	29.7	17.5	40.0	242
German lenders	13.4	9.6	10.7	12
Genoese lenders	23.9	15.9	23.9	246
Spanish lenders	24.0	11.8	44.4	143

Loan characteristics explain few of the differences in profitability; variations between different loan types seem small compared to the standard deviation of profitability. While not satisfactory overall, these results are similar to those found in the modern finance literature.[19]

On average, the general settlements caused losses for the lenders. What explains the cross-section of these differences? We define the variable LOSS_MIRR as the difference between the MIRR according to the settlement and the promised MIRR, as per the original agreement. LOSS_PI is defined analogously. Table 18 regresses these measures on our standard set of explanatory variables. Loans with a foreign exchange component typically did poorly. Defaults happened in times of intense military conflict, when most loans were disbursed near foreign battlefields. Loans with a high collateral component showed higher returns; since the settlements took the presence of collateral into account when determining the haircuts, this is not surprising. Longer

and Genoese attest to their "insider" role, or reflect the fact that German lenders only participated in particularly safe loans.

19 Allen Berger and Gregory Udell (1995) and Mitchell Petersen and Raghuram Rajan (1994, 1995) find R-squared values of around 0.06 to 0.15 in modern-day data. See also Eugene White 2001a.

Table 18. Correlates of losses during the defaults

	(1)	(2)	(3)	(4)	(5)	(6)
Dependent Variable	LOSS_MIRR (MIRR-based losses)			LOSS_PI (PI-based losses)		
Foreign exchange	-0.036*** (-2.58)	-0.036*** (-2.61)	-0.044*** (-2.76)	-0.055* (-1.85)	-0.056* (-1.93)	-0.076** (-2.34)
Collateral		0.037*** (2.88)	0.039*** (2.84)		0.063* (1.92)	0.065* (1.75)
Duration		-0.002*** (-3.00)	-0.002*** (-3.00)		-0.003*** (-3.01)	-0.004*** (-3.00)
Duration squared		1.47E-5*** (2.67)	1.36E-5** (2.43)			
Loan size			4.68E+8** (2.18)			9.72E-8* (1.70)
Genoese			0.011 (0.72)			0.050 (1.36)
Germans			0.005 (0.19)			0.000 (0.00)
Constant	-0.041*** (-7.21)	-0.020 (-1.61)	-0.025** (-2.08)	-0.117*** (-6.84)	-0.042* (-1.75)	-0.055** (-2.29)
N	400	400	400	400	400	400
R^2	0.020	0.048	0.057	0.009	0.082	0.094

Significance levels: *10%, **5%, ***1%

durations were unambiguously associated with greater losses, while larger loans did somewhat better. Nationality did not confer a clear-cut advantage when negotiating the settlements, nor were specific families favored over others. In combination, these two sets of regressions suggest that the rates of return were determined by a specific loan's features and did not reflect the particular negotiating position of a given set of bankers. The same is true of the losses sustained during the defaults.

PROFITABILITY OVER TIME

How did lending rates change over time? Did the defaults make lending more expensive for the king? In other words, is there evidence of mounting "debt intolerance" (Reinhart, Rogoff, and Savastano 2003)? Figure 19 plots the volume of lending and its profitability over time. The line, indexed to the left-hand axis, shows the weighted average of the ex post MIRRs of contracts ac-

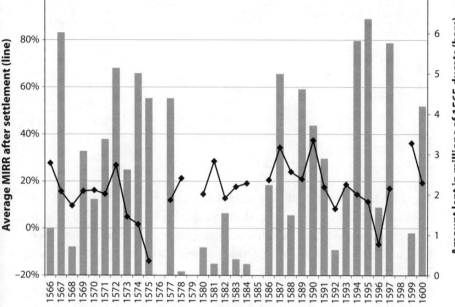

FIGURE 19. Profitability and volume of lending

cording to the year in which they were signed. The bars show the volume of actual lending every year.[20]

MIRRs fluctuated between 15 and 30 percent. The exceptions are the defaults. Only contracts signed in 1573, 1574, 1575, and 1596 failed to earn the juro rate. There is virtually no connection between MIRRs and lending volume—the correlation coefficient is -0.16. With the exception of the dips around the defaults, rates do not show major fluctuations.

Table 19 shows the average differential between ex ante and ex post MIRRs for contracts signed in the years leading up to each bankruptcy. The 1575 default was more severe than the 1596 one. Consequently, the gap between contracted and actual rates was higher in the years leading up to 1575. Many contracts of long duration were affected; maturities ranged up to seven years in 1575 versus a maximum of four in 1596. The amount defaulted on in 1575 was 14.6 million ducats and the average haircut was 38 percent; in 1596, the

Table 19. Difference between average contracted and actual MIRRs

Year contract was signed	1575 default	1596 default
Year of default	30.9%	24.7%
t–1	16.8%	9.4%
t–2	11.6%	1.4%
t–3	3.1%	1.2%
t–4	1.7%	0.0%
t–5	0.7%	0.0%
t–6	0.9%	0.0%
t–7	4.3%	0.0%

king stopped servicing 7 million ducats of debt and negotiated a reduction of outstanding claims by 20 percent. These numbers reflect the severity of each fiscal crisis. In 1575, two simultaneous campaigns, three unusually poor fleets, and the reluctance of the Cortes to increase taxes led to a serious cash flow shortfall. In 1596, in contrast, taxes had already increased substantially. The liquidity shortfall was caused largely by renewed military activity, while accounting errors may have contributed to the sense that the situation was critical. As is the case with any insurance contract, the losses suffered by lenders were larger when the fiscal situation was more pressing.

Net Rates of Return

In our benchmark scenario, bankers obtained an average ex post gross MIRR of 15.5 percent. To derive a net measure of profitability, we need to subtract costs. Unfortunately, we do not observe most costs at the contract level. We instead use the available information on their general range to estimate the effect on the average rate of return: the costs were not sufficient to overturn the result that lending was profitable. Nevertheless, they likely reduced some apparently high rates of return to a normal range.

The most important cost—financing—is captured by the long-term bond rate. Next, we need to consider the costs of intermediation. Lenders relied on a correspondent network. The cost of using this network is reflected in the charges for issuing letters of exchange. Between 1566 and 1575, most contracts required disbursements either in cash at the treasury or via a letter of exchange drawn on a specific fair. When the latter was requested, the king was charged an additional 0.5 percent of the principal.[21] In addition, most bankers did not risk their own capital but instead acted as intermediaries, splitting the contracts into smaller parts and selling them to individual investors. Their typical fee for this service was 1 percent.

Currency conversions and the need to transport bullion also added to costs. Contracts with a foreign exchange component often specified that the banker would be reimbursed for "what is customary among businessmen."[22] Sometimes the king requested an affidavit signed by three or four independent bankers attesting to the costs incurred. The king often provided free space on his ships. Other costs were either reimbursed on top of all other payments to the bankers or covered directly by the king. These costs thus do not affect the rate of return.[23]

Several contracts include specific allowances for other costs. Our sample contract with the Maluenda brothers is a good example. The king agreed to pay the bankers a total of 5,490 ducats to cover any costs they might incur, without demanding that they account for the expenses. This amount was 1.6 percent of total payments by the king. We don't know whether cost allowances covered actual costs or whether they were merely used as a way to increase the rate of return. In our cash flows, we treat them in the same way as any other payment to the bankers. Hence, their effect is incorporated in the gross profitability figures. They typically amounted to 1 to 2 percent of the principal.

Finally, our rates of return are nominal. The second half of the sixteenth century witnessed the price revolution, as inflows of American silver caused a general increase in the price level. Existing price indices are not accurate enough at yearly frequencies, preventing us from calculating real rates of return for each contract. Period averages are more reliable. Between 1556 and 1600, prices rose at an annualized rate of 1.7 percent (Drelichman 2005).

---

21 When a cash disbursement at the court was requested, the specific language was "en esta corte en reales de contado." Because bankers or their agents resided at and collected their payments whenever the court was stationed, this type of transaction would have carried the lowest transaction costs. When a disbursement was needed at a payments fair, either in Castile or abroad, the language was "en feria de [specific fair], en banco con cinco al millar"—that is, as a bank draft with a five per thousand surcharge.

22 The standard language is that the king will pay the bankers for "hasta lo que se acostumbra entre hombres de negocios."

23 This would only be problematic for our results if the bankers systematically undercharged the king for these services. There is no evidence to suggest this.

We can now calculate the net rates of return. The starting point is our benchmark estimate of 15.5 percent, which already takes into account the effect of the bankruptcies. We subtract the 7.14 percent opportunity cost, up to 1.5 percent in intermediation costs, up to 2 percent in other transaction costs, and 1.7 percent for inflation. This yields a real net return of 3.16 percent in a scenario involving high costs. If intermediation or transaction costs for a specific contract were lower, the net real rates of return could have been as high as 5 percent. While stressing that these are rough estimates, we note that they remain positive, in line with our general results, and they are relatively modest values considering the risky nature of short-term lending.[24]

RAISING THE FUNDS

All the calculations in this chapter were presented as if Genoese bankers lent directly, with the Spinola or Maluenda effectively writing large checks to Philip II, and then waiting to be repaid. In actual fact, bankers seldom offered a loan using only their own capital. Rather, much as modern banks do, they would tap a variety of financing sources, including demand deposits and the sale of participations in the sovereign's lending ventures. In this fashion, they could offer much larger loans than their own resources allowed, while simultaneously limiting their exposure as well as spreading the risk among their customers and equity partners. These arrangements can also have an important impact on the rate of return for the bankers.

The profitability of individual loans could differ significantly from the gains for the international bankers who were in charge of organizing large, multilayered syndicates that lent to the king of Spain. Returns for final investors could again be different: a chain of financial intermediation linked the king to investors small and large throughout Europe, and they ultimately bore the risks. The available information on this aspect of lending is much more fragmentary than the data on asientos themselves.

In our opening chapter, we recounted the story of the Di Negro–Pichenotti partnership—the small merchants from Genoa who purchased shares in two asientos extended by Agustín Spinola and Nicolás De Negro in 1596. Here we take a closer look at their transactions and show how the risks of lending to

---

24 We do not know to what extent bankers sold the loans that they issued. If they sold the loans at lower rates of interest, their profits would have been higher still. In the absence of reliable information, we refrain from speculation.

the king were spread through several layers of financial intermediation. In good times, a large number of investors, big and small, benefited from the asientos. When payments were suspended, many parties shouldered the losses with diversified portfolios, ensuring that most would weather the storm unscathed.

In February and July 1596, Agustín and Nicolás jointly underwrote the two asientos we analyze here.[25] As discussed above, the Spinola were the largest lenders to Philip II. They alone accounted for over 20 percent of the total short-term borrowing over the period. While the De Negro lent money on a more modest scale, amounting to some 770,000 ducats in total, they were also among the leading business families in Genoa.[26] Agustín and Nicolás lived permanently in Madrid, and were in charge of managing the financial operations that their families entered into with the king. This management included negotiating new loans, arranging the disbursements promised in Madrid, and issuing the necessary letters of exchange to authorize disbursements abroad. They were also responsible for collecting the repayments, which required skill at navigating the royal bureaucracy and trustworthy agents in many places where treasurers in charge of different royal revenue streams were stationed. Finally, the bankers had to obtain the necessary permits to remit the proceeds back to their families in Italy or wherever else they were needed, and had to ensure that the bullion was delivered to a port of exit and shipped safely.

The first asiento was concluded on February 24, 1596. Spinola and De Negro initially agreed to deliver 90,000 ecus in Milan. Half the amount was due immediately and payable on presentation of the letters of exchange by the royal officials. The other half would be disbursed in three equal payments over the months of April, May, and June. In addition, the bankers promised to deliver 112,500 ducats in Madrid in six equal payments. The first two payments had already been made on January 1 and February 1, 1596; the remaining four installments were to be paid once a month.[27] The contract valued the Italian

---

25 These contracts are located in the AGS, Contadurías Generales, Legajo 92.

26 We report cumulative sums actually disbursed by the Spinola and De Negro families rather than contracted ones. For example, in the second contract we examine in this section, Spinola and De Negro agreed to lend over 1 million ducats, but only disbursed 127,000 before the payment stop of 1596 put a premature end to the contract. We use the latter amount in our calculations.

27 It was not unusual for disbursements and payments to predate the actual signing of an asiento. The contracts carried the date on which they were signed by the king. Bankers and royal

ecus at 404 maravedíes each, which represented a 1 percent premium over their gold content of just under 400 maravedíes (1.067 ducats). The combined principal of the contract therefore amounted to 209,460 ducats.

The king promised to repay the capital using the proceeds of the three graces from the years 1597 and 1598 as well as those from the ordinary and extraordinary servicios.[28] The contract stipulated that the proceeds of these taxes would be disbursed to bankers in six installments, starting in July 1598, and every four months thereafter. The interest rate was 1 percent per month, not compounding; each capital repayment would also be accompanied by the accrued interest on that part of the capital only. The first installment would include an extra two months of interest as well. As additional compensation, the bankers were allowed to swap juros worth up to 485 ducats for other bonds of their choice. They could therefore purchase nonperforming bonds at bargain prices, exchange them at the treasury for choice securities, and net a substantial profit.[29]

The contract included a number of additional provisions. First, the bankers were allowed to export bullion equivalent to the value of the principal. Although 112,500 ducats were to be delivered in Castile, the bankers would be raising the necessary funds outside the kingdom and hence would need to export the repayments to satisfy their own liabilities. The bankers were also given permission to export another 60,000 ducats to Portugal. These export licenses were valuable, as they allowed their holders to arbitrage between different currency markets. Bankers could sell them to other businessmen. If a license went unused, the treasury would on occasion buy it back.

Spinola and De Negro were given the option of collecting their repayments from alternative income streams, too. In particular, they were allowed to choose to be repaid from the fleets of 1596 and 1597. In this fashion, they

---

officials, however, might have come to an agreement weeks or months earlier, and several of the promised cash flows might have already happened by the time the documents were formally signed.

28 As discussed in chapter 3, the three graces were three income streams (cruzada, subsidio, and excusado) that the church collected on behalf of the Crown and forwarded to the royal treasury. The servicios were direct taxes approved by the Cortes.

29 Since this transaction would have taken place in March 1596, the bankers would have collected the entire yearly interest of the new juro in November 1596, although they would have held it only for nine months. This would have increased the present value of the operation from 485 to 502 ducats. The small amount of this transaction suggests that the bankers already had a nonperforming juro worth exactly 485 ducats in hand and took advantage of this asiento to dispose of it.

could have begun to collect funds a few months earlier, at the cost of forfeiting the extra 2 percent on the first installment. Alternatively, the bankers could request that repayment be made in the form of lifetime juros. This would have allowed them to receive payment almost immediately, but at a higher cost.[30] The bankers, according to the contract, also could opt for perpetual juros, but they would have to wait until the originally promised repayment dates to receive them. This last option would only be valuable if, for some reason, the original income streams failed. Finally, the contract allowed the bankers the use of one or two royal galleys to convey bullion to Italy.

Table 20 shows the agreed-on cash flows from the asiento of February 24. All the disbursements took place in the first six months of the contract, and with the exception of the small profit from the juro operation, no repayments were promised until July 1598, a full thirty months after the beginning of the contract. In laying out the cash flows, we abstract from the several options that the bankers could exercise, such as choosing different repayment streams or converting part of their credits into juros. Most of these would have resulted in some small modification of the contract's profitability. The actual sign and magnitude of the change depended on unobservable conditions. In order to produce a conservative estimate of the rate of return, we also omit the value of the license to export bullion.[31]

Had the contract been honored as originally signed, the bankers would have realized a yearly rate of return of 10.4 percent.[32] If they chose to exercise some of the built-in options—for example, requesting payment from the fleets while forfeiting the extra months of interest—the returns could have climbed to 11.7 percent per year. The bankruptcy decree of November 1596 came once the bankers had disbursed the entire principal, but had not yet received a single repayment. In terms of timing, this is the worst scenario

---

30 For accounting purposes, juros were valued as perpetual streams. Lifetime bonds, however, stopped performing at the death of their holders and hence had a lower present value than perpetuities.

31 This would have likely yielded between 1 and 2 percent of the 60,000 ducats under license, and hence perhaps enhanced the overall profitability of the contract to the order of 0.2 to 0.4 percent annually, depending on the timing and actual yield of the transaction. Since the actual return would have depended on the relative conditions of the Spanish and Italian money markets, which we do not observe, we refrain from including this additional profit in our calculations.

32 We calculate the profitability of asientos using the MIRR, with a finance rate of 5 percent and reinvestment rate of 7.14 percent. For a detailed discussion of the properties of the MIRR and justification of our choice of parameters, see Drelichman and Voth 2011b.

Table 20. Agreed-on cash flows from the asiento of February 24, 1596

Month	Disburse-ments	Repay-ments	Net cash flow	Description
January 1596	18,750		−18,750	First Madrid disburse-ment (presigning)
February 1596	18,750		−18,750	Second Madrid disburse-ment (presigning)
March 1596	66,688	502	−66,186	Third Madrid disburse-ment; first Milan disbursement; profit from the juro operation
April 1596	34,729		−34,729	Fourth Madrid disburse-ment; second Milan disbursement
May 1596	34,729		−34,729	Fifth Madrid disburse-ment; third Milan disbursement
June 1596	34,729		−34,729	Sixth Madrid disburse-ment; fourth Milan disbursement
July 1598		46,081	46,081	First repayment plus interest (including the one time payment of two months of additional interest)
November 1598		46,779	46,779	Second repayment plus interest
March 1599		48,176	48,176	Third repayment plus interest
July 1599		49,572	49,572	Fourth repayment plus interest
November 1599		50,969	50,969	Fifth repayment plus interest
March 1600		52,365	52,365	Sixth repayment plus interest

that bankers could find themselves in. The settlement of 1597 gave the bankers juros worth 80 percent of the outstanding debt. The promised profits evaporated. Evaluated at its terminal date of March 1600, considering the reduction in principal and yield of the juros, the operation resulted in a loss of 1.08 percent annually.[33]

The second asiento was signed on July 26, 1596. This was a much larger contract. Spinola and De Negro agreed to deliver 1 million ecus of 57 plaques in Flanders in fourteen payments. The first thirteen payments were to amount to 65,000 ecus each, and the fourteenth would have consisted of the remaining 155,000 ecus. The disbursements were to start on September 1, 1596, and continue at a monthly frequency. For accounting purposes, the Flemish ecus were being valued at 1.088 ducats each, although their theoretical gold content only amounted to 0.977 ducats. The contract thus provided for a potential profit of 10.5 percent in the exchange operation alone, although the actual profit would have depended on the market value of the Flemish ecus.

The king agreed to repay a total of 1,088,267 ducats of principal, which represented 1,000,245 ecus at the agreed-on conversion rate.[34] As with the February contract, interest would be added to each installment at the time of repayment. Because of the size of the loan, the king had to use several revenue sources to repay it. He promised the bankers:

- 75,133 ducats from the royal direct and indirect taxes corresponding to the year 1595, and payable by the end of 1596
- 75,133 ducats in the taxes owed by the city of Seville and charged on the goods brought by the fleet, also payable by the end of 1596
- 75,000 ducats from the proceeds of the goods of Cardinal Don Gaspar de Quiroga.[35]

---

33 Because the MIRR incorporates the opportunity cost of funds, its value depends on the terminal date of the contract. We use the terminal date originally specified in the contract to calculate the losses sustained in the restructurings. The reason is that the bankers expected to have their funds tied up until that time, and would have made their original investment decisions based on that terminal date. This also ensures comparability between the expected and actual rates of return.

34 The additional 245 ecus are a rounding error due to the specific unit of account used.

35 Quiroga y Vela was a towering figure in the Spanish ecclesiastical hierarchy. He held its two most coveted posts—those of inquisitor general and archbishop of Toledo. He enjoyed large rents and possessions, many of which reverted to the Crown on his death in November 1594. This contract shows that the Crown did not transfer these assets entirely to the new archbishop but instead chose to use part of them to satisfy its financial obligations.

- 466,667 ducats from the fleet expected between September and November 1596
- 263,000 ducats from the proceeds of the three graces and servicios, in three installments beginning in July 1598 and continuing every four months
- 133,333 ducats payable in the same fashion as the previous clause, but in 1599

The yearly interest rate applied to each payment was 12 percent (simple, not compounding), calculated from July 1596. Payments from the three graces received an extra month of interest, while payments from the servicios received an extra two months of interest and an additional two months for not otherwise-specified "costs." The bankers were given broad authority to collect their payments from alternative revenue streams, but they could only convert up to 100,000 ducats of repayments into juros, and another 100,000 ducats from the 1596 payments into silver from the Indies. The king also provided galleys for the transportation of the bullion. Table 21 shows the agreed cash flows from the asiento of July 26.

The second asiento is different from the one signed on February 24. A large proportion of the repayments are stipulated early in the life of the contract—in November and December 1596. In fact, if those two repayments had actually taken place, the bankers would have had a cash surplus until September 1597. There are only two time periods during which the bankers would have found themselves in the red: September–October 1596, and between October 1597 and March 1599. In effect, this contract can be thought of as having three components:

1. A relatively small loan of 127,000 ducats disbursed in September–October 1596, and repaid in November 1596
2. A large transfer to Flanders, for which the king prepays in November and December 1596 (with an additional disbursement in July 1597), and which the bankers actually carry out between November 1596 and August 1597[36]
3. A loan of some 215,000 ducats in September–October 1597

---

36 This contract illustrates how both parties to the contract bore risks. The bankers were cash flow positive for ten months, as they gradually transferred to Flanders the large sum that the king had given them up front. Had Spinola and De Negro gone bankrupt, the king would have lost money.

Table 21. Agreed-on cash flows from the asiento of July 26, 1596

Month	Disbursements	Repayments	Net cash flow	Description
September 1596	63,488		−63,488	Monthly disbursement of 65,000 ecus, valued at their gold content of 0.977 ducats
October 1596	63,488		−63,488	Monthly disbursement
November 1596	63,488	485,333	421,845	Monthly disbursement; repayment from the fleet (clause 4) plus four months' interest
December 1596	63,488	236,530	173,042	Monthly disbursement; repayments from clauses 1 to 3 plus five months' interest
January 1597	63,488		−63,488	Monthly disbursement
February 1597	63,488		−63,488	Monthly disbursement
March 1597	63,488		−63,488	Monthly disbursement
April 1597	63,488		−63,488	Monthly disbursement
May 1597	63,488		−63,488	Monthly disbursement
June 1597	63,488		−63,488	Monthly disbursement
July 1597	63,488	99,940	36,452	Monthly disbursement; first installment from clause 5 plus interest
August 1597	63,488		−63,488	Monthly disbursement
September 1597	63,488		−63,488	Monthly disbursement
October 1597	151,395		−151,395	Final disbursement of 155,000 ecus
November 1597		103,447	103,447	Second installment from clause 5 plus interest
March 1598		106,953	106,953	Third installment from clause 5 plus interest
July 1598		56,000	56,000	First installment from clause 6 plus interest
November 1598		57,778	57,778	Second installment from clause 6 plus interest
March 1599		59,556	59,556	Third installment from clause 6 plus interest

It is not possible to separate the compensation for each of the three components, as they are not identified in the contract itself. The profit nonetheless was all back loaded, as the bankers swung decisively into surplus with the last six repayments. The options built into the contract only allowed the bankers to switch the source of the repayments; since they did not affect their timing or amount, they would not have affected the rate of return. Had the contract been honored as agreed on, the annualized rate of return would have been 17.6 percent.

This contract mirrored a number of other loans, which called for large repayments in November–December 1596. Indeed, it is quite likely that the time of the payment stop was dictated by this fact.[37] The bankers actually managed to collect part of the first payment prior to the November 1596 suspension, and recovered 80 percent of the remaining amount in 1597. When evaluated at the terminal date of March 1599, the operation resulted in an annualized loss of 4.82 percent.

Families like the Spinola regularly entered into asientos worth hundreds of thousands of ducats. Even if they had had the financial wherewithal to remain liquid whenever the king declared a payment stop, lending such enormous amounts to a single borrower may not have been a good business strategy. During the first and second of Philip's bankruptcies, for example, the Fugger had been caught between largely illiquid claims on the Spanish Crown, on the one hand, and their own creditors, on the other. Only massive injections of private funds saved their banking business (Ehrenberg 1896). In the previous section, we calculated the excess return from asiento lending overall. After the opportunity cost of funds and losses from the bankruptcies, it amounted to 3.16 percent. While such a return compared favorably to other available financial instruments and even to some commercial ventures, it came with the considerable risk of extended periods during which loans were not serviced. The solution adopted by international bankers was to sell shares in asientos in exchange for a fee. This allowed them to spread the risk among several investors while fine-tuning their own exposure. Parceling out the risk was central to the asiento system. Most large contracts gave bankers lead time of a few months before the main disbursement. This allowed them to tap the European payment fairs for the needed funds. In some cases, the king

---

37 The king had received net inflows for 3.1 million ducats between January and October 1596. In November and December, he was expected to have net outflows of 1.5 million ducats. The payment stop, declared just before the end of November, froze these disbursements.

even advanced "working capital" to the bankers, providing them with a sum of money that could be used to round up prospective investors.[38]

While the original asiento contracts preserved at the Archive of Simancas only identify the main underwriters, it is possible to find shares of Spanish asientos in the account books of merchant families based in Genoa. One such source is the *libro mastro* of the partnership formed by the brothers Lazzaro and Benedetto Pichenotti along with Gio Girolamo Di Negro, who we encountered at the beginning of the book.[39] The Pichenotti belonged to a well-known merchant family that never lent directly to the king of Spain. Gio Girolamo was a member of the De Negro family that participated in the asientos, although his name is never found in the contracts themselves.[40]

The Pichenotti–Di Negro society purchased shares in both the asientos described above. It contributed 5,265 ducats and 4,500 ecus to the one concluded on February 24, and 30,000 ecus to the one signed on July 26. The Pichenotti brothers supplied half the capital, and Di Negro contributed the other half. The society would make the disbursements and collect repayments under the same conditions that the Spanish bankers had stipulated with the king. The intermediation fee payable to the Spanish bankers was 1 percent.

The suspension decree was published on November 29, 1596. At that point, Spinola and De Negro had not yet collected any repayments from the February 24 asiento. They nevertheless forwarded 12,200 ducats to the Genoese society on account of a partial repayment of their share in the July 26 contract. This indicates that the king had already made a partial repayment himself, even though none was expected before the end of November. The most likely reason for this is that the fleet must have arrived a month earlier than expected, thereby allowing the bankers to collect the 466,667 ducats that had been promised from that source before the payment stop.[41]

---

38 For example, on July 1, 1572, the king entered into a contract with Pablo de Grimaldo for 800,000 ducats, to be delivered in October 1573. The agreed-on repayment structure shows that the king was to make the first repayment of 125,000 ducats in July 1573, three months before the banker made his initial disbursement. This practice was not uncommon in large contracts, particularly those involving international transfers.

39 ADG, Inventario Doria 193. For a detailed study of this book, see Felloni 1978. Our description closely follows his account.

40 When referring to bankers based in Genoa, we use the Italian spelling of their names.

41 The asientos at Simancas only allow us to observe the promised cash flows, not the actual ones. The Pichenotti–Di Negro account book thus provides a rare window into what actually transpired after the contracts had been signed. This example makes it clear that deviations from

The default froze all further cash flows on the Pichenotti–Di Negro participation. The situation began to be resolved with the settlement of November
1597, in which the bank debt was converted into juros. Two-thirds of the debt
was repaid in 7.14 percent bonds, which largely traded at par. The remaining
third was repaid through a bond swap, reducing the interest rate on juros
acquired or already held by the bankers, and entailing a net loss of 20 percent
of the original capital of the outstanding asientos. The Spanish bankers collected the bonds corresponding to the settlement, calculated the share of
principal and interest corresponding to the Genoese society, deducted their
fees, collection, and conveyance expenses, and forwarded the remainder to
Genoa using the same mix of assets they had received from the king. This was
the provision of la misma moneda, which we mentioned earlier. Since bankers received bonds in the settlements, requiring them to pay their creditors
back in cash would have created serious liquidity problems. The arrangement of la misma moneda allowed international lenders to forward the bonds
to the smaller investors who had supplied capital. This applied regardless of
whether investors had purchased specific shares in an asiento or just made a
demand deposit with the banking house (Neri 1989).

The accounts of the Pichenotti–Di Negro society were finalized and closed
in 1600. By that time, with no more credits outstanding, the society had received a total of 38,741 ducats net of costs in cash and bonds of different
characteristics. This represented a loss of 8.4 percent of the original capital.[42] Because the loss was spread over several years, however, the annualized
rate of loss was substantially smaller. While we do not observe the actual
dates of every cash flow for the Genoese venture, we can exploit the fact that
its investment was structured to mimic the Spanish asientos, whose cash
flows we have reconstructed before. After adding the 1 percent intermediation fee, Pichenotti and Di Negro obtained an annualized return of -1.32 percent for their share in the February 24 contract, and -5.19 percent for their
participation in the July 26 one.[43] Their overall (weighted) annualized return
was thus -4.27 percent.

---

the letter of the contracts did not always harm the bankers. The early arrival of the fleet meant
that they collected a portion of their debts ahead of schedule, hence mitigating the impact of the
bankruptcy.

42 In the Pichenotti–Di Negro account book, the ecus are valued at the exchange rate agreed
to between the king and Madrid bankers rather than at their metallic content. This suggests that
the Madrid bankers did not pass through the profits obtained in the exchange operation.

43 To obtain conservative estimates, we assume the intermediation fee was front loaded.

The true test of any risk-sharing system comes in bad times. The rhetoric during the bankruptcies was harsh enough. Bankers complained loudly to the king about how poorly he rewarded their loyalty. On December 22, 1575, for example, Lorenzo Spinola wrote to the king to maintain that he had been enormously harmed by the suspension decree, and to remind him of the many services and favors he had provided over the years. He then asked the king to make good on his promises because "the word of a king is a law."[44] Contemporary business commentators bemoaned the plight of the widows and orphans of Genoa. For instance, Venetian merchant Giovanni Domenico Peri (1672), describing the effects of the 1627 bankruptcy, wrote: "In addition to the ruin of the bankers, several other financiers who provided them with funds exited the business. Between ones and the others, many rich families were exterminated, and many widows and orphans were at the same time reduced to miserable poverty."[45] Later scholars such as Braudel concluded that the suspension decrees were catastrophic events, periodically ruining the cream of Europe's financial elite. This is not what the contract with Spinola and De Negro suggests. While the bankruptcies caused short-term losses on specific contracts, these were more than offset by high profits during normal times. This result applies to prominent banking families that kept representatives in Madrid and dealt directly with the king. It is entirely possible that the bankruptcies had a stronger impact on smaller financiers. This is where a second archival document can shed more light.

Gio Girolamo Di Negro also kept his own master account books, as was customary. These *libri mastri* detailed all the assets, liabilities, and profits or losses for the relevant period. The book covering the period between April 1596 and October 1598 is preserved in the Doria Archive, giving us a glimpse of the 1596 default's impact.[46] At the end of the period, in October 1598, Di Negro had not yet received the settlement payments corresponding to his participation in the asientos.[47] He recorded his participation in the society with the Pichenotti brothers as an asset worth 7,500 Genoese lire and also

---

44 "Pues la una le yes la palbra de v.m. y me la dio de que esto se haria assi conmigo por mis muchos servicios y los que tengo de hazer." Instituto Valencia de Don Juan, Envío 22, Caja 33, TB 144.

45 "Oltre la rovina degli Assentisti, hanosi questi ritirato a dietro molti, che gli soccorevano di rivelantissime partite, e fra gli uni, e gli altri, sono restate esterminate molte ricche famiglie, e molte Vedove, e pupilli insiememente ridotti a miserabile povertà."

46 ADG, Inventario Doria 192.

47 This is consistent with the society's book, which records the final settlement in 1600.

had another 1,116 lire invested in a different asiento.[48] The final balance sheet shows that Di Negro had total assets worth 96,252 Genoese lire. He turned a profit of 6,025. Since these funds had been earned over a period of thirty months, the annual profit was 2.4 percent. Di Negro was not doing particularly well by the standards of the day. Investing in long-term bonds would have netted him 7 percent or more, with little risk (but also less of a chance to receive the principal back anytime soon or without a discount). While Gio Girolamo Di Negro did not report any juros among his assets, most businessmen kept a diversified portfolio that included Spanish bonds backed by various income streams. For example, his relative Ambrogio Di Negro in 1560 had juros backed by the taxes on silk in Granada, internal customs of Seville, sales taxes of Carmona, royal taxes on wool, and yearly payments that the king received from the shepherds' guild.[49]

Overall, Di Negro's relatively mediocre performance must have been caused by commercial ventures, to which he committed over 90 percent of his capital. More important, he was in no danger of financial ruin as a result of Spain's default. Had Philip II completely repudiated his debts, Di Negro would have lost less than 9 percent of his assets. Over the period covered in the account book, this would have translated into annualized excess losses of 3.5 percent. This result is consistent with our findings for the top-level bankers and yields a powerful insight into the strength of the overall system. While the defaults of Philip II caused substantial losses, no link in the chain of financial intermediation was exposed to catastrophic risk when they occurred.

CONCLUSIONS

Lending to the king of Spain made good business sense; it was hugely profitable on average, despite periodic defaults and restructurings. According to our estimates, the typical contract during the second half of Philip's reign cost 20.3 percent annually—or 13.1 percent over and above the return on long-term debt. About 9 percentage points of the return was absorbed by

---

48 This contract is identified as the *assiento del millione*—a common name given to contracts for 1,000,000 ducats or ecus. Since there were four different asientos for that amount open at the time of the 1596 suspension, it is not possible to identify the exact one that Di Negro had invested in.

49 ADG, Ambrogio Di Negro, Libro Mastro, Inventario Doria 342.

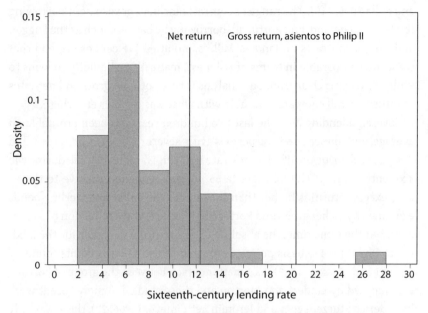

FIGURE 20. Interest rates on sixteenth-century loans and returns on asientos

write-offs, interest not received, and the delay in settling old debts. This left a net return of 11.6 percent for Philip II's bankers—or 4.4 percent above the return on long-dated juro debt.

The same conclusion emerges from analyzing the profitability of loans by the banking dynasty. Of the sixty families that lent to Philip, only five failed to earn their likely opportunity cost of capital—and these bankers provided only a negligible proportion of the short-term loans taken out by the king. It therefore is no surprise that so few bankers stopped lending to the king of Spain. While our figures cannot take into account the profitability of lending before 1566—a period hit by two bankruptcies—it is unlikely that additional information would overturn our results. Even the Fugger family, whose laments have been echoed by Ehrenberg (1896), was not so disappointed with the returns that it stopped lending altogether.

How do these returns compare to those available to lenders at other times, or elsewhere? Genoese and German lenders could have easily extended credit to other borrowers. While few had funding needs on the scale of Philip II, the general demand for credit was not low. In figure 20, we compare the average lending rate to Philip II with other sixteenth-century interest rates (Homer and Sylla 2005, 119). The range of contracts includes government borrowing (by France, England, and Portugal), borrowing by bankers such as the Fugger, and census contracts on land as well as annuities. We cannot pretend that these are comparable in terms of riskiness, maturity, or liquidity to loans to Philip II. What is clear from our analysis is that both the gross and net rates of return overall compare favorably with what was on offer elsewhere.[50]

Sovereign lending over the last two hundred years has been profitable on average, but punctuated by periods with severe losses (Eichengreen and Portes 1989b). Our results demonstrate that this was already true during the sixteenth century. The loss rate (a 65 percent reduction relative to the ex ante excess return) is higher than the one for the dollar and sterling bonds examined by Eichengreen and Portes (ibid.), who found a reduction of 34 percent.[51] At the same time, the absolute excess return was higher for the lenders to Philip II—460 basis points, compared to the 44 basis points found by Lindert and Morton (1989). As a matter of fact, between the group of borrowers analyzed by Lindert and Morton and those studied in more recent work by Federico Sturzenegger and Jeromin Zettelmeyer (2006, 27), there was only one country with a higher rate of excess return, achieved for a short period of time: Brazil paid a premium of 1,623 basis points between 1992 and 2001. The fact that excess returns were high ex post, over a long time, suggests the high ex ante rates were not simply a compensation for risk. Market power— the ability of the Genoese network to extract favorable terms and conditions from a borrower heavily dependent on credit—must be an important part of our story.

What underpinned the power of Genoese lenders was a remarkably effective way of raising funds. Lending took place with loans that the leading bankers syndicated, selling on participations to smaller investors. We used two investments during Philip II's fourth and final default, in 1596, to gain insight into actual gains and losses for the final investors. The Pichenotti–Di Negro partnership bought participations in two short-term loans to the king, underwritten by Agustín Spinola and Nicolás De Negro. They were affected by the payment stop. We carefully reconstruct the profitability of these two

---

50 To compare like with like, we should remember that the plotted interest rates are gross rates of return, prior to any haircuts, defaults, or restructurings. Since most were arguably safer than lending to the king of Castile, we also give the net rate of return on loans to Philip II. Even with this standard of comparison, business with Madrid appears an attractive proposition.

51 A full comparison would have to take into account that Castile's juros were not defaulted on at all in the sixteenth century.

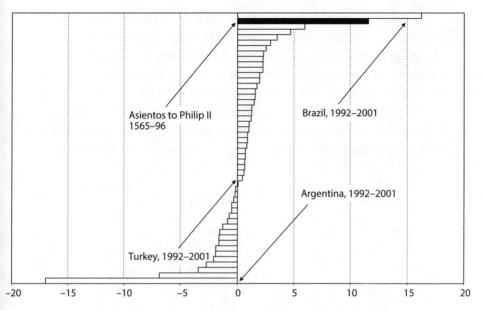

FIGURE 21. Excess returns to sovereign lending, 1850–2001

investments and interpret them in the context of the investors' portfolio overall.

The original underwriters achieved a full risk transfer. They only owed the partnership the respective proportion of the money that they received from the king. Losses were modest overall; investments in these loans did not constitute a large fraction of the partners' wealth. While a sudden payment stop was not a small matter for investors, there was no domino effect—a wave of defaults as one creditor after another sees a large share of their assets disappear or turn illiquid.

Remarkably, the Genoese system of repackaging and reshuffling risk worked better than securitization did after 2000. As the financial crisis since 2008 has made clear, new securities consisting of repackaged mortgages actually failed to provide risk diversification. Losses in a small corner of the financial system soon threatened to overwhelm it in its entirety (Gorton and Metrick 2012). The sixteenth century instead produced a successful example of how financial intermediation can "work" by offering a combination of attractive returns and relatively modest, well-diversified risk. In part, it did so by passing on some of the exposure from bankers to final investors.

By effectively selling "shares" in loans made to the king of Spain, Genoese bankers could achieve a dual objective. They continued to monopolize access to the short-term lending market. This was necessary for lending to be sustainable, as we argued in chapter 5. It also cannot have been bad for profitability. At the same time, selling on parts of the loans reduced the principal lender's risk. Securitization was thus remarkably successful: it provided funds to the Spanish monarchy at the height of its powers, and the system weathered the effect of temporary, negative shocks such as the 1596 bankruptcy.

CHAPTER 7

RISK SHARING WITH THE MONARCH

In early October 1591, lookouts near Cadiz could see the sails of the Spanish treasure fleet on the horizon. After crossing the Atlantic from Havana, the galleons' final leg of their journey saw them sailing up the Guadalquivir River. They put into harbor under the walls of Seville and unloaded their well-guarded cargo: many tons of silver, mined in modern-day Bolivia using the latest chemical processes as well as forced labor. At the Casa de la Contratación, the value of imports was assessed in detail; one-fifth had to be paid as tax.

The previous year, two rich fleets had reached Spain, bringing up to 2.5 million ducats with them (Morineau 1985). Whenever the fleets did not sail or came in with smaller silver cargoes than expected, the royal income was also lower; the king, strapped for cash, had to take even more short-term loans from his Genoese bankers. In some years, much more silver came in than anyone expected. In 1595, for example, the fleet arriving in March carried more silver and gold than the Casa de la Contratación could store. The overflow had to be stockpiled in the courtyard (Deforneaux 1979). Nor could anyone predict the fleet's date of arrival with any accuracy; news traveled with the same ships that brought the silver from the Americas.[1] Also, prior to Piet Heyn's successful raid in 1628, pirates never captured an entire Spanish treasure fleet. The principal determinant of the size and timing of the galleons' arrival was weather in the Atlantic in the summer and fall.

One person who waited for the news of the fleet's arrival in 1591 with particular interest was Tomás Fiesco. A Genoese banker who would eventually rise to the role of *factor general*, he had agreed to provide 300,000 ecus

---

1 Sometimes a faster ship (a frigate or sloop) would sail ahead of the main fleet and inform the authorities in Seville of its imminent arrival (Perez-Mallaina 1998).

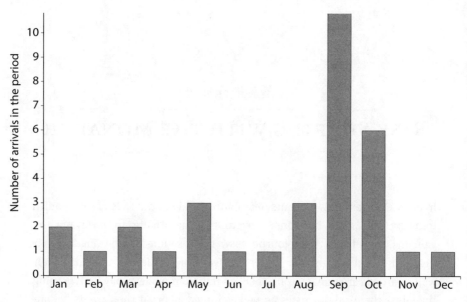

FIGURE 22. Frequency of fleet arrivals, 1587–1600. *Source*: Morineau 1985.

(some 293,000 ducats) to Philip II.[2] These funds were to be paid out to the military commander in Flanders, the Duke of Parma. The king had promised to repay a substantial part of the loan with the proceeds of the 1591 silver fleet.

Typically, Spanish silver fleets arrived in September or October, as shown in figure 22. The contract specified that one month after the convoy's arrival, the king had to repay the loan. If he failed to do so within thirty days, the banker could stop all future disbursements. The king had the right to delay payment if the fleet did not reach Seville by October in exchange for a penalty of 1 percent additional interest per month. Eventually, the banker could demand repayment in the form of long-dated juros.

In this chapter, we ask what the sighting of the silver fleet off Cadiz and the king's contract with Fiesco can teach us about history of sovereign debt in early modern Europe, and about the nature of cross-border lending more generally.

---

2 The factor general was in charge of raising loans to meet the king's financing needs and often provided part of those loans themselves.

THE PROBLEM OF NONCONTINGENT DEBT

Philip II and his bankers effectively solved a problem that defeats bonds market today: how to link repayment terms for sovereigns to a borrower's financial situation while avoiding perverse incentives. We first summarize the nature of the concern in order to appreciate how remarkable this sixteenth-century feat of "financial engineering" was. We then show how the contractual structures worked and what they can tell us about cross-border lending in the age of monarchs.

The issuance of noncontingent sovereign debt can be destabilizing. It requires procyclical fiscal policies, which aggravate recessions (Eichengreen 2002). In the extreme, outstanding noncontingent debts can no longer be serviced in bad times. After defaults, GDP typically falls, trade plummets, and banking systems have to be recapitalized (Eaton and Fernandez 1995; Rose 2005). Economists and policymakers alike have argued that the issuance of debt indexed to GDP (or export prices) could reduce the risk of bankruptcy and smooth consumption (Borensztein and Mauro 2004; Borensztein et al. 2004; Kletzer, Newbery, and Wright 1992). While state-contingent debt is conceptually attractive, few GDP-indexed bonds have actually been issued (Griffith-Jones and Sharma 2006).[3] Most instances—such as Argentina's and Greece's GDP-linked bonds—occurred in the aftermath of defaults.[4] Overall, there is substantial skepticism that the problems with governments issuing state-contingent debt can be overcome.

Why did a sixteenth-century monarch and his financiers succeed where modern states and investment banks fail? We argue that two factors were key. First, the king's need to spend ahead of revenue was particularly large. Expenditure—dominated by war financing—fluctuated wildly from year to year; revenue was broadly stable.[5] The need for intertemporal barter (Kletzer and Wright 2000) was acute. In this environment, the principal risk for the monarch was a shortfall of liquidity. Risk sharing was especially valuable, and negative shocks were most likely to be temporary.[6] Second, the sixteenth-century fiscal environment generated easily observable, verifiable

---

3 Some scholars have argued that all sovereign debt is de facto contingent (Grossman and Van Huyck 1988).
4 Greece avoided an outright default through a "voluntary" restructuring.
5 Silver revenues were highly volatile; we describe them below.
6 Elsewhere, we have shown that Philip II's famous defaults do not reflect insolvency but instead were caused by liquidity crises (Drelichman and Voth 2010).

state variables reflecting the strength of the monarch's finances. The arrival and size of silver fleets from the Americas as well as the yield from individual tax streams controlled by third parties, for instance, served as a ready reference for payments due.

Bad news was effectively translated into lower payment obligations or later due dates; risk sharing between borrowers and lenders worked. This arrangement also survived Philip II's famous defaults. The king suspended payments no less than four times during his long reign, but defaults were excusable in Grossman and Van Huyck's (1988) sense. Debt was de facto state contingent even under circumstances not specified in loan contracts. Defaults involved larger shocks than the contracted ones in individual contingent loans. They also entailed contingencies that were difficult to write into contracts—principally the outbreak and outcome of wars. Our data show that the pricing of loans did not change adversely after the payment stops; lenders did not update their priors about the type of borrower Philip II was. This fact along with the prevalence of contingency clauses in loan contracts offers support for interpretations of sovereign lending emphasizing implicit risk sharing in cross-border debt.

Scholars working on debt restructuring have highlighted that the process can be long and inefficient (Benjamin and Wright 2009). On the other hand, Kovrijnykh and Szentes (2007) argue that repeated cycles of borrowing and default may be an efficient outcome, with lenders having an incentive to let borrowers escape from debt overhang. Patrick Bolton and Olivier Jeanne (2009) suggest that contracts that are ex post excessively difficult to restructure can be the result of efficient bargaining ex ante. Philip II's defaults were restructured unusually quickly and with moderate haircuts, indicating that the payment suspensions were closer to an implicit contingent contract than to full-scale breakdowns in debt markets.

CONTINGENT LENDING TO PHILIP II

In this chapter, we work with the 393 contracts for which we were able to observe every single clause and repayment scenario.[7] Of these, 270 have at least one contingency clause; many contain several. There were a total of 408

---

7 We were not able to do so for 41 contracts. This is mostly due to material damage to the documents. In a few cases, the clauses were too vague to allow an accurate estimation of cash flows and rates of return.

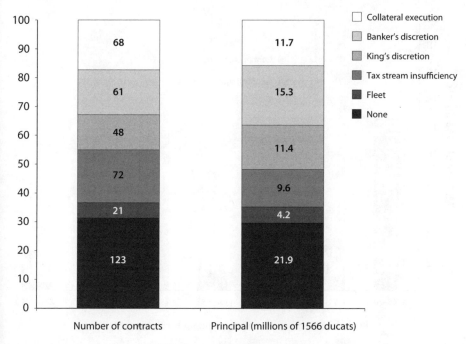

FIGURE 23. Distribution of the major contingent scenario,
by number of contracts and by principal

different scenarios over which the king and bankers contracted. We first
summarize the types of contingencies written into contracts and then analyze their economic effects.

TYPES OF CONTINGENCIES

The loans contain a wide variety of scenarios allowing the king and bankers
to deviate from the baseline payment schedule. We can distinquish five
broad categories. The first two are associated with events outside the control
of either king or bankers: the arrival of the fleet and the performance of specific tax streams. Two more types are actually options, given to either the
king or bankers. In some cases, the king can delay payments, usually in exchange for some penalty. In others, the banker can request to be paid in juros
ahead of the loan maturity date. We call these options "king's discretion"
and "banker's discretion." Finally, contracts involving collateral also have an
"execution" clause, which specifies under what conditions the banker may
seize and sell the collateral. Figure 23 plots the main type of contingency for

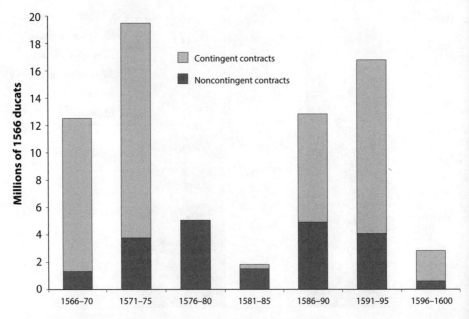

FIGURE 24. Contingent and noncontingent borrowing over time

each contract, showing both simple frequencies and the principal-weighted distribution.

Less than a third of the contracts were issued without a contingency clause. About 31 percent of these contingent scenarios refer to insufficient revenue for the Crown—either because some taxes fall short, or because the treasure fleets do not arrive on time or in sufficient size. Slightly over 40 percent of the contingent clauses give either the king or banker discretion to change the timing or nature of the payments. The remaining ones give the banker the right to seize and sell collateral if the king fails to repay.

The use of collateral clauses was not constant over time. As figure 24 portrays, it fluctuated heavily over time. While a dominant feature during the entire period, the use of contingency clauses was curtailed between 1576 and 1585. In the run-up to both the 1575 and 1596 bankruptcies, in contrast, contingencies were quite common.

We now illustrate the working of contingency clauses using specific examples from the primary sources. In 1566, the king entered into a contract with Lucián Centurión and Agustín Spinola. They agreed to disburse 38,000 and 57,000 ducats in Flanders in, respectively, May and September of that year, and were meant to receive one repayment in August from the first silver fleet.[8] If the fleet did not arrive by the end of July, the king promised to pay a penalty rate of 1 percent per month until the full repayment was made. The bankers also received a juro that covered the full value of the contract, which they were allowed to sell in case the king failed to meet his obligations. The original contract without contingency clauses produced an annualized MIRR of 24.1 percent. If the contingency clauses were invoked, this fell to 15.6 percent. The king thus could insure part of the income risk that came from the highly volatile silver revenue stream. At the same time, the bankers' financial position was largely safeguarded against the risk that the king could or would not pay through the use of collateral juros.[9]

Another asiento demonstrates how variable tax revenue could also trigger contingency clauses. In October 1581, Juan Ortega de la Torre lent 60,000 ducats to the king. He was to be repaid from the second payment of the excusado.[10] De la Torre was not first in line; the contract specified that Baltasar Cattaneo should collect his money first. Importantly, the banker would have to collect payments himself, to which end the king provided him with the necessary documentation. Should the revenue from the excusado be insufficient, the banker had the right to be repaid from the *perlados y cabildos* (a minor revenue stream levied on ecclesiastical rents). Other contracts in this category specified that if the tax revenue in one year was insufficient, the king would pay a penalty interest rate until he could repay with the following year's taxes.[11]

We now turn to a more complex asiento. We already met the lender— Tomás Fiesco, the Genoese banker waiting for the silver fleet to arrive at the

8 This asiento also shows how loans were combined with transfers. The bankers first disbursed 38,000 ducats, the king next repaid the principal and interest on 95,000 ducats, and only afterward did the bankers disburse the final 57,000 ducats in Flanders. Therefore, the latter disbursement is a transfer rather than a loan, since the bankers had already received the money from the king.

9 The deeper reason for collateralizing with juros is that fiscal centralization in Castile was limited—the king could sometimes not pay the bankers directly, but the city of Seville, say, would still pay holders of juros. Hence, the fragmentation of fiscal authority facilitated the continuation of lending. The incentives that supported the collateralization of one type of debt instrument with another are similar to those in Broner, Martin, and Ventura 2010.

10 As mentioned earlier, the excusado is a tax levied on church revenue, one of the so-called three graces, introduced in 1567.

11 This example also shows the importance of weak tax-collecting powers in determining lending arrangements, with the king effectively outsourcing the right to access taxes already collected.

beginning of this chapter. His contract with the Crown showcases how multiple contingent clauses could be used to provide insurance for both king and bankers under a variety of scenarios. In 1591, Fiesco had agreed to provide 300,000 Flemish ecus.[12] Of these, 200,000 ecus were paid out in Flanders, while the rest were delivered at the payment fairs of Besançon. The king advanced 75,000 ducats at the contract's signing, which meant that the actual loan was for 218,000 ducats (the rest was a mere transfer of funds). The first disbursement by the banker, also in April, was for 61,500 ecus. It was followed by nine equal monthly payments of 26,500 ecus each.

The king promised to repay the loan from a variety of sources. Several of these payments were not contingent: 84,700 ducats from the new millones excises in November 1591 and May 1592; another 60,000 from the cruzada ecclesiastical tax in October and November 1592; 12,000 ducats from the sale of vacant lands; and 30,000 ducats from the extraordinary service. The single-largest payment, for 90,100 ducats, was to come from the proceeds of the silver fleet of 1591, which was expected in late summer or early fall. This was followed by a fleet contingency clause: if the silver did not arrive by October, a penalty of 1 percent per month would apply until the banker was repaid from alternative tax streams—specifically the subsidio, excusado, and ordinary and extraordinary services. The treasury disbursed payments from these sources every four months, in March, July, and November.

Even if the fleet arrived on time, the king could unilaterally choose to delay repayment until the maturity of the loan, twelve months later. This is what we have labeled king's discretion. It came at a steep cost: if the contingency was invoked, the banker had the right to stop the remaining disbursements (for a total of 53,000 ecus) while still being entitled to collect all the promised repayments on earlier disbursements. Finally, from January 1592, the banker had the right to request repayment of up to 100,000 ducats of principal and interest in perpetual juros—a banker's discretion clause. This contingency allowed the banker to receive safe bonds instead of promised cash payments.

Table 22 shows the cash flows for the Fiesco contract under the baseline scenario, and under each of the fleet's and king's discretion contingencies. Because the banker's discretion contingency only affects the payment instruments but not the actual timing or values, we do not report it in a separate column.

---

12   AGS, Contadurias Generales, Legajo 90.

Table 22. Net cash flows from the Fiesco contract under three repayment scenarios

	Baseline scenario	Fleet contingency	King's discretion
April 1591	14,931	14,931	14,931
May 1591	−25,884	−25,884	−25,884
June 1591	−25,884	−25,884	−25,884
July 1591	−25,884	−25,884	−25,884
August 1591	−25,884	−25,884	−25,884
September 1591	−25,884	−25,884	−25,884
October 1591	−25,884	−25,884	−25,884
November 1591	124,283	34,183	34,183
December 1591	−25,884	−25,884	0
January 1592	−13,948	−13,948	0
February 1592	0	0	0
March 1592	0	31,535	0
April 1592	0	0	0
May 1592	54,767	54,767	54,767
June 1592	0	0	0
July 1592	0	32,736	0
August 1592	0	0	0
September 1592	0	0	0
October 1592	30,033	30,033	30,033
November 1592	30,033	63,971	120,133
Yearly MIRR	23.2%	24.0%	39.8%

Note: Figures are in ducats; 1 ducat = 1.023 ecus.

The baseline scenario gave bankers a 23.2 percent return. While higher than average, this was not an unusual cost for a contract that included transfers to multiple locations, deliveries in several currencies, and repayments sourced from many different tax streams. Under the fleet contingency scenario, the king misses the largest part of the November payment (some 90,100 ducats) in 1591, and makes up the shortfall in March, July, and November 1592 with 1 percent monthly interest. In this case, the rate of return on the contract increases slightly, to 24 percent.

The king's discretion scenario is markedly different. The king additionally misses the payment of 90,100 ducats in November 1591, causing the banker to cancel the December and January disbursements. The king is still obliged to make all promised repayments, including the 90,100 ducats, which are now due in November 1592. The banker gets paid much later than promised, but since he skips two disbursements totaling over 50,000 ducats, his rate of return increases to 39.8 percent.

It is useful to contrast the two contingencies. The cash flows are identical up to and including November 1591. The missed payment is exactly the same. In one case, however, the reason is an exogenous, verifiable event: the fleet has not arrived. The banker continues to make the disbursements as scheduled, while the repayments are delayed. The cost of the contract rises marginally. In the second case, though, the fleet has arrived. If the king fails to pay in this particular instance, he has much less of an excuse. The cost of the contract in this scenario goes up substantially.

The fleet contingency insures the king against factors outside his control, such as adverse Caribbean weather and disruptions to silver production. Because these factors are self-equilibrating in the medium term, the bankers do not charge high insurance premiums. The king's discretion contingency is different. It gives the king the option to extend the maturity of his debts without having to borrow fresh funds, even if the fleet arrived in time. The king is now protected against an unexpected need for liquidity or the prospect of a rollover crisis. Because these situations would signal mounting pressure on the king's finances (or a lower willingness to use available funds for repayments), the banker demanded a hefty premium in exchange for providing that insurance. Finally, the banker's discretion contingency insures the lender against a downturn in the king's ability to pay. After the first eight months of the contract, the banker can swap almost all his remaining claims for relatively safe long-term bonds of the same present value.

THE ECONOMIC IMPACT OF CONTINGENCY CLAUSES

What is the economic purpose (and impact) of the different contingencies? In this section, we examine the effect of contingent clauses on cash flows. We also analyze cost and maturity modifications as a function of the Crown's and bankers' interests as well as in response to the arrival of new information. Contingent clauses provided ample, bidirectional risk sharing between the king and his bankers. Their use is interesting: they reveal a preference to deal with eventualities ex ante, before they materialize, instead of having to renegotiate ex post. This implies that frequent recontracting (in the spirit of Bulow and Rogoff 1989) was not costless in the eyes of Crown and financiers.

How exactly did contingencies influence cash flows? For each contingent scenario, we compare the rate of return to that of the noncontingent cash flow scenario. Loans that feature contingent scenarios have a baseline return of 20.5 percent. In aggregate, contingencies do not affect the returns substantially. The median change in the cost of a contract is close to zero under the average contingent scenario.[13] Panel A in figure 25 plots the distribution of cost changes. While some contracts saw their cost rise or fall by 20 percent or more annually, most changes were much smaller; the bulk of observations involve changes of around 5 percent per year.

Contingent scenarios also affected the maturity of the loans (panel B). On average, the maturity of loans changed little: an increase of two months with a standard deviation of nine. One hundred and twenty one scenarios allowed for a longer maturity, giving the king an average of 9.7 additional months to repay. In 18 cases, there was an early termination date, either because the king could exercise an early repayment clause or because a missed payment allowed bankers to cancel future disbursements. In these situations, the average termination date preceded the original one by 17.6 months. The remaining 269 scenarios do not affect the maturity date either because they shuffle intermediate repayments or because they specify a swap of payment instruments.

Table 23 summarizes the contingent changes in the MIRR and the maturity of loans. The modifications reflect the changes in the king's fiscal position associated with each contingency type. In case of a fleet-related event, the maturity of the loan was extended for an average of 2.6 months. The cost increased only by a small amount.[14] On average the bankers received some compensation, reflecting only a minor increase in risk. Fleets would eventually arrive, and delays did not convey new information about the king's solvency. At the same time, bankers on average required some additional compensation *entering* into contracts that had a fleet contingency written into them; on average, the baseline cost was 4.1 percent higher (even if variability was high and the difference is not statistically significant).

Tax revenue shortfalls were a different matter. Most taxes were collected directly by cities or tax farmers, which had an incentive to maximize reve-

---

13 By comparison, the median return of loans that do not have contingent clauses is 19 percent.
14 The increase is a mere 0.4 percent; the difference in cost compared to the baseline is not statistically significant.

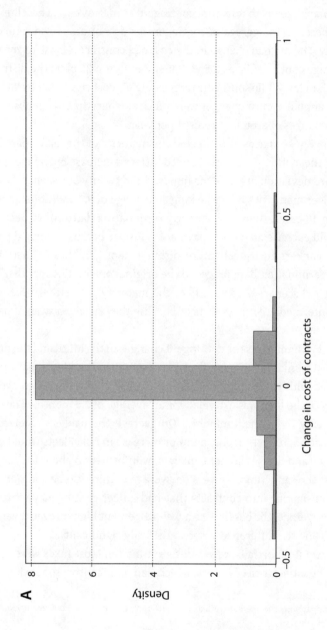

A
Density
Change in cost of contracts

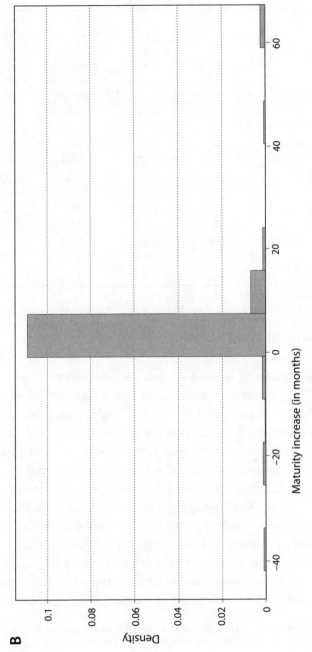

B

Density

Maturity increase (in months)

FIGURE 25. Changes in the cost of contracts and in maturity after contingency clauses are invoked

Table 23. Baseline MIRR, differential MIRR, and maturity (in months) by type of contingency

| Contingency type | Frequency | MIRR differentials | | Maturity differential |
		Baseline minus noncontingent average*	Contingency minus baseline	Contingency minus baseline
Fleet	26	4.1% (0.72)	0.4% (0.75)	2.6 (0.00)
Tax stream insufficiency	100	−1.6% (0.10)	−1.7% (0.06)	4.6 (0.00)
King's discretion	63	4.3% (0.03)	4.1% (0.06)	1.6 (0.30)
Banker's discretion	102	1.6% (0.08)	1.5% (0.04)	−0.2 (0.84)
Collateral execution	118	−2.1% (0.03)	−2.3% (0.01)	2.1 (0.00)
Total/average	408	0.0%	−0.1%	2.1

Note: P-values in parentheses.
*The coefficient is from a regression of MIRR on contingency type dummy, use of foreign exchange clause, duration, and loan size. The standard errors are clustered at the contract level.

nue. The performance of revenue streams was independently verifiable by the lenders. The incentives of bankers and those of tax collectors were compatible, and there was no possibility for the king to manipulate the total yields.[15] Tax stream insufficiencies were bad news on the fiscal front, but they did not convey information about what type of borrower the king was. The associated contingent scenarios gave the king an extra 4.6 months to repay, while reducing the rates of return by 1.7 percentage points. Consistent with a risk-sharing arrangement, a negative shock in terms of fiscal revenue resulted in a reduction of borrowing costs. The baseline cost of loan agreements with a tax shortfall clause was 1.6 percentage points below the average; bankers were willing to offer this type of "insurance" without a premium.

King's discretion scenarios involve nonpayment without an externally verifiable trigger. This was followed by a rearrangement of cash flows. The

---

15 The king, however, could manipulate the order in which lenders were paid. Contracts were therefore quite specific in establishing the collection priority of individual lenders with respect to specific tax revenues.

arbitrary postponement of payments by the king was undoubtedly bad news, either because of new, urgent spending needs or because other loans were receiving priority for repayment. Unlike the case of tax stream insufficiencies, the cause of the need for extra liquidity was uncertain, and moral hazard could not be ruled out. The risk to the bankers was increasing compared to the original contract. Risk sharing implies that this additional risk should be associated with a transfer to the bankers. The large increase in returns—4.1 percent on average—is consistent with this interpretation. Contracts with a postponement option for the king were also more expensive in the baseline scenario, by an average of 4.3 percent.

The effect of banker's discretion is more difficult to evaluate, as there are liquidity considerations to take into account. These clauses typically allowed bankers to collect part or all repayments in juros instead of cash. There was often no reduction in the amount payable, and bankers were allowed to collect the entire current-term interest of the juros.[16] This accounts for the increase of 1.5 percent in the rate of return. In practice this accounting profit probably did not translate into an actual cash flow advantage. Bankers would have had to sell juros on the secondary market—a costly operation that could nullify the 1.5 percent gain. If they chose to keep the bonds, they would have had to wait for and oversee the collection of the coupon payments. A reasonable guess is that banker's discretion clauses allowed lenders to switch their repayments to safer assets without a substantial impact on their cash flow. Bankers typically asked for these clauses when they had reason to be concerned about the future yield of extraordinary revenues.[17] Whenever asientos contained banker discretion clauses, they were on average 1.6 percent more expensive initially for the king.

The final contingency type was collateral executions, which were triggered by the king missing the final loan payment. Because the event was predefined in the contractual clauses, it was not considered a default. When it was exercised, the cost of the contract fell. Sometimes the contracts specified that the bankers had to wait before being able to sell collateral juros—hence the two-month average maturity increase, which reduced profitabil-

16 Juro interest was paid twice yearly. If the banker received juros in October, he would be allowed to collect the entire December interest payment rather than the portion corresponding to the three months he had held the bond. This increases the profitability of the contract relative to a cash payout in December.

17 The maturity of the loan for the king changed differently from the one for the bankers. The king would now only repay through tax revenue foregone, which means at a slow pace.

ity. Bankers also lost because the collateral was not always sufficient to cover the last repayment. When bankers and the king's representatives entered into contracts with a collateral execution clause, the cost was on average 2.1 percentage points lower. This reflects the additional security of holding a collateralized loan.

Our findings indicate that the king was mainly concerned with the risk of a liquidity shortfall; the cost of borrowing mattered relatively less. The majority of short-term loan contracts envisaged the option to postpone the payment or swap payment instruments. Return differences by the type of contingency strongly suggest that these options allowed for effective risk-sharing arrangements. Instead of having to find fresh funds to redeem maturing debt, the king had the right to extend the maturity of his borrowing either by delaying payments or swapping short-term debt for perpetual bonds. At the same time, the bankers reduced the risks from the king changing his spending priorities. The most costly eventualities—combining higher baseline cost and the expense of the contingency cost—were those triggered at the king's discretion. Here, bankers received an extra 8.4 percent in interest. In other words, when the Crown postponed payments without "just cause" in the form of late fleet arrivals or tax insufficiencies, the increase in borrowing costs was greater than average. Bankers realized that writing an option on such eventualities did not imply good news about the king's finances and demanded to be compensated accordingly.

We now take a closer look at the effect of contingent clauses on loan maturities. In table 24, we regress the change in the loan's due date (in months) on its original maturity, plus a host of controls.

Longer durations are not strongly associated with maturity extensions in case a contingency clause is invoked; the coefficient is significant but small. When contingency clauses are invoked, contracts with a foreign exchange component typically offered extensions of over a month and a half. Fleet contingencies extend the due date by two months on average—roughly the time it took to tap an alternative repayment source. Tax stream shortfalls are associated with even longer extensions—four months on average. Collateral executions add only one month. King and banker discretion clauses mainly reshuffled payments before the maturity of the loan, and as such, were not significantly correlated with changes in the due date.

When was each particular type of contingency clause used? In figure 26, we examine the evolution of contingency clauses by five-year intervals. In

Table 24. Loan duration modifications in case of contingency

	Maturity increase
Constant	−1.97
	(−2.31)**
Fleet	2.14
	(2.19)**
Tax stream insufficiency	4.07
	(6.19)***
King's discretion	0.44
	(0.28)
Banker's discretion	−1.03
	(−0.97)
Collateral execution	1.19
	(2.02)**
Principal (real)	−1.13
	(−0.96)
Duration	0.07
	(1.72)*
Foreign exchange	1.58
	(1.88)*
R^2	0.09
N	531

Note: The standard errors are clustered at the contract level. The t-statistics are in parentheses.
Significance: *0.1, **0.05, ***0.001

the beginning, for the years before the 1575 bankruptcy, over half the clauses were associated with collateral executions. At the same time, almost 25 percent referred to shocks that reduce the Crown's revenue, such as fleet arrival and revenue shortfalls. Collateral execution clauses vanished as a category after the 1575 default. There was little borrowing—and hence few contingencies—up to 1585, when the preparations for the invasion of England resulted in a new round of asientos. In the last fifteen years of the sample, banker discretion clauses became the top category, followed by revenue shortfalls.

The use of contingent loans was not affected by the 1575 default; their share was roughly constant before and after.[18] Their composition, however, changed significantly. Before 1575, most contingent contracts had collateral

18 The exception was the 1576–80 period, when most lending came from the 1577 settlement.

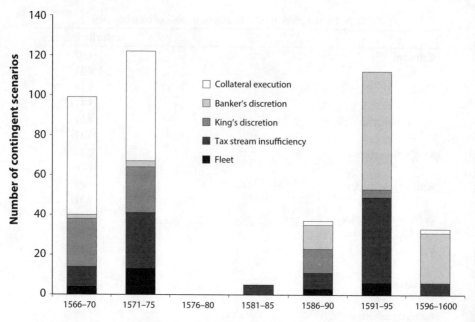

FIGURE 26. Number of contingent scenarios by type and period

clauses. During the 1575 bankruptcy, the Crown declared that asientos had been illegal and thus payments on the collateral bonds were suspended. Bankers were prevented from selling them in the secondary market. These juros were reinstated with the 1577 settlement. Nonetheless, few bankers were interested in collateral execution clauses afterward. They instead used banker's discretion clauses, which allowed for juros to be obtained and sold off at will in advance of the contract's maturity. Banker's discretion clauses were also priced to offset the cost of collecting and transferring the juros. In essence, bankers learned how to better protect themselves. If before they had to wait for the king to miss a payment to switch to safe assets, now they could do it at the slightest hint of trouble.

Why was it in the interest of bankers and the king to write these contracts? We emphasize three key facts. First, there was an absence of asymmetric information as a result of primitive means of communication along with the extraordinary opportunities for intertemporal barter at a time of urgent, sudden spending needs and variable revenue. Second, the pricing of loans and effect of duration on interest cost suggests that the Crown principally struggled with liquidity issues, not solvency problems. Third, the fragmented nature of fiscal authority ensured that the Crown's borrowing could be effectively collateralized by other debts.

Both silver revenue and tax farming facilitated the writing of contingent contracts. Silver taxes were a major source of revenue for servicing asientos. Since news from the New World about the production of the mines traveled at the same speed as the galleons laden with bullion, the king had no informational advantage vis-à-vis his bankers. There was also no way to hide the arrival of a fleet from the Indies.

The key reasons that favored conditional contracts written on fleet revenues—new information about the king's fiscal position was independently verifiable and neither party had advanced knowledge—also encouraged tax farming. Tax farmers had strong incentives to maximize revenue and were not in the king's employ. Relevant news might have been obtained from them ahead of time, but it is highly unlikely that there was much scope for manipulation. Overall, the existence of tax farming (combined with typically low volatility in nonsilver revenue) would have made it much more likely that shortfalls reflected genuine adverse shocks to the king's fiscal position.

CONTINGENT DEBT AND EXCUSABLE DEFAULTS

Having analyzed the conditional nature of many loans to Philip II, we now shed light on sovereign lending and the nature of defaults. King and bankers contracted over a large number of different states of the world; they found an effective way to share risks. Nevertheless, some eventualities could not be written into loan covenants.[19] Default under these conditions was a form of risk sharing, but it did not differ fundamentally from the contingencies foreseen in loan documents; it simply extended the sharing arrangements already in place to a different situation. We argue that the defaults of Philip II were excusable (in the sense of Grossman and Van Huyck 1988).[20] While violations of the letter of lending contracts occurred, these were anticipated by both sides and did not violate lenders' original expectations. To support this argument, we need to demonstrate that defaults took place in times of exog-

---

19 Shocks arising from military defeat are an obvious case in point. It would be hard, for instance, for the Crown to contract on the possibility of the Armada sinking.

20 Strictly speaking, in chapter 5 we surmised that defaults were excusable; here, we actually argue the case based on a closer reading of loan and fiscal conditions.

enous, independently verifiable adverse shocks and that there were no significant negative changes in loan conditions after an actual default.[21]

Modern-day sovereign bonds issued in New York or London are said to be in default when the borrower misses a single agreed-on payment. No such definition existed in sixteenth-century debt markets. At the time, neither banker nor Crown could firmly commit to servicing debts or taking deposits. Actual outcomes could fall somewhere on a spectrum between full compliance and default. It helps to think in terms of five possibilities: full compliance with the baseline scenario, as detailed in the original contract; use of one or more of the contingency clauses; violation of one or more of the clauses, followed by a rescheduling; full suspension of payments to all creditors, followed by a general settlement; and outright repudiation.

We argue that because contracts already considered a wide range of states of the world, both parties were aware that repayment according to the original agreement was not always possible. At the same time, the fact that contingencies were written into loan documents suggests that the Crown attached considerable importance to not violating explicit loan conditions. If defaults are excusable, financial outcomes for the lenders should reflect the borrower's fiscal position. Crucially, differences in outcomes should be driven by exogenous shocks—that is, events that are beyond the borrower's control. The king should live up to the letter of his obligations during normal times. When some minor shocks occur, he will invoke some of the emergency clauses in the contracts, which we document extensively. Larger shocks will see him violate some of these clauses, only to compensate lenders later. Full-blown moratoriums reflect even larger negative shocks and in this sense are driven by events that cannot be contracted over ex ante. Finally, for defaults to be excusable, outright repudiation should never be observed, unless it was preceded by a negative shock so large that no further payments can happen. This is the easiest part of the argument; there is no single case of outright debt repudiation in our database.

We first demonstrate that payment stops occurred in poor states of the world for Philip II, which were caused by exogenous shocks. Excusable defaults also imply that lenders' expectations are not disappointed. These are

---

21 If there had been changes in the actual loan conditions, these could also be rationalized by Bayesian updating (about, say, the strength of the Spanish navy). In this sense, demonstrating that rates did not change requires the "strong" version of our hypothesis to hold.

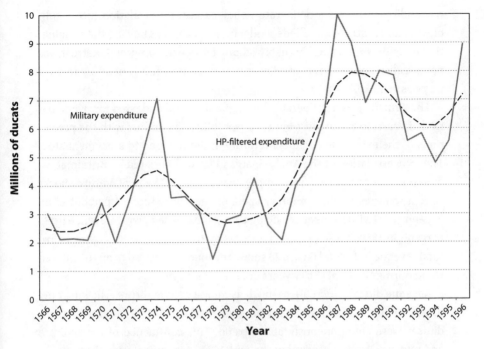

FIGURE 27. Military expenditure, actual and HP filtered, 1566–96

not directly observable; instead, we analyze how the pricing of loans changed after the 1575 default.

DEFAULT IN VERIFIABLY BAD STATES OF THE WORLD

For the Grossman and Van Huyck interpretation to be correct, defaults have to take place in verifiably bad states of the world. This was true in the case of Philip II. Twin shocks hit the Spanish monarch's finances in both 1575 and 1596—military expenditures surged and revenue from the New World was below trend.

In figure 27, we show military expenditures during the period 1566–96. From year to year, expenditures on armies and fleets varied considerably. Three spikes are clearly visible: 1572–75, 1587–88, and 1596. These reflect the escalation of the Dutch Revolt, the Armada, and the outbreak of war with Britain. In two of these cases, the king defaulted. The exogeneity of these shocks varied. The Dutch Revolt had been simmering for a few years, and responding to it was a deliberate policy choice. Its escalation into a full-blown—and costly—war of independence, however, was beyond the imagination of Spain's ruler (and arguably among European observers). Retreat was not a realistic option, as control over important revenue-generating territories was at stake.[22]

The Armada was a deliberate choice, planned and budgeted for over a period of years. Its failure was always a possibility, and in line with the predictions of the excusable defaults literature, it did not lead to a payment stop. The 1596 escalation of the Anglo-Spanish War was initiated by Britain; it required a major military effort on the part of Spain. The expenditure shocks were also large. In 1574, military spending accounted for 93 percent of all expenditure (without debt-servicing costs); it exceeded Crown revenue by 25 percent. In 1588, it also exceeded revenue by 16 percent (while staying below total revenue in 1596).[23] Figure 28 shows revenues compared to an HP-filtered trend during the final thirty years of Philip II's reign.

Revenue did not fluctuate as much as military expenditure. The king only defaulted in those years when revenue was markedly below trend and expenditures were simultaneously above trend. This confluence of expenditure and revenue shocks occurred in the mid-1570s, for several years in a row. As figure 28 shows, there were also many years when revenue was significantly below trend and the king did *not* default. This does not contradict our hypothesis that the king's defaults were excusable because they occurred in bad states of the world. For it to be correct, the king does not have to default in *all* bad states; it is enough that he never defaults in good times. The observation is also easy to rationalize: silver revenues contributed substantially to volatility in the 1580s. Years of low revenue typically alternated with years of high revenue. Extra asiento borrowing smoothed over normal fluctuations. Combined with risk-sharing elements in the loan contracts (such as the one with Fiesco), the Crown coped with most fluctuations. In years of extraordinary pressure, a payment stop was declared and a general renegotiation became necessary.

The events that caused fiscal difficulties were easy enough to confirm and identify. Only one or two silver fleets reached Spain every year. The cargo of the arriving ships was a key determinant of Crown revenue. Once the ships

---

22 For a detailed analysis of Philip's military strategy, see Parker 1998.
23 All figures are from the analysis in chapter 4 and the appendix in Drelichman and Voth 2010.

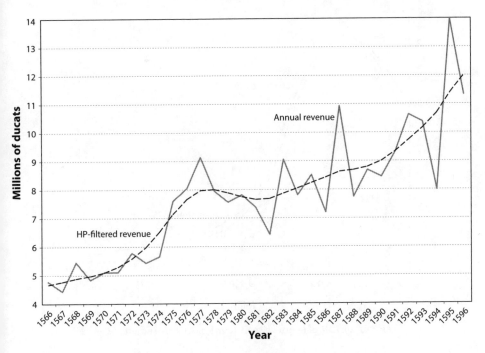

FIGURE 28. Crown revenue, actual and HP filtered, 1566–96

had arrived, it proved impossible to suppress information on the size and value of the fleet (Morineau 1985). Commercial gazettes all over Europe carried details on the value of treasure brought from the Indies; a major determinant of the king's fiscal position became public knowledge almost instantly. Military events such as the escalation of fighting in the Netherlands after 1568 were also simple to verify. While not all years of high military expenditure or revenue shortfalls led to payment stops, every default during Philip II's reign happened when the king's fiscal position was poor. Strained finances always reflected exogenous events and not poor fiscal policy. They were caused by the Dutch rebellion flaring up as well as Caribbean storms.

NO ADVERSE CHANGE IN LOAN CONDITIONS

We have established that defaults occurred in bad times and that bankers to Philip II shouldered some fiscal risks that the monarch was exposed to, thereby effectively providing insurance. In interpreting the defaults, the key question is the extent to which these were de facto anticipated. If so, they were simply

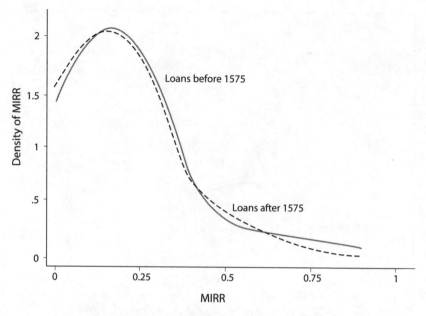

FIGURE 29. Rate of return on short-term loans, before and after 1575

another instance of claims falling due on an insurance policy; with the Crown's finances stretched due to a lack of liquidity, contracts could not be honored to the letter. We now demonstrate that this is what happened.

If lenders did not understand that they were de facto holding contingent debt, and if the defaults were not excusable, then loan conditions after 1575 should have changed for the worse.[24] This is the null hypothesis that we examine. Figure 29 presents the distribution of interest rate (MIRR) on asientos before and after the 1575 default. As is readily apparent, there was no systematic shift in the cost of loans. The range, means, and medians of both distributions are virtually identical. A t-test finds no evidence that the king's access to credit became more expensive.[25]

Alternatively, the quantity lent could have gone down even while the cost stayed the same. This is not what we find. The principal of loans made did not decline. In figure 30, we plot the log size of loans before and after 1575. The average dropped from a log value of 11.86 to 11.83 (p-value 0.78). While the

---

24 As Alfaro and Kanczuk (2005) argue, rising interest rates after a default act as a punishment for borrowers who violated the original loan contract in a context of contingent lending.
25 We obtain a value of 0.68 (p-value 0.49).

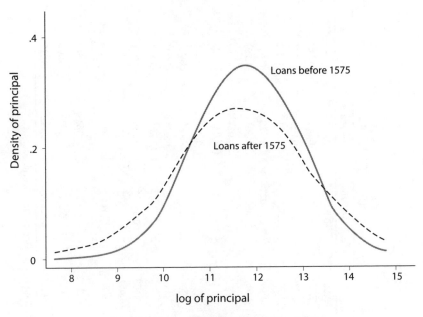

FIGURE 30. Size of loans, before and after 1575

distributions are not identical, there is no evidence that loans are systematically smaller.[26]

Next we examine the cost of borrowing more formally. In the first column of table 25, we regress rates of return on the principal lent, foreign exchange clauses, and duration as well as a dummy for lending after 1575.[27] We find that longer-duration lending, on average, was less expensive—a result that is consistent with the fixed cost of underwriting asientos and relatively cheaper alternatives available to the king for long-term borrowing. The size of a loan was not a significant determinant of its cost. Foreign exchange transactions raised the cost of borrowing by over 6 percent on average—a result of both the cost of operating overseas and use of foreign exchange transactions as a way to circumvent usury laws. Lending became 5 percent cheaper on average after the 1575 default. If we estimate with banker fixed effects (column 2), we find that the dummy variable for post-1575 loses its significance. This implies that the same bankers lent at the same rates as before, but that the number

26 A t-test has a value of 0.48 (p-value 0.63).
27 Our data for these regressions end in 1596, as no fiscal indicators are available after that date. As a result, we are unable to explore the effects of the 1596 bankruptcy.

Table 25. Correlates of borrowing costs (dependent variable: MIRR)

	(1) OLS	(2) OLS	(3) Robust regression	(4) OLS	(5) OLS	(6) OLS	(7) OLS
	All years	All years	All years	<1576	<1575	All years	All years
Duration	-0.0025***	-0.0027***	-0.0006***	-0.0023***	-0.0035**	-0.0025***	-0.0025***
	(-6.65)	(-6.03)	(-3.27)	(-3.93)	(-4.39)	(-6.35)	(-4.10)
Foreign exchange clause	0.066***	0.048**	0.024***	0.029	0.071**	0.059**	0.040
	(3.82)	(2.35)	(2.63)	(0.99)	(2.34)	(2.40)	(1.05)
Principal	0.035	0.065	0.026	-0.145	0.150**	0.372	0.048
	(1.05)	(1.58)	(1.44)	(-1.56)	(2.69)	(1.30)	(1.20)
After 1575 Dummy	-0.050***	-0.089	-0.066***			-0.051***	-0.067*
	(-3.01)	(-1.62)	(-2.69)			(-3.08)	(-1.82)
Debt/revenue Ratio						0.010**	0.008
						(2.21)	(1.09)
Fiscal Balance						0.001	-0.001
						(0.26)	(-0.21)
Constant	0.264***	0.461***	0.212***	0.403***	0.359***	0.206***	0.206***
	(14.45)	(4.30)	(4.42)	(4.65)	(3.98)	(5.18)	(4.06)
Banker fixed effects	No	Yes	Yes	Yes	Yes	No	Yes
N	393	393	383	181	212	381	381
Prob <F	0.000	0.000	0.000	0.010	0.012	0.000	0.001
Adj. R^2	0.137	0.130		0.133	0.146	0.149	0.155

Notes: The standard errors are clustered at the year level in columns (6) and (7). The t-statistics are in parentheses.
Significance: *0.1, **0.05, ***0.001

of bankers willing to only provide "dear" credit now played a smaller role. The post-1575 dummy becomes significant if we use robust regression estimation instead, and the size and significance of the coefficient is similar to simple OLS (column 3). The results so far do not suggest that the default caused bankers to suddenly update their beliefs about the riskiness of lending to Philip II. They did not begin charging more to compensate for higher perceived risk. If anything, the cost of borrowing dropped substantially after the resolution of the bankruptcy.

In specifications (4) and (5), we estimate the basic regression for the period before and after 1575. In both periods, lending for a longer period was associated with a significantly lower cost of financing. Before 1575, extending a contract's duration by one year (roughly one standard deviation) was associated with a 2.4 percent fall in the cost of borrowing; thereafter, the predicted decline was by 4 percent. These two coefficients are statistically different from each other (beta coefficient -0.015; t-statistic -3.05). Column 5 also shows a significant coefficient for principal. This is in contrast to the result prior to 1575. At the same time, if we interact the post-1575 dummy with the size of principal offered, we do not find a statistically significant shift in terms of loan pricing in response to lending volume. Overall, the only major changes in loan pricing after 1575 favored the Crown.

In columns (6) and (7), we add two fiscal indicators as explanatory variables: the debt-to-revenue ratio and fiscal balance.[28] In column (6), the debt-to-revenue ratio is significant at the 5 percent confidence level. The coefficient suggests that a unit rise of the ratio resulted in an additional 1 percent in borrowing costs for the king. Once banker fixed effects are added, however, the coefficient is no longer significant. This implies that as debts mounted, only a subset of "premium" bankers continued to operate in the short-term debt market. The fiscal balance, in contrast, is never significant; bankers did not take year-to-year fluctuations in the budget into account when pricing loans.[29]

In sum, we find that sixteenth-century Spanish defaults occurred in bad times; they did not adversely influence the pricing of loans, and the Crown's ability to borrow did not suffer. Combined with the evidence on the extensive

---

28 These data are discussed in chapter 4.
29 It should be noted that neither the debt-to-revenue ratio nor the fiscal balance were readily available statistics. Estimating the latter is substantially more difficult.

use of contingency clauses, this makes it likely that the defaults were excusable in Grossman and Van Huyck's (1988) sense.

THE TIMING OF DEFAULT

Why did Philip II default when he did? There can be no question that he suspended payments when revenue was unusually low and expenditure was high. Here we examine an additional factor that entered the king's calculus: the structure of maturing debts. So far, the implication of our reasoning was that Spain simply could not pay its debts at a particular moment because of a combination of pressing spending needs and revenue shortfalls. Before such a toxic blend leads to a default, though, one more problem typically needs to materialize: an inability to roll over maturing debts. We do not know with certainty that this contributed to the timing of the 1575 default, but the archival record provides some tantalizing hints that point in this direction.

Few borrowers can cope with a sudden need to repay maturing debt instead of merely paying off old creditors with new borrowings. Spain in the age of Philip II was no different. In a classic paper, Kehoe and Cole (2000) argue that rollover crises will be more likely the shorter the maturity profile of debt is. A short maturity profile raises the risk that repayments will be high in the absence of new debt contracts being signed. Interestingly, the borrower's optimal decision in this setting depends on the possibility of rolling over the debt. If the market offers a chance to repay old bonds with new borrowing, it is typically best to repay. In contrast, if the maturing debt needs to be paid by reducing expenditure or increasing taxes, the cost may be too high. Cole and Kehoe (1996) point out that Mexico's crisis in 1994–95 occurred with relatively low outstanding debt, but after a massive shortening of the maturity profile of the debt outstanding. If all loans had been contracted with a single lender, that lender would always roll over the debt to avoid the cost of default; a larger group of lenders cannot easily coordinate to the good equilibrium, since it is individually optimal to "run" on the sovereign and demand repayment.

We now show that this logic at least partly applied to Spain's famous default of 1575. As a result of reconstructing all cash flows, we have a good idea of how high the repayment burden implied by scheduled payments was on the eve of the decree—and how much worse things became as few contracts were signed as the debt burden mounted. Table 26 shows the pattern of inflows and outflows per year as specified in the loan covenants:

Table 26. Short-term debt inflows and outflows (in ducats)

	Inflows	Outflows	Total
1568	1,075,791	1,922,955	−847,163
1569	2,212,168	1,690,146	522,023
1570	3,389,018	4,055,424	−666,405
1571	4,204,295	3,338,327	865,968
1572	2,962,373	3,064,128	−101,755
1573	3,590,391	5,218,367	−1,627,975
1574	4,238,107	7,141,147	−2,903,040
Jan-Aug 1575	5,221,784	2,775,257	2,446,527
September 1575	417,888	40,000	377,888
October 1575	227,876	1,018,095	−790,219
November 1575	0	1,005,113	−1,005,113
December 1575	922,818	2,415,391	−1,492,574

Positive and negative net flows alternated over time, as expenditures and tax revenues ebbed and flowed. In a growing economy and with rising tax revenue, this does not indicate a fiscal problem. The balance remained positive for the first eight months of 1575. For the last three months of the year, however, the outflows would have been massively negative. The total repayments implied by the signed contracts amounted to 4.4 million ducats; at the same time, there were contractual arrangements for inflows to the tune of more than 2 million ducats. This was a much faster rate of net outflow than in 1574, when the entire year saw a liquidity drain from asiento borrowing of 2.9 million.

The fact that lots of debt was maturing itself offers only limited information about the nature of the 1575 crisis. Earlier years had seen sustained periods when the gross monthly liquidity drain was above 0.5 million ducats— but matching inflows had reduced the net figure substantially. In the last quarter of 1575, there were few commitments for fresh funds. This suggests that some bankers at least had begun to suspect that a decree suspending payments was in the offing. Indeed, in an undated memorandum of one royal official, Francisco Gutiérrez de Cuéllar, there is a hint of a building crisis of confidence among the bankers during the run-up to the default. The memorandum observes that there is "gran rumor" and growing concern about a coming suspension, and that Nicolao de Grimaldo and Lorenzo Spinola in particular had begun preparations in advance of a default.[30]

---

30 Instituto de Valencia de Don Juan, E22, C33, TB, 142. Lovett (1980) argues that Spinola even sold juros de resguardo in the run-up to the crisis.

Gutiérrez himself apparently only learned about the decree later than even the bankers concerned—a sign of the great secrecy surrounding the decision, which was largely taken by the king himself with only minimal advice from officials (Lovett 1980). It also shows that some information had begun to leak out. Plans about how to solve the problem of the floating debt had been circulating since the 1573 discussions about an increase in the sales tax, and many of them included measures against the bankers. While bankers were willingly rolling over maturing debt, these plans came to naught; once some of the better-informed bankers like Lorenzo sought to salvage their own position, the cost of paying out maturing contracts at a time of general cash shortage became too big—a classic rollover crisis created by a scramble for the exit by the biggest and most-informed lenders.

If our interpretation is correct, one question arises: Why could bankers coordinate during defaults (as argued in chapter 5), but not in the run-up to a default? We argue that the structure of incentives was different. Lending during a moratorium would be easily observed and could possibly lead to a permanent ostracism in the community of Genoese lenders. Failing to lend, on the other hand, may have had many reasons, including a lack of available funds. Since lenders did not have to step forward on a fixed schedule, the failure to join in a common enterprise was less visible, and at the best of times, coordination was more indirect. Finally, the balance of risks and returns was arguably different; lending in the run-up to a default offered only average returns in exchange for high risks. Lending during a default combined sky-high risks with substantial rates of return. Lenders could be perfectly rational in having an appetite for one but not the other combination of risks and returns.

CONCLUSION

Over the last eight hundred years, many periods of debt accumulation have been followed by default (Reinhart and Rogoff 2009). Despite these disruptions, the market for sovereign debt did not disappear. What accounts for this resilience? We argue that at least in the case of asiento lending to Philip II, excusable defaults were an important factor. Studying the loan documents directly, we show that a significant share of short-term loans contained contingency clauses. We analyze the different types of loan modifications along with their impact on cash flows and loan maturity. These modifications allowed effective risk sharing between king and bankers—an institutional solution that offered many of the desirable properties that contingent debt would have today (Borensztein and Mauro 2004).

Genoese bankers effectively offered insurance to the king. They charged relatively high interest rates in normal times, but offered a service that the king valued when times were bad: de facto insurance. Loan contracts often included clauses that modified loan terms if financial conditions worsened in an unforeseen manner. One contingency that featured prominently in the documentation for short-term loans was fleet arrival. If the king's ships put into harbor later than expected (or not at all in a single year), then the repayment clauses could automatically be adjusted. Similar clauses covered low tax receipts and the like. In addition, there were numerous possibilities to extend payment horizons at the king's discretion.

The system of state financing under Philip II was not without shortcomings. The 1575 bankruptcy was probably caused by a combination of negative fiscal shocks—high spending coupled with low revenue—and a "run" by bankers on the treasury. There is some indirect evidence that financiers stopped offering fresh funds as the Crown's financial situation deteriorated. The short maturity profile of asiento borrowing then made it optimal for the king to stop servicing his debts, since a high share of outstanding debts would have to be redeemed from other sources (instead of simply rolled over). In this sense, a combination of coordination failure and a negative liquidity shock may well account for the timing of the 1575 default.

The fact that an early modern monarch and his financiers could effectively write state-contingent debt contracts—providing insurance—is remarkable in its own right. This insight can also inform our understanding of Philip's famous defaults. In all likelihood, they were excusable.[31] They occurred in a context that involved loans that were individually rescheduled with some frequency, they happened in verifiably bad states of the world, and they reflected events beyond the control of the sovereign. The early Spanish defaults were far from synonymous with a one-sided abrogation of contracts, as Reinhart and Rogoff (2009) imply.[32] Instead, the defaults healed a form of market incompleteness: not all possible states of the world can be contracted on. When some unspecified—or perhaps unspecifiable—contingency arises,

---

31 In the sense of Grossman and Van Huyck (1988).
32 Reinhart and Rogoff (ibid., 86) treat early French and Spanish defaults as equivalent, and use the terms abrogate and default interchangeably.

it is rational for the borrower to default. Since lenders realize this before the fact, the default—while violating the letter of the contract—does not go against the spirit of the original agreement. Payment stops thus are not followed by higher interest rates or lengthy exclusion from loan markets. "Business as usual" should resume quickly once the temporary, adverse shock that caused the default in the first place has dissipated. This is what happened in the case of both the 1575 and 1596 bankruptcies.

CHAPTER 8

TAX, EMPIRE, AND THE LOGIC
OF SPANISH DECLINE

Non sufficit orbis—the world is not enough. When Sir Francis Drake's men stormed the Spanish governor's palace in Santo Domingo in 1586, they found a coat of arms displaying a map of the world. It was adorned with a horse rising triumphantly on its hind legs; the Latin motto was prominently displayed above.[1] What sounds like hubris to modern ears (and will remind readers of a James Bond film) was not an exaggeration for contemporaries: in the days of Philip II, Spain's empire had no equal. After the takeover of Portugal, Philip II ruled virtually all of the Americas, numerous trading posts along the African coast and in India, the Philippines, and a string of possessions in Italy and the Low Countries. Philip II's Portuguese ships dominated the spice trade and Indian Ocean; Spanish ships led the fleet that defeated the seemingly unstoppable Ottoman expansion at the Battle of Lepanto; Spanish armies won glittering victories against France. Spain's armed forces, numbering 163,000 troops, were three times larger than that of the next European power (Karaman and Pamuk 2010). No other power in the world controlled a territory as large, armed forces as powerful, or financial resources as vast as those of Habsburg Spain.

And yet within little more than a century, Spain's empire was a shadow of its former self. By 1700 already, its armed forces numbered no more than 63,000 troops—a third of their former size. France, in contrast, had raised the number of soldiers under arms from 57,000 to 342,000—from one-third of the Spanish figure to a number almost seven times greater. Britain was not far behind, increasing the size of its army and navy more than threefold, from

---

1 One of Drake's soldiers published a sketch of the coat of arms in *A Summarie and True Discourse of Sir Francis Drake's West Indian Voyage* (Bigges 1589). The English apparently amused themselves by repeatedly asking the Spaniards to translate the Latin inscription (Parker 2001).

Table 27. Europe's great powers: Measures of might

	Armed troops[*]			Fiscal revenue[**]		
	1550	1700	Change	1600	1700	Change
England	66	191	125	66	559	494
France	57	342	285	294	878	584
Spain	163	63	−100	431	219	−212

Source: Karaman and Pamuk 2010.
* in thousands
** in tons of silver per year

66,000 to 191,000 (ibid.). While still controlling vast territories, Spain's standing had taken a beating. Portugal broke away in 1640; northern Catalonia and the Franche-Comté had to be ceded to France as a result of peace treaties in 1659 and 1678. Rebellions in Catalonia and Sicily along with conspiracies against the Crown in Andalusia and Aragon underlined the imperial center's fragile grip on its possessions in Europe and the Iberian Peninsula. Gone were the trading outposts in India and control of the spice trade.

Revenues had declined—from more than four hundred tons of silver per year in the heyday of imperial Spain to barely half that figure. Other powers had succeeded in raising more revenue. England, where the total tax income was a mere 15 percent of the Spanish figure in 1600, raised revenue almost tenfold. It now commanded financial resources that were 150 percent greater than Spain's. France similarly went from 68 to 400 percent of Spanish tax revenue.

There can be no doubt that by 1800, in the European concert of powers, Spain had become a bit player; it "failed" where England succeeded. England came to control dominions every bit as vast as those held by Philip II; its frigates and ships of the line ruled the waves more absolutely than Spanish galleys and galleons ever had.

Two of the great empires during the early modern period ended up on radically different trajectories. Spain under the Habsburgs, in the sixteenth and seventeenth centuries, is today a byword for poor governance, profligacy, economic stagnation, and military decline, from which Spain even now has not fully recovered. Eighteenth- and nineteenth-century Britain serves as a paragon of good institutions, fiscal probity, economic growth, and military prowess.

One of the main factors underlying Spain's poor performance as a great power was economic decline. Since Earl Hamilton's (1938) famous essay, many studies have examined and documented the slowdown after 1600.

What was a vigorously expanding economy in the fifteenth and sixteenth centuries, with rising per capita incomes and expanding population, first stagnated and then began to shrink. Hamilton attributed much of the decline to monetary mismanagement following the influx of American silver. Elliott (1961) later reexamined the evidence, and found it overwhelmingly in favor of eventual decline—but stressed that Castile, not Spain as a whole, was its principal victim.[2]

Elliott emphasized that high real rates of return on government bonds diverted capital away from trade and production, and created a rentier class. Warfare, in his view, was responsible for the continuously high interest rates. This created what amounted to a siren song for Spanish entrepreneurs. This argument, while plausible, does not stand up to scrutiny. Spaniards often held long-dated debt, but much of it was also placed abroad; entrepreneurs everywhere in Europe should have been equally tempted to become rentiers. After 1610, interest rates on public debt also were progressively lowered, declining to 2.75 percent by the eighteenth century (Alvarez Vázquez 1987). There is therefore no reason to think that the crowding-out effects west of the Pyrenees should have been greater than elsewhere.

The leading interpretation of Spanish decline—put forward by economists working in the new institutional economics tradition—highlights the overwhelming strength of the Crown. According to this view, Spain's rulers were already more powerful than other monarchs by the time the Americas were discovered. The influx of silver revenues then strengthened their position further. Ruinously costly and unnecessary wars, the high-handed breaking of contracts, frequent defaults and payment stops, and a disregard for the sanctity of property eventually undermined growth and prosperity.[3] In contrast, where rulers in 1500 were initially weaker—such as in England—Atlantic trade strengthened the merchant class, which eventually wrested power from the rulers, improving the institutional quality and facilitating growth (Acemoglu, Johnson, and Robinson 2005).

---

2 In recent years, the decline of Spain in the seventeenth century has continued to attract scholarly attention. For three recent examples, see Kamen 2003; Marcos Martín 2000; Yun Casalilla 2004. Robert Allen (2001) provides a long-run comparative analysis of the economic performance of several European economies, including Spain.

3 This argument is found, for example, throughout the work of Stanley Stein and Barbara Stein (2000, viii), who write, "While Spain's silver-based transatlantic system at first provided a primary source of Hapsburg preeminence, it was also a basic structure of Spain's relative political, social, and economic backwardness as the metropole grew dependent on its colonial world."

Remarkably, the leading interpretation of Spain's "failure" is a blend of the same ingredients typically invoked to rationalize British success. In both cases, there is a focus on many wars fought, territories acquired, fiscal resources directed toward the military, preferential trading agreements, and the exploitation of colonies. According to Patrick O'Brien (2001), Britain's bellicose policies and aggressively mercantilist strategy propelled its rise as an economic power. John Brewer (1988) underscored the importance of the English Crown controlling ever-greater resources through the tax system in an effort to finance more wars. Philip Hoffman (2012) has argued that efficiency improvements in weapons spilled over into production processes. Even the mountain of debt accumulated by Britain during the eighteenth century apparently had surprisingly few negative effects, as some of the literature observes.[4]

Seemingly, what was good in one case turned out to be poisonous in another situation. Some of the contradiction can be explained by the way in which the writing of history is organized. Country specialists typically write history; they look for explanations in unique tales. As a consequence, the field as a whole has provided a deeply contradictory explanation of the rise and fall of Europe's early modern empires. Here, we will first review Spain's fiscal performance, together with that of other European great powers. We find little evidence of policy failure. Next, we offer an alternative explanation of Castilian decline. It was not excessive powers in the Crown's hands that led to eventual doom but rather a failure to successfully centralize the Spanish administration, integrate heterogeneous territories into a larger whole, and pursue an "absolutist" agenda. The reasons for this failure were, according to our view, a greater initial level of political heterogeneity on the Iberian Peninsula than elsewhere and the deleterious effect of silver on state capacity.

SPAIN'S FISCAL PERFORMANCE IN COMPARATIVE PERSPECTIVE

A central part of the institutionalists' indictment of Spain rests on that country's seemingly disastrous fiscal performance. Spain defaulted time and again between 1550 and 1913 (Reinhart, Rogoff, and Savastano 2003). There is also no doubt about the country's economic decline in the seventeenth century, during and after a string of payment stops. Whether defaults can be

---

4 Robert Barro (1987) argued for Ricardian equivalence. Some authors have considered that "crowding out" was unimportant (Heim and Mirowski 1987), in contrast to the arguments by Jeffrey Williamson (1987) and Peter Temin and Hans-Joachim Voth (2005).

regarded as a sign of imprudent fiscal policy and the violent breaking of property rights is at least debatable from a theoretical perspective.[5] It also bears repeating that the first four of Spain's "defaults" only affected 15 percent of total borrowing—the short-term debt. As chapter 7 argued, these defaults were excusable and in all likelihood anticipated by the lenders. Hence, they did not violate the initial implicit contract struck between the Crown and lenders. Nothing demonstrates this more clearly than the fact that Philip II never lost access to credit, except for brief periods during the payment stops; in other words, the ultimate test of the sustainability of his debts was that he managed to sustain access to debt markets.

In addition, we show here that Spain actually conducted its finances before 1600 in a *more* prudent manner than many other early modern European powers. This reinforces our conclusions in chapter 4, arguing that debts were sustainable and the payment stops reflected liquidity shocks. Our comparison does not look at various powers at the same point in time. Instead, we try to make our comparison more appropriate by examining a set of European states at the height of their power (during the early modern period), comparing sixteenth-century Castile with the imperial incarnations of Holland, France, and Britain in later centuries. The date ranges are mostly determined by data availability. This does not bias our comparisons; France, for example, would arguably look even worse if the final years prior to the revolution had been included (White 1989).[6]

In table 28, we use a variety of fiscal indicators.[7] Two measures frequently used in assessing the strength of fiscal systems are the debt-to-revenue and debt-service-to-revenue ratios (Sargent and Velde 1995). The Netherlands marks one extreme with an average debt-service-to-revenue ratio of 68 percent; fully two-thirds of tax revenue was spent on the Low Countries' debts.[8] France is at the opposite end of the spectrum, with a relatively low debt-service-to-revenue ratio of 38 percent in the eighteenth century.[9] The figure for France may be too low; the average excludes the period prior to the 1720 rescheduling, when debt service accounted for more than 80 percent of reve-

---

5 See the discussion in chapter 1.
6 For an analytic narrative comparing Castile to other contemporary European nations, see Yun Casalilla 2004.
7 We draw on several sources from the "European State Finance Database" (Bonney 2007) as well as fiscal estimates in other work.
8 Calculated from the data in the "European State Finance Database" compiled by Marjolein 't Hart (1999).
9 Inferred from figure 1 in Sargent and Velde 1995.

Table 28. International comparisons

	United Kingdom****	Netherlands	Castile	France
Average debt service/revenue	43% (1698–1793)	68% (1601–1712)	51% (1566–96)	38% (1720–80)
Maximum debt service/revenue	70% (1784)	194% (1713)	75% (1574)	81% (1718)
Growth rate of tax revenue	1.47% (1692–1794)	0.36% (1601–1712)	3.30% (1566–96)	1.26%++ (1661–1717)
Primary surplus/ revenue	19.5% (1698–1794)	Negative	31.50% (1566–96)	14.2%++ (1662–1717)
Revenue/GDP	9.1%	21.2%+	2.7*–9.5%**	6.8%*** (1788)
Debt/GDP	74% (1698–1793)		14.7*–51.4%** (1566–96)	81.1%+++ (1789)

Note: Data taken from the "European State Finance Database" (Bonney 2007).
+ per capita tax as a percentage of income of an unskilled laborer, as calculated by Jan De Vries and Ad Van der Woude (1997)
++ based on data used by Francois Velde (2007), as kindly provided by the author
+++ Sargent and Velde 1995, table 1
* GDP based on the lower bound in Alvarez Nogal and Prados de la Escosura 2007
** GDP from Carreras 2003
*** Based on data analyzed by David Weir (1989), as compiled by N.F.R. Crafts (1995)
**** GDP data from Crafts 1995; fiscal data from Mitchell 1988

nue. Sixteenth-century Castile falls in the middle of the range, with a ratio of 51 percent. This makes it more similar to the United Kingdom than to the Netherlands.[10] Compared to the other great powers in early modern Europe, Castile was not spending an especially high proportion of its revenue on debt service.[11]

The same conclusion emerges from the maximum debt-service-to-revenue ratio. This ratio peaks at 75 percent for Castile, the second-lowest value among this set of competitors—and only marginally higher than the 70 percent registered in Britain.[12] France saw a maximum of 81 percent.[13] The Neth-

10 We compare the cases of Spain and the United Kingdom in greater depth in Drelichman and Voth 2008.
11 While we are biasing this number downward by taking the effects of the restructurings into account, we show in chapter 4 that even if we added the debt service saved by them back in, the overall numbers would look similar.
12 Note that by 1815, Britain's ratio was probably much higher; using the debt-to-GDP estimate by Barro (1987) suggests approximately 185 percent. By excluding the period of the Napoleonic Wars, we are biasing our results against finding high fiscal pressure in France and Britain.
13 By the late eighteenth century, this figure was actually lower in France than in Britain, amounting to 52 percent in 1788.

erlands sustained high levels of close to 200 percent for a short period while accumulating debts during the War of the Spanish Succession.

During Philip II's reign, Castilian tax revenues grew quickly—more quickly than in the United Kingdom, France, or Holland. Fiscal pressure increased approximately twice as fast as in the United Kingdom during the eighteenth century. This is all the more remarkable since historians have long held up Britain's willingness and ability to raise taxes as one of the key factors for its success in both the wars with France and avoiding default (Brewer 1988; O'Brien 2009). Admittedly, the Castilian figures are for a shorter period than in the case of Holland or the United Kingdom, but the time span is similar to the one available for France.

The maximum fiscal pressure relative to the GDP in Britain and Castile was also broadly comparable. Even when we use the (pessimistic) GDP estimates from Carreras (2003), the Castilian Crown extracted a much smaller proportion of national income than Holland, where the government revenue reached more than 20 percent of the national income. By this measure, both the United Kingdom and Castile collected a little less than a tenth of national product in taxes and contributions. Since a significant share of Crown revenue in Castile was effectively a tax on foreign mining, the actual fiscal pressure on the domestic economy was even lower than what the raw numbers imply. If we use the GDP figures by Alvarez Nogal and Prados de la Escosura (2007), which are more optimistic than Carreras's, the Castilian revenue-to-GDP ratio was half the British figure and markedly lower than in Holland.

Debt-to-GDP ratios (tentative as they are) tell a similar tale. Relative to the economy's total output, government debt in Castile was low—lower than in France or the United Kingdom. Scaling by revenue does not alter our conclusions. In 1801, for example, Britain's debt stood at 13.7 times annual fiscal revenue (Mitchell 1988). In 1822, the ratio still stood at 12.96, while the Castilian number fell in the range of 5 to 6.

Castile's primary surpluses were also high, even by elevated English and French standards.[14] Castile under Philip II actually allocated a higher proportion of its revenue to paying interest and repaying debt than either the United Kingdom or France. It could be argued that this is stacking the deck in Castile's favor; the high primary surpluses were partly necessary because of the markedly higher interest rates paid by Castile compared to eighteenth-

14 Prerevolutionary France also achieved significant primary surpluses under Anne-Robert-Jacques Turgot, if only for a time. See White 1989.

century England. Keeping the debt from exploding thus required a greater effort. Low borrowing costs in England were indeed important for debt sustainability there, but they did not reflect the market's fair assessment of risk. Instead, there is ample evidence that fiscal repression—forcing private lenders to underwrite government debt at below-market prices—was critical for the United Kingdom's debt management.[15]

So far we have examined a range of indicators and pointed out the relative position of the different powers. There is not a single indicator of fiscal probity on which Castile emerges as worst among the competitors; on several, it is at or near the top. If there is another state that looks broadly similar—in terms of average debt service, maximum debt service, and the revenue-to-GDP ratio—it is Britain, which has long been regarded as the benchmark for responsible financial management.

While there is no single measure of fiscal behavior that can serve as a summary measure of policy, there is an indicator more powerful than the mélange of different measures we already discussed. One crucial factor for debt sustainability is the reaction of fiscal policy to a buildup of debt. For debts to remain sustainable, a higher debt burden must be met with a greater primary surplus—if not immediately, then not too long thereafter. This insight is at the heart of the literature on fiscal policy functions (Bohn 1998). For example, the United States during the twentieth century accumulated enormous debts—essentially during World War I and II, and again after 1980. After these debt buildups, it ran large primary surpluses over a long time, bringing down the debt burden gradually.

Typically, scholars estimate fiscal policy reaction functions econometrically to determine how much the primary surplus rises as debt accumulates. Because of the logic we used in compiling annual fiscal accounts for Habsburg Spain, this is not feasible.[16] Instead, we can examine how different powers performed according to the basic logic of fiscal reaction functions. In figures 31 and 32, we plot primary surpluses and debt stocks for Castile and Britain. Both powers show debt accumulation at a fairly rapid pace—with Britain going from a debt of 14 million pounds sterling in 1700 to 244 in 1790, while Castile saw an increase from 25 to 72 million ducats between 1566 and 1595.

---

15 For a further discussion of this issue, see Drelichman and Voth 2008; Temin and Voth 2008.
16 In our fiscal accounting exercise in chapter 4, we calculated debt accumulation as a residual of a fiscal identity. Because of this, whenever the primary surplus increases, our estimate of debt accumulation automatically goes down.

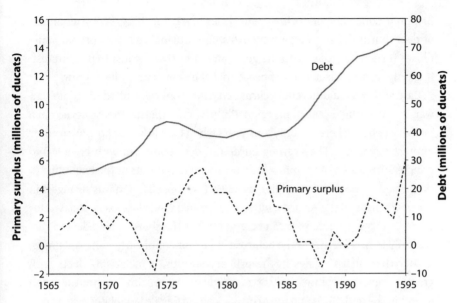

FIGURE 31. Primary surpluses and debt stock in sixteenth-century Castile

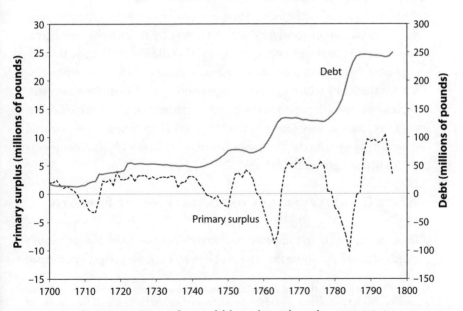

FIGURE 32. Primary surpluses and debt stock in eighteenth-century Britain

Britain produced higher primary surpluses to pay for this growing mountain of debt, but it did so in a particular fashion. During each war, primary surpluses turned negative, with the government borrowing just to pay interest. It is only during select years of peace that the primary surpluses grew.

Castile showed a different cyclical behavior from the United Kingdom's; at war in every single year of his reign, Philip II nonetheless almost never ran a primary deficit. There are only four years when Castile had to borrow to cover interest payments. The growing burden of debt coincided with greater and greater surpluses, rising from a little over 1 million ducats at the beginning of the period to more than 5 million by 1595. The consolidation was strongest in the years prior to the Armada, when high primary surpluses accumulated for years in a row. Therefore, it can be argued that Habsburg Spain adapted successfully in fiscal terms to the bellicose environment of early modern Europe. Rather than sharp swings in the primary surplus, it met rising debts with greater primary surpluses. Only extraordinary emergencies—such as the Dutch Revolt in the mid-1570s and the Armada—caused Castile to violate the first rule of fiscal probity (never to borrow to pay interest). By the standard of fiscal policy reactions, Castile was every bit as prudent as Britain, if not more so.[17]

The conclusion from these international comparisons has to be that Castile's finances in the second half of the sixteenth century were not in worse shape than those of other major European powers in their respective heydays. There was ample room for Castile's tax-to-GDP ratio to grow, and grow it did. To a striking extent, ordinary expenditure did not catch up with revenue, producing large surpluses that were used to service the debt. While Castilian fiscal infrastructure was not as highly developed as Holland's or Britain's, revenue growth provided the breathing room to cope with high debts. On average, the Castilian Crown in the 1580s and 1590s commanded financial resources that were on the same scale (relative to the size of the economy) as Britain's in the eighteenth century.

STATE CAPACITY VERSUS CONSTRAINTS ON THE EXECUTIVE

If fiscal recklessness and imperial overstretch are not to blame for Spain's decline, what is? We argue that the problem was not despotism but instead

---

17 Our conclusions echo those of White (2001b), who also emphasized that France's position was nowhere near as poor compared to the British one, as much of the literature has made it out to be.

weak, incompetent, incoherent governance. Rather than the new institutional economics' emphasis on too much power in the hands of an absolute monarch (Acemoglu, Johnson, and Robinson 2005; De Long and Shleifer 1993), the key shortcoming was almost exactly the opposite: a lack of state capacity, of a government's ability to successfully assert a monopoly of violence, defend its borders, impose uniform taxation, administer justice, and obtain resources for carrying out these tasks.

In early modern Europe, constraints on the executive were not a key determinant of economic performance—otherwise Poland, where a single noble in the Sejm, the national assembly, could veto policy, should have grown faster than the rest of Europe (Mokyr and Voth 2011). Instead, it languished economically before being carved up by its neighbors and disappearing from the map altogether. Predation—the despotic breaking of contracts and seizing of property—was exceedingly rare in Europe ever since the High Middle Ages (Epstein 2000; Clark 2007). Spanish kings sometimes seized American silver in times of distress (as discussed in chapter 3), but compensated the owners with long-dated debt of equivalent value. This behavior of the Spanish Crown is broadly comparable to the infamous raid on the Tower of London in 1638. Normally the wrong was acknowledged and attempts at righting it were made.[18]

Nor were the poor defenseless in any sense. Courts often sided with the underprivileged against magnates, rulers, and rich burghers (Grafe 2012). At the same time, corruption limited the extent to which laws were actually applied. The Duke of Alba, writing in 1573, argued that decisions in court cases were frequently sold "like meat in a butcher's shop" (Braudel 1966, 693). While many European powers suffered from corruption on a vast scale before the nineteenth century (Mokyr and Nye 2007), Spain was widely acknowledged to be particularly poor because of the weakness of its central ruler. Throughout much of early modern European history, constraining princes was not crucial; building an effective state whose writ ran to the furthest corner of the land was, as Stephan R. Epstein (2000, 15) argued in *Freedom and Growth*: "Jurisdictional fragmentation . . . gave rise to multiple coordination

---

18 A more subtle argument holds that "absolutist" tax regimes were not predatory as such but instead poorly designed—putting extreme pressure on some activities while exempting others. In this context, strong property rights can be distortionary. This is the contention in Hoffman and Rosenthal 1997. We would argue that these are common difficulties. Many tax systems (including modern ones) have to contend with them. Deviations from the principles of Ramsey taxation may or may not have been more common under the Old Regime, but they are different from predatory behavior and distortions that come from poor property right protection.

failure. [R]ather than autocratic rule[, it] was the main source of institutional inefficiency of 'absolutism' before the 19th century." Our interpretation also connects with recent developments in political economy. Instead of the simple dichotomy of absolutist versus constrained governments, it is increasingly recognized that strong states can be good for growth and that weak states struggle to provide the conditions for economic development (Acemoglu 2005; Besley and Persson 2009, 2010).

There is no doubt that Spain scored poorly in terms of governance. Contemporaries already saw administrative reality for what it was. An English observer commented in 1681: "Spain is a clear example that misgovernment . . . will soon bring the mightiest Kingdoms low" (Bethel 1681, cited in Elliott 1989). Similarly, Thomas Babington Macaulay (1833, cited in Elliot 1989) remarked that "all the causes of the decay of Spain resolve themselves into one cause, bad government." The problem of state capacity was acute throughout early modern Europe. This is because states as we know them today did not exist in 1500. Instead, there was a collection of minor and major territories, ruled by princes subject to multiple feudal allegiances; local power holders frequently acted as judges, often commanding bodies of armed troops and controlling major fortresses. Exemptions from taxation and other duties for large segments of the population, based on ancient rights and traditions, created highly uneven tax burdens. Taxes were rarely collected directly; rather, they were either farmed out or their collection was delegated to cities in exchange for lump-sum payments. Out of this system of weak, fragmented, unsystematic governance emerged a handful of powerful, consolidated, centralized nation-states by the nineteenth century. These successfully tore up the spider web of ancient "liberties" and exemptions, monopolized military power, and collected significant amounts of revenue by applying the same taxation rules to every citizen.

There is one simple measure that allows for comparisons of state capacity: the ability to tax. From K. Kivanc Karaman and Sevket Pamuk (2010), we compile data on the total tax take per capita in the early modern period. In figure 33, we plot the total tax revenue; in figure 34, we depict revenue per capita. France stands out for the high total amount of taxes raised; in terms of per capita taxation, the Dutch Republic takes first prize. Taxes were rising almost everywhere after 1500 as the power of the political center grew, and states struggled ever harder for resources to fight their foes (Tilly 1990). Every single European state with the exception of Spain collected higher taxes per

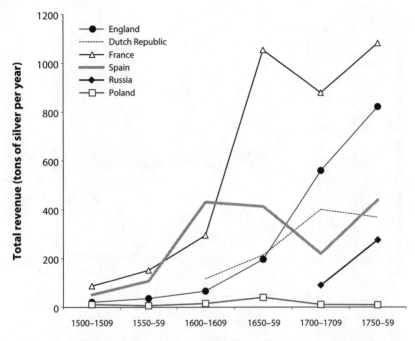

FIGURE 33. Total tax revenue, various European powers. *Source*: Karaman and Pamuk 2010.

capita in 1700 than it had done in 1600. As we discussed in the introduction, Spain went from one of the most successful revenue collectors to no more than a middling position—not as far behind as Russia, the Ottoman Empire (not shown), or Poland, but nowhere near the performance of the Dutch Republic or England. While Spain's sixteenth-century performance is flattered somewhat by taxes on mineral wealth, the overall picture remains unaltered if one corrects for it. Spanish decline in terms of taxes raised, then, had two components: a weakening grip of the tax authorities and disappointing demographic performance.

State borrowing—especially in the form of asientos—had some deleterious effects on the ability to tax. The estates of the military orders, over which the Crown held the right of patronage, were administered by the Fugger family, as were the quicksilver mines at Almadén (Ehrenberg 1896). As part of the resolution of Philip's first bankruptcies, the Genoese received the monopoly for the sale of playing cards (Braudel 1966). These forms of administrative outsourcing did not help to raise state capacity. Yet they were part of a much bigger problem for Spain: it largely failed to build an integrated tax system

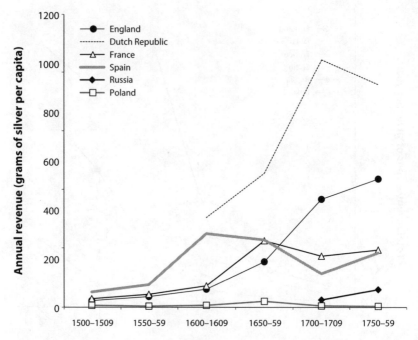

FIGURE 34. Revenue per capita, various European powers. *Source*: Karaman and Pamuk 2010.

that directly collected information on taxpayers; almost all taxes were farmed out or assessed wholesale for larger cities.

Many historians of early modern Europe have observed that states made war, and war made states (Tilly 1990). War could also unmake them in short order: As a result of 350 years of nearly constant warfare, Europe became a collection of a few, consolidated nation-states. Weak powers disappeared; those that built effective tax-and-spend infrastructures survived and prospered. Timothy Besley and Torsten Persson (2009, 2010) argue that a history of warfare is one of the reasons why some countries today have much more capable states than others. Early modern history suggests that the link between warfare and institutional improvements was not straightforward. Some states survived and prospered despite being at peace, such as Switzerland. If war was the key driver of institutional improvements, Spain, France, and Britain should have emerged with wonderful institutions. All three fought numerous wars between 1500 and 1800, and had enormous financing needs. And yet their institutional paths diverged dramatically. This suggests that more attention needs to be paid to the fact that war could not only unmake states by seeing them destroyed as independent entities; it could also undermine state building depending on the exact historical circumstances.

Underlying the broad patterns traced out in figure 33 were different approaches to state building. The path to capable states differed by country. The English model saw a consensually strong executive—a monarch whose parliament permitted a tremendous increase in the debt burden, taxation, and scale of military ambitions, in exchange for greater control over the legislative process, independence of the courts, and a recognition of parliament's power to chose the monarch. The French absolutist model, begun by Cardinal Richelieu and perfected under Louis XIV, has frequently been portrayed as pushing through far-reaching reforms against the continuous, often-violent opposition of major groups in society. Revisionist historical research has suggested a more nuanced picture (Mousnier 1979; Oestreich 1969), stressing the extent to which even absolutist rulers governed a polycentric system based on a consensus among the elites. While some of the legal writings and official propaganda—from Denmark to France and beyond—emphasized the sole power of the sovereign, the emergence of a strong state (with the support of major social groups) is not altogether different from the English path.[19]

One key difference between England and France, on the one side, and Spain, on the other, was the degree to which the political center successfully asserted its dominance—over independent-seeking regions as well as individual magnates. In other words, state building was much more successful outside the Iberian Peninsula than within it. As a simple example, it is useful to compare the progress in unifying taxation, jurisdiction, and representation in Britain after the Act of Union (1707) with the Unión de las Armas, the Count-Duke of Olivares's attempt to centralize fiscal and military power in 1624. After 1707, the Scottish church was integrated into the Church of England; Scottish peers and Members of Parliament sat in Westminster; taxation quickly became unified; and Britain's extensive eighteenth-century wars were fought with Scottish and English taxes, using Scottish and English troops.[20] In contrast, Spain remained a composite state after 1492 (Elliott

---

19 It could be claimed that the French Revolution shows that the French model could not work in the long run. We believe that there is more scope for accident in history than this reasoning allows. For example, the final fiscal crisis of the ancien régime could arguably have been avoided if fiscal consolidation had not been abandoned in the 1770s and 1780s (White 2001b).

20 This is not to deny that making Scotland pay was not a trivial act. As late as the 1750s, during the debate of the Scottish bill, the lord chancellor said, "Some method should be taken to make Scotland pay the taxes but could any ministry hit upon that method?" (Walpole 1822).

1992)—and arguably, to the present day. While the Crown's political position in Castile was relatively strong after the Comuneros Revolt had been vanquished, the Cortes—representing the cities—regularly turned down royal requests for higher taxation. Outside Castile, the Crown's position was even weaker; the oath of allegiance, sworn by the Aragonese nobles after the accession of a new king, famously declared,

> We, who are as good as you,
> swear to you, who are no better than us,
> to accept you as our king and sovereign,
> provided you observe all our liberties and laws,
> but if not, not. (Herr 1974)

This is not the language of absolute monarchy. Until the arrival of the Bourbon kings, there was no successful attempt to unify representation, legal systems, or taxation. In one famous episode, the Madrid government tried to raise taxes on the non-Castilian territories in a major way. During the Thirty Years' War, under the Count-Duke of Olivares, the government was strapped for cash and tried to increase contributions (Elliott 1986). After being refused by the representative assemblies outside Castile, it invoked royal prerogative to allocate military costs directly through the Unión de las Armas. Revolts in Portugal, Catalunia, and Naples followed over the next decade; Portugal regained its independence in 1640, and the other two rebellious territories could only be brought back into the fold by backtracking on reform. Despite eventually repressing two of the revolts, Olivares's experiment in fiscal burden sharing and centralization was a failure—and a costly one. For another two-thirds of a century, until the Bourbon reforms of the early eighteenth century, the ancient freedoms—and this increasingly meant freedom from taxation—were left essentially untouched.

Such a patchwork of privileges combined with high taxes on the remaining individuals and income categories created huge inefficiencies (Grafe 2012). In the language of economics, they violate the principle known as Ramsey taxation, which states that distortions created by tax should be equalized across sectors and individuals so as to minimize overall efficiency losses.

Internal tariff barriers remained in place. Some of these were part of a broader set of ancient "liberties" (*fueros*). For example, the *fueros de Bizkaia* created a customs barrier between Vizcaya, Guipuzcoa, and Alava, on the one hand, and Castile, on the other (Grafe 2008). Similarly, the system of *puertos secos* continued to exist into the late seventeenth century. Despite some tinkering, a system that maximized internal market fragmentation remained untouched for centuries after the marriage of the Catholic Kings and even after the Bourbon accession to throne. The terms of unification with the crowns of Aragon, Navarre, and Portugal in each case required the continuation of such arrangements.

The persistence of these ancient "freedoms" are not only responsible for the continuation of economically harmful rules; they also serve to illustrate a particular type of internal weakness, and one that goes to the heart of Spain's early modern failure to build a more capable state. As Grafe (2012) points out, officials in all Spanish-ruled territories happily disregarded direct royal directives if they undermined long-standing exemptions and privileges. This practice made perfect legal sense; since the king was bound to uphold the old liberties as part of his compact with his subjects, he could not legally require officials to do the opposite. In these cases, as the Spanish phrase has it, the king's law would be obeyed, but not put into practice: *la ley se obedece, pero no se cumple* (MacLachlan 1988).

Of course, such reluctance to follow orders could only persist because officials feared no direct sanctions from the center. Being fined, removed, stripped of honors, or sent to prison was not even a remote prospect; the whole apparatus of sanctions that a sovereign state typically applies to run its administrative machinery were almost never within the reach of the court in Madrid. Spain failed to develop an administrative infrastructure that could overcome opposition based on old custom and ancient legal agreements. Even in terms of collecting taxes, there was no centralization of administrative processes and no homogenization of rules; Spain never developed the equivalent of the French intendants, introduced by Cardinal Richelieu, who supervised the collection of direct taxes. Significant revenue bypassed royal coffers. Elliott (1963a, 99–110) estimated that the Spanish church controlled up to three times the resources available to the Spanish Crown under Ferdinand and Isabella. While the ratio shrank in later years, the Catholic Church in Spain continued to receive significant income. Its influence was so widespread that it actually served as one of the most important fiscal arms of the states. The so-called three graces were taxes collected by the church on behalf of the Crown. Together with the *tercias reales*—taxes on the salaries of ecclesiastics—they accounted for a full third of fiscal revenue in the sixteenth century.[21]

Far from being able to impose its will with ease, and riding roughshod over the opposition of merchants, nobles, and clergy, the Spanish monarchy often found it impossible to force through the application of royal decrees and directives. Every attempt to centralize, tax more equitably and efficiently, and do away with the patchwork of ancient privileges that undermined the efficiency of the Spanish state and economy was quickly met with attempts at rebellion (Portugal, Catalonia, Vizcaya, and Sicily) or conspiracies (Andalusia and Aragon) (Elliott 1963b). The ease with which local resistance could be organized, the inability of the Crown to fully disarm local magnates, and the gentle touch—at least under the Habsburgs—with which rebellious regions were treated all suggest that the government in Spain was simply too weak to mount an effective attempt to centralize, streamline, and professionalize tax collection as well as the administering of the judicial process. As Elliott (1963a) elegantly put it, "Such strength as it [the Spanish monarchy] possessed derived from its weakness."[22]

To understand why state capacity stagnated in Spain while it surged elsewhere, we need to take a closer look at a contrasting example: Britain. There, the rise of a unified, bureaucratized, centralized tax structure was not a simple or linear process (Brewer 1988). In the sixteenth century, tax farming was used for indirect taxes; local agents often supervised the collection of local direct taxes. Charles I's experiment with ship money ran into massive opposition (Kimmel 1988). Challenges were not just based on the dubious legal basis for the writs but also the supposed, regionally based special privileges (Braddick 2000). London, for example, claimed to be exempt from ship money payments due to its special status, just like Seville or Zaragoza would have argued that any rise in the excise taxes of Castile was not relevant, since they had agreed on a lump sum in lieu of ordinary taxation. In other words, before the civil war, Britain's tax system did not look particularly streamlined or efficient.

It was only in the 1680s and 1690s that an effective end was put to tax farming in England. Brewer (1988) argues that by 1700, the process of re-

---

21 Under an arrangement know as *patronato*, Spanish kings could appoint bishops; they were effectively political heads of the church in Spain. For further discussion, see chapter 2.

22 María Alejandra Irigoín and Regina Grafe (2008) have called this mode of interaction "bargaining for absolutism."

forms after the Glorious Revolution had produced an efficient and effective bureaucracy—one that was centrally directed, paid regular salaries, and monitored agents using a fixed hierarchy with clear incentives. William Pitt's reforms in the 1780s, a good century later, achieved similar benefits by streamlining the collection of direct taxes—and laid the foundation for the introduction of the first income tax in history to be successfully collected on any significant scale.[23] By the end of the period, the single most impressive feature of the British state was arguably its ability to raise taxes, and do so in a way that not only failed to snuff out economic growth altogether but also actually allowed it to proceed—no matter how slow the process may have been.

WINDMILLS OF DECLINE: HETEROGENEITY, STATE CAPACITY, AND SILVER

What accounts for these differences? Why did Britain successfully centralize its administration, streamline tax collection, and build a more powerful, capable state apparatus than Spain? The pressures of war—the leading explanation in the tradition of Tilly (1990)—cannot be the answer, since both powers were frequently at war (with each other and the rest of Europe). We emphasize two factors: different starting conditions and the availability of silver revenues in the case of Spain.

HETEROGENEITY

The lands ruled by Spain's Habsburg and Bourbon kings were vastly more heterogeneous than those ruled by English monarchs from Henry V to George III. While both had inherited territories with preexisting linguistic, cultural, and economic differences, these were arguably much greater on the Iberian Peninsula. A simple statistic bears this out: the territory ruled by Philip II contained seven predecessor states in 1300; in England, it was one (or three if we use Britain as a unit of observation, and add Scotland and Ireland).[24] Linguistic fragmentation in England was also much lower—0.05 instead of 0.41 in Spain on the Alesina et al. (2003) scale. In both places, local magnates con-

---

23 On the evolution of tax farming and tax collection in England, see also Noel D. Johnson and Mark Koyama (2012).

24 We do not count Wales as an independent predecessor state.

trolled significant armed forces for some time. And yet this phenomenon disappeared in England after the civil war. In seventeenth-century Spain, though, the arsenals of grandees, such as the one of the Duke of Medina-Sidonia, were once sufficient to equip small armies (Anderson 1988).

Why should initial heterogeneity matter? Nicola Gennaioli and Hans-Joachim Voth (2012) build a simple model of investments in fiscal capacity that rationalizes the importance of starting conditions. Assume that two rulers try to centralize tax collection, but are faced with different levels of domestic opposition. Domestic opposition—potential and real—makes it more costly to push through centralizing reforms, such as the abolition of customs barriers, application of general rules of taxation, and so on. To obtain greater revenues in the future, rulers have to invest up front. Both rulers have the same incentive to raise more revenue, driven in part by the threat of war.

If one country is more heterogeneous than the other, with more powerful grandees and greater linguistic, cultural, and administrative fragmentation, the cost of centralization will be greater. In this case, the ruler of the more homogeneous territory will be more inclined to undertake investments in fiscal infrastructure—and state building will be greater. These effects will be amplified by military competition. The more important money becomes for winning wars—a direct result of the military revolution after 1500—the greater the importance of raising revenue. The more costly war is, the more difficult it will be for a state to recover from a string of adverse shocks to its position, such as a bad draw in a military confrontation.

If growing financial resources strengthen the center's military might, as they typically did in the early modern period, then each successful centralizing step makes the next one less costly; vanquishing the opposition becomes progressively easier. According to the logic of the model in Gennaioli and Voth (2012), small differences as a result of luck on the battlefield, say, or a consequence of different starting conditions can produce large divergence in state capacity over the long run. In this framework, initial fragmentation determines the path of state building as international competition heats up. While tax pressure is low, the incentive to improve tax collection and push aside local magnates is low, too. As warfare become more intense and more costly, stronger states have an incentive to improve their institutions and strengthen tax collection.

Weaker powers, on the other hand, may find it optimal to "give up" and not even try to improve state capacity. Those that started the race with greater obstacles—having inherited more powerful local institutions and a greater diversity of old state infrastructures as a result of recent territorial expansion—will be increasingly hamstrung. An excess of local power, the ability to defy the center, and the capacity to check an absolutist agenda were more damaging to both economic performance and political development, especially in the case of Spain. In this sense, the marriage of equals between Ferdinand and Isabella cast a long shadow over Spain's development in the early modern period. While it initially concentrated power in the Catholic Kings' hands, it also hampered the forging of a unified, functional state with a large internal market and effective, incentive-compatible taxation.

SILVER

The second key explanation for declining state capacity in Spain emphasizes the *incentives* to push through reform against potential opposition. Spain's treasury, in contrast to Britain's, had access to significant mineral wealth. The silver mines of Potosí, once they could be successfully exploited, created a torrent of silver; a substantial share of it found its way into the coffers of the Castilian Crown.

We are not the first to argue that silver was bad for Spain. Contemporaries already saw American silver as a poisoned chalice. Writing in 1600, Martín González de Cellorigo (1600) observed that

> Our Spain has set her eyes so strongly on the business of the Indies, from where she obtains gold and silver, that she has forsaken the care of her own kingdoms; and if she could indeed command all the gold and silver that her nationals keep discovering in the New World, this would not render her as rich and powerful as she would have otherwise been.

There can be no question that in general, many countries around the globe and throughout history suffered from a "resource curse." Figure 35 illustrates the basic pattern in a cross-section of countries today: growth is systematically lower the higher the share of primary exports in GDP. The resource curse theory's origins can be traced back to the 1950s' dependency theory of H. W. Singer (1949) and Raúl Prebisch (1950). The fact that resource abundance and poor economic performance go hand in hand is well documented in the empirical literature.[25] The resource curse literature first underscored

---

25 See, for example, Sachs and Warner 1995; Auty 2001.

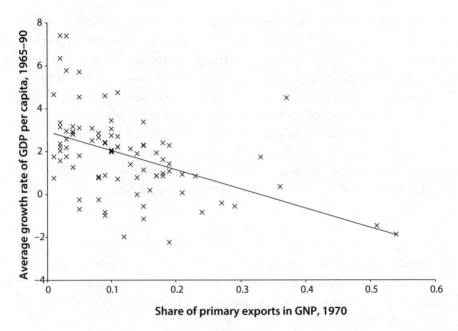

FIGURE 35. The resource curse

the deterioration in the terms of trade—a phenomenon labeled "Dutch disease" after the 1970s' natural gas boom in the Netherlands (Corden and Neary 1982). Yet this rise in the terms of trade is an optimal response: a country that becomes richer will increase its consumption; in the face of a relatively inelastic supply of domestic factors of production, this can only be accomplished through increased imports of traded goods and a corresponding deterioration in the terms of trade. This situation is reversed if the resource abundance disappears; Dutch disease on its own cannot account for long-term economic decline.

Instead, the literature offers three alternative explanations. One strand argues that resource-abundant countries invest less abroad and lose out as a result. A second approach emphasizes learning by doing in the traded goods sector (van Wijnbergen 1984; Krugman 1987). Efficiency losses here are a result of agents optimizing their utility and ending up in an equilibrium that is socially suboptimal. Similarly, Patrick Asea and Amartya Lahiri (1999) emphasize the detrimental effects of resource booms on human capital accumulation decisions. A third strand in the literature considers negative political economy externalities, such as greater incentives for rent seeking (Baland

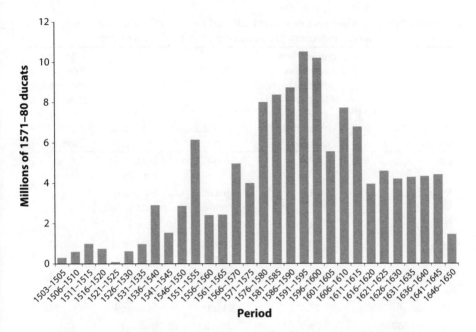

FIGURE 36. Crown treasure, 1503–1650. *Sources:* Hamilton 1934; Drelichman 2005.

and Francois 2000; Torvik 2002). Halvor Mehlum, Karl Moene, and Ragnar Torvik (2006) generalized this approach, introducing institutional quality as a determinant of rent seeking. James Robinson, Ragnar Torvik, and Thierry Verdier (2006) explicitly model the incentives of politicians, as shaped by institutions, as a conduit for the resource curse.[26]

Spain experienced a resource boom that was large even by modern standards. Silver revenues became significant in the 1540s, and then reached values of 4 million ducats or more in every quinquennium from the 1560s onward. Eventually, imports were so large that the Crown's share reached more than 2 million ducats per year at its peak, or more than 10 million every five years (figure 36). For comparison, Henry VIII's sales of confiscated church lands produced revenues of only 375,000 pounds over six years—or no more than 4 million ducats (Hoyle 1995).

How does this resource boom compare with modern-day examples? In table 29, we compare the share of revenue from silver in Castile at the peak

---

26 For another examination of the institutionally detrimental effects of resource windfalls, see Tornell and Lane (1999).

Table 29. Government revenues from hydrocarbon and mineral sources in selected
resource-rich countries, as percentage of total fiscal revenue

Hydrocarbon-rich countries	Hydrocarbon revenue as percentage of total fiscal revenue (2000–2003 average)	Mineral-rich countries	Mineral resources	Mineral revenue as percentage of total fiscal revenue (2000–2003 average)
Colombia	9.0	Sierra Leone	Diamonds, bauxite	0.5
Kazakhstan	21.0	Jordan	Phosphates, potash	1.6
Norway	24.4	Chile	Copper	3.9
Ecuador	26.4	Kyrgyz Republic	Gold	4.1
Cameroon	26.6	Mongolia	Copper, gold	6.1
Trinidad and Tobago	27.4	Namibia	Diamonds	10.0
Castile 1587–89	**29.0**	Mauritania	Iron ore	10.6
Indonesia	31.3	Papua New Guinea	Gold	16.1
Vietnam	31.8	Guinea	Bauxite/ alumina	18.3
Mexico	32.2	**Castile 1587–89**	**Silver**	**29.0**
Russia	39.7	Botswana	Diamonds	56.2
Venezuela	52.7			
Iraq	58.4			
Iran	59.3			
Bahrain	71.2			
Qatar	71.3			
Libya	72.5			
United Arab Emirates	76.1			
Nigeria	77.2			
Saudi Arabia	81.6			
Equatorial Guinea	84.0			
Brunei Darussalam	85.8			

Source: IMF Guide on Resource Revenue Transparency, June 2005.

(1587–89) with contemporary oil exporters and mineral producers. Castile was never as dependent on silver as Saudi Arabia and Nigeria in 2000–2003 were on oil, but it still generated a higher proportion of revenue from resources than Norway. Compared to the mineral-rich countries, Castile scores near the top; only diamond-exporting Botswana has a higher share of government revenue derived from a mineral resource.

Silver had an enormous impact on the economy of Castile, Europe, and indeed the whole world. The silver price differentials between Europe and the Far East stimulated long-distance trade. Some scholars see this period as the "birth of globalization" (Flynn and Giráldez 2004). The bullion that was retained in Europe roughly doubled the monetary stock in the course of a century; the ensuing "price revolution," a sustained increase in the price level of virtually all European economies, had large effects on fiscal systems, trading arrangements, and monetary institutions (Hamilton 1934; Flynn 1978; Fisher 1989).

The strongest effects of the resource windfall were felt in Castile. The large increase in the supply of silver coupled with the new sources of demand from the Far East prompted factors of production to be diverted from export industries, such as fine wool and manufactures, and into the extraction and service industries associated with the silver trade. This classic case of Dutch disease afflicted Castile for much of the second half of the sixteenth century (Forsyth and Nicholas 1983; Drelichman 2005), but the resource boom had costs in terms of economic as well as political development that went far beyond factor allocation and balance of payments effects.

Silver's greatest downside was that it weakened the bargaining position of the Cortes vis-à-vis the Crown. Because of silver revenues, Castile's rulers could spend freely using borrowed funds and effectively present the Cortes with the bill. Throughout the sixteenth century, the Crown resorted twice to the same "hardball" bargaining. It borrowed short term through asientos against silver and other extraordinary revenues, without the Cortes' consent. As a debt crisis loomed and short-term loans became hard to roll over, it requested increases in ordinary taxation to be able to issue more long-dated juros. Long delays or outright refusals to approve these tax increases would have resulted in a rapid deterioration of the military situation—a political cost that the Cortes was seldom prepared to bear. Also, debt holders in the cities—many of them of elevated social status—were affected by the default and probably saw a tax rise as a much smaller evil than a continued moratorium.

The first such episode was triggered by the suspension of payments of 1575. As we discussed in chapter 4, the proximate cause of rapid borrowing was the flare up of the Dutch Revolt.[27] Philip convened the Cortes and requested a threefold increase in the value of the alcabalas sales tax. During the payment suspension, the military situation in the Netherlands deteriorated. The Cortes eventually granted a doubling of the alcabalas with an additional extraordinary levy in the first two years. Despite hard bargaining, the Cortes received no additional control over the Crown's expenditures.

One might ask whether silver was instrumental in this outcome. Ultimately, the Cortes was forced to grant a tax increase. Couldn't Philip II have borrowed against these future tax revenues, used the proceeds to lead Castile into the same expensive campaigns, and requested money from the Cortes later? We argue that the nature of the early modern sovereign debt markets ruled out such a scenario. Sixteenth-century monarchs who wanted to venture into the international credit markets had two options. The first one was to hand over control of the revenue sources that guaranteed repayment. This usually happened in the framework of a multiyear arrangement and secured the lowest interest rates. Castilian juros were usually issued under such arrangements.

The second route was uncollateralized, short-term borrowing with high interest. Bankers typically imposed tight credit limits; neither Henry VIII nor Charles V borrowed more than twice their annual revenues. American bullion taxes were paid to the Crown, leading to massive increases in its ability to borrow short term. Genoese bankers would not have lent to Philip II on the chance that the Cortes might later pay; they took a calculated gamble in lending to him because the steady silver flows meant that the Crown would be liquid enough to repay a good part of the loans. Silver allowed borrowing to take place, war to be declared, and Philip to lead Castile into military adventures that left the Cortes with little choice but to grant additional taxes in case events took a turn for the worse—as they often did. Without silver, Spain's military adventures under Philip II would almost certainly have been fewer and cheaper.

The second example is similar. After the Armada's defeat in 1588, Philip again convened the Cortes and requested emergency taxation to protect Castile. The millones, as the new excises were called, departed from earlier practice. The Cortes succeeded in attaching strings to the millones' renewal (Jago

---

27 See also Lovett 1980, 1982.

1981). The scheme consisted of multiyear agreements negotiated between the Crown and Cortes. The new taxes were collected at the local level and, in theory, transferred to the Crown provided that the conditions in the previous agreement had been met. An independent commission staffed by city representatives was to monitor compliance.

The revival of parliamentary authority took place mainly on paper and did not make itself felt in the Crown's coffers. Although the millones commission repeatedly sought instruments to control the use of the funds, it never gained the ability to restrain the Crown from diverting them to its preferred uses. Starting in the 1620s, the king gradually packed the commission with his own representatives. As the Crown declared its sixth bankruptcy in 1647, the Council of Finance absorbed the commission (Jago 1981). The following year the Peace of Westphalia would mark the end of Castile's imperial adventures, and usher in a period of internal strife and disintegration of state institutions. The Cortes never recovered the influence it lost; after 1663, it was only convened on ceremonial occasions.

Silver made it harder to strike the mutually advantageous deal that emerged in other countries—a bargain that saw the representative assembly agreeing to greater centralization and higher taxes in exchange for effective oversight as well as control. City-states first overcame the collective bargaining problem and created "consensually strong" executives; the Dutch Republic and England eventually followed suit. Such a bargain could not be struck in Spain, despite false starts. Ultimately, because of silver revenues, the Crown's hand was just too strong to compromise. A better tax system, funding a more effective executive, would have also been a more equitable system—one that distributed burdens more equally between Castile and the other territories ruled by Philip II, leading to less distortionary taxation within Castile.

DETERMINANTS OF DECLINE

Spain's decline as an economic and military power is one of the critical themes of early modern history. It has variously been claimed as a case in point by monetary historians emphasizing the negative effects of inflation and terms-of-trade effects, cultural historians arguing for the dilatory effects of enforced insularity, financial historians and macroeconomists highlighting the dangers of default and fiscal overstretch, and institutional economists underlining the dangers of unconstrained, absolutist monarchs.

Compared to the other great European powers after 1500, Spain's fiscal policy showed no signs of imperial overstretch. We demonstrated that its finances were no worse—and better in a variety of ways—than those of other countries at the height of their power. According to several criteria, Castilian finances were managed with greater probity than even those of Britain, with primary surpluses being maintained during wartime and rapid improvements in the budget position when debts accumulated. There is also no evidence of the supposedly deleterious effects of serial default; after each payment stop, the Crown's revenues increased, suggesting no decline in fiscal capacity.

Castilian rulers' despotic powers mainly exist on the movie screen and pages of scholarly journals. It was the weakness of the imperial center, not the omnipotence of Habsburg rulers, that was crucial for economic and political decline—its inability to force through change, centralize, streamline, and tax effectively and evenly (Grafe 2012; Epstein 2000). The failure to build a more capable state on the Iberian Peninsula reflects two underlying weaknesses: initial heterogeneity and the influx of silver. The first made it more costly for the ruler of a composite state to wrest control from local power holders as well as to abolish ancient privileges and freedoms, remove internal customs barriers, and expand the tax net (Gennaioli and Voth 2012). Second, silver revenues were large enough to give the Crown a way out of having to compromise with the Cortes; a consensually strong executive did not emerge west of the Pyrenees because an efficiency-enhancing grand bargain between the representative assembly and ruler was not struck (Drelichman and Voth 2008). The situation was made worse by major strokes of bad luck in the military arena.

EPILOGUE

FINANCIAL FOLLY AND SPAIN'S BLACK LEGEND

Financial folly. The very words conjure up images of overpaid bankers, venal politicians and ruined savers, economic chaos and disastrous collapses in market confidence. Financial folly is a common explanation for booms and busts, bubbles and irrational exuberance in stock and bond prices. Reinhart and Rogoff's monumental *This Time Is Different* puts excessive optimism of financiers at the heart of financial crises. Recurrent crises, in their view, reflect swings in investor sentiment: as good returns accumulate, initially skeptical investors gradually become blue-eyed optimists who start to believe that this time is indeed different. Once a crisis hits, sentiment collapses and extreme pessimism reigns. For decades, risky behavior all but disappears; stability gradually convinces everyone of a new age of high, stable returns. Investors let down their guard, and the cycle repeats.

Philip II's debts are often invoked as an egregious example of financiers' gullible optimism and fiscal recklessness. The editorial from the *Economist* cited above (September 23–29, 2006) used the Genoese loans to Philip II to argue that "lending is a sober business punctuated by odd moments of lunacy." Philip failed to honor his debts four times. Many earlier scholars have attributed Philip II's continued access to funds to cunning manipulation, starry-eyed bankers, and the general novelty of lending to powerful princes.

In addition, Habsburg Spain's defaults have typically been regarded as catastrophic financial events, causing major economic disruptions while ruining scores of bankers and small investors. Philip II, to exaggerate only a little, is usually cast as the villain of a morality play—an absolute monarch who squandered the wealth of his realms on fanciful dreams of European hegemony. Spain's decline and eventual fall as a European great power is generally linked with imperial overstretch—the excessive ambitions and financial irresponsibility of the Habsburg monarch whose courtiers flattered him with the moniker "the biggest brain in the world."

This book draws on new archival documents, advances in sovereign debt theory, and fresh insights in early modern historiography to offer a reinterpretation of Philip II's finances. Taking our lead from earlier scholars—such as Thompson—who already argued that default cycles must have been anticipated, we show that Castile was solvent throughout Philip's reign. A complex web of contractual obligations designed to ensure repayment governed the relationship between the king and his bankers. The same contracts allowed great flexibility for both the Crown and bankers when liquidity was tight. The risk of potential defaults was not a surprise; their likelihood was priced into the loan contracts. As a consequence, virtually every banking family turned a profit over the long term, while the king benefited from their services to run the largest empire that had yet existed.

We began with a historical overview of sixteenth-century Spain, with particular emphasis on the origins and evolution of state institutions as well as the distribution of political power. Philip II was not an absolute monarch by any standard; neither Cardinal Richelieu nor the famous theorists of absolutist rule, Bodin and Pufendorf, would have recognized him as such. Raising taxes and issuing long-term debt required the consent of Castile's representative assembly, the Cortes. In contrast to the arguments in some of the new institutional economics literature, the rulers of Castile were every bit as constrained in the sixteenth century as, say, the kings of England, if not more so. The dynamics of bargaining between the king and Cortes resulted in a safe, tax-backed system of long-term debt (juros), on which Philip never defaulted. It was underpinned by rapidly rising fiscal revenue, which increased with the consent of the principal cities of Castile.

In addition, the king had access to several revenue streams not controlled by the Cortes. The most important of these was a tax on silver remittances from the Indies. These resources were used to back short-term loans, called asientos. At their peak, they accounted for a quarter of total borrowing. Philip II only ever defaulted on this relatively small share of total debt. To understand these defaults, we constructed a database using information from every single short-term contract subscribed during Philip II's reign preserved in the Archive of Simancas. Earlier research never used all the information in these lending contracts. For each loan we transcribed every single contractual clause, reconstructed the associated cash flows, and coded up to ninety additional variables.

Based on these new data, we first examined the king's ability to pay. If the Crown was insolvent—with no hope of bridging the gap between unavoidable expenditures and available revenues—lending would have been either irrational or naive. Using our new borrowing series along with a combination of primary and secondary sources, we reconstruct the fiscal position of Habsburg Castile on an annual basis between 1566 and 1596—the earliest such series for a sovereign state in history. With these data in hand, it is easy to show that Castile passes several key tests of fiscal sustainability. The king's ministers—without knowing even the exact quantity of money received or borrowed—managed to run a primary surplus in almost every year of Philip's reign. This means that the Castilian Crown almost never had to borrow to pay interest; it serviced debt out of regular revenue. Equally important is the fact that as debt levels increased, the primary surplus on average rose as well; the more debt had to be serviced, the greater the amount of money made available to this end. The final proof of probity is the long-run outcome. At the time of Philip's death, the debt-to-revenue ratio was broadly unchanged from the one he had inherited from his father.

The defaults reflect illiquidity—and not an unsustainable debt burden or insolvent borrower. Cash could run out for several reasons; typically, a combination of adverse military developments—boosting required spending—and revenue shortfalls was necessary to send Castile's treasury over the edge. This confluence of negative factors was generally counterbalanced by increases in revenue and adjustments in expenditure thereafter. During Philip's long reign, his resources were both large and increasing, and he ran a tight fiscal ship. Lenders had little risk of facing an utterly bankrupt monarch who could not pay even if he wanted to.

The king could service his debt. But what were his incentives to do so? The sovereign debt literature argues that repayment must be enforced either through reputational concerns, economic disruptions, or the threat of sanctions above and beyond the loss of access to credit. We use the contracts in our database to document the legal and economic environment in which lending took place. Borrowing and lending in the age of Philip II took place under "anarchic" conditions—neither the king nor bankers could credibly commit to honor contracts to the letter. The king sometimes defaulted on or postponed payments; bankers also took deposits and then declared bank-ruptcy, leaving the king with losses, or made promises of loans that were not fulfilled.

The majority of Philip II's bankers were Genoese. They engaged in a par-ticular form of syndicated lending. They issued joint loans in overlapping constellations, and used cross-collection and cross-posted collateral to fur-ther strengthen the bonds between members of these informal syndicates. In addition to the manifold linkages of blood and marriage between these bank-ing dynasties, there was a near certainty that they would act in unison dur-ing a crisis. Despite numerous, often-desperate attempts to strike side deals with powerful lenders, this arrangement prevented the king from negotiat-ing separate terms with any of his Genoese financiers. Unable to break the coalition of lenders that provided over 70 percent of his funds, Philip in the end had to repay his loans in full most of the time. After each default, he also had to offer a settlement acceptable to the lenders to regain access to credit. The lenders' coalition was a private-order institution in the sense of Avner Greif (1993). Our case study of what sustained sovereign lending in its earliest days lends powerful support to models of sovereign debt stressing the impor-tance of lenders' market power in combination with reputational concerns. It is also one of the first studies that can provide empirical support for reputation-based approaches, which are by their very nature hard to verify.[1]

In contrast, we find no support for the sanctions-based view of sovereign debt; the threat of cutting the king off from further lending was sufficient to align incentives and ensure the operation of a successful, sustainable system of sovereign borrowing. Conklin (1998) had concluded that a transfer mora-torium by the Genoese, caused by the 1575 bankruptcy, directly led to a mu-tiny in the Army of Flanders. The unpaid soldiers then sacked and plundered the loyalist city of Antwerp, dealing a major blow to Spain's position in the Low Countries. In Conklin's view, therefore, the penalty of a transfer morato-rium could bring the king of Spain to heel. A close reading of the historical record, however, suggests that the transfer stop was never effective; other bankers filled the void and transferred funds (without ever lending). Muti-nies were common in the Army of Flanders; the only reason this one got out of hand was a power vacuum caused by the governor-general's death. Penal-ties and sanctions played no role in convincing Philip II to pay his bankers.

---

1 For an exception, see the evidence in Tomz 2007.

The conclusion has to be that the king could pay his creditors, and most of the time had no choice but to pay merely to retain access to lending services. Yet defaults happened, and settlements featured significant reductions in principal and interest. Short-term loans were converted into perpetuities. Most contracts caught in a bankruptcy posted negative rates of return. Why did bankers continue to lend in the face of these repeated defaults? Our answer is simple: because it was good business. To assess the profitability of lending, we painstakingly transcribed every single clause in 438 contracts, reconstructed the agreed-on cash flows, and calculated the implied rates of return. Based on an assessment of the default's impact, we calculated ex post rates of return. The losses suffered during the defaults were more than offset by the returns obtained in tranquil times. No banking family that maintained a long-term relationship with the Crown lost money overall during the period 1566–98; virtually all earned over 7.14 percent, the yield on safe perpetuities that we use as a benchmark. Over the long run, real returns on short-term lending averaged just over 10 percent after accounting for the effect of the defaults and reschedulings, leaving a healthy premium over the risk-free rate.

The key to understanding the nature of Philip II's defaults lies in the peculiar structure of his loans. The contractual clauses show that lending was contingent on a wide variety of circumstances, including the timing of the arrival of the silver fleets and the performance of specific tax streams. The contracts also gave the king and his bankers several options for delaying repayment, or changing delivery locations and maturities. The clauses speak of a rich contracting environment. Both parties understood they lived under uncertainty, and tried to anticipate and price as many states of the world as possible. Defaults were nothing more than an extension of this uncertainty. Some shocks were large enough to be unanticipated or noncontractable. Examples include the opening up of two simultaneous war fronts, delay of several silver fleets in a row, or disastrous defeat of the Invincible Armada. Some of these events prompted an across-the-board rescheduling of outstanding debt. Bankers understood that these were one-off occurrences and that business would resume as usual as soon as the negative shocks had dissipated. Negotiations were thus swift, settlements were moderate, and lending resumed as soon as the Crown's liquidity was restored. Philip's defaults were hence excusable in the sense of the modern sovereign debt literature (Grossman and Van Huyck 1988).

Toward the end of Philip's reign, primary surpluses were no longer sufficient to stabilize the debt-to-income ratio. By this relatively narrow standard, debts were no longer sustainable. This does not mean that Philip was insolvent; it merely implied the need for a fiscal adjustment. We calculate that the necessary changes were relatively small compared to the ones that had been carried out several times during his reign. Since four ducats out of five were spent on war, any reduction in the scale of the military effort could have quickly improved Philip's fiscal position. The massive expenditure cuts and revenue measures implemented during the 1570s, for example, reduced the debt problem quickly. On average during Philip's reign, higher debt levels had always been met with greater primary surpluses. Compared to other early modern European powers, Habsburg Spain conducted its finances in a highly responsible manner: it raised primary surpluses more in the face of mounting debts than England or France did at the height of their military ambitions. By this standard, sixteenth-century Spain was on a more solid financial footing than eighteenth-century England, often regarded as a paragon of fiscal virtue.

One key difference between England and Spain was military success on the battlefield. England frequently won; in contrast, Spain's few victories failed to deliver major gains. The fog of war clouded Spain's fiscal outlook, but it was not a reflection of military weakness as such; Philip II won glittering victories against France and the Ottoman Empire, for instance. The fact that victories did not translate into peace and defeats produced the need for further spending reflects the nature of great power politics at the time along with the severity of religious strife. None of the military outcomes is a fair judgment of financial probity. Spain could have easily coped with its fiscal situation had the Dutch War (or the Armada) gone slightly better.

We also argue that the long-run performance of Spain—typically interpreted through the lens of sixteenth-century fiscal turmoil—suffered more from an inability to strengthen state capacity than from financial ineptitude and serial defaults. All early modern monarchs faced the same basic problem: to outspend their military rivals required new, higher taxes. These were best collected with the consent of powerful magnates, cities, and the clergy—all to some extent "veto players" in the game of early modern politics. The absolutist strategy—as far as it existed—gradually hammered away at the ability of dispersed power holders to resist the monarch's centralizing agenda. In contrast, some polities evolved a different strategy—one of compromise with the potential adversaries, allowing much higher taxes in exchange for power sharing. City-states had long pioneered such a bargain (Stasavage 2011); both the Dutch Republic and England (after 1688) found ways of combining strong state power with constraints on the executive (North and Weingast 1989).[2]

Such a grand bargain was never struck in early modern Spain. Why? We emphasize the political economy of the silver remittances. The king alone controlled silver revenue. It was not subject to oversight by the Cortes, the representative assembly of Castile. Time and again, when the king was under pressure to compromise, the Cortes offered bargains that would have increased its power in exchange for higher fiscal revenues for the king. In almost all cases, this came to naught. Philip II ultimately avoided compromise because American silver strengthened his hand. During one episode, a power-sharing and revenue-raising deal was almost implemented. The provisions for the millones tax allowed independent budget oversight of the royal finances by the Cortes. As the flood of American silver continued, the Crown gradually undermined the commission's influence, co-opting key players and sidelining others. While this neutering of the budget commission meant that the same deal would not be on the table in the future, the king could afford not to care. Spain's institutions did not gradually decline and degrade under hammer blows struck by bankruptcies and fiscal incompetence, as the serial default view would argue; instead, a resource windfall strengthened the executive at a crucial moment, when it would have been more beneficial for it to be constrained in the long run.

Our conclusions challenge two strands of scholarly literature. First, we find little evidence of financial folly. Rather than emphasizing animal spirits and crowd psychology, we argue that lending and defaults were not signs of bankers' folly. This conclusion is based on a close analysis of the earliest and most famous case of serial default: the payment stops of Philip II. We show that lending to him actually made excellent economic sense. Occasional losses were more than compensated by rich pickings during the long periods when the king serviced his debts. Defaults were largely anticipated. Bankers de facto wrote insurance contracts that allowed the Crown to reduce payments in bad times, such as when military setbacks occurred. Despite all the hue and cry of bankers during the sixteenth-century crises, there was nothing irrational about either continued lending or the defaults of the Crown. In

---

2 For a detailed examination of the nature of this bargain, see Gennaioli and Voth 2012.

effect, at the dawn of sovereign borrowing, lenders and borrower evolved an effective system of risk sharing that offered attractive returns to the bankers, rapid access to funds for the Crown, and a quick as well as simple resolution mechanism in times of crisis.

The second strand of the literature that we challenge is the economic history version of Spain's Black Legend—*la leyenda negra*. The term "Black Legend" refers to Protestant propaganda going back to the early 1500s that emphasized, exaggerated, and embellished willful cruelty along with lawless behavior by the conquistadores in the Americas and Spanish troops in the Netherlands. While often containing a kernel of historical truth, it became a genre full of huge exaggerations—such as the caricature by Jean de Bry, a Dutch Calvinist, depicting a Spaniard feeding a murdered infant to his dogs. Challenged by historians a century ago, the Black Legend nowadays serves more as a case study in religious propaganda than as an organizing principle of historical analysis.[3]

The economic history version of the Black Legend emerged from a marriage of two narratives: a rich historical tradition analyzing the decline of Spain as an economic and military power from the seventeenth century onward, combined with new institutional analysis highlighting the unconstrained power of the monarch (and contrasting it unfavorably with England after the Glorious Revolution). Hamilton (1938, 170) famously emphasized "the abundant evidence that agriculture, industry and commerce declined sharply in the seventeenth century." Later work by Jaime Vicens Vives (1959), Elliott (1961), and Kamen (1978) largely reinforced this conclusion.[4]

This research rests on a firm empirical foundation. And yet it also served as a basis for Spain's Black Legend in economic history terms. With the rise of new institutional economics, Spain's indisputable decline of the seventeenth century became increasingly seen as the just punishment for the country's institutional weaknesses during its heyday. According to this view, imperial Spain was an absolutist monarchy that destroyed the country's economic prospects as a result of poor institutions coupled with a blatant disregard for property rights and proper incentives. When comparing the performance of Spain with other European powers, Douglass North and Robert Paul

---

3 The term "Black Legend" as well as its critical assessment was introduced in the scholarly literature by Julián Juderías (1914).

4 For later work on the effect of silver on Spain's competitiveness, see Forsyth and Nicholas 1983; Drelichman 2005.

Thomas (1973, 101) classify the country as an "also-ran," and argue that "contrasting sets of property rights . . . on the one hand produced sustained growth in the Netherlands and England and on the other led to . . . stagnation and decline in the instance of Spain."[5] The executive, according to this view, was so strong that it could trample on ancient freedoms, ignore merchant interests, break contracts at will, and push through massive tax rises (Acemoglu, Johnson, and Robinson 2005). All this eventually crippled the Spanish economy.

Spain's economic Black Legend is so powerful because the string of bankruptcies under Philip II seemingly bear witness to the disregard for property rights and due process as well as the willful breaking of contracts. Serial default, seen through this lens, showed the absolutist colors of Habsburg Spain, incompetence of its rulers, and unsustainable nature of fiscal excesses. In the work of Carmen Reinhart, Kenneth Rogoff, and Miguel Savastano (2003), Spain emerges as the record holder in terms of defaulting—the key example for their argument that once a default occurs, the next one is more likely because a country's fiscal infrastructure suffers and the economy declines, undermining sustainability.

We are not the first to point out the many incongruities in this picture. Our analysis demonstrates that serial defaults did not damage Spain's fiscal capacity; indeed, they had remarkably few negative effects. As far as the documentary record can tell, it is likely that defaults were anticipated and constituted part of an efficient risk-sharing structure: in good times, bankers were paid well for lending to the Crown, and in bad times, the king could postpone payments or even renegotiate his debts without violating the implicit contract. The fact that the same banking dynasties lent to Philip II throughout his reign—with no sign of any major lenders exiting, contrary to Braudel's claims—speaks powerfully in favor of our interpretation. Also, the absence of any change in interest rates after the 1575 default (the largest of Philip's reign) again suggests that lenders did not learn anything negative about the Crown's behavior or financial situation as a result of the payment stop.

We are not the first to point out that the institutionalist interpretation suffers from further weaknesses. The economic slowdown of Spain after 1600 is largely a Castilian phenomenon; most other regions under Habsburg rule

---

5 A variant of the economic history version of the Black Legend underscores the moral and cultural shortcomings of the Spanish people as a leading cause of economic decline. This view was articulated most recently by David Landes (1998).

performed well.[6] During the sixteenth century, Castile also showed a re-markable degree of economic dynamism—at the very moment when it was allegedly overtaxed and misgoverned the most. Recent research by Alvarez Nogal and Prados de la Escosura (2007) indicates that per capita incomes expanded between 1500 and 1600, and that population increased rapidly. It was only after 1600 that these growth rates declined, before eventually turning negative. More recently, Grafe (2012) also reassessed the power of the Castilian Crown, reevaluating measures of market integration and economic performance during the early modern period.

If neither imperial overstretch (Kennedy 1987) nor the willful breaking of contracts was to blame for Spain's eventual loss of momentum, then what was responsible? Modern-day economic theory argues that institutions conducive to growth should deliver a strong state with a constrained executive (Acemoglu 2005). We argue that imperial Spain's difficulties do not reflect the evils of an unconstrained executive and were more about the failure to build a consensually strong state—one where those paying taxes gained some degree of control over expenditure in exchange for massively higher contributions. Taxation, while high in Castile, was often low in Aragon, Navarre, Portugal, and the Crown's other territories—and the resulting inefficiencies did much to misallocate resources. Recent research has pointed out just how economically damaging Spain's internal fragmentation was. A more successful state could have implemented a tax regime that followed Ramsey's rule, lowered taxes on Castile, raised them in other territories on the Iberian Peninsula, and abolished internal customs barriers. In our view, the inability to raise state capacity must ultimately be traced back to a resource windfall—silver. It kept the Crown fiscally sound without the need to strike a bargain that would have helped to build a stronger, more capable state in the long run.

---

6 The causal effect is likely less; Ugo Panizza and Eduardo Borensztein (2008) estimate it at around 1 percent, similar to the decline in growth rates in countries with debt crises found by Reinhart and Rogoff (2009).

REFERENCES

Acemoglu, Daron. 2005. "Politics and Economics in Weak and Strong States." *Journal of Monetary Economics* 52: 1199–226.

Acemoglu, Daron, Simon Johnson, and James Robinson. 2005. "The Rise of Europe: Atlantic Trade, Institutional Change, and Economic Growth." *American Economic Review* 95 (3): 546–79.

Aguiar, Mark, and Gita Gopinath. 2006. "Defaultable Debt, Interest Rates, and the Current Account." *Journal of International Economics* 69 (1): 64–83.

Aizenman, Joshua, and Brian Pinto. 2005. *Managing Economic Volatility and Crises: A Practitioner's Guide.* Cambridge: Cambridge University Press.

Alesina, Alberto, Arnaud Devleeschauwer, William Easterly, Sergio Kurlat, and Romain Wacziarg. 2003. "Fractionalization." *Journal of Economic Growth* 8: 155–94.

Alfaro, Laura, and Fabio Kanczuk. 2005. "Sovereign Debt as a Contingent Claim: A Quantitative Approach." *Journal of International Economics* 65 (2): 297–314.

Allen, Robert C. 2001. "The Great Divergence in European Prices and Wages from the Middle Ages to the First World War." *Explorations in Economic History* 38 (4): 411–47.

Alvarez Nogal, Carlos. 1997. *El Crédito de la Monarquía Hispánica en el Reinado de Felipe IV.* Ávila, Spain: Junta de Castilla y León.

———. 2003. "The Role of Institutions to Solve Sovereign Debt Problems: The Spanish Monarchy's Credit (1516–1665)." Universidad Carlos III Working Paper 03-08.

Alvarez Nogal, Carlos, and Leandro Prados de la Escosura. 2007. "The Decline of Spain (1500–1850): Conjectural Estimates." *European Review of Economic History* 11 (3): 319–36.

Alvarez Vázquez, José Antonio. 1987. *Rentas, Precios y Crédito en Zamora en el Antiguo Regimen.* Zamora: Colegio Universitario de Zamora.

Anderson, M. S. 1988. *War and Society in Europe of the Old Regime, 1618–1789.* New York: St. Martin's Press.

Arellano, Cristina, and Jonathan Heathcote. 2010. "Dollarization and Financial Integration." *Journal of Economic Theory* 145 (3): 944–73.

Artola, Miguel. 1982. *La Hacienda del Antiguo Régimen.* Madrid: Alianza.

———. 1988. *Enciclopedia de Historia de España.* 3 vols. Madrid: Alianza.

Asea, Patrick K., and Amartya Lahiri. 1999. "The Precious Bane." *Journal of Economic Dynamics and Control* 23:823–49.

Ashraf, Quamrul, and Oded Galor. 2011. "Dynamics and Stagnation in the Malthusian Epoch." *American Economic Review* 101 (5): 2003–41.

Atkeson, Andrew. 1991. "International Lending with Moral Hazard and Risk of Repudiation." *Econometrica* 59 (4): 1069–89.

Auty, Richard M. 2001. *Resource Abundance and Economic Development.* Oxford: Oxford University Press.

Baker, Wayne E. 1984. "The Social Structure of a National Securities Market." *American Journal of Sociology* 89 (4): 775–811.

Bairoch, Paul, Jean Batou, and Pierre Chèvre. 1988. *La population des villes européennes 800 à 1850.* Geneva: Droz.

Baland, Jean-Marie, and Patrick Francois. 2000. "Rent-Seeking and Resource Booms." *Journal of Development Economics* 61:527–42.

Barber, Malcolm. 2001. *The Trial of the Templars.* 2nd ed. Cambridge: Cambridge University Press.

Barro, Robert J. 1987. "Government Spending, Interest Rates, Prices, and Budget Deficits in the United Kingdom, 1701–1918." *Journal of Monetary Economics* 20 (2): 221–47.

———. 2001. "Economic Growth in East Asia before and after the Financial Crisis." NBER Working Paper 8330.

Benabou, Roland. Forthcoming. "Groupthink: Collective Delusions in Organizations and Markets." *Review of Economic Studies.*

Benassar, Bartolomé. 2001. *La España de los Austrias (1516–1700).* Barcelona: Crítica.

Benjamin, David, and Mark Wright. 2009. "Recovery before Redemption: A Theory of Delays in Sovereign Debt Renegotiations." UCLA Working Paper.

Berger, Allen N., and Gregory F. Udell. 1995. "Relationship Lending and Lines of Credit in Small Firm Finance." *Journal of Business* 68 (3): 351–81.

Bernstein, Lisa. 1992. "Opting Out of the Legal System: Extralegal Contractual Relations in the Diamond Industry." *Journal of Legal Studies* 21 (1): 115–58.

Besley, Timothy, and Torsten Persson. 2009. "The Origins of State Capacity: Property Rights, Taxation, and Politics." *American Economic Review* 99 (4): 1218–44.

———. 2010. "State Capacity, Conflict, and Development." *Econometrica* 78 (1): 1–34.

Bethel, Slingsby. 1681. *The Interest of the Prices and States of Europe.* London: John Wickins.

Bigges, Walter. 1589. *A Svmmarie and Trve Discovrse of Sir Frances Drake's West Indian Voyage, Wherein Were Taken, the Townes of Saint Iago, Sancto Domingo, Cartegena, and Saint Augustine, with Geographicall Mappes Exactly Describing Each of the Townes Made by Baptista Boazio.* London: Roger Ward.

Blockmans, Wim. 2001. *Emperor Charles V: 1500–1558.* London: Bloomsbury Academic.

Blockmans, Wim, and Nicolette Mout. 2005. *The World of Emperor Charles V.* Chicago: University of Chicago Press.

Bohn, Henning. 1998. "The Behavior of US Public Debt and Deficits." *Quarterly Journal of Economics* 113 (3): 949–63.

Bolton, Patrick, and Olivier Jeanne. 2009. "Structuring and Restructuring Sovereign Debt: The Role of Seniority." *Review of Economic Studies* 76 (3): 879–902.

Bonney, Richard J. 1987. "Absolutism: What's in a Name?" *French History* 1 (1): 93–117.

———. 2007. "European State Finance Database." http://www.le.ac.uk/hi/bon/ESFDB/.

Boone, Marc. 2007. "The Dutch Revolt and the Medieval Tradition of Urban Dissent." *Journal of Early Modern History* 11 (4–5): 350–75.

Borensztein, Eduardo, Marcos Chamon, Olivier Jeanne, Paolo Mauro, and Jeromin

Zettelmeyer. 2004. "Sovereign Debt Structure for Crisis Prevention." IMF Occasional Paper 237.

Borensztein, Eduardo, and Paolo Mauro. 2004. "The Case for GDP-Indexed Bonds." *Economic Policy* 38:165–206, 211–16.

Borensztein, Eduardo, and Ugo Panizza. 2009. "The Costs of Sovereign Default." *IMF Staff Papers* 56:683–741.

Boyajian, James C. 1993. *Portuguese Trade in Asia under the Habsburgs: 1580-1640*. Baltimore: Johns Hopkins University Press.

Boyer-Xambeu, Marie-Thérèse, Ghislain Deleplace, and Lucien Gillard. 1994. *Private Money and Public Currencies: The 16th-Century Challenge*. Armonk, NY: M. E. Sharpe.

Braddick, Michael J. 2000. *State Formation in Early Modern England, c. 1550-1700*. Cambridge: Cambridge University Press.

Braudel, Fernand. 1966. *The Mediterranean and the Mediterranean World in the Age of Philip II*. Glasgow: William Colins and Sons.

Brewer, John S. 1988. *The Sinews of Power*. Cambridge, MA: Harvard University Press.

Broner, Fernando, Alberto Martin, and Jaume Ventura. 2010. "Sovereign Risk and Secondary Markets." *American Economic Review* 100 (4): 1523–55.

Bulow, Jeremy, and Kenneth Rogoff. 1989. "A Constant Recontracting Model of Sovereign Debt." *Journal of Political Economy* 97 (1): 155–78.

Buringh, Eltjo, and Jan Luiten Van Zanden. 2009. "Charting the 'Rise of the West': Manuscripts and Printed Books in Europe, a Long-Term Perspective from the Sixth through Eighteenth Centuries." *Journal of Economic History* 69 (2): 409–45.

Carande, Ramón. 1987. *Carlos V y sus banqueros*. Barcelona: Crítica.

Carreras, Albert. 2003. "Modern Spain." In *The Oxford Encyclopedia of Economic History*, ed. Joel Mokyr, 546–53. New York: Oxford University Press.

Carretero Zamora, Juan Manuel. 1988. *Cortes, Monarquía, Ciudades: Las Cortes de Castilla a Comienzos de la Época Moderna (1476-1515)*. Madrid: Siglo XXI.

Casado Alonso, Hilario. 1994. "El Comercio Internacional Burgalés en los siglos XVI y XVII." In *Actas del V Centenario del Consulado de Burgos (1494-1994)*, 175–247.

Casado Soto, José Luis. 1988. *Los Barcos Españoles del Siglo XVI y la Gran Armada de 1588*. Vol. 4. Madrid: Instituto de Historia y Cultura Naval.

Castillo, Alvaro. 1963. "Los Juros de Castilla: Apogeo y fin de un Instrumento de Crédito." *Hispania* 23 (89): 43–70.

———. 1972. "'Decretos' et 'Medios Generales' dans le Système Financier de la Castille. La Crise de 1596." In *Melanges en l'honneur de Fernand Braudel*, 1:137–44. Toulouse: Privat Éditeur.

Chabot, Benjamin R., and Christopher J. Kurz. 2010. "That's Where the Money Was: Foreign Bias and English Investment Abroad, 1866–1907." *Economic Journal* 120 (547): 1056–79.

Chamley, Christophe. 2011. "Interest Reductions in the Politico-Financial Nexus of Eighteenth-Century England." *Journal of Economic History* 71 (3): 555–89.

Chamley, Christophe, and Carlos Alvarez Nogal. 2012. "Debt Policy under Constraints between Philip II, the Cortes, and Genoese Bankers." Universidad Carlos III de Madrid Working Paper.

Clark, Gregory. 2007. *A Farewell to Alms: A Brief Economic History of the World*. Princeton, NJ: Princeton University Press.

Cohen, D. 1992. "The Debt Crisis: A Postmortem." In *NBER Macroeconomics Annual*, ed. Olivier Blanchard and Stanley Fisher, 65–114. Cambridge, MA: MIT Press.

Cohn, Henry J. 2001. "Did Bribes Induce the German Electors to Choose Charles V as Emperor in 1519?" *German History* 19:1–27.

Cole, Harold L., and Patrick J. Kehoe. 1995. "The Role of Institutions in Reputation Models of Sovereign Debt." *Journal of Monetary Economics* 35 (1): 45–64.

———. 1996. "A Self-Fulfilling Model of Mexico's 1994–1995 Debt Crisis." *Journal of International Economics* 41 (3–4): 309–30.

———. 1998. "Models of Sovereign Debt: Partial versus General Reputations." *International Economic Review* 39 (1): 55–70.

Conklin, James. 1998. "The Theory of Sovereign Debt and Spain under Philip II." *Journal of Political Economy* 106 (3): 483–513.

Corden, W. Max, and J. Peter Neary. 1982. "Booming Sector and De-Industrialization in a Small Open Economy." *Economic Journal* 92:825–48.

Cortes de Castilla y León. 1989. *Las Cortes de Castilla y León en la Edad Moderna*. Valladolid, Spain: Cortes de Castilla y León.

Crafts, N.F.R. 1995. "Exogenous or Endogenous Growth? The Industrial Revolution Reconsidered." *Journal of Economic History* 55 (4): 745–72.

Dandelet, Thomas James. 1995. "Roma Hispanica: The Creation of Spanish Rome in the Golden Age." PhD diss., University of California at Berkeley.

———. 2001. *Spanish Rome, 1500–1700*. New Haven, CT: Yale University Press.

De Abreu, Pedro. 1866. *Historia del Saqueo de Cádiz por los Ingleses en 1596*. Cádiz: Revista Médica.

De Carlos Morales, Carlos Javier. 2008. *Felipe II: El Imperio en Bancarrota*. Madrid: Dilema.

Deforneaux, Marcelin. 1979. *Daily Life in Spain in the Golden Age*. Stanford, CA: Stanford University Press.

De Lamar, Jensen. 1964. *Diplomacy and Dogmatism: Bernardino De Mendoza and the French Catholic League*. Cambridge, MA: Harvard University Press.

———. 1988. "The Spanish Armada: The Worst-Kept Secret in Europe." *Sixteenth-Century Journal* 19 (4): 621–41.

De Long, J. Bradford, and Andrei Shleifer. 1993. "Princes and Merchants: European City Growth before the Industrial Revolution." *Journal of Law and Economics* 36 (October): 671–702.

De Vries, Jan. 1976. *Economy of Europe in an Age of Crisis, 1600–1750*. Cambridge: Cambridge University Press.

De Vries, Jan, and Ad Van der Woude. 1997. *The First Modern Economy*. Cambridge: Cambridge University Press.

Diamond, Jared. 1997. *Guns, Germs, and Steel: The Fates of Human Societies*. New York: W. W. Norton and Company.

Díaz-Alejandro, Carlos F. 1983. "Stories of the 1930s for the 1980s." In *Financial Policies and the World Capital Market: The Problem of Latin American Countries*, ed. Pedro Aspe Armella, Rudiger Dornbusch, and Maurice Obstfeld. Chicago: University of Chicago Press.

Dickson, P.G.M. 1987. *Finance and Government under Maria Theresia, 1740–1780*. Oxford: Oxford University Press.

Dincecco, Mark. 2011. *Political Transformations and Public Finances: Europe, 1650–1913.* Cambridge: Cambridge University Press.

Domínguez Ortiz, Antonio. 1985. *Las Clases Privilegiadas en el Antiguo Régimen.* 3rd ed. Madrid: Itsmo.

Drelichman, Mauricio. 2005. "The Curse of Moctezuma: American Silver and the Dutch Disease." *Explorations in Economic History* 42 (3): 349–80.

———. 2007. "Sons of Something: Taxes, Lawsuits, and Local Political Control in Sixteenth Century Castile." *Journal of Economic History* 67 (3): 608–42.

———. 2009. "License to Till: The Spanish Mesta as a Case of Second-Best Institutions." In *Explorations in Economic History* 46 (2): 220–40.

Drelichman, Mauricio, and David González Agudo. 2013. "What Price a Roof? Housing and the Cost of Living in Sixteenth-Century Toledo." UBC Working Paper.

Drelichman, Mauricio, and Hans-Joachim Voth. 2008. "Debt Sustainability in Historical Perspective: The Role of Fiscal Repression." *Journal of the European Economic Association* 6 (2–3): 657–67.

———. 2010. "The Sustainable Debts of Philip II: A Reconstruction of Castile's Fiscal Position, 1566–1596." *Journal of Economic History* 70 (4): 813–42.

———. 2011a. "Lending to the Borrower from Hell: Debt and Default in the Age of Philip II." *Economic Journal* 121 (557): 1205–27.

———. 2011b. "Serial Defaults, Serial Profits: Returns to Sovereign Lending in Habsburg Spain, 1566–1600." *Explorations in Economic History* 48 (1): 1–19.

———. 2012. "Risk Sharing with the Monarch: Excusable Defaults and Contingent Debt in the Age of Philip II, 1556–1598." UBC Working Paper.

———. Forthcoming. "Funding Empire: Risk, Diversification, and the Underwriting of Early Modern Sovereign Loans." In *Festschrift in Honour of Joel Mokyr*, ed. John V. C. Nye and L. Lynne Kiesling.

Eaton, Jonathan, and Raquel Fernandez. 1995. "Sovereign Debt." NBER Working Paper 5131.

Eaton, Jonathan, and Mark Gersovitz. 1981. "Debt with Potential Repudiation: Theoretical and Empirical Analysis." *Review of Economic Studies* 48 (2): 289–309.

Ehrenberg, Richard. 1896. *Das Zeitalter der Fugger: Geldkapital und Creditverkehr im 16 Jahrhundert.* Jena.

Eichengreen, Barry. 2002. *Financial Crises and What to Do about Them.* Oxford: Oxford University Press.

Eichengreen, Barry, and Richard Portes. 1989a. "After the Deluge: Default, Negotiation, and Readjustment of Foreign Loans during the Interwar Years." In *The International Debt Crisis in Historical Perspective*, ed. Barry Eichengreen and Peter Lindert, 12–47. Cambridge, MA: MIT Press.

———. 1989b. "Settling Defaults in the Era of Bond Finance." *World Bank Economic Review* 3 (2): 211–39.

Ekelund, Robert B., and Robert D. Tollison. 1997. *Politicized Economies.* College Station: Texas A&M University Press.

Elliott, John H. 1961. "The Decline of Spain." *Past and Present* 20:52–75.

———. 1963a. *Imperial Spain, 1469–1716.* London: Penguin Books.

———. 1963b. *The Revolt of the Catalans: A Study in the Decline of Spain, 1598–1640.* Cambridge: Cambridge University Press.

Elliott, John H. 1986. *The Count-Duke of Olivares: The Statesman in an Age of Decline.* New Haven, CT: Yale University Press.

———. 1989. *Spain and Its World, 1500-1700: Selected Essays.* New Haven, CT: Yale University Press.

———. 1992. "A Europe of Composite Monarchies." *Past and Present* 137:48–72.

Epstein, Stephan R. 2000. *Freedom and Growth: The Rise of States and Markets in Europe, 1300-1750.* London: Routledge.

———. 2001. *Genoa and the Genoese, 958-1528.* Chapel Hill: University of North Carolina Press.

Felloni, Giuseppe. 1978. "Asientos, Juros y Ferias de Cambio Desde El Observatorio Genovés (1541–1675)." In *Dinero y Crédito (siglos XVI Al XIX): Actas del Primer Coloquio Internacional de Historia Económica.* Madrid.

———. 2006a. *La Casa di San Giorgio: Il Potere del Credito.* Genoa: Brigati Glauco.

———. 2006b. *A Series of Firsts.* Genoa: Brigati Glauco.

Ferguson, Niall. 2001. *The Cash Nexus: Money and Power in the Modern World, 1700-2000.* London: Allen Lane.

Fernández Alvarez, Manuel. 1979. *Corpus Documental de Carlos V.* 5 vols. Salamanca: Ediciones Universidad de Salamanca.

———. 2004. *Carlos V, el César y el Hombre.* Madrid: Espasa Calpe.

Fisher, Douglas. 1989. "The Price Revolution: A Monetary Interpretation." *Journal of Economic History* 49 (4): 883–902.

Flynn, Dennis O. 1978. "A New Perspective on the Spanish Price Revolution: The Monetary Approach to the Balance of Payments." *Explorations in Economic History* 15 (4): 388–406.

Flynn, Dennis O., and Arturo Giráldez. 2004. "Path Dependence, Time Lags, and the Birth of Globalisation: A Critique of O'Rourke and Williamson." *European Review of Economic History* 8 (1): 81–108.

Forsyth, Peter J., and Stephen J. Nicholas. 1983. "The Decline of Spanish Industry and the Price Revolution: A Neoclassical Analysis." *Journal of European Economic History* 12 (3): 601–10.

Fortea Pérez, José Ignacio. 2009. *Las Cortes de Castilla y León Bajo los Austrias: Una Interpretación.* Junta de Castilla y León.

Frederiksen, M. W. 1966. "Caesar, Cicero, and the Problem of Debt." *Journal of Roman Studies* 56:128–41.

Fritschy, Wantjie. 2003. "A 'Financial Revolution' Reconsidered: Public Finance in Holland during the Dutch Revolt, 1568-1648." *Economic History Review* 56 (1): 57–89.

Gachard, Louis-Prosper. 1861. *Correspondance de Philippe II sur les affaires des Pays-Bas [1558-1577] pub. d'après les originaux conservés dans les archives royales De Simancas; précédée d'une notice historique et descriptive de ce célèbre dépôt et d'un rapport à m. le ministre de l'intérieur.* Brussels: Librairie ancienne et moderne.

García Gallo, Alfonso. 1950. "La Unión Política de los Reyes Católicos y la Incorporación de las Indias." *Revista de Estudios Políticos* 30:178–93.

García Sanz, Angel. 1980. "Bienes y Derechos Comunales y el Proceso de su Privatización en Castilla durante los siglos XVI y XVII: El Caso de las Tierras de Segovia." *Hispania* 144:251–99.

Gelabert, Juan E. 1997. *La Bolsa del Rey: Rey, Reino y Fisco en Castilla (1598-1648)*. Barcelona: Crítica.

———. 1999a. "Castile, 1504-1808." In *The Rise of the Fiscal State in Europe, c. 1200-1815*, ed. Richard Bonney, 201–41. Oxford: Oxford University Press.

———. 1999b. "The King's Expenses: The Asientos of Philip III and Philip IV of Spain." In *Crises, Revolutions, and Self-Sustained Growth: Essays in European Fiscal History, 1130-1830*, ed. W. M. Ormrod, Margaret Bonney, and Richard J. Bonney, 233–59. Stamford, UK: Shaun Tyas.

———. 2013. "Cuentas para una Guerra." In *El Alimento del Estado y la Salud de la República: Orígenes, Estructura y Desarrollo del Gasto Público en Europa (siglos XIII-XVIII)*. Madrid: Instituto de Estudios Fiscales.

Gelderblom, Oscar. 2013. *Cities of Commerce: The Institutional Foundations of International Trade in the Low Countries, 1250-1650*. Princeton, NJ: Princeton University Press.

Gennaioli, Nicola, and Hans-Joachim Voth. 2012. "State Capacity and Military Conflict." UPF Working Paper.

Glaeser, Edward L., and José A. Sheinkman. 1998. "Neither a Borrower nor a Lender Be: An Economic Analysis of Interest Restrictions and Usury Laws." *Journal of Law and Economics* 41 (1): 1–36.

González de Cellorigo, Martín. 1600. *Memorial de la Política Necesaria y Útil Restauración a la República de España y Estados de Ella, y del Desempeño Universal de estos Reinos*. Valladolid, Spain: Iuan de Bostillo.

Gorton, Gary, and Andrew Metrick. 2012. "Securitized Banking and the Run on Repo." *Journal of Financial Economics* 103 (3): 425–51.

Grafe, Regina. 2001. *Northern Spain between the Iberian and the Atlantic Worlds: Trade and Regional Specialisation, 1550-1650*. London: University of London Press.

———. 2008. "Stuck in the Past or Looking towards the Future?" Inaugural Epstein Lecture, London School of Economics.

———. 2012. *Distant Tyranny: Markets, Power, and Backwardness in Spain, 1650-1800*. Princeton, NJ: Princeton University Press.

Grafe, Regina, and María Alejandra Irigoín. 2006. "The Spanish Empire and Its Legacy: Fiscal Re-Distribution and Political Conflict in Colonial and Post-Colonial Spanish America." *Journal of Global History* 1 (2): 241–67.

Greif, Avner. 1993. "Contract Enforceability and Economic Institutions in Early Trade: The Maghribi Traders' Coalition." *American Economic Review* 83 (3): 525–54.

———. 1994. "On the Political Foundations of the Late Medieval Commercial Revolution: Genoa during the Twelfth and Thirteenth Centuries." *Journal of Economic History* 54 (2): 271–87.

———. 2006. *Institutions and the Path to the Modern Economy: Lessons from Medieval Trade*. Cambridge: Cambridge University Press.

Griffith-Jones, Stephany, and Krishnam Sharma. 2006. "GDP-Indexed Bonds: Making It Happen." United Nations-DESA Working Paper 21.

Grossman, Herschel I., and John B. Van Huyck. 1988. "Sovereign Debt as a Contingent Claim: Excusable Default, Repudiation, and Reputation." *American Economic Review* 78:1088–97.

Gutmann, Myron P. 1980. *War and Rural Life in the Early Modern Low Countries*. Princeton, NJ: Princeton University Press.

Haliczer, Stephen. 1975. "The Castilian Aristocracy and the Mercedes Reform of 1478–1482." *Hispanic American Historical Review* 55 (3): 449–67.

———. 1981. *The Comuneros of Castile: The Forging of a Revolution, 1475–1521*. Madison: University of Wisconsin Press.

Hamilton, Earl J. 1929. "Imports of American Gold and Silver into Spain, 1503–1660." *Quarterly Journal of Economics* 43 (3): 436–72.

———. 1934. *American Treasure and the Price Revolution in Spain, 1501–1650*. Cambridge, MA: Harvard University Press.

———. 1938. "The Decline of Spain." *Economic History Review, 1st Series* 8:168–79.

Heim, Carole E., and Philip Mirowski. 1987. "Interest Rates and Crowding-Out during Britain's Industrial Revolution." *Journal of Economic History* 47 (1): 117–39.

Henderson, Ernest F. 1910. *Select Historical Documents of the Middle Ages*. London: George Bell and Sons.

Herr, Richard. 1974. *An Historical Essay on Modern Spain*. Berkeley: University of California Press.

Hoffman, Philip T. 2011. "Prices, the Military Revolution, and Europe's Comparative Advantage in Violence." *Economic History Review* 64 (1): 39–59.

———. 2012. "Why Was It Europeans Who Conquered the World?" *Journal of Economic History* 72:601–33.

Hoffman, Philip T., and Jean-Laurent Rosenthal. 1997. "The Political Economy of Warfare and Taxation in Early Modern Europe: Historical Lessons for Economic Development." In *The Frontiers of New Institutional Economics*, ed. John N. Drobak and John V. C. Nye, 31–55. Waltham, MA: Academic Press.

Homer, Sydney, and Richard Sylla. 2005. *A History of Interest Rates*. Vol. 4. Hoboken, NJ: John Wiley and Sons.

Hoyle, Richard. 1995. "War and Public Finance." In *The Reign of Henry VIII: Politics, Policy, and Piety*, ed. Diarmaid MacCulloch, 75–100. Houndmills, UK: Palgrave Macmillan.

IMF. 2003. *World Economic Outlook*. Washington, DC: IMF.

Irigoín, María Alejandra, and Regina Grafe. 2008. "Bargaining for Absolutism: A Spanish Path to Empire and Nation Building." *Hispanic American Historical Review* 2:173–210.

Jago, Charles. 1981. "Habsburg Absolutism and the Cortes of Castile." *American Historical Review* 86 (2): 307–26.

———. 1985. "Philip II and the Cortes of Castile: The Case of the Cortes of 1576." *Past and Present* 109:22–43.

Johnson, David A., and Karl Whittle. 1999. "The Chemistry of the Hispanic-American Amalgamation Process." *Journal of the Chemical Society: Dalton Transactions* 23:4239–43.

Johnson, Noel D., and Mark Koyama. 2012. "Standardizing the Fiscal State: Cabal Tax Farming as an Intermediate Institutions in Early-Modern England and France." George Mason University Working Paper.

Juderías, Julián. 1914. "La Leyenda Negra y la Verdad Histórica: España en Europa." *La Ilustración Española y Americana* (January–February).

Kagan, Richard L. 1981. *Lawsuits and Litigants in Castile, 1500–1700*. Chapel Hill: University of North Carolina Press.

Kamen, Henry. 1978. "The Decline of Spain: A Historical Myth?" *Past and Present* 81:24–50.

———. 1999. *The Spanish Inquisition: A Historical Revision*. New Haven, CT: Yale University Press.

———. 2003. *Empire: How Spain Became a World Power, 1492–1763*. New York: HarperCollins.

Kantorowicz, Ernst H. 1957. *The King's Two Bodies: A Study in Mediaeval Political Theology*. Princeton, NJ: Princeton University Press.

Karaman, K. Kivanc, and Sevket Pamuk. 2010. "Ottoman State Finances in European Perspective: 1500–1914." *Journal of Economic History* 70 (3): 593–629.

Karnehm, Charles. 2003. *Die Korrespondenz Hans Fuggers von 1566 bis 1594: Regesten der Kopierbücher aus dem Fuggerarchiv 1574–1581*. Munich: Quellen zur Neueren Geschichte Bayerns.

Kehoe, Timothy J., and Harold L. Cole. 2000. "Self-Fulfilling Debt Crises." *Review of Economic Studies* 67 (1): 91–116.

Kellenbenz, Hermann. 1967. *Die Fuggersche Maestrazgopacht (1525–1542): Zur Geschichte der spanischen Ritterorden im 16. Jahrhundert*. Tübingen: Mohr.

Kennedy, Paul M. 1987. *The Rise and Fall of the Great Powers: Economic Change and Military Conflict from 1500 to 2000*. New York: Random House.

Kimmel, Michael S. 1988. *Absolutism and Its Discontents: State and Society in Seventeenth-Century France and England*. London: Transaction.

Kirshner, Julius. 1996. *The Origins of the State in Italy, 1300–1600*. Chicago: University of Chicago Press.

Kletzer, Kenneth M. 1984. "Asymmetries of Information and LDC Borrowing with Sovereign Risk." *Economic Journal* 94 (374): 287–307.

Kletzer, Kenneth M., D. Newbery, and Brian D. Wright. 1992. "Smoothing Primary Exporters' Price Risks: Bonds, Futures, Options, and Insurance." *Oxford Economic Papers, New Series* 44 (4): 641–71.

Kletzer, Kenneth M., and Brian D. Wright. 2000. "Sovereign Debt as Intertemporal Barter." *American Economic Review* 90 (3): 621–39.

Koenigsberger, H. G. 1951. *The Government of Sicily under Philip II of Spain: A Study in the Practice of Empire*. London: Staples.

Kovrijnykh, Natalia, and Balázs Szentes. 2007. "Equilibrium Default Cycles." *Journal of Political Economy* 115 (3): 403–46.

Krugman, Paul. 1987. "The Narrow Moving Band, the Dutch Disease, and the Competitive Consequences of Mrs. Thatcher." *Journal of Development Economics* 27:41–55.

Lanau, Sergi. 2008. "Essays on Sovereign Debt Markets." PhD diss., Universitat Pompeu Fabra.

Landers, John. 2003. *The Field and the Forge: Population, Production, and Power in the Pre-Industrial West*. Oxford: Oxford University Press.

Landes, David S. 1998. *The Wealth and Poverty of Nations: Why Some Are So Rich and Some So Poor*. New York: W. W. Norton and Company.

Lane, Phillip. 2004. "Empirical Perspectives on Long-Term External Debt." *Topics in Macroeconomics* 4 (1): 1152.

Lapeyre, Henri. 1953. *Simón Ruiz et les "Asientos" de Philippe II*. Paris: Librairie Armand Colin.

Levy-Yeyati, Eduardo, and Ugo Panizza. 2011. "The Elusive Costs of Sovereign Defaults." *Journal of Development Economics* 94 (1): 95–105.

Lindert, Peter, and Peter J. Morton. 1989. "How Sovereign Debt Has Worked." In *Devel-*

oping Country Debt and Economic Performance, ed. Jeffrey Sachs, 39–106. Chicago: University of Chicago Press.

Lovett, A. W. 1980. "The Castilian Bankruptcy of 1575." *Historical Journal* 23:899–911.

———. 1982. "The General Settlement of 1577: An Aspect of Spanish Finance in the Early Modern Period." *Historical Journal* 25 (1): 1–22.

Lunenfeld, Marvin. 1970. *The Council of the Santa Hermandad: A Study of the Pacification Forces of Ferdinand and Isabella*. Coral Gables, FL: University of Miami Press.

Lynch, John. 1961. "Philip II and the Papacy." *Transactions of the Royal Historical Society* 11:23–42.

———. 1991. *Spain, 1516-1598: From Nation State to World Empire*. Cambridge: Basil Blackwell.

Macaulay, Thomas Babington. 1833. *Critical and Historical Essays*. Vol. 2. London.

MacLachlan, Colin M. 1988. *Spain's Empire in the New World: The Role of Ideas in Institutional and Social Change*. Berkeley: University of California Press.

Maravall, José Antonio. 1963. *Las Comunidades de Castilla: Una Primera Revolución Moderna*. 2nd ed. Madrid: Revista de Occidente.

Marcos Martín, Alberto. 2000. *España en los siglos XVI, XVII y XVIII: Economía y Sociedad*. Barcelona: Crítica.

Marques, A. H. de Oliveira. 1979. *Historia de Portugal, Vol. II*. Lisbon: Palas.

Marsilio, Claudio. 2008. *Dove Il Denaro fa Denaro: Gli Operatori Finanziari Genovesi Nelle Fiere di Cambio del XVII Secolo*. Novi Ligure, Italy: Città del Silenzio.

———. 2013. "European State Finance (1348 to 1700): Genoa." In *Handbook of Key Global Financial Markets, Institutions, and Infrastructure*, ed. Gerard Caprio. Vol. 1. Oxford: Elsevier.

Martínez Hernández, Santiago. 2010. "Ya no hay Rey sin Privado Cristóbal de Moura, un Modelo de Privanza en El Siglo de los Validos." *Librosdelacorte.es* 2 (2): 21–37.

Mattingly, Garrett. 1959. *The Armada*. New York: Houghton Mifflin.

Mehlum, Halvor, Karl Moene, and Ragnar Torvik. 2006. "Institutions and the Resource Curse." *Economic Journal* 116:1–20.

Mitchell, Brian R. 1988. *British Historical Statistics*. Cambridge: Cambridge University Press.

Mitchener, Kris James, and Marc D. Weidenmier. 2005. "Empire, Public Goods, and the Roosevelt Corollary." *Journal of Economic History* 65 (3): 658–92.

———. 2010. "Supersanctions and Sovereign Debt Repayment." *Journal of International Money and Finance* 29 (1): 19–36.

Mokyr, Joel, and John V. C. Nye. 2007. "Distribution Coalitions, the Industrial Revolution, and the Origins of Economic Growth in Britain." *Southern Economic Journal* 74 (1): 50–70.

Mokyr, Joel, and Hans-Joachim Voth. 2011. "Understanding Growth in Early Modern Europe." In *The Cambridge Economic History of Europe*, ed. Stephen Broadberry and Kevin O'Rourke. Cambridge: Cambridge University Press.

Mommsen, Theodor. 1881. *The History of Rome*. Vol. 3. London: Richard Bentley and Son.

Moore, Lyndon, and Steve Juh. 2006. "Derivative Pricing 60 Years before Black-Scholes: Evidence from the Johannesburg Stock Exchange." *Journal of Finance* 61 (6): 3069–98.

Morineau, Michel. 1985. *Incroyables Gazettes et Fabuleux Metaux*. London: Cambridge University Press.

Mousnier, Roland. 1979. *The Institutions of France under the Absolute Monarchy, 1598–1789.* Chicago: University of Chicago Press.

Munro, John H. 2005. "Spanish Merino Wools and the Nouvelles Draperies: An Industrial Transformation in the Late Medieval Low Countries." *Economic History Review* 58:431–84.

Nadal i Oller, Jordi. 1984. *La Población Española: Siglos XVI a XX.* Barcelona: Ariel.

Nader, Helen. 1990. *Liberty in Absolutist Spain: The Habsburg Sale of Towns, 1516–1700.* Baltimore: Johns Hopkins University Press.

Neri, Enrica. 1989. *Uomini d'affari e di Governo tra Genova e Madrid.* Milano: Vita e Pensiero–Pubblicazioni dell'Università Cattolica.

Netanyahu, Benzion. 2001. *The Origins of the Inquisition in Fifteenth-Century Spain.* 2nd ed. New York: New York Review of Books.

Nicolau, Roser. 2005. "Población, Salud y Actividad." In *Estadísticas Históricas de España,* ed. Albert Carreras and Xavier Tafunell, 77–154. 2nd ed. Madrid: Fundación BBVA.

North, Douglass C. 1991. "Institutions, Transaction Costs, and the Rise of Merchant Empires." In *The Political Economy of Merchant Empires,* ed. James D. Tracy, 22–40. Cambridge: Cambridge University Press.

North, Douglass C., and Robert Paul Thomas. 1973. *The Rise of the Western World: A New Economic History.* Cambridge: Cambridge University Press.

North, Douglass C., and Barry R. Weingast. 1989. "Constitutions and Commitment: The Evolution of Institutional Governing Public Choice in Seventeenth-Century England." *Journal of Economic History* 49 (4): 803–32.

O'Brien, Patrick K. 2001. "Mercantilism and Imperialism in the Rise and Decline of the Dutch and British Economies, 1585–1815." *Economist* 148 (4): 469–501.

———. 2003. "Political Structures and Grand Strategies for the Growth of the British Economy, 1688–1815." In *Nation, State, and the Economy in History,* ed. Alice Teichova and H. Matis, 1–33. Cambridge: Cambridge University Press.

———. 2009. "Mercantilist Institutions for the Pursuit of Power with Profit: The Management of Britain's National Debt, 1756–1815." In *The Fiscal Military State in Eighteenth-Century Europe: Essays in Honour of P.G.M. Dickson.* Farnham, UK: Ashgate.

Oestreich, Gerhard. 1969. *Geist und Gestalt des Frühmodernen Staates.* Berlin: Duncker and Humblot.

Ormrod, W. M. 1995. *Political Life in Medieval England.* London: Macmillan.

Panizza, Ugo, and Eduardo Borensztein. 2008. "The Costs of Sovereign Default." IMF Working Paper 08/238.

Panizza, Ugo, Federico Sturzenegger, and Jeromin Zettelmeyer. 2009. "The Economics and Law of Sovereign Debt and Default." *Journal of Economic Literature* 47 (3): 651–98.

Parker, David. 1983. *The Making of French Absolutism.* London: E. Arnold.

Parker, Geoffrey. 1970. "Spain, Her Enemies, and the Revolt of the Netherlands, 1559–1648." *Past and Present* 49 (1): 71–95.

———. 1972. *The Army of Flanders and the Spanish Road, 1567–1659: The Logistics of Spanish Victory and Defeat in the Low Countries' Wars.* Cambridge: Cambridge University Press.

———. 1973. "Mutiny and Discontent in the Spanish Army of Flanders, 1572–1607." *Past and Present* 58:38–52.

———. 1976. "The 'Military Revolution,' 1560–1600: A Myth?" *The Journal of Modern History* 48: 195–214.

Parker, Geoffrey. 1977. *The Dutch Revolt*. New York: Penguin Books.

———. 1979. *Spain and the Netherlands, 1559-1659*. London: William Collins and Sons.

———. 1996. *The Military Revolution: Military Innovation and the Rise of the West, 1500-1800*. Vol. 2. Cambridge: Cambridge University Press. http://www.loc.gov/catdir/descrip tion/cam027/95024970.html.

———. 1998. *The Grand Strategy of Philip II*. New Haven, CT: Yale University Press.

———. 1999. "The Political World of Charles V." In *Charles V and His Time, 1500-1559*. Antwerp: Mercatorfonds.

———. 2001. *The World Is Not Enough: The Imperial Vision of Philip II of Spain*. Waco, TX: Baylor University Press.

———. 2002. *Philip II*. 4th ed. Peru, IL: Open Court.

———. 2004. *The Army of Flanders and the Spanish Road, 1567-1659: The Logistics of Spanish Victory and Defeat in the Low Countries' Wars*. Cambridge: Cambridge University Press.

Pérez, Joseph. 1970. *La Révolution des "Comunidades" de Castille (1520-1521)*. Bordeaux: Institut d'Etudes Ibériques et Ibero-Américaines de l'Université de Bordeaux.

———. 2003. *Breve Historia de la Inquisición Española*. Barcelona: Crítica.

Perez-Mallaina, Pablo. 1998. *Spain's Men of the Sea: Daily Life on the Indies Fleets in the Sixteenth Century*. Baltimore: Johns Hopkins University Press.

Peri, Giovanni Dominco. 1672. *Il Negotiante*. Venice.

Petersen, Mitchell A., and Raghuram G. Rajan. 1994. "The Benefits of Lending Relationships: Evidence from Small Business Data." *Journal of Finance* 49 (1): 3–37.

———. 1995. "The Effect of Credit Market Competition on Lending Relationships." *Quarterly Journal of Economics* 110 (2): 407–43.

Pezzolo, Luciano, and Giuseppe Tattara. 2008. "'Una Fiera Senza Luogo': Was Bisenzone an International Capital Market in Sixteenth-Century Italy?" *Journal of Economic History* 68 (4): 1098–122.

Phillips, Carla Rahn, and William D. Phillips. 1997. *Spain's Golden Fleece: Wool Production and the Wool Trade from the Middle Ages to the Nineteenth Century*. Baltimore: Johns Hopkins University Press.

Pierson, Peter. 1989. *Commander of the Armada: The Seventh Duke of Medina Sidonia*. New Haven, CT: Yale University Press.

Prebisch, Raúl. 1950. "Economic Development of Latin America and Its Principal Problems." UN Document No. E/CN.12/89/Rev.1.

Rawlings, Helen. 2006. *The Spanish Inquisition*. Oxford: Blackwell Publishing.

Rei, Claudia. 2011. "The Organization of Eastern Merchant Empires." *Explorations in Economic History* 48 (1): 116–35.

Reinhart, Carmen M., and Kenneth Rogoff. 2009. *This Time Is Different: Eight Centuries of Financial Folly*. Princeton, NJ: Princeton University Press.

Reinhart, Carmen M., Kenneth S. Rogoff, and Miguel A. Savastano. 2003. "Debt Intolerance." *Brookings Papers on Economic Activity* 2003 (1): 1–74.

Rich, E. E., and C. H. Wilson. 1967. *The Cambridge Economic History of Europe*. Vol. 4. London: Cambridge University Press.

Robinson, James, Ragnar Torvik, and Thierry Verdier. 2006. "Political Foundations of the Resource Curse." *Journal of Development Economics* 79 (2): 447–68.

Rodríguez-Salgado, M. J. 1988. *The Changing Face of Empire: Charles V, Philip II, and Habsburg Authority, 1551-1559*. Cambridge: Cambridge University Press.

——. 1990. "The Spanish Story of the 1588 Armada Reassessed." *Historical Journal* 33 (2): 461–78.

Roesler, Konrad. 1967. *Die Finanzpolitik des Deutschen Reiches im Ersten Weltkrieg.* Berlin: Duncker and Humbolt.

Rose, Andrew. 2005. "One Reason Countries Pay Their Debts: Renegotiation and International Trade." *Journal of Development Economics* 77:189–206.

Rubin, Nancy. 2004. *Isabella of Castile: The First Renaissance Queen.* New York: ASJA Press.

Ruiz Martín, Felipe. 1965. "Un Expediente Financiero entre 1560 y 1575: La Hacienda de Felipe II y la casa de Contratación de Sevilla." *Moneda y Crédito* 92:3–58.

——. 1968. "Las Finanzas Españolas durante el Reinado de Felipe II." *Cuadernos de Historia: Anexos de la revista Hispania* 2:181–203.

Ruiz Martín, Felipe, and Angel García Sanz. 1998. *Mesta, Transhumancia y Lana en la España Moderna.* Barcelona: Crítica.

Sachs, Jeffrey, and Andrew M. Warner. 1995. "Natural Resource Abundance and Economic Growth." NBER Working Paper 5398.

Saginati, Liana. 2004. *L'Archivio dei Doria di Montaldeo.* Genoa: University of Genoa.

Sanz Ayán, Carmen. 1998. *Los Banqueros de Carlos II.* Valladolid, Spain: Universidad de Valladolid.

——. 2004. *Estado, Monarquía y Finanzas: Estudios de Historia Financiera en Tiempos de los Austrias.* Madrid: Centro de estudios políticos y constitucionales.

Sargent, Thomas J., and Francois R. Velde. 1995. "Macroeconomic Features of the French Revolution." *Journal of Political Economy* 103 (3): 474–518.

Schmitt, Carl. 1954. *Gespräch über die Macht und den Zugang zum Machthaber.* Stuttgart: Klett-Cotta.

Serrão, Joaquim Verissimo. 1982. *Historia de Portugal, Vol. IV.* Lisbon: Verbo.

Singer, H. W. 1949. "Economic Progress in Underdeveloped Countries." *Social Research: An International Quarterly of Political and Social Science* 16 (1): 1–11.

Stasavage, David. 2011. *States of Credit: Size, Power, and the Development of European Polities.* Princeton, NJ: Princeton University Press.

Stein, Stanley J., and Barbara H. Stein. 2000. *Silver, Trade, and War: Spain and America in the Making of Early Modern Europe.* Baltimore: Johns Hopkins University Press.

Strayer, Joseph. 1970. *On the Medieval Origins of the Modern State.* Princeton, NJ: Princeton University Press.

Sturzenegger, Federico, and Jeromin Zettelmeyer. 2006. *Debt Defaults and Lessons from a Decade of Crises.* Cambridge, MA: MIT Press.

——. 2008. "Haircuts: Estimating Investor Losses in Sovereign Debt Restructurings, 1998–2005." *Journal of International Money and Finance* 27 (5): 780–805.

Swart, Koenrad Wolter. 1978. "William the Silent and the Revolt of the Netherlands." Historical Association: General Series 94.

Temin, Peter, and Hans-Joachim Voth. 2005. "Credit Rationing and Crowding Out during the Industrial Revolution: Evidence from Hoare's Bank, 1702–1862." *Explorations in Economic History* 42 (3): 325–48.

——. 2008. "Interest Rate Restrictions in a Natural Experiment: Loan Allocation and the Change in the Usury Laws in 1714." *Economic Journal* 118:743–58.

Tenace, Edward Shannon. 1997. "The Spanish Intervention in Brittany and the Failure of Philip II's Bid for European Hegemony, 1589–1598." PhD diss., University of Illinois at Urbana-Champaign

Tenace, Edward Shannon. 2003. "A Strategy of Reaction: The Armadas of 1596 and 1597 and the Spanish Struggle for European Hegemony." *English History Review* 118:855–82.

't Hart, Marjolein. 1999. "The United Provinces, 1579–1806." In *The Rise of the Fiscal State in Europe, c. 1200–1815*. Oxford: Oxford University Press.

Thompson, I.A.A. 1969. "The Appointment of the Duke of Medina Sidonia to the Command of the Spanish Armada." *Historical Journal* 12 (2): 197–216.

———. 1976. *War and Government in Habsburg Spain*. London: Athlone Press.

———. 1992. *War and Society in Habsburg Spain: Selected Essays*. Brookfield, VT: Ashgate Publishing Company.

———. 1993. *Crown and Cortes: Government, Institutions, and Representation in Early-Modern Castile*. Aldershot, UK: Variorum.

———. 1994a. "Castile: Absolutism, Constitutionalism, and Liberty." In *Fiscal Crises, Liberty, and Representative Government, 1450–1789*, ed. Philip T. Hoffman and Kathryn Norberg, 181–225. Stanford, CA: Stanford University Press.

———. 1994b. "Castile: Polity, Fiscality, and Fiscal Crisis." In *Fiscal Crises, Liberty, and Representative Government, 1450–1789*, ed. Philip T. Hoffman and Kathryn Norberg, 140–80. Stanford, CA: Stanford University Press.

Tilly, Charles. 1990. *Coercion, Capital, and European States, AD 990–1990*. Cambridge, MA: B. Blackwell.

Toboso Sánchez, Pilar. 1987. *La Deuda Pública Castellana durante el Antiguo Régimen (juros) y su Liquidación en el siglo XIX*. Madrid: Instituto de Estudios Fiscales.

Tomz, Michael. 2007. *Reputation and International Cooperation: Sovereign Debt across Three Centuries*. Princeton, NJ: Princeton University Press.

Tomz, Michael, and Mark Wright. 2007. "Do Countries Default in 'Bad Times'?" *Journal of the European Economic Association* 5 (2–3): 352–60.

Tornell, Aaron, and Philip R. Lane. 1999. "The Voracity Effect." *American Economic Review* 89 (1): 22–46.

Torvik, Ragnar. 2002. "Natural Resources, Rent Seeking, and Welfare." *Journal of Development Economics* 67:455–70.

Tracy, James D. 1985. *A Financial Revolution in the Habsburg Netherlands: Renten and Renteniers in the County of Holland, 1515–1565*. Berkeley: University of California Press.

———. 1990. *Holland under Habsburg Rule, 1506–1566: The Formation of a Body Politic*. Berkeley: University of California Press.

———. 2002. *Emperor Charles V, Impresario of War: Campaign Strategy, International Finance, and Domestic Politics*. Cambridge: Cambridge University Press.

Ulloa, Modesto. 1977. *La Hacienda Real de Castilla en el Reinado de Felipe II*. Madrid: Fundación Universitaria Española, Seminario Cisneros.

van Wijnbergen, Sweder. 1984. "The Dutch Disease: A Disease after All?" *Economic Journal* 94:41–55.

Vassberg, David E. 1975. "The Sale of Tierras Baldías in Sixteenth-Century Castile." *Journal of Modern History* 47 (4): 629–54.

———. 1984. *Land and Society in Golden Age Castile*. Cambridge: Cambridge University Press.

Vázquez de Prada, Valentín. 1962. *Lettres Marchandes d'Anvers*. Paris: S.E.V.P.E.N.

Velde, Francois. 2003. "Government Equity and Money: John Law's System in 1720 France." Unpublished manuscript, Federal Reserve Bank of Chicago.

———. 2007. "John Law's System." *American Economic Review* 97 (2): 276–79.

Verbruggen, J. F. 1997. *The Art of Warfare in Western Europe during the Middle Ages.* 2nd ed. Woodbridge, UK: Boydell Press.

Vicens Vives, Jaime. 1959. *Manual de Historia Económica de España.* Barcelona: Teide.

Vidal-Robert, Jordi. 2011. "An Economic Analysis of the Spanish Inquisition's Motivations and Consequences." Unpublished manuscript, Boston University.

Voigtländer, Nico, and Hans-Joachim Voth. 2013. "The Three Horsemen of Riches: Plague, War, and Urbanization in Early Modern Europe." *Review of Economic Studies* 80: 774-811.

Wade, Robert. 1987. *Village Republics: Economic Conditions for Collective Action in South India.* Cambridge: Cambridge University Press, 1987.

Walpole, Horatio. 1822. *The Works of Horatio Walpole, Earl of Orford . . . : Memoirs of the Last Ten Years of the Reign of George the Second.* London: John Murray.

Weir, David R. 1989. "Tontines, Public Finance, and Revolution in France and England, 1688–1789." *Journal of Economic History* 49 (1): 95–124.

White, Eugene N. 1989. "Was There a Solution to the Financial Crisis of the Ancien Regime?" *Journal of Economic History* 49 (3): 545–69.

———. 2001a. "California Banking in the Nineteenth Century: The Art and Method of the Bank of A. Levy." *Business History Review* 75 (2): 297–324.

———. 2001b. "France and the Failure to Modernize Macroeconomic Institutions." In *Transferring Wealth and Power from the Old to the New World: Monetary and Fiscal Institutions in the 17th through the 19th Centuries,* ed. Michael D. Bordo and Roberto Cortés Conde, 59–99. Cambridge: Cambridge University Press.

Williamson, Jeffrey G. 1987. "Has Crowding Out Really Been Given a Fair Test? A Comment." *Journal of Economic History* 47 (1): 214–15.

Wright, Mark. 2002. "Reputations and Sovereign Debt." Stanford Working Paper.

Yun Casalilla, Bartolomé. 2004. *Marte contra Minerva: El Precio del Imperio Español, c. 1450-1600.* Barcelona: Crítica.

INDEX

Pages followed by "f" refer to figures; pages followed by "t" refer to tables.

THE PRINCETON ECONOMIC HISTORY
OF THE WESTERN WORLD

JOEL MOKYR, SERIES EDITOR